word·spy

word·spy

The Word Lover's
Guide to Modern Culture

PAUL McFEDRIES

BROADWAY BOOKS

NEW YORK

Library of Congress Cataloging-in-Publication Data

McFedries, Paul.
Word spy : the word lover's guide to modern culture /
Paul McFedries.—1st ed.
p. cm.
1. English language—New words. 2. English language—Terms and
phrases. 3. Civilization, Modern—Terminology. 4. Language and culture.
5. Vocabulary. I. Title.
PE1583.M34 2004
428.1—dc21
2003052206

ISBN 0-7679-1466-X

1   3   5   7   9   10   8   6   4   2

FOR KAREN

Contents

Preface

This book examines our world by shining the light of modern culture through the prism of new words and phrases. So just what on the earth *is* a "new word"? Lexicographers and linguists have wildly different definitions, but for this book, a word is "new" if it meets the following criteria:

- It doesn't appear in any general dictionary.
- It first appeared in the written record of the language no earlier than about 1980.
- It has a track record in the language. This means it has to have appeared in at least three different media publications, in at least three different articles, written by at least three different authors. (By "media publication," I mean newspapers, magazines, newsletters, journals, books, TV and radio transcripts, websites, and newsgroups.)

I may as well confess up front that I fudge each of these criteria shamelessly throughout the book. Some of the new words *do* appear in dictionaries; some of them first popped up in the 1970s; and a few have only a couple of mainstream media citations. In any case, I've taken pains to avoid *stunt words*—coinages created only to show off one's cleverness or dexterity with a pun—and *nonce words*—terms made up on the spot that are either unrecorded or appear only once.

Conventions Used in This Book

I'm a simple guy, so this is a simple book. Each chapter is self-contained, so feel free to dip in and out of the text at will. There are just two things you need to bear in mind as you're dipping:

1. I wanted the book's new words and phrases to stand out from the regular text, so those terms appear in **bold** type.
2. The year that appears in parentheses after all the new words (and even some old words) represents the year in which (as near as I can figure) each word first appeared in print. This doesn't necessarily mean the word was coined in that year because many words appear first in ephemeral contexts such as conversations, television or radio broadcasts, and, nowadays, chat rooms and instant messaging confabs.

Acknowledgments

A book like this doesn't get written without a lot of help from an embarrassingly large number of people. It may have just my handle on the cover, but if you could peel back my name you'd see the names of dozens of people who had a finger in this book's pie. The list of those who lent a helping hand has to begin with my wife, Karen, whose generous and unstinting encouragement would have been enough to sustain me through this project, but who also served as an excellent sounding board, reader, and editor. Karen is, in addition, one of the best researchers I know, and many of the statistical and narrative gems in this book were unearthed by her considerable research skills. This book probably would still be a vague thought in the back of my mind if it wasn't for my agent, Bob Mecoy, who firmly believed that my Word Spy site had a book in it somewhere and who then went out and found someone who could do something about it. That someone was my editor at Broadway Books, Gerry Howard, whose enthusiasm for this project inspired me to work harder and better, and whose love of words made him the perfect person to help this book see the light of day.

The thousands of people who have written to me over the years to suggest words or comment on the site are all present in this book, at least indirectly. Of those who offered direct assistance, I'd like to single out the following for heartfelt thanks: David Barnhart, Grant Barrett, Gareth Branwyn, James Callan, Hal Davis, Richard Dooling, Mike Elgan, Jane Farrow, Robert Faulkner, Lucy Fisher, Tom Gally, Anu Garg, Jack Kapica, June Langhoff, Margaret Lee, Bob Levey, Erin McKean, Alan Metcalf, Joel Miller, Kathleen Miller, Laurie Mullikin, Haya El Nasser, Victoria Neufeldt, Jack Nilles, Paul Overberg, Thomas Paikeday, Dan Pink, Mike Pope, Barry Popik, Delma Porter, Michael Quinion, David Rowan, Rakesh Satyal, Fred Shapiro, Jesse Sheidlower, Barbara Wallraff, and Mark Worden.

I hope you enjoy *Word Spy*. If you like what you see here, there's more where this came from at my Word Spy website (www.wordspy.com). It's always open, so feel free to drop by any time you like.

Chapter 1

A Mosaic of New Words

A community is known by the language it keeps, and its words chronicle the times. Every aspect of the life of a people is reflected in the words they use to talk about themselves and the world around them. As their world changes—through invention, discovery, revolution, evolution, or personal transformation—so does their language. Like the growth rings of a tree, our vocabulary bears witness to our past. —*John Algeo*

The bold and discerning writer who, recognizing the truth that language must grow by innovation if it grow at all, makes new words and uses the old in an unfamiliar sense, has no following and is tartly reminded that "it isn't in the dictionary" although down to the time of the first lexicographer (Heaven forgive him!) no author ever had used a word that was in the dictionary. —*Ambrose Bierce*

ne•ol•o•gism *noun* A meaningless word coined by a psychotic. —*Merriam-Webster's Collegiate Dictionary*

What could be more relevant, more interesting, more *fun* than new words? Well, yes, lots of things. However, for many people a newly minted word is one of life's little pleasures, something that can be counted among what James Boswell called "the small excellencies." But then there are those of us who have been stricken with a malady that I call *neologophilia,* the intense attraction—oh, why not say it?—the *love* of new words.

This ailment's happy sufferers exhibit an unvarying collection of symptoms: an untrammeled glee at coming across a new word in a book or newspaper; an unquenchable curiosity about life, because, as you'll see, new words lead us into new worlds; an unending wonder at the amazing plasticity of the language and at the relentless creativity of those who use it; and an unceasing urge to coin new words (and, of course, an unabashed desire to weave these new coinages into cocktail party conversations).

I came down with this affliction many years ago, and I've been clam-happy ever since. I enjoy words and language in general, but what sets my crank a-turning is, as H. L. Mencken said, "the biology of language, as opposed to its paleontology." I love the *living language* more than the fossilized variety with its hardened meanings and set-in-stone lexicon. To put it another way, although I get as much pleasure as anyone out of a dictionary, the words it contains are, well, domesticated. I love the wild, untamed neologisms that romp around the linguistic wilderness. When I see a new word in an article or book, I get a little jolt of excitement, a mental shock akin to seeing an animal live for the first time while walking in the woods. I'm not looking to hunt the word, or tame it, or capture it for inclusion in some kind of lexical zoo. Instead, I take a snapshot of the word—I record the source and the citation—that shows the word in its natural environment.

And that, more than anything, explains what this book is all about. It's a series of cultural snapshots, with the lens focused on new words and phrases that tell us something about our world. These snapshots cover various slices of modern life, including relationships, business, technology, war, aging, multiculturalism, and even fast food. I define each word, tell you when it first appeared in print, provide a citation from the media that shows how the word is used, and give you some cultural background—stats, stories, trends, and tidbits—that put the word into context. Taken together, I hope these snapshots will form a larger picture of our modern culture. Have you ever seen one of those images that, when examined closely, turns out to be made up of thousands of smaller pictures? It's called a *mosaic,* and that's the metaphor that underlies this book. It's a mosaic of new words.

Why go to all this trouble? After all, aren't new words, at best, mere trifles soon to be forgotten or, at worst, signs of linguistic decay? I have to respond with a big, fat "No!" on both counts. It's my unshakable belief that, putting it as simply as I can, *new words matter.* Why? Two reasons: new words reflect our culture, and they have universal appeal.

New Words Reflect Our Culture

> Words are a mirror of their times. By looking at the areas in which the vocabulary of a language is expanding fastest in a given period, we can form a fairly accurate impression of the chief preoccupations of society at that time and the points at which the boundaries of human endeavour are being advanced. —*John Ayto*

Language wears many hats, but its most important job is to help us name or describe what's in the world. As the American writer and editor Howard Rheingold says, "Finding a name for something is a way of conjuring its existence, of making it possible for people to see a pattern where they didn't see anything before." So we have nouns for things, verbs for actions, and adjectives and adverbs for describing those things and actions. But the world changes. Constantly. New things are created; old things are modified; light bulbs are appearing over people's heads all the time, signaling new ideas and theories; people do things differently; they look at existing things from new perspectives. Today's world is different in a thousand ways from yesterday's world.

So if language describes the world, and if the world changes, then language must also change as a way of keeping up with the world. We're compelled to create new words to name and describe our new inventions and ideas and institutions; we're driven to create new meanings for existing words to accommodate our newly modified things and actions.

It follows then—and this is the central premise of this book—that you can understand the culture by examining its new words, by going out to what one linguist calls the "vibrant edges" of language. However, it's not enough just to note the existence of a neologism and move on to the next one. Each new word reflects something about the culture, but you have to examine the word closely to see the details of that reflection. How is the word being used? Who is using it? What are the cultural factors that gave rise to and nourish the word's existence? Each new word opens a door (one writer likened them to "the doorbells of the mind") that leads you to a room with various cultural and sociological artifacts. The Czech playwright Daniela Fischerova said it best: "Every new word is a new reality."

New words both reflect and illuminate not only the subcultures that coin them, but also our culture as a whole. New words give us insight into the way things are even as they act as linguistic harbingers (or canaries in the cultural coal mine), giving us a glimpse of (or a warning about) what's to come. Here's the lexicographer Victoria Neufeldt on this neologism-as-cultural-reflection idea:

> The neologisms that especially capture our attention are indeed often remarkable; some with their metaphorical baggage can constitute miniature sociological studies in themselves—like *McJob,* for instance, which for comprehension depends on all the associations and connotations of the name McDonald's, as well as an awareness of the difficulties of the current em-

ployment situation, in particular for new graduates wanting to enter the workforce.

New Words Have Universal Appeal

> Slang . . . is a monument to the language's force of growth by creative innovation, a living example of the democratic, normally anonymous process of language change, and the chief means whereby all the languages spoken today have evolved from earlier tongues. —*Mario Pei*

Each new word is a story that tells us something about our lives and our times, but there are, as they say, a million stories in the naked city. New words and new meanings are coined with a breathtaking frequency and trying to catalog them all is like herding cats. Lexicographer Wendalyn Nichols says that language "is as easy to nail as Jell-O. It changes all the time."

My focus in this book and in my neological work in general is on new words that appear in print, since these records have some staying power and can be read and searched. But the brain of every person on the planet is a miniature word factory, and new coinages appear spontaneously as a natural part of everyday speech. Consider the following hypothetical snippet of conversation:

"Did you read MacWhoozit's column today?"
"Yeah, the man is a *master* at stating the obvious."
"I *know*. I counted no less than four, uh, *obviosities*."
"Obviosities? Is that a word?"
"Hmmm, let's see. If you can describe something as curious, then you can call that thing a curiosity, right?"
"Right."

"So, if you can describe something as obvious, then why not call that thing an obviosity?"

"Okay. But is it *really* a word?"

"Well, it is now!"

People do this kind of thing all the time. The linguist W. D. Whitney once called it "the natural delight of language-making." Human beings have this uncorkable creative streak that revels in creating new words (such as "uncorkable"). Victoria Neufeldt calls this "everyday" neology and says that it "produces the bulk of our neologisms. Such neology, far from being a separable linguistic phenomenon that manifests itself periodically or sporadically in response to social stimuli, in fact rises out of *ordinary linguistic competence,* what might be called the linguistic collective unconscious of the speech community" (emphasis added).

I view language not as a solid mountain to be admired from afar, but rather as an active volcano to be studied up close. This volcano is constantly spewing out new words and phrases; some of them are mere ash and smoke that are blown away by the winds; others are linguistic lava that slides down the volcano and eventually hardens as a permanent part of the language. But although volcanoes have periods of intense activity followed by periods of inactivity, word creation never stops. As the linguist Allan Metcalf has said, "You can hardly spend a day without coining a new word or two."

The universal appeal of neologisms is also reflected in their popularity. For example, my Word Spy mailing list, which is devoted to new words, has over 15,000 members. The Word Spy website (wordspy.com) gets over half a million visits each month. As well, many newspapers and magazines include lists of new words to accompany articles, and quite a few—including *Wired, Time, Newsweek,* and *The Guardian*—even include new word sections as a regular feature.

Then there is the phenomenon of the *sniglet*, "a word that doesn't appear in the dictionary, but should." This concept was created by the comedian Rich Hall in the 1980s and was for several years a part of the HBO comedy series *Not Necessarily the News*. Example sniglets include *lactomangulation*, "manhandling the 'open here' spout on a milk carton so badly that one has to resort to using the 'illegal' side," and *peppier*, "the waiter at a fancy restaurant whose sole purpose seems to be walking around asking diners if they want ground pepper." These coinages were collected into several books: *Sniglets* (1984), *More Sniglets* (1985), *Unexplained Sniglets of the Universe* (1986), *Angry Young Sniglets* (1987), and *When Sniglets Ruled the Earth* (1989). By 1990 these five slim volumes (they all weighed in under 100 pages) had sold an eyebrow-raising 1.4 million copies and had appeared collectively for more than 60 weeks on the *New York Times* bestseller list.

Clearly humans, as linguist Jean Aitchison has said, "mop up words like sponges." But it's also true that folks love creating new words and, in particular, they can't resist a contest. Ask people to come up with a new name or a new word for something, throw in a token prize, and stand back the next time the mail arrives.

Name contests are always popular. When the city of Toronto held a "Name the Dome" contest in 1987 to come up with a moniker for its newly built sports stadium (featuring a retractable roof), it received over 150,000 entries suggesting nearly 13,000 unique names. (The winning name was *Skydome*.) In 1996 the owners of the Washington Bullets basketball team decided it was time for a new team nickname, so they announced a contest that eventually garnered more than 500,000 entries, with the winner being the disappointingly dull name "Wizards." In 1947, when Borden Foods asked consumers to come up with a name for the new calf born to Borden's spokescow, Elsie, more than 3 million people replied.

Unfortunately, the poor thing ended up being saddled with the unwieldy name Beauregard.

If there's one thing people hate, it's a gap in the language. What do you call the adult with whom you regularly go out on dates? ("Girlfriend" and "boyfriend" are too juvenile, and "lover" is too intimate, too romance-novelish.) What should we call the first decade of the 2000s? (We have the sixties, seventies, eighties, nineties, and then . . . what?) Why is there no gender-less third-person singular pronoun? ("He" is traditional but is now considered politically incorrect; "they" is grammatically controversial.) Despite the language's half a million words, these kinds of gaps are legion, and contests to fill these gaps are a thriving cottage industry.

One of the earliest such contests was launched by a teetotaler named Delcevare King, who in 1923 was alarmed at the number of people who were flouting the U.S. Constitution's Eighteenth Amendment, which prohibited the manufacture and sale of liquor. Mr. King decided that what the world needed was a word to name these "lawless drinkers," these "scoffers." He offered a $200 prize (a princely sum in those days) for the best word. By the contest deadline, more than 25,000 people had responded with suggestions ranging from *boozlaac* to *hooch-sniper* to *law-loose-liquor-lover*. The winning entry, submitted independently by Kate Butler of Dorchester, Massachusetts, and Henry Dale of Andover, Massachusetts, was *scofflaw*, a word that found a permanent place in the language, although today it refers to anyone who ignores or disregards the law.

In a 1940 contest people were asked to come up with a name for the porters who worked at the Airlines Terminal in New York. According to an article in the December 24, 1940, edition of the *New York Herald Tribune* (unearthed by etymologist Barry Popik and posted to the American Dialect Society mailing list), 2,780 people vied for the $100 prize, which was won by Willie

Wainwright of New Orleans, Louisiana. His suggested word was *skycaps*, another neologism that's still in use today.

One-time-only contests generate a lot of responses, but there is enough interest in coining new words to support contests that run regularly. The veteran of this genre is Bob Levey of the *Washington Post,* who has been running a monthly neology contest for over 20 years. He describes a person or situation for which a word doesn't exist and asks his readers to coin a suitable term. (Example: The sound made when pulling two strips of Velcro apart. The winning term: *velch.*) The first contest, announced on November 19, 1982, elicited 1,089 suggestions. These days he gets over 3,000 responses for each contest.

Another regular neology feature appeared on CBC Radio, Canada's public broadcaster. "Wanted Words" was a weekly contest run by Jane Farrow, who at the time was a CBC producer. (Ms. Farrow calls neologists the "do-it-yourselfers of language building . . . Where's there's a will, there's a word.") The show began in October 1999 and ran until June 2002. Each segment would outline a *challenge:* a "language gap" that listeners were asked to fill with a new word or phrase. (For example, what do you call those anti-gardeners who, despite their best efforts, kill any plant they bring home? The winning submission was *herbicidal maniacs.*) These challenges would receive between 400 and 1,500 e-mails, letters, and faxes each week. The show also produced a couple of books (*Wanted Words* and *Wanted Words 2*) that were national bestsellers in Canada.

Another ongoing contest is presided over by Barbara Wallraff of *The Atlantic Monthly,* who has been conducting the bi-monthly "Word Fugitives" column on the back page of the magazine since February 2001 (an online version existed before that). She describes word fugitives as "empty mental spaces waiting to be filled by neologisms" and says that she typically gets several hundred suggestions each month.

New word contests appeal to a wide swath of the population because neology is a democratic art. Oil painting and sculpting, for example, are arts that require years of study and practice, but coining new words requires nothing but a willing mind and "ordinary linguistic competence." We all have within us what Virginia Woolf called "the word-coining genius, as if thought plunged into a sea of words and came up dripping."

Of course, there's also the siren song of linguistic fame (if not fortune). Who wouldn't want to go down in history, as have Kate Butler, Henry Dale, and Willie Wainwright, as the coiner of a word that has found a permanent place in the lexicon?

Not that a contest is required for that. Sometimes ordinary people capture neological lightning in the language jar. Consider professor Paul Lewis, of Newton Center, Massachusetts, who wrote the following letter to the editor, which appeared in the June 16, 1992, edition of the *New York Times:*

> To the Editor:
> "Tomatoes May Be Dangerous to Your Health" (Op-Ed, June 1) by Sheldon Krimsky is right to question the decision of the Food and Drug Administration to exempt genetically engineered crops from case-by-case review. Ever since Mary Shelley's baron rolled his improved human out of the lab, scientists have been bringing just such good things to life. If they want to sell us Frankenfood, perhaps it's time to gather the villagers, light some torches and head to the castle.

The cheeky and evocative coinage *Frankenfood* caught on almost immediately. By the end of the summer of 1992, it had appeared in the *Boston Globe,* the *Los Angeles Times,* and *Newsday.* Ten years later the word is ensconced in at least three major dictionaries. (Professor Lewis was so pleased with the success of his new word that he tried to foist another upon the world: *schmoozeoisie,* the class of people who make their living by talking. Alas, this blend of *schmooze,* "to talk persuasively to some-one, especially for personal gain," and *bourgeoisie,* "the affluent middle class," was too clever by half, and resides now in the lex-ical Dead Letter Office.)

The universal appeal of new words is leavened by the happy fact that neologisms are often just plain fun. What's not to like about a word such as *zitcom,* a television sitcom aimed at or fea-turing teenagers? Or consider the *torpedo,* an inept employee who quits to go work for a rival company.

These neological high jinks come from what H. L. Mencken described (when discussing slang formation) as "a kind of lin-guistic exuberance, an excess of word-making energy." In a sim-ilar vein, American writer Jerry Dunn has said that "the exuberance that leads human beings to create and enjoy new language is part of our nature. Since lingo is pithy and often funny, it adds freshness and zest to life." He goes on to relate a great story: "Humorist S. J. Perelman once got in a traffic acci-dent that wrecked his car. He quickly forgot being upset when a mechanic at the repair garage described his car as 'totaled.' Perelman, who had never heard this term, was nearly ecstatic. 'Totaled!' he went around repeating. 'Totaled!' The word was perfect."

The first person who saw a stand of trees under which the permafrost had melted, causing the trees to tilt at various angles, and called them *drunken trees* was someone for whom language is more toy than tool. Or consider the waggish woman or man who invented the *clue stick,* a metaphorical stick used to "hit" a person in an effort to remedy that person's ignorance or incom-petence. This is jubilance made manifest and, as the linguist Allen Walker Read once said, "Jubilance is an explanation for a lot of the things that happen in language."

New Word Metaphors

> The metaphor is perhaps one of man's most fruitful potentialities. Its efficacy verges on magic, and it seems a tool for creation which God forgot inside one of His creations when He made him.
> —*José Ortega y Gasset*

Human beings love making metaphors. "Life . . . is a tale told by an idiot, full of sound and fury, signifying nothing" (Shakespeare). "Nature is an infinite sphere in which the center is everywhere, the circumference is nowhere" (Pascal). "If Love Were Oil, I'd Be a Quart Low" (country song title). We make metaphors for many things, but when we make many metaphors for one thing, it's a sign that that thing is important to us. And we make metaphors for new words almost as readily as we make new words. Perhaps that's because, as psychologist Julian Jaynes says, language itself is a metaphorical business: "Because in our brief lives we catch so little of the vastness of history, we tend too much to think of language as being solid as a dictionary, with a granite-like permanence, rather than as the rampant restless sea of metaphor which it is."

So far in this introduction I've likened new words to animals, a mirror, doorbells, lights, a volcano, canaries, and stories. Over the years, many language writers have set their minds free to conjure the appropriate imagery that captures what new words mean to them, and I'll look at a few of these metaphors in this section.

Earlier I mentioned that I prefer the "living language" to the dead. That phrase is a favorite of linguists and lexicographers for whom language change is a kind of lifeblood, and only living things are capable of changing. Here are a few quotations that capture this sense of language being alive:

Language is a living thing that evolves. Like species, words gradually may shift their meanings. This is no problem if meanings are clear but can be trouble if the usage confuses or misleads people. After all, evolution of species commonly produces mutants that live briefly but become extinct because they are not well adapted to their environments. —*Boyce Rensberger*

The words of a living language are like creatures: they are alive. Each word has a physical character, a look and a personality, an ancestry, an expectation of life and death, a hope of posterity. —*Morris Bishop*

A living language is like a man suffering incessantly from small haemorrhages, and what it needs above all else is constant transactions of new blood from other tongues. The day the gates go up, that day it begins to die. —*H. L. Mencken*

If language is alive, sometimes it takes a specific form, such as a particular kind of animal:

Words are chameleons, which reflect the colour of their environment. —*Learned Hand*

For the most part our words came deviously, making their way by winding paths through the minds of generations of men, even burrowing like moles through the dark subconsciousness. —*John Moore*

Or perhaps words are akin to skin, a part of our anatomy that constantly changes:

But don't blame me if some of these neologisms have hit the lexical dumpster even as you read them. Such is the nature of neology. . . . For words are the living tissue of any language. Just like our skin cells, words have a life, wear out, and slough off. Then new verbal tissue takes their place. —*Bill Casselman*

The linguist Allan Metcalf is fond of botanical metaphors that compare new words to seeds and plants:

Every year there are many thousands of potential new words, some of them deliberately coined, others spontaneously created in response to new situations. They are like seeds in the ground, waiting for rain and favorable weather to sprout. —*Allan Metcalf*

It may help to think of language as a great field of word plants. Whenever most people focus their attention on one subject, it's like a great dose of fertilizer and rain on that portion of the field. Existing words grow and flower into new meanings. Nouns sprout verbs. —*Allan Metcalf*

In other cases, writers liken language not to plants, but to the soil that supports them:

Language is like soil. However rich, it is subject to erosion, and its fertility is constantly threatened by uses that exhaust its vitality. It needs constant reinvigoration if it is not to become arid and sterile. —*Elizabeth Drew*

Words as water is another common theme:

The development of vocabulary has been compared to the tide. Words wash up and fade as activities of a society flow and then ebb, each tide reaching a high point in its generation, then subsiding into the oceanic swirl of language. Some words sink in the sand; others join the body of the language for an effect ("foodie"), for a generation ("Savings Bond," "McCarthyism"), for a lifetime ("H-bomb"), for an age ("acronym"). —*Robert K. Barnhart*

Most new words simply disappear, like raindrops falling and soaking into the ground. Only a few get caught in the bucket of public attention, and make their way into dictionaries. —*Jean Aitchison*

Finally, the connection between new words and cultural or social change is a fruitful source of useful and poetic metaphors:

New words are the birth certificates of change— change in attitudes, in mores, in human relations, in technology, in the social and economic landscape, in the natural world. —*Cullen Murphy*

Words are the bugles of social change.
—*Charles Handy*

English, like all languages, is a sign of the times— present or past. It is also a record of the invention and imagination, the poetic or playful fantasies, the sly or sardonic humor, of the known and unknown people who have shaped it. —*Robert Claiborne*

How New Words Are Created

Of all the words that exist in any language only a bare minority are pure, unadulterated, original roots. The majority of "coined" words are forms that have been in one way or another created, augmented, cut down, combined, and recombined to convey new needed meanings. The language mint is

> more than a mint; it is a great manufacturing center,
> where all sorts of productive activities go on unceas-
> ingly. —*Mario Pei*

Where do new words come from? Sometimes we're lucky enough to know the answer to that question. Earlier I told you about some words that originated as contest winners, and another that was a letter to the editor. But for every *scofflaw, skycap,* and *Frankenfood* that made the linguistic grade, there are thousands of coinages like *scadink, skivlines,* and *fraznit* that died unmourned deaths. Those three words are typical examples of the sniglets that I mentioned a few pages back. Of the hundreds of words coined on the show and in the five books, not a single sniglet has found a place in the language, much less made it into a dictionary. Creating new words is easy; getting other people to use them is not.

And yet, as any linguist will tell you, we're living in a time of neological frenzy, where words are being coined at a faster rate than in any other period of history. (The only time comparable to ours would be the Elizabethan age, when thousands of new words entered—and remained in—the language. Shakespeare alone is credited with coining over 1,500 words in his plays, from *academe* to *moonbeam* to *zany.*) You can give at least partial credit for this new-word explosion to technology as a whole and to the Internet in particular. What appears to be happening is that two very potent forces are hard at work: a field (technical terms and jargon) that is rich in new vocabulary and a medium (the Internet and all its various communications channels) that makes it extremely easy to disseminate new words. In the pre-Internet world, new words would tend to stay within whatever subculture coined them, and only a few would "leak out" to the mainstream. Now we have a subculture—the Internet—that includes hundreds of millions of people and so by definition is part of the mainstream. This means it's easier than it used to be for new words and phrases to catch on.

That isn't to say that the technology is the only source of new words. Stockbrokers, for example, seem to be word-coining Einsteins who revel in fanciful phrases such as *angel investor* and *underwater options,* to name two that appear in this book. However, in the 1980s we would never have heard these words. They hit our lexical radar screens now because there is so much financial news available, not only on the Web, but on television stations such as CNNfn.

So just how does a word get the "household" adjective attached to it? Nobody really knows for sure, sad to say. From my own experience, people seem to take a shine to a new word if it meets certain conditions:

- **It's easy to pronounce.** If people can't figure out how to pronounce a word, they're unlikely to use it in conversation, which reduces the word's word-of-mouth possibilities. For example, consider the word *democrazy,* a democracy that has absurd or inequitable characteristics or in which senseless or unjust events occur. I have no idea how to pronounce this word. Is it di•MOK•ray•zee or di•MOK•ruh•zee or DEM•uh•kray•zee or dem•uh•KRAY•zee? Insert perplexed shrug here.

- **It's easy to understand.** The problem with so many coined words is that their meaning can't be gleaned just by examining the word. What does *fraznit* mean? Who knows? But if you come across a word such as *pollutician,* you can "see" the components *pollution* and *politician* in there, and you can sort of guess its meaning. (For the record, it's a politician who supports initiatives and policies that harm the environment.) *Frankenfood* is similarly transparent.

- **It's short.** Short words are easier to remember than long words, so they're more likely to appear in articles and pop up in dinner table conversations. *Gynobibliophobia,* "the dislike of women writers," is a useful term, but it's a real mouthful so you don't see it very often. *Gaydar,* "an intuitive sense that enables gay people to identify other gays," is short and pithy, which at least partially explains why it's now relatively commonplace.

▪ **It fills a gap in the language.** Earlier I mentioned that just because there's a language gap, it doesn't mean that a word will arise to fill it. However, many successful coinages are ones that *do* fill a gap. They're successful usually because the underlying phenomenon is a part of many people's lives, and if the coined word is well suited to that phenomenon, then the word finds a place in the language. One of my favorite new words is *speako,* an error in speaking, especially when dictating to a voice recognition system. This play on *typo* is a useful addition to the language that nicely fills a gap and will likely be seen more often as people use voice recognition software.

New words that meet some or all of these conditions must then somehow propagate through the culture. They do this in various ways, but the most effective are pop culture; the mainstream media; Internet technologies such as e-mail, chat rooms, newsgroups, and websites; and old-fashioned word of mouth. In each case, however, the key is the extent to which people participate in or share the experience associated with the new word. Someone can come up with a neological gem on an obscure cable show and it won't go anywhere. But put "yada, yada, yada" on *Seinfeld,* and it doesn't take long before everyone's using it. This explains why, for example, business words always have a good chance of spreading throughout the culture: We live in a business-oriented society, so a snappy word or phrase will resonate in a lot of minds.

New word propagation also depends on whether people understand the associated experience. If they get the details of it, then they'll easily set up in their minds an association between the word and the event. If they don't understand it, the word won't have anything to hang its linguistic hat on. For example, in 2002 many Enron-related words and phrases sprang up like so many lexical mushrooms after a spring rain (*Enronomics, Enronitis,* and so on). Unfortunately, the average man and woman on the street didn't have a clue what went wrong with Enron or even what Enron's business was in the first place. As a result, these Enronish coinages have no linguistic legs.

But how are words coined in the first place? Linguists have identified a number of mechanisms that people use, consciously and unconsciously, to forge new words. Here's a summary.

Combining

The process of combining marries a word either with one or more affixes (a prefix, infix, or suffix) or with another word. Bolting on a prefix or suffix (or both) to an existing word is probably the easiest and most common method for making new words. English has dozens of affixes—*anti-, pre-, un-, -able, -ing, -ness,* and so on—and most of us know how to wield these to give an existing word a makeover.

Getting two existing words to shack up together to create a *compound* is also a prolific source of new terms. Some of the new compounds that appear in this book are *wildposting, superbrand, self-gift, bash-and-build, media-wrenching, summit-hop, gender-ender, dolphin-safe, greenspeak,* and *day-extender.*

Finally there's the process called *blending,* which usually combines the first part of one word with the last part of another word. For example, *brunch* is a blend of *breakfast* and *lunch.* In this book, *fritterware, deskfast, celliquette, fictomercial, advertainment, brandscape, affluenza, privatopia, hacktivist, subvertisement, permalancer,* and *flexecutive* are just a few of the blends that appear.

Shortening

The process of shortening is based mostly on a kind of linguistic laziness called *clipping* that causes us to lop off great chunks of words. Usually the victims are unstressed syllables or nonprimary stress syllables. For example, we end up with *fridge* from *refrigerator* and *flu* from *influenza*. More commonly, we clip everything after the first syllable: *abs, dis, rad, exam, gym, lab, prof, condo,* and so on. A relatively new form of shortening is to clip stressed syllables. For example, *phone* from *telephone, za* from *pizza, rents* from *parents,* and *burger* from *hamburger.*

A related process is the creation of *acronyms,* which create a pronounceable word using the first one (or sometimes two) letters of each word in a phrase; for example, UNICEF from United Nations International Children's Emergency Fund, and NATO from North Atlantic Treaty Organization. This book's acronym examples include *domo, BANANA, NIMBY, SOHO,* and *TOHO.*

If the first letters of the phrase can't be pronounced as a word, then the result is an *initialism,* such as NHL from National Hockey League and NYPD from New York Police Department. Some initialisms you'll find in this book are *DWY, TRA, PC, OTPOTSS, PPC, DWB, FWA,* and *MTBU.*

Shifting

One of the things that most vexes language purists and other professional tsk-tskers is when the meaning of a word changes over time. For example, it appears that the traditional sense of the word *nonplussed,* "bewildered and at a loss as to what to think," is slowly giving way to a new (and opposite) sense: "unfazed." Even experienced writers are using the new sense. For example, here's a snippet from the February 20, 2000, edition of the *New York Times* by veteran journalist Gina Kolata: "The owner happens to be a computer security expert [who] knows about the attacks because his computer has a fire wall, which keeps intruders out and tells him when they have come by. Yet he was nonplussed by the number of attacks on that single day last week. 'I think it's fairly typical,' he said."

No doubt the *Times* received more than a few letters complaining about the "misuse" of the word. But if linguistic history tells us anything, it's that language "correctness" is, over time, determined solely by usage. If enough people use *nonplussed* to mean "unfazed," then that will be the "correct" meaning and no amount of chest-beating or hair-pulling will change it.

Linguists call this kind of thing a *semantic shift,* and it isn't even remotely rare. For example, the word *nice* once meant "foolish or stupid"; people originally used *silly* to mean "deserving of pity"; a *hearse* has over the years referred to a candlestick, a framework for holding tapers, a coffin, and a corpse.

In some cases, the meaning of a word broadens. For example, *bird* originally meant "a small fowl," and now it means "any winged creature." Similarly, *dog* went from "a hunting breed" to "any canine." The opposite process—semantic narrowing—also goes on under our noses. *Meat* used to mean "any type of food," and now it means "flesh of an animal." *Disease* once referred to "any unfavorable state," and it now means "an illness."

The human love of metaphor also gives words new meanings. *Down* means, in the metaphorical sense, "depressed"; *dull* means "stupid"; *grasp* means "understand"; *high* means "on drugs"; and *yarn* means "story."

Finally, there's also the process of *grammar shift,* where a word takes on a new grammatical category. For example, nouns often become verbs: *brush, butter, father, nail,* and *ship.* Verbs also become nouns, although they also often change the stress of their syllables. The verb conDUCT begets the noun CONduct; the verb subJECT is cloned as the noun SUBject.

This book includes a few new words arising from shifts, such as the noun *teardown.* There are also lots of new verbs, including *background, cocooning, caving, skulling, monkey-wrenching, pie, redlining, dilbert,* and *Nasdaq.*

Borrowing

English has a genius not only for creating new words, but also for welcoming foreign guests into its home and then convincing them to stay for a while. These are called *loanwords,* and it has been estimated that something like half of the most common words in English were borrowed from non–Anglo-Saxon languages. ("Borrowing" is a peculiar name for this activity, since it's tough to see any way in which a loan is involved. Someone once said that "not only does the English language borrow words from other languages, it sometimes chases them down dark alleys, hits them over the head, and goes through their pockets.")

Dozens of languages have graciously donated words to English. French has been especially generous over the years, giving us hundreds of words, including "naturalized" terms such as *attorney, grenade, magic,* and *soldier,* as well as terms that retain a distinct French feel, such as *déjà vu, faux pas,* and *nom de plume.* From German we've taken in *blitz, dachshund, kindergarten, hinterland, pretzel,* and *schnapps,* all of which are recognizably German. However, that language has also provided us with *bum, cookbook, fresh* ("impertinent"), *rifle, noodle, poodle,* and *seminar.* Italian has handed over *artichoke, balcony, carnival, casino, mafia, malaria, motto, piano,* and *studio.* Spanish has lent us *banana, cannibal, comrade, guitar, marijuana, mosquito, potato, rodeo,* and *tornado.*

Note, too, that words from other languages influence existing English words. For example, the word *dumb* originally meant "lacking the power of speech," but now it's usually taken to mean "stupid" (except in phrases such as "struck dumb" and "deaf, dumb, and blind"). This change was caused by the German word *dumm,* which means "stupid." Enough German immigrants used this word (for example, *dummkopf*) that it became associated with *dumb* and the "stupid" sense took over.

Onomatopoeia

Onomatopoeia means, literally, "name-making," but it refers to the specific process of creating words from the sounds associated with things. (This is also called *echoism.*) The letter Z seems to figure in many of these coinages: *buzz, fizz, sizzle, whizz, zap, zing, zither, zip, zoom.* Animals are popular onomatopoeic targets: *bow-wow* (dog), *bleat* (sheep), *cheep* (bird), *clip-clop* (horse), *coo* (pigeon), *gobble* (turkey), *purr* (cat), and *quack* (duck). (Not that these are necessarily accurate interpretations. In fact, it's amazing how varied these kinds of words are from culture to culture. In French, a dog's "bow-wow" is *oua-oua* [pronounced "wah-wah"]. In Italian, it's *bu-bu,* and in Romanian, *ham-ham.* Vietnamese dogs *gau-gau,* and Turkish ones *hov-hov.* Tagalog dogs *aw-aw,* Japanese hounds *wau-wau,* and Indonesian breeds *gong-gong.*)

There are onomatopoeic words for thing sounds—*beep, boom, clang, gurgle, slosh,* and *splatter*—and for people sounds— *brrr, burp, giggle, harrumph, sniff, snort,* and *sob.* In fact, there's a whole category of onomatopoeic words for idle chatter: *babbling, blah* (or *blah blah blah*), *flibbertigibbet, yackety-yack,* and, of course, *yada yada yada.* (The jurist Oliver Wendell Holmes memorably described the sounds of an afternoon tea as "giggle, gabble, gobble, and git.")

Some newer additions to the onomatopoeic lexicon are *oomph* (1937), *bebop* (1945), *bleep* (1953), *yuck* ("to vomit";

1963), *vroom* (1967), *doo-wop* (1969), *yech* (1969), and *squodgy* ("soft and soggy"; 1970).

Mistakes

Sometimes new words are created simply by a person (or a bunch of people) making a "mistake." (I use quotation marks here because this is a natural process that goes on all the time, so it shouldn't have a fully negative stigma attached to it.) An interesting subset here are the *ghost words,* or words that are entered erroneously in a dictionary. The classic example is *dord,* "density," which should have been "D or d," the short forms for density. This appeared in the 1934 *Merriam-Webster International Dictionary* after someone misread a handwritten note. The *Oxford English Dictionary* calls these *spurious words* and lists over 300 of them, including *banket* (banker), *corf* (coif), *lolion* (lotion), and *munity* (mutiny). There's also *finiteless,* which sounds useful, possibly as a negatively charged synonym for *infinite;* alas, it was merely a misreading of *fruitless.* Then there's *coysell,* which sounds like a good word for a teasingly shy sales pitch; nope, it's just a mistake for *cayser* (an alternative form of *kaiser*).

Happily, ghost words rarely infiltrate the language. They usually remain hunkered down within the original dictionary (sometimes making appearances in other dictionaries that recklessly copy the original), but eventually they're hunted down and exiled to some haunted house of language.

Other kinds of mistakes have more long-lasting effects on the language. The most common of these errors is something called *back-formation* or *false analogy.* This means that someone sees an existing word, falsely places it in a particular grammatical category, and then proceeds to modify the word based on that false assumption. For example, the noun *pease* originally meant what we know of today as the pea. However, the word *pease* was both singular and plural (something like *pants* or *scissors*). But some-time around 1600 someone thought *pease* was plural, so they started using the word *pea* as the singular.

The *Oxford English Dictionary* lists over 700 such back-formations, including *agoraphobe* from agoraphobia, *exurb* from exurban, *sleaze* from sleazy, *burgle* from burglar, *enthuse* from en-thusiasm, *televise* from television, *couth* from uncouth, *ept* from inept, and *gruntled* from disgruntled. Other examples are *sur-veil, baby-sit, diagnose, donate,* and *reminisce.*

Another error that results in new words is mishearing an exist-ing word. For example, the verb *to buttonhole,* "to detain a person in conversation and not allow them to escape," was originally *button-hold,* as though the accosting conversationalist had taken hold of a button on the victim's coat or shirt to prevent them from leaving. See *undertoad* in this book for an example (although a lit-erary one) of a word formed by mishearing an existing word.

Retronyms

A *retronym* is a word formed from an older word by attaching a previously unnecessary modifier. For example, there was a time when the words *guitar, mail,* and *transmission* were unambigu-ous. However, the advent of the electric guitar, e-mail, and the automatic transmission forced the creation of the retronyms *acoustic guitar, snail mail,* and *manual transmission.* For an ex-ample of a retronym in this book, see *p-book* in Chapter 8, "Weapons of Mass Distraction."

Genericide

Genericide is the process by which a brand name becomes a generic name for an entire product category. Hoover, tabloid, cellophane, heroin, zipper, aspirin, escalator, granola, yo-yo, and linoleum were all once trademarked names, but are now just regular words.

Ex Nihilo

Producing neologisms *ex nihilo* means creating words out of thin air (literally, "from nothing"). That is, these are words that don't arise out of any of the other processes mentioned above. Linguist Mario Pei calls these words "the illegitimate children, the bastards of the lexicological family." The *Oxford English Dictionary* contains several thousand words that are classified as "of obscure origin," "origin obscure," "origin unknown," "of doubtful origin," or "uncertain origin" (the *OED*'s etymological descriptions aren't very consistent). This list includes obscure words such as *bazoo, gongoozler,* and *pilliwinks,* but it also contains many surprisingly common words, including the following: *aye, beach, bet, boy, capsize, caucus, charade, condom, cub, dog, dud, garbage, gravy, hog, hug, job, lad, moniker, muffin, niche, oat, plot, puke, pun, queer, sleet, slush, slut, smidgen, sneak, stooge,* and *wife.* Modern words with unknown origins include *jazz* (1909), *bozo* (1920), *hijack* (1923), *gig* (1926), *gimmick* (1926), *jive* (1928), *pizzazz* (1937), *raunchy* (1939), *gizmo* (1943), *hoagie* (1955), *scam* (1963), *dork* (1964), *zit* (1966), *reggae* (1968), *humongous* (1970), and *mosh* (1987).

Brand names are occasionally created *ex nihilo.* Examples include *Camry, Pyrex,* and *Kodak.* Here's George Eastman on coining the name Kodak:

> I knew a trade name must be short, vigorous, incapable of being misspelt to an extent that will destroy its identity, and, to satisfy trademark laws, it must mean nothing. The letter K had been a favorite with me—it seemed a strong, incisive sort

of letter. Therefore, the word I wanted had to start with K. Then it became a question of trying out a great number of combinations of letters that made words starting and ending with K. The word Kodak is the result.

Another relatively modern word created out of thin air is the mathematical term *googol,* which represents the number 1 followed by 100 zeroes. It was coined by nine-year-old Milton Sirotta in 1938, who made it up when his uncle, the mathematician Edward Kasner, asked him to think of a word for a very large number.

Finally, there are words that writers, particularly novelists, invent for their stories. This happens all the time (remember that Shakespeare fellow), but only a few of these coinages demonstrate linguistic staying power. Some recent examples include *Shangri-La* (1933, from James Hilton's book *Lost Horizon*); *hobbit* (1937, from J. R. R. Tolkien's *The Hobbit*); and *muggle* (1997, from J. K. Rowling's *Harry Potter* series).

Chapter 2

The Accelerated Culture

The wish to live as intensely as possible has subjected humans to the same dilemma as the waterflea, which lives 108 days at 8 degrees Centigrade, but only 26 days at 28 degrees, when its heartbeat is almost four times faster, though in either case its heart beats 15 million times in all. Technology has been a rapid heartbeat, compressing housework, travel, entertainment, squeezing more and more into the allotted span. Nobody expected that it would create the feeling that life moves too fast. —*Theodore Zeldin*

They're busy making bigger roads,
and better roads and more,
so that people can discover
even faster than before
that everything is everywhere alike.
—*Piet Hein*

We are a nation that shouts at a microwave oven to hurry up. —*Joan Ryan*

For most of human history, the world has been a slow place. Humans walked to where they needed to go or they cajoled a nearby animal—horse, donkey, camel, elephant, sled dog—to do the work. Journeys from here to there, depending on how far away "there" was, could take days or even weeks. This didn't seem to bother too many people, but I'm guessing it rankled a few folks with impatient streaks because I imagine they were the ones who invented both the steam engine and the internal combustion engine. With trains and cars now loosed upon the world, "the acceleration of just about everything" (to borrow the subtitle of James Gleick's 1999 book *Faster*) began in earnest.

Not that things became startlingly fast overnight. In 1865 (when the few steam-powered automobiles that were around were known as *road locomotives*), the British Parliament passed the Locomotives and Highways Act, part of which established the world's first speed limits: four miles per hour in the country and two miles per hour in towns and villages. These were apparently still alarming speeds, because the act also decreed that each vehicle must be preceded by a person walking 60 yards in front and waving a red flag to warn others of the vehicle's rapid approach. (Not surprisingly, the legislation became known popularly as the Red Flag Act.)

By the late 1800s, doctors were noticing a remarkable number of cases of *neurasthenia,* a disease characterized by exhaustion, muscle and joint pain, headaches, and poor memory or concentration levels. The source? They didn't think the human body was made to withstand travel at the speeds trains were going, and they didn't think the mind could withstand the hectic pace of the world, with its telegraphs and telephones.

The world has seemed like a too-fast place ever since. In the 1920s, for example, many people claimed they were too busy to read lengthy stories and articles. So *Reader's Digest* was created in 1922 to give people condensed versions of articles that they could fit into their busy schedules. The need for speed was responsible for the popularity of TV dinners (an otherwise inexplicable phenomenon) in the 1950s and '60s, the rise of the push-button phone and the remote control in the 1970s and '80s, and the move of both Federal Express and United Parcel Service from next-day delivery to next-morning delivery to same-day delivery in the 1990s. (They've also shortened their names to FedEx and UPS, thus saving the population as a whole untold millions of syllables.)

When the cardiologists Meyer Friedman and Ray Rosenman

were researching personality types in the 1950s, they coined the term *hurry sickness,* where a person feels chronically short of time and so tends to perform every task faster and to get flustered when encountering any kind of delay. By 1959 they had refined this to the now-classic *Type A personality,* a key element of which was a "harrying sense of time urgency."

Nowadays "time urgency" has a familiar ring to it. That familiarity comes from most of us having felt this "harrying sense" at one time or another, and for many of us it's becoming the way we approach the world. Perhaps, then, we now live in a Type A culture, or an **accelerated culture** (1985):

> The convention makes Burana realize that stripping has changed along with the rest of the world: "Stripping today is more athletic—less subtle and high energy. We're an **accelerated culture** now. Who's got ten minutes to spend taking off a glove?" (*Palm Beach Post,* September 30, 2001)

This phrase became popular in the early 1990s after Douglas Coupland published his famous book, *Generation X: Tales for an Accelerated Culture.* This acceleration has also affected the adjectives we use to describe the world. The rat race is no longer merely *fast-paced,* but **amphetamine-paced** (1993) or **meth-paced** (1997; *meth* is short for *methamphetamine,* a stimulant).

The only way to keep up is to **multitask** (2000)—to do two or three things at once:

> [Mark] Cuban pounds out up to 1,000 e-mail letters a day. Even in the middle of an interview, he doesn't stop. "Go ahead," he tells a reporter, "I can **multi-task.**" (*New York Times Magazine,* March 5, 2000)

For example, if you're on the phone but the call isn't all that important, isn't it tempting to keep working on that memo or to answer an e-mail or two? (This is particularly true for those of us who have perfected the modern art of noiseless typing or mouse-clicking.) There's a new verb for people who succumb to this temptation:

> **background** *v.* (1999) To surreptitiously perform a task in the background while one's attention is supposed to be on another task. *Ever rung a colleague or client and found that the only response your questions are soliciting is the occasional "Hmmm"? You've just been **"backgrounded"**! To **background** someone is to deny them your full attention while multi-tasking.* (*The Guardian,* London, February 13, 1999)

Even clicking a mouse, that keystroke- (and, hence, time-) saver, has become a burden. A few years ago Microsoft Windows introduced a new "single-click" feature that reduced the number of times people had to perform the apparently onerous task of double-clicking. Online retailer Amazon.com touts their "1-click ordering" feature. On the rest of the Web, a quick click of a link can take you to a site across town, across the country, or across the ocean. Clicking—you literally don't even have to lift a finger!—has become a symbol of the modern love of convenience and speed, of our **one-click culture** (2002):

> There's nothing like a book on why marriages fail to leave you staggered by how much the institution of marriage is up against. Not what marriage is up against "now," in the fast-paced, **"one-click" culture** of modern America, blah, blah, blah. No. Consider how much marriage is up against as a concept. How is it that we can decide at 25 or 30 or even 35 what we want for the rest of our lives? (*Washington Post,* January 31, 2002)

When you ask someone how they're doing these days, the answer more often than not is an exasperated "Busy!" (Which reminds me of a cartoon I once saw where a man walks along the beach holding a woman's hand while with the other hand he speaks into a cell phone: "Don't tell me about busy—I'm on my freaking honeymoon!") Sociologists call this tendency toward constant activity the **busy syndrome** (1989):

> She said individuals would know if they had **Busy Syndrome** if they could identify with the following: Their average working day is 9.1 hours; They determined success by the way a person handled stress; Their social calendar is fully booked for the next five weeks; They sent an average of 22 text messages a day; They became irritated when something slows down the daily pace; They described their lives as hectic and yet felt fulfilled; They worked hard and played hard. (*Western Mail*, Cardiff, Wales, May 28, 2002)

Variations on the theme include **too-busy syndrome, I'm busy syndrome, I'm too busy syndrome, constantly busy syndrome, mummy's busy syndrome,** and **terminal busy syndrome.** Related syndromes include the **frantic family syndrome** (1993) and the **hurried woman syndrome** (2002).

One of the consequences of being terminally busy is that we increasingly shun civic or social duties in favor of more solitary pursuits. We are, in other words, increasingly **bowling alone** (1995):

> Individuals now lead more atomised and anonymous lives in which they are more likely to be watching television and **"bowling alone"** than participating in collective activities alongside politicians. (*The Gleaner,* Kingston, Jamaica, February 16, 2003)

This phrase was popularized by Robert Putnam in an essay called "Bowling Alone: America's Declining Social Capital," which appeared in the January 1995 issue of the *Journal of Democracy.* (An expanded version is available in book form.) Putnam argued that civil society was eroding because people were becoming increasingly disconnected from their neighbors and communities. His whimsical symbol for this was the fact that, at the time, more Americans than ever were bowling, but bowling league participation was down 40 percent since 1980.

The ambitious among us work long hours to get ahead; the anxious work long hours to avoid getting laid off; and everyone else works long hours because they can't afford not to. The evidence for this isn't just anecdotal. In her 1997 book *The Time Bind,* sociologist Arlie Russell Hochschild reported that, from 1989 to 1996, the average working couple in the United States increased their total annual working time by 135 hours, the equivalent of nearly three-and-a-half 40-hour workweeks. In her 2001 book *White Collar Sweatshop,* journalist Jill Andresky Fraser reports that over 25 million Americans now work more than 49 hours a week and at least 8.5 percent of the workforce chalks up at least 60 hours a week.

There's always an element of one-upmanship involved when you talk to someone about working hard. If you tell them you usually work 50 hours a week, they'll invariably counter by telling you they work 60 hours. (The general formula seems to be to add 10 hours to whatever number someone else provides.) This is why some researchers pooh-pooh the conventional wisdom that says people (read: Americans) are working longer hours than ever before. They say that these numbers can't be trusted because people generally overreport how many hours they work each week.

Either way, people *feel* harried and rushed. They sense that all the lanes in life's highway have become fast lanes, and it seems as though there are just not enough hours in the day to do everything they want or need to do. They abandoned **quality time** (1977) ages ago and would be happy to settle for a little **quantity time** (1977). They're caught in a **time bind** (1986), and they feel **time-starved** (1983) to the point of famine:

> **time famine** *n* (1987) A chronic lack of time. *These are the days of the **time famine**. As demands on time mount, activ-*

*ities like daydreaming, reading novels, taking long walks or
spending afternoons goofing off with the family have disappeared. For the two-income, middle-class family in particular, time has become more precious than money. As work
pressures increase, more people are complaining about their
lives being out of balance. According to a Lou Harris survey,
the average American had 37 percent less leisure time than in
1973.* (San Francisco Chronicle, December 9, 2001)

Over and above working long hours, there are so many other
activities that demand temporal attention: longer commutes,
aerobics and yoga classes, kids' parties and play dates, and on
and on. These activities suck up huge handfuls of time:

time suck *n.* (1995) An activity that takes up, or is perceived to take up, a large amount of time. Also: **time-suck,
timesuck.** *Lunch in the Bay Area is dead—or at least on life
support. No need to tell that to vending machine mechanic
Luis De La O. All day, on a route that includes offices from
Petaluma to Palo Alto, he stands witness to what remains of
the traditional lunch hour. "No one's going anywhere except
down the hall to the machines," he says. De La O often doesn't
have time to break at noon, either. On a recent Tuesday, he
grabbed a slice at Blondie's Pizza on Powell Street, where 15
minutes is considered a long lunch. Across Market Street, in
the halls of Bay Area dot-com businesses, stopping to eat is considered a* **time suck,** *a ritual for losers who simply don't have
enough to do.* (San Francisco Chronicle, August 16, 2000)

time sucker *n.* (1995) Also: **time-sucker, timesucker.** *I
could drone on about all the usual arguments for not having
a TV. It's a* **time-sucker,** *luring you into program after program once you've switched it on.* (Pittsburgh Post-Gazette,
April 22, 2001)

The time so lost is called a **time sink** (1989), **time suckage** (1994), or **time leakage** (1990):

> Have you ever been to the cashpoint in the morning, taken out £10 and then, by 6pm, found you've got no money left? "But I didn't buy anything!" you exclaim, until you remember that train ticket, the sandwich, the magazine, the soft drink, all of which mount up to about nine quid. The same thing goes for time. Sometimes our working day seems to just slip by. Just like the magazine and the soft drink, it goes on the little things—tiny **time-leakages** that all eat into the hours we've set aside for work tasks. This is known as **"time suckage."** (*Sunday Herald,* Glasgow, Scotland, February 4, 2001)

Computers were supposed to save us time, but we end up spending half of our days either trying to figure out how they work or recovering from the inevitable crashes. Then there's the annoying software that causes us to fritter away vast amounts of what would otherwise be productive time:

> **fritterware** *n.* (1988) Feature-laden software that seduces people into spending inordinate amounts of time tweaking various options for only marginal gains in productivity. *A couple of years ago, Sun Microsystems Chairman Scott McNealy declared, "The massive slowdown in production and fall in the standard of living in the Eighties and Nineties is going to be blamed entirely on Microsoft Office." He railed about wasted "person-centuries in manipulation of clip art." Now McNealy has* **fritterware** *of his own, thanks to Sun's acquisition of Star Division Corp., and its StarOffice "productivity suite."* (*Forbes,* October 4, 1999)

Time leaks, but time is also often stolen right out from underneath our watches:

time thief *n.* (1997) A person or activity that takes a significant amount of time. *I've noticed a significant increase in spam over the past year. An informal survey of friends revealed that I'm not alone. The feeling was confirmed when my online research found that Gartner Inc. estimates that spam increased five-fold during 2001. Others estimate that spam is doubling every five months. Spam is much more than an inconvenience. Spam is a **time thief**. It takes time to download unwanted e-mail, review it and send it to the trash bin. It's time that is wasted—diverted from more productive or relaxing pursuits.* (*Occupational Hazards*, June 1, 2002)

We used to *pass the time,* as though it was something free that we were only too happy to share with others; now we *spend time* as though it's some kind of commodity to be bought and sold. So if a time thief takes away too much time, a person becomes time-impoverished:

time poor *adj.* (1983) Describes a person who lacks the time to perform basic tasks and chores. Also: **time-poor.** *"The reality is, for those of us who are cash rich and **time poor,** midnight may be the only time we can shop," adds Ira Matathia, CEO of the Intelligence Factory, a business research unit of advertising giant Young & Rubicam. "But we're still in an environment of immediate gratifiers. We want everything exactly the way we want it, and want it immediately.* (*The Christian Science Monitor,* August 7, 2000)

Someone who is time poor can make up his or her **time deficit** (1997) by **borrowing time** (2000) from a friend or neighbor (that is, asking the other person to perform a task). He or she can they repay this **time debt** (1997) by doing the other person a **time favor** (2000) later on:

Research in Liverpool indicated that in order to meet their journey requirements, women from low-income households often joined forces . . . and exchanged **time-favours.** Typically, in order to enable a neighbour or a friend to undertake her shopping, one woman would take care of the children of two households. When she in turn needed to **"borrow time"** in order to meet a hospital appointment or undertake her shopping, she would call in the **"time-debt."** (*Urban Studies,* September 1, 2000)

If a person becomes chronically time poor, he or she may have to declare **time bankruptcy** (2001):

In an economy awash in capital and information, time is scarce. And scarcity, as any Econ 101 graduate can tell you, generally makes something more valuable. For many people today, time is more valuable than money, because throughout the workforce, Americans seem to be suffering from **time bankruptcy.** (Daniel Pink, *Free Agent Nation,* 2001)

Elevators are a major example of time suckage. The *Wall Street Journal* reported in 2002 that the "vertical-transportation industry" (the highfalutin name preferred by elevator professionals) has studied the amount of time people are willing to wait for an elevator before they get "antsy." The results? In a residential building, people will wait patiently for about 50 to 60 seconds, but in office buildings frustration sets in around the 25-second mark.

Of course, there are always those caricatures of impatience, the people who press the elevator call button and, a few seconds later, begin stabbing the button frantically in an apparent effort to transmit the urgency of their situation to the elevators' consciousness. In his book *Faster,* James Gleick talked about a method that elevator engineers have devised to calm these tortured souls (and prolong the usable life span of elevator call buttons): "Japan has pioneered another feature, called 'psychological waiting-time lanterns': as soon as someone presses a call button, a computer determines which car will reach the floor first and lights the appropriate signal well in advance of its arrival. This gives the illusion of an instantaneous response and, as a side benefit, herds riders into position for quick loading."

Once inside, a new delay awaits the impatient:

door dwell *n.* (1999) The amount of time it takes for the door to close after having boarded an elevator. *"Door dwell" typically lasts two to four seconds. Do you reach for the door-close button anyway? Would you still reach for it if you knew that most building managers disable the buttons out of fear of trapped limbs and lawsuits? (Austin American-Statesman, October 4, 1999)*

Given all this, I guess it's not surprising that I feel absurdly pleased with myself if I press the elevator call button and a car arrives immediately, as though it had been the car's turn this time to wait tediously for *my* arrival.

People love this kind of thing: the subway or bus arriving just as we reach the station or stop; the clerk who becomes free just as we arrive at the cash register; the box of fresh corn that gets put out just as we arrive at the vegetable stand.

When things happen "just in time," we feel good because we've entered a rare credit item in our personal time accounting ledger. We're a little less time poor. This has worked in the business world for many years in the form of **just-in-time manufacturing** (1982): the manufacturing of goods without keeping large inventories of raw materials or the finished product. (That is, raw materials are delivered just when they're needed, and goods are built just when customers order them.)

The mistake many people make is to try to expand this just-in-time approach to their entire lives. If it typically takes 10 minutes to drive to the office, they'll leave exactly 10 minutes before they're supposed to be there. That's fine if it's a typical drive, but if there's an accident or the traffic is heavier than usual, they end up late and angry at themselves for not leaving sooner (see *road rage* in Chapter 4, "Modern Angst and Anger"). This kind of lifestyle has it own name:

> **just-in-time lifestyle** *n.* (1999) A modern lifestyle in which people expend only the minimum effort to complete a task and rush from one appointment to another. *Leslie Charles, a corporate consultant and author of* Why Is Everyone So Cranky?, *speculates that more people are running late these days because of what she terms "**just-in-time lifestyles,**" after a manufacturing process that has materials arriving at a plant as needed to save storage expenses. In humans, she says, it works this way: "They make plans to get there just in time—and something happens." (Atlanta Journal–Constitution, May 22, 2001)*

Our obsession with saving time and the inordinate attachment we feel for free time has turned time into a kind of fetishistic object. When we hurry from one appointment to another during the day, we see people walking along, standing around, or sitting in outdoor patios. "Don't these people have jobs?!" we cry, the jealousy only barely concealed. We become covetous of their free time, we want it *real* bad:

> **time porn** *n.* (1994) Television shows and other media that portray characters as having excessive amounts of spare time. **—time-porn** *adj.* Also: **leisure-time porn** (1998), **leisure porn** (1999). *Call it **time porn.** Just as sexual pornography titillates us with images from a forbidden world in which casual sex is there for the taking, do modern images, on television shows and in advertising, show us free time, a thing we covet but cannot have? The characters of*

*"Seinfeld" wallow obscenely in unscheduled time, as did the characters on "Cheers," probably the mother of all **time-porn** shows. (Hartford Courant, May 16, 1994)*

In the twenty-first century, we live by an amended version of Parkinson's Law: "Life expands to fill the time available." We become gluttons for time and ask, semiseriously, "When is someone going to invent the 48-hour day?" Or we become time junkies, always looking for a fix of free time so that we can do more, see more, be more. When time addicts look for ways to score a bit more time during the day, sleeping less is the most obvious source. Our culture has a sleep-is-for-sissies attitude that isn't helped by legendary sleep habits of some highly effective people. We read that the likes of Napoleon, Edison, and Churchill needed only a few hours of sleep a night. Leonardo da Vinci, the genius's genius, allegedly slept for 20 minutes every four hours.

A kind of temporal New Math comes into play: "If I sleep six hours a night during the week instead of eight, that's an extra ten hours a week! Nothing will stop me then, bwah ha ha ha!" We become a new kind of creature:

sleep camel *n.* (1999) A person who gets little sleep during the week and then attempts to make up for it by sleeping in and napping on the weekend. *Silicon Valley refers to the pressured people who store up enough sleep on weekends to manage a 60-hour-plus week as **sleep camels.** The term brings to mind beasts of burden, expendables expected to die beneath you in pursuit of some higher purpose.* (Business Day, July 11, 2000)

The problem, of course, is that the human body requires sleep. You can only saw off so much slumber before the body begins to rebel and the mind turns to mush. The body in its wisdom knows this, so it often forces the issue:

microsleep *n.* (1982) A brief period (usually only a few seconds) in which the brain enters a sleep state regardless of the activity the person is performing at the time. Also: **micro sleep, micro-sleep.** *"No one, not even CEOs, are resistant to the effects of sleep loss," said J. Catesby Ware, professor of Eastern Virginia Medical School and director of the Sleep Disorders Center at Sentara Norfolk General Hospital. "As CEOs get less and less sleep, they become more moody, grouchy and irritable." Sleep-deprived people can perform routine tasks, Ware said. In new or challenging situations, however, they are less likely to come up with novel or the most appropriate decisions, he said. They will have "micro sleeps" or attention lapses, Ware said. "They're not processing what's going on around them."* (*Richmond Times-Dispatch,* July 23, 2001)

If a person is dangerously sleep-deprived, the body will resort to more drastic measures:

sleep seizure *n.* (1990) A long period of unexpected sleep. *For his part, Cornell University sleep researcher James Maas wonders whether we weren't initially programmed to conk out for even longer . . . "It's one thing to function," he notes, "another to be alert, creative and not have an unintended **sleep seizure** driving down the freeway." He recommends a little more than nine hours a night for teenagers, and for most adults, 71/2 to eight hours.* (*Seattle Times,* April 7, 2002)

An earlier (and more dramatic) term is **sleep attack** (1976):

Sleeping too little also takes a serious toll on mental acuity, said David Dinges, president of the Sleep Research Society. He found that after seven days on six hours a night of sleep, nearly one-fourth of experimental subjects began to experience **"sleep attacks,"** where they nodded off uncontrollably for up to 30 seconds. The greater the sleep deprivation, the more frequent the sleep attacks. (*Tacoma News Tribune,* June 12, 2002)

Too little sleep may lead to exhaustion and other symptoms that may land a person in the hospital. Unfortunately, things don't slow down there, either:

beeper medicine *n.* (1999) The practice of medicine by responding primarily to pages and other emergency calls. *Other professions, other technological speed-ups: medicine has been profoundly altered by the simple pocket pager . . . Some doctors worry about the rise of what they call "beeper medicine"; they see an addiction to paging and quick fixes.* (James Gleick, *Faster,* 1999)

sicker and quicker *adj.* (1985) Describes a hospital discharge in which a patient is released before having completely recovered. *Hospitals used to care for us until we got better—even if it took a couple of weeks. Then we went home. But almost 20 years ago, Congress passed a little-known law that changed all this by changing how hospitals get paid. Until the mid-'80s, hospitals were paid for every day we were there. But then the law changed, and hospitals began getting a flat fee based on our diagnosis. A heart attack had one price tag, a broken foot another. If we recovered quickly, the hospital kept the leftover dollars as profit. If we lingered, the hospital took a loss. Like magic, hospital lengths of stay plummeted. Patients were discharged "sicker and quicker," often to nursing homes, which became centers of rehabilitation.* (*Seattle Times,* July 24, 2002)

hit-and-run nursing *n.* (1998) An aspect of managed health care in which nurses attend to a greater number of patients and attempt to speed those patients through the system by performing tasks—such as drawing blood—previously assigned to specialists. *Many traditional nurses say they are appalled by having more patients to watch, relying on aides to take up the slack. They worry that managed care, without restraints, leads to what they call **hit-and-run nursing** and to mistakes, abuses and oversights. Patients are discharged sooner, and so they need more vigilance, not less, said Kit Costello, president of the California Nurses Association in Sacramento.* (*New York Times,* April 9, 1998)

This is also called **accelerated-care nursing** (2001), which brings us back to our starting point: the accelerated culture. We live in a world where the VCR's fast-forward mode is too slow, where people speed-walk along moving sidewalks, where a second's delay when the light turns green elicits a chorus of impatient honking from the cars behind. Is all this bad? The neologist, ever the disinterested chronicler of linguistic change, takes the easy way out and shuns such value judgments. "It's all good," as the kids say (for a while, anyway; because slang changes constantly, it's the "accelerated culture" of language).

Chapter 3

Faster Food

A nation's diet can be more revealing than its art or literature. —*Eric Schlosser*

Terence, this is stupid stuff:
You eat your victuals fast enough;
There can't be much amiss, 'tis clear,
To see the rate you drink your beer.
—*A. E. Housman*

The phrase *fast food* entered the English language in the early 1950s, just a few short years after the brothers Richard and Maurice McDonald opened their first *McDonald's Famous Hamburgers* restaurant. (Yes, we're talking here about *the* McDonald's.) For all of its 50-plus-year history, the emphasis in the fast food industry has almost always been on the word "fast" instead of the word "food." The McDonald brothers started it all by developing their "Speedee Service System" that took the methods and principles of a factory assembly line and applied them to food. (One employee worked the grill, another added the condiments—which were exactly the same on all orders, no exceptions—a third poured the drinks, and so on.)

Nowadays, fast-food emporiums routinely time how long it takes workers to perform certain tasks (and issue stern reprimands when those tasks take longer than the officially prescribed time), and they spend millions each year researching and developing new machines that will fry, grill, or pour faster or

more efficiently. This emphasis on speed is no mystery; it's ax-
iomatic in the industry that the faster a restaurant gets customers in and out, the more money it will make. So it's no
wonder that when they talk among themselves, fast-food operators prefer to call their establishments **quick service restaurants**
(1991) or **fast-feeders** (1982).

And the good news for fast food franchisees is that their customers have fully embraced this faster-is-better ethos. North
American culture is now in large part a fast food culture because
fast food fits in with our hectic lifestyles. Hungry, but running
short on time? Then just take a quick run over to the nearest
KFC or Taco Bell, where you'll be eating in a just a few minutes.
(Eric Schlosser, author of the book *Fast Food Nation,* conserva-
tively estimates that each day about one-quarter of the U.S.
adult population eats at least one fast-food meal.)

But lately it seems that even fast food isn't enough to satisfy
our need for speed. When the time-starved are starving, they
want their food served more quickly, cooked more conveniently,
and eaten more efficiently. They want, in short, even *faster* food,
and the world's culinary capitalists have been only too eager to
accommodate them. This chapter looks at the numerous words
and phrases that have sprung up in the fertile fields of this faster
food movement.

The Car as Dining Room

Before they opened *McDonald's Famous Hamburgers* in 1948,
the McDonald brothers owned a drive-in restaurant, which was
a natural business to go into in California in the 1930s and '40s.
In 1923 the owner of a Sacramento A&W had a lightbulb-over-
the-head moment and hired waiters to run mugs of frothy root
beer out to customers waiting in cars. By 1930 the word *drive-in*

had entered the lexicon, and the it-could-only-happen-in-America notion of getting served and eating in one's car became a bona fide fad.

However, McDonald's "Speedee" system marked the beginning of the end for the drive-in as people—especially families—took almost immediately to the new combination of fast service and cheap prices. Although only a few drive-in restaurants still exist (happily, the "waiters" in these establishments are still called *carhops,* a term that dates from 1937), the combination of cars and eating has seen a resurgence over the past few years. This time, however, the focus isn't on eating while merely *sitting* in a car. Rather, it's on eating while *driving* a car, or **dashboard dining** (1985):

> The average American now eats 27 meals a year while on the road. That's up from 17 meals in 1984, according to the NPD Group, a Port Washington, N.Y.-based consulting company. . . . Among young adults the number is probably much higher than 27, says Harry Balzer, vice president of the NDP Group. Eating in the car is so much a part of our lives there's even a catch phrase for it: **dashboard dining.** (*Baltimore Sun,* September 18, 2002)

There are also verb **(dashboard dine;** 1997) and noun **(dashboard diner;** 1995) variations:

> Of course, you can avoid the desire to **dashboard dine** by just eating in. (*Orange County Register,* October 24, 1997)

> Was the **"dashboard diner"** concept created because people are becoming more and more mobile? (*Franchising World,* November/December 1995)

To the efficiency experts of the world, dashboard dining—or **drive-time dining** (1997)—must make a lot of sense. After all, many commuters spend great hunks of time stuck in traffic.

According to the 1990 U.S. Census data, nearly one-third of commuters spend at least 30 minutes driving to work. And other than listening to music (nonproductive) or talking on a cell phone (dangerous), there isn't much for a driver to do with all that **windshield time** (1991)—work-related time spent in a car, including commuting time.

So why not inhale a quick meal in between the imprecations and gesticulations that accompany the typical commute? That's exactly what people are doing. In fact, dashboard dining has become so popular that the food industry now has a separate **food-in-the-car** (1998) category to keep an eye on the latest trends. Here dashboard diners often are referred to, unflatteringly, as **mobile stomachs** (1998), and marketers fight for **stomach share** (1984) instead of market share. They also use the following terms for the meals people are eating while they're on the move:

carfast *n.* (2000) A breakfast eaten while driving a car. *Instead of those creaky old three squares, more studies than you can shake a pretzel stick at have shown that the majority of us are more or less behaving like teen-agers, devouring what amounts to anytime, anywhere energy fixes. Thus the terms . . . "dashboard dining" and "carfast" have emerged. (Snack Food and Wholesale Bakery, June 2000)*

dashboard breakfast *n.* (1991) A breakfast eaten while driving. *The Laguna Hills couple say they planned their October vacation during their commute on the Santa Ana (I-5) Freeway. They did it over a **dashboard breakfast.** (Orange County Register, July 21, 1991)*

commuter food *n.* (1987) A meal eaten while commuting to or from work. *Sammy's also serves the best corn dogs in town—slightly sweet and delivered to you fresh from the fryer. They are the perfect **commuter food:** You can eat them easily in a car without fear of spraying mustard all over your*

clothes. *You don't even have to get your hands dirty.*
(*Milwaukee Journal Sentinel,* August 27, 1999)

The *New York Times* once called such food *no-think food*
(1987), but the phrase never caught on. That's a shame because
it would be nice not to have to think too much about the food
you're eating while behind the wheel. Yes, eating in the car may
be convenient, but it turns out that it's also downright dangerous. These days it's common for people to complain about drivers who are driving while talking on cell phones (see *DWY* in
Chapter 4). However, there is evidence to suggest that what we
might call "DWE" (driving while eating) is much more dangerous. A 2001 study published by the American Automobile
Association's Foundation for Traffic Safety analyzed more than
26,000 crashes that occurred between 1995 and 1998. Of the
accidents that were attributed to driver distraction, a mere 1.5
percent were caused by cell phone use, but a whopping 19 percent were caused by eating or drinking.

Here's a more general term for the wheel meal deal:

drive-through cuisine *n.* (1994) The food prepared for
and served through a restaurant's drive-through window.
Be warned: This is a strict vegan cookbook—anyone raised on
takeout and **drive-through cuisine** *will run screaming from*
dishes created with tempeh, tofu or spelt flour. (*Denver Post,*
October 25, 2000)

The *drive-through* (or *drive-thru*) concept—pulling your car
up to a special window in a fast-food restaurant to pay for and
receive a meal—is almost as old as fast food itself. (The *Oxford*
English Dictionary's earliest citation for drive-through/drive-thru
is from 1949 and mentions something called, tantalizingly, the
"Beer Vault Drive-Thru.") However, it didn't become popular
until Wendy's made it a standard part of each restaurant in the

1970s. Now most fast-food restaurants generate anywhere from 50 to 70 percent of their revenues from drive-through sales.

The phenomenal success of the drive-through can be attributed to two factors. First, drive-throughs are fast. According to *QSR Magazine*'s annual "Drive-Thru Time Study" for 2001, fast-food outlets can process a drive-through stomach, oops, I mean customer—meaning from the moment the person stops the car at the **menuboard** (1980) until she or he drives off with food—in an average of 188 seconds, or just over three minutes. The speed demon of the group was Wendy's, which moved 'em in and moved 'em out in an average of just 135 seconds.

Second, the restaurants have begun adapting their menus to suit the drive-through crowd. For example, you now see cups— even **supersized** (*adj.*; 1994) ones—tapered to fit into car cup holders and foods placed into special packages to make them easier to eat. Taco Bell recently reengineered its taco shells so they'd be less prone to shattering. What's happening here is the triumph of a new kind of consumable:

> **one-handed food** *n.* (1987) Food that is small enough to hold in one hand and is not messy to eat so that it can be consumed while driving or working. *Grabowski of GMA, who says that 2000 was the year of "one-handed foods," expects more to come. There's a "great premium" placed on anything that can be prepared or eaten while holding a baby or driving a car, he says. (Washington Post, January 3, 2001)*

A much rarer synonym is **one-fisted food** (1996). On a slightly more general level, there's the following popular term:

> **handheld food** *n.* (1982) Food that can be consumed without utensils. Also: **hand-held food.** *Manufacturers are responding with foods that can be more easily consumed with one hand and foods that are less messy, decreasing the likeli-*

hood that you'd show up for a parent-teacher conference with salsa on your pants or a for a job interview with coffee splashes on your tie. . . . Production of **handheld foods** *has grown about 8 percent a year since 1995 and is expected to reach $2.3 billion in sales by 2004.* (*Chicago Daily Herald,* May 15, 2002)

Handheld food is big business. Early in 2000 the market research firm Kalorama Information published a report titled "The U.S. Market for Frozen and Refrigerated Hand-Held Foods." They concluded that the annual retail sales of such products are expected to reach $2.3 billion by 2004. That's a lot of **handheld meals** (1987) and **handheld lunches** (2001).

Some handheld food is designed to be eaten while walking, and this ambulatory nourishment has its own term of art:

portable food *n.* (1983) Food that can be eaten while walking. *Whatever brings people back, tasty walking-around food is essential for the ultimate fair experience. This year more than 40 food vendors will provide a variety of* **portable foods** *including waffle-on-a-stick, shrimp-on-a-stick, frozen cheesecake-on-a-stick and the all-time favorite, hot-dog-on-a-stick.* (*Spokesman-Review,* Spokane, Wash., September 6, 2002)

As with dashboard dining, the popularity of portable food is directly attributable to the time crunch that most people feel. For example, the National Restaurant Association's 1999 "Lunch Study" found that 27.3 percent of full-time employees often spend their lunch hours shopping or running errands (up from 24.4 percent just three years earlier). That leaves little time for a sit-down meal, so the preferred repast is an **on-the-go meal** (1988). For that, you need **walkabout food** (1994) or **street food** (1977). (The latter is most often used to refer to the food that's available from street locations such as hot dog vendors and ice cream trucks.)

Need an example? Okay, how about macaroni and cheese shoehorned into a microwaveable cardboard tube that has a push stick on the bottom? After cooking, you use the stick to push the food up the tube and you munch away on what squeezes out of the top. (You're sorry you asked, right? Lucky for you I decided not to describe the scrambled eggs version.) This is called a **push and eat** (*adj.*, 2000) product or a **tube food** (1993). This tube-and-push-stick contraption is an example of a **self-server** (1999). Besides tubes, handheld food has also been crammed into bags, stuffed into pockets and pouches, nestled in wraps, and adhered to sticks (where it's called, naturally, **stick food**).

Macaroni and cheese qualifies as a **comfort food**. The on-the-go version of such a meal is called—give me a "duh"— **portable comfort food** (1999) or **portable comfort cuisine** (2000). Higher-quality portable food has its own term:

> **portafuel** *n.* (2001) A portable and nutritious meal or snack. *Raymond sees opportunities for more "portafuels," foods that are both portable and healthful, such as Athenos Foods' new pita triangles and hummus that comes in a compartmentalized plastic container.* (*Washington Post,* January 3, 2001)

Handheld foods are the only way to go if you're eating a meal at your desk, which half of all employees have done at one time or another. Here are a couple of terms related to this desk-as-dining-table trend:

> **deskfast** *n.* (1996) Breakfast eaten at a desk. *A soaring number of Britain's workers have replaced breakfast with "deskfast," a new report found yesterday. The report by bread makers Nimble shows that one in 10 people arrive early*

at work to eat brekkie at their desk while they read e-mails and open post. (*Daily Star,* London, January 26, 2001)

cubicle cuisine *n.* (1999) A meal eaten within an office cubicle. *Dilberitos are, in the words of the manufacturer, Scott Adams Foods of Newton, N.J., "cubicle cuisine."* (*New York Times,* July 7, 1999)

dining al desko *pp.* (1981) Eating at one's desk (cf. *alfresco,* "outdoors"). *Crunch. Munch. Slurp. Crunch. Munch. Slurp. What's that? It's the guy at the next desk having lunch. The number of folks who have taken to **dining al desko** is causing some new problems in the workplace.* (*Philadelphia Daily News,* March 29, 1994)

Let's hope desk-based diners aren't influenced by the commercial showing a cubicle-dweller eating a Kellogg's Pastry Swirl. A dollop of the food's internal goo drops on his pants and, later, the cleaning lady catches him with his pants off sucking the sweet stuff out of the fabric. The tag line: "They're that good."

Not only are people changing *where* they eat, but also *how often.* For example, the majority of people no longer eat the traditional three square meals a day. Instead, these folks have a new way of eating:

grazing *pp.* (1984) Eating a number of small meals throughout the day. *Eating frequent, small meals (200 to 500 calories) instead of larger ones (1,000 calories) boosts the body's fat-burning ability by up to 30 percent in some women, research has shown. . . . While you're **grazing,** make sure to stay hydrated. Drinking eight to 10 cups a day of water or other noncaffeinated, nonalcoholic beverages aids metabolism, since the body needs water to help burn calories.* (*Chicago Daily Herald,* November 26, 2001)

When they're at home, time-sensitive grazers will often resort to a **sink meal** (1991), which is a quick but potentially spillable meal (such as cereal) that is eaten over the kitchen sink. The food eaten by a grazer is sometimes called a **meal bridge** (1995), which refers to any food that people eat when they don't have the time either to cook a meal or to sit down and eat one leisurely.

Speed Comes to the Kitchen

Speaking of cooking, if our time-deficient lifestyles dictate eating meals while driving, walking, or sitting at our desks, then it isn't the least bit surprising to learn that this **fast-food mentality** (1982) means we're also spending far less time preparing meals. According to the market research firm the NPD Group, more than 44 percent of households prepare their weekday meals in 30 minutes or less. For young couples and singles, that number rises to over 54 percent.

For many years, time-challenged cooks could cobble together a quick dinner by preparing a **skillet meal** (1984), a meal in which the ingredients come prepackaged and are cooked in a skillet or pot. However, many cooks missed the satisfaction of cooking from scratch. So how did they reconcile this with the fact that they lacked the time required to cook the old-fashioned way? They found a new way:

> **speed scratch** *n.* (1994) Meal preparation in which the basic ingredients come pre-measured in a package and only need to be combined with one or more fresh ingredients and then cooked. Also: **speed-scratch.** —*adj. Time-pressed cooks are driving the trend toward "speed scratch," using convenience products like mixes and frozen dinners that call for a handful of fresh ingredients to turn out fast meals.*

*U.S. consumers used **speed scratch** techniques to prepare
food 24.4 times a month in 2000, up from 15.7 in 1998, according to the Riedel Marketing Group in Phoenix.* (Cox
News Service, October 26, 2001)

For example, one company offers a lasagna **meal kit** (1989)
that comes with just the right amount of noodles, sauce, and
cheese. Add the optional meat, combine everything in the usual
way, and then pop the concoction into the oven. The result is a
quick meal, but one that makes the cook feel as though they
cooked it from scratch. This is also known as **component cooking** (1991), and the results are often called, unappetizingly, **assembly meals** (1990). Gourmands and other cookery snobs
take a good long look down their noses at these items and declare them to be mere **toy food** (1983).

A nice salad would go great with that lasagna, but who has
time to mess around with various heads of lettuce and other veg-
gies? No problem, just get yourself a **salad-in-a-bag** (1997), a
bag that contains preshredded lettuce, precut vegetables, as well
as other ingredients such as croutons and dressing (which comes
in its own single-serving pouch).

Grocery stores wasted no time in jumping on this **meal solution** (1991) or **just-in-time meal** (1995) bandwagon. For
example, they located meal kits conveniently in the meat
department for one-stop shopping. Similarly, they gathered related food items—such as the ingredients for a stir-fry or an
Italian food dish—into special "theme" areas. Other perks that
the grocers have been mulling over include allowing customers
to order what they need in advance and having meal components gathered by a store employee while you shop for other
things.

Then there are the hungry hurriers who don't even have time
to shop for groceries and who can't stomach the thought of ordering yet another pizza or chowing down on last night's chow

mein. A quick check in the fridge and the cupboards turns up some basic ingredients: leftover chicken, some cans of soup, the usual spice suspects. What's a would-be chef to do? The Campbell Soup Company has an answer: a toll-free line that you can call to speak to a **recipe representative** (1997), who'll be happy to take down your ingredients list and turn it into an honest-to-goodness recipe.

If you're too tired to talk to a live person, the Campbell's website offers a "Quick Recipe Finder," an online form in which you check off the ingredients you have on hand (including, of course, the Campbell's products you have kicking around the kitchen) and then choose the type of meal you want (such as a main dish or a dessert). The site then displays one or more recipes, most of which can be prepared in 30 minutes or less. Not to be outdone, the Betty Crocker website has a "What's On Hand" feature that does basically the same thing.

Once you have that ad hoc recipe, you can cook it even faster by getting yourself a newfangled **rapid-cooking oven** (1999), which doesn't require preheating and which, through the combination of convection and microwave technologies, can bake things up to five times faster than a conventional oven.

For those times when there's nothing in the cupboard and there's no slack in your schedule, the grocery stores came up with yet another solution:

home meal replacement *n.* (1993) A full, cooked meal purchased at a grocery store or other food outlet. *Jerry Bockwinkel, owner of two downtown groceries, said people who live in condos tend to shop for groceries more frequently, so their purchases are smaller. They're also more apt to buy single servings or prepared foods. "The current jargon is '**home meal replacement**,' " he said. "Those sales have gone up 70-fold over the last five years." (Chicago Tribune, July 17, 2002)*

This is also called a **replacement meal** (1994), although don't confuse this with **replacement dining** (1990), which refers to eating at a restaurant when you can't be bothered to cook.

Vittles that can be turned into a meal quickly and easily have long been known as *convenience foods* (1961). However, for modern sustenance-seekers who are perpetually in hurry-up mode, mere convenience is no longer good enough. They need food to go to the next level:

> **hyperconvenience food** *n.* (2000) Food that is ready-to-eat or that requires only minimal preparation. *Now, with the pace of life near warp speed, it's time for something marketers call **hyperconvenience food***. (*New York Times,* May 28, 2000)

Examples of **hyperconvenient** (*adj.;* 1994) foods include tube-bound yogurt that you squirt into your mouth, **toaster foods** (1993)—which now go beyond the traditional waffles and bagels to comestibles such as pizza, sandwiches, and even eggs—and **energy bars** (1977), a candy bar–shaped food that contains an energy-boosting combination of dried fruit, nuts, and seeds.

The big problem with hyperconvenient meals is that they tend to lack nutritional balance. If you don't have time to go the balanced meal route, the world's scientists have come up with an alternative that combines both convenience and nutrition:

> **functional food** *n.* (1989) A food product that has been enhanced with vitamins or pharmaceuticals to provide specific health benefits. *Scientists asked: If foods can boost risk of illness, can they reduce it as well? Modern lab techniques offer proof of what had been mere theory, identifying compounds in foods that have physiological effects. This accomplishment, coupled with an aging and health-conscious*

*population, has helped fuel the popularity of **functional
foods.** (San Jose Mercury News,* April 23, 2002)

This good-for-you food is also known by a whole host of
aliases, including **therapeutic food** (1980), **medical food** (1983),
prescriptive food (1990), **nutraceutical** (1990), **foodaceutical**
(1991), **pharma food** (1992), **pharmafoodical** (1992), and
food/drug hybrid (1993). For example, one recent innovation
is **golden rice** (1999), a strain of rice that has been genetically
modified to increase its Vitamin A content.

You've seen in this chapter that we satisfy our alimentary speed
cravings with everything from quick-service restaurants to speed
scratch meals. We drive along eating commuter food, walk
along eating handheld food, and hurry along eating hypercon-
venience food. For the sake of saving a few seconds here and a
few minutes there, we subject our bodies to the indignities of
tube foods, toy foods, and toaster foods. We eat in front of our
dashboards, at our desks, and over our sinks. The good news is
that if this fast-food mentality causes our nutrition-starved bodies to crash and burn, we can always turn to functional foods to
repair the damage.

Chapter 4

Modern Angst and Anger

Now is the age of anxiety. —*W. H. Auden*

On an average weekday, a major newspaper contains more information than any contemporary of Shakespeare's would have acquired in a lifetime. —*Anonymous*

When angry count four; when very angry, swear.
—*Mark Twain*

History buffs have a mania for applying "Age of" labels to epochs gone by: the Age of Enlightenment, the Age of Reason, the Age of Aquarius. When historians look back on the current age, what label will they choose? Some psychologists are already suggesting that the *Age of Anxiety* would be an appropriate moniker. (They've also suggested *Century of Stress,* proving, if nothing else, that the joys of alliteration are not lost on the psychology profession.)

True, the name has already been used. W. H. Auden's famous poem *The Age of Anxiety* was published in 1948, and Leonard Bernstein's symphony based on that poem was first performed in 1949. These works reflected the worries of a world only a few short years removed from a devastating war and a few short years into a new and particularly worrisome kind of conflict: the Cold War.

But now, with World War II a distant historical event for most people and the Cold War long ago won by the good guys, we seem to be more stressed out than ever. Gentle souls bottle up the stresses and end up living in a state of near-perpetual anxiety. And the breakneck pace of modern society has caused a virtual epidemic of rage as people who used to get mad at the drop of a hat now don't even wait for the hat to start falling. As you'll see in this chapter, when the going gets tough nowadays, the tough either get anxious or get mad.

The Anxious Generation

That anxiety levels are rising fast is well documented in the psychological community. In one of the most comprehensive studies, psychologist Jean Twenge examined anxiety research on children and college students from 1952 to 1993. Writing in the *Journal of Personality and Social Psychology,* Dr. Twenge estimated that anxiety levels are roughly 50 percent higher now than they were in the 1950s, and she found that the "change in anxiety is so large that by the 1980s normal child samples were scoring higher than child psychiatric patients from the 1950s." So it's not surprising that we now have a new generation of anxious citizens:

anxious generation (1994) The class of people who exhibit a general anxiousness about the world or about specific issues such as job security, crime, and money. *The Anxious Generation; A new study finds that living alone, stress, fear of AIDS, and other modern-day traumas are making Americans unhealthily edgy.* (*Business Week Online,* January 10, 2001)

This group is also called the **anxious class** (1992):

The American middle class is disintegrating. In its place are emerging three new strata of society: an underclass of desperately poor, almost entirely disconnected from the world of work; an overclass of the well-educated, who take full advantage of advancing technologies and global markets; and in between an **anxious class** of Americans who are steadily losing ground. (Speech to Dartmouth College graduates, June 12, 1994)

Although he didn't invent the phrase *anxious class,* it was popularized by economist Robert Reich (whom I've quoted in the above citation) when he was secretary of labor under Bill Clinton.

The anxious often report feelings of angst, so now they have their own adjective:

angsty *adj.* (1980) Relating to someone who feels the anxiety or dread associated with angst. *There's a kind of romantic futurism in all things '80s. It was a Euro-trash space-age, a make-up drenched experiment in passion liberated by gallant naiveté. In music, behind the industry-powered superstars, wonderful things were happening. The Fall, The Cure, The Smiths and New Order were turning the angst that lurked behind the scenes in previous generations into underground hymns. The **angsty** poetry was the elixir of a legion of teenagers who wore black on the outside "because black is how I feel on the inside"—Morrissey. (Toronto Star, May 7, 2002)*

The anxious and the angsty usually get that way because they feel a tremendous amount of stress in their lives. Sometimes it's just one thing causing the stress—what psychologists call *state anxiety,* a short-term anxious response experienced in a particular situation. But more often these days, we have a whole collection of stressors, from work to relationships to outside influences such as traffic jams and talk radio participants. What we have, in other words, is a

stress portfolio *n.* (1998) The collection of events and situations that cause stress in a person's life. *First Chicago is* *about to merge with Banc One Corp. and employees already are worried about their futures even though no layoffs have been announced, said Conti, a psychologist. He calls the economic uncertainties, "one more piece of personal stress. We're building a **stress portfolio**." (Wall Street Journal, October 20, 1998)*

State anxieties usually go away when the stress-causing experience goes away. But psychologists also study a more insidious form called *trait anxiety,* which deals with how prone a person is to become anxious and stressed out. Some folks score very high on the trait anxiety scale:

stress puppy *n.* (1995) A person who complains about the stress in his or her life, yet does little to change it. *All the excitement of the holidays can be nothing but a lot of stress for animals. Your pets don't understand why you're running around, slamming doors, muttering under your breath, yelling at your phone, dumping boxes all over the place, throwing clothes around and not getting enough sleep. There's a payoff for you (I hope!), but the only payoff for them is stress over the fact that you're stressed. So if the holidays turn you into a **stress puppy,** try to get rid of your anxieties away from home. (Orange County Register, November 23, 2000)*

Inside the Stress Portfolio

So what's in our personal stress portfolios these days? A big one is technology:

techno-angst *n.* (1984) Feelings of dread and anxiety caused by technology. Also: **techno angst, technoangst.** *As online privacy fears have exploded into a national wave of **techno-angst,** Web companies have tried to stave off new* *federal regulations by promising self-policing measures to keep Internet snooping under control.* (*Business Week,* May 15, 2000)

techno-stress *n.* (1983) Feelings of frustration and stress caused by having to deal with computers and other technologies. Also: **techno stress, technostress.** *Technostress strikes in many different ways. Communications technology, for instance, is great for keeping in touch away from the office but it's a two-way street—before you know it, colleagues and bosses call you at home, you feel guilty switching off your mobile and your private life all but vanishes. "Down time" is becoming a scarce commodity.* (*The Mirror,* London, January 18, 2002)

This is also called **IT stress** (1995), where *IT* is short for *information technology:*

According to a recent study by *CIO Canada* magazine and Athabasca University, only 20% of managers and professionals believe that information technology hasn't increased stress for employees. "The complexity and difficulty of doing many jobs has increased due to IT," says Athabasca University's Peter Carr, who led the research team. IT departments themselves are partly to blame. "**IT stress** has a lot to do with an IT system that hasn't been properly implemented," says Paul Zonneveld, KPMG's senior manager of information risk management in Calgary. (*National Post Business,* April 2001)

Another synonym is **technology-related anxiety** (1999), which is often shortened to **TRA:**

The causes of **TRA,** as suggested in the survey, are intriguing: Fourteen percent of the respondents said computer problems interrupted their work more than once a day. Seventeen percent said it often takes more than an hour to resolve the problems. Twenty-one percent claimed to have missed work dead-lines in the previous three months because of computer or soft-ware problems. Forty-six percent were unhappy because error messages appeared in technical jargon rather than plain English. (*Washington Post,* June 7, 1999)

Against all the evidence, people expect technology to work perfectly all the time. After all, the microwave oven does what it's supposed to do every day, so why can't the computer? And when it doesn't, people get anxious and stressed out. (They also tend to get very, very upset. See "Rage against the Machines" later in this chapter.)

But it's not just recalcitrant hardware and software that cause our stress levels to soar. Our stress portfolios are also bulging at the seams with *way* too much data. First, the total amount of knowledge in the world is expanding at an ever-increasing rate. Up to the twentieth century, it was thought that knowledge doubled every 100 years or so. By the 1950s, the doubling rate was down to 25 years. Now knowledge doubles about every 10 to 12 years.

Of course, the total amount of knowledge in the world has long been far greater than any one person can assimilate. What causes problems isn't the total amount of *available* information, but total amount of *required* information. Our **information overload** (1977) is caused by the books, magazines, newspapers, documentaries, contracts, licenses, by-laws, and manuals that we must take in each day to get through our lives. Eventually, we just get tired of dealing with the onslaught:

> **information fatigue syndrome** *n.* (1994) The weariness
> and stress that result from having to deal with excessive
> amounts of information. Also: **IFS, information fatigue**
> (1991). *Information overload is said to be the disease of the 21st
> century. "Information Fatigue Syndrome" is the medical*

term for the pariah of the modern age, symptoms include ex-
haustion, anxiety, failure of memory and shortness of attention.
A growing number of psychologists are warning that our brains
simply aren't geared for the onslaught of information zapped at
us on a daily basis. (*Birmingham Post,* June 26, 2001)

The information deluge hasn't been helped one bit by the
Internet. Now there are websites to surf, newsgroups to read, instant messages to handle, and the worst offender of them all,
e-mail messages to read and respond to. A recent Gartner, Inc.,
survey found that the average employee spends nearly an hour a
day doing nothing else but handling e-mail chores. For managers,
e-mail tasks usurp close to two hours each day. It's no wonder that
people are complaining about **e-mail fatigue** (1997):

> **E-mail fatigue** *has become a common business complaint.*
> *Increasingly, co-workers seem to figure there's no point in*
> *walking 10 feet to a colleague's desk and having a brief con-*
> *versation when a 300-word e-mail mini-essay will do.* (*The*
> *Irish Times,* December 12, 1997)

One of the big factors that make e-mail so tiresome is **spam**
(1994), those unsolicited commercial messages selling everything from preapproved credit cards to Viagra to pictures of
people having sex with animals. But anyone who has spent even
a short time using a corporate e-mail system will be quite familiar with a different kind of spam:

> **occupational spam** *n.* (2001) Unwanted or unnecessary
> messages sent over a corporate e-mail system. *Respondents*
> *to a recent survey conducted by Gartner, Inc. . . . report that*
> *34 percent of the internal business e-mail they receive is un-*
> *necessary. Gartner analysts refer to this e-mail intrusion as*
> *"occupational spam," and advise that managers take*
> *proactive steps to reduce it.* (*Business Wire,* April 19, 2001)

Spam originally meant flooding a newsgroup with irrelevant or inappropriate messages. This original sense derived from the overuse of the word *spam* in a sketch performed by Monty Python's Flying Circus. The sketch begins as follows:

Mr. Bun: Morning.

Waitress: Morning.

Mr. Bun: Well, what you got?

Waitress: Well, there's eggs and bacon; egg, sausage and bacon; egg and spam; egg, bacon and spam; egg, bacon, sausage and spam; spam, bacon, sausage and spam; spam, egg, spam, spam, bacon and spam; spam, sausage, spam, spam, spam, bacon, spam, tomato and spam.

Vikings (starting to chant): Spam spam spam spam . . .

Waitress: . . . spam spam spam egg and spam; spam spam spam spam spam spam baked beans spam spam spam . . .

Vikings (singing): Spam! Lovely spam! Lovely spam!

Waitress: . . . or Lobster Thermidor au Crevette with a Mornay sauce served in a Provençale manner with shallots and aubergines garnished with truffle pâté, brandy and with a fried egg on top and spam.

Wife: Have you got anything without spam?

Waitress: Well, there's spam egg sausage and spam, that's not got much spam in it.

In case you don't know, Spam is a luncheon meat consisting of compressed pork shoulder with a bit of ham tossed in.

This scourge also goes by the names **workplace spam** (1998) and **office spam** (2001). *Spam* doesn't seem like the right term for this kind of e-mail nuisance, because spam traditionally refers to *commercial* messages. Occupational spam is usually noncommercial, so some people have opted for a different term:

meatloaf *n.* (1999) Forwarded messages, jokes, lists, and other unsolicited noncommercial e-mail messages sent by an individual to a large number of people. *In the online world,* **meatloaf** *refers to unsolicited mass e-mail sent out by an individual. These people post their personal rants and raves to an extensive mailing list compiled by collecting personal addresses from discussion groups, chat parties and so forth. These are then fired off at any time of the day or night, regardless of whether the receiver cares for what's inside. Linguistically, it is related to "spam"—the term used for unsolicited e-mails used for marketing and advertising, except that* **meatloaf** *is "home made."* (*The Herald,* Glasgow, Scotland, January 24, 2001)

The information tsunami is huge, but it's also eerily quiet, which leads to yet another addition to the stress portfolio:

pin-drop syndrome *n.* (1999) Extreme quietness in an office, which leads to worker stress because the significance of even the smallest noises is magnified.

In some offices, the solution, believe it or not, is a contraption called a **mutter machine** (1999), a machine that plays office background sounds, such as chatting and laughing:

Some of the accountants complained of feeling lonely and said they found the hushed atmosphere in their carpeted, air-conditioned new office suite at White City extremely stressful—a problem known as **"pin-drop syndrome."** In a response that sounds like something out of a Dilbert cartoon, the BBC decided to install a special **"mutter" machine** that will provide soothing artificial background noise in the form of simulated human conversation punctuated by light laughter to improve the workplace environment. (*The Christian Science Monitor,* October 26, 1999)

Stressing out over specific things such as computer melt-downs, e-mail overload, and overly quiet offices is common enough, but the truly anxious believe this strategy is *way* too hard. Instead, they prefer more of a "big picture" approach:

> **undertoad** *n.* (1982) Anxiety characterized by an over-arching fear of the unknown in general and one's personal mortality in particular. *[Timothy Findley's] genuine self-doubt is forever near the surface, threatening to pull him down, and if not destroy him, silence him for good. This is his personal **undertoad**. (Quest,* October 1982)

This word comes from the phrase *Under Toad,* which was coined by John Irving in his 1976 book *The World According to Garp.* In the book, the youngest child, Walt, is constantly being warned to "watch out for the undertow" while playing in the surf, but he mishears the word as "Under Toad": "Garp . . . realized that all these years Walt had been dreading a giant toad, lurking offshore, waiting to suck him under and drag him out to sea. The terrible Under Toad."

Feel the Fear

Anxiety and stress can be debilitating, so how do sufferers cope with these feelings? Most often, the anxious resort to therapy to treat their problems, so it's not surprising that we now have the **therapy generation** (1993), people who grew up with, and are comfortable with, using therapy to solve personal problems.

The writer Cameron Tuttle, author of *The Paranoid's Pocket Guide,* suggests dealing with fears by **niche worrying** (1997), or worrying about one thing at a time:

> **Niche worrying** is a means of conveniently organizing one's paranoia. It's concentrating on a specific fear or phobia at an

appropriate time, like focusing on getting Legionnaires' disease from inhaling steam containing Legionella pneumophila bacteria while taking a shower at the gym. (*New York Times,* July 13, 1997)

Here's another strategy, first outlined by the psychologists Julie K. Norem and Nancy Cantor in 1986, and later (2001) published in book form as *The Positive Power of Negative Thinking:*

> **defensive pessimism** *n.* (1986) A strategy that anticipates a negative outcome and then takes steps to avoid that outcome. —**defensive pessimist** *n.* *Defensive pessimism can be reduced to a three-step mental rehearsal. First, approach the anxiety-producing task with lowered expectations, certain that it will go badly. . . . Then, imagine in detail all the ways in which it will go awry. . . . Finally, map out ways to avert each catastrophe.* (*New York Times Magazine,* December 9, 2001)

The Age of Rage

Cram enough anxiety and aggravation into your stress portfolio, and eventually it will burst open, resulting in an at best cathartic, at worst catastrophic, paroxysm of anger. The news is jampacked with such outbursts, but perhaps a better indicator is the following list of recent book titles:

- *Anger Busting 101* (Bayou Publishing, 2002)
- *Boiling Point* (Health Communications, 1999)
- *Control Yourself!* (Indus Publishing, 1997)
- *The Little Voodoo Kit: Revenge Therapy for the Over-Stressed* (Griffin, 1997)

- *Road Rage to Road-Wise* (Forge, 1999)
- *Since Strangling Isn't an Option* (Perigee, 1999)
- *Why Is Everyone So Cranky?* (Hyperion, 1999)

Clearly, the Age of Anxiety is turning into the Age of Rage; the stressed-out are replacing their angst with attitude:

attitude-y *adj.* (1989) Relating to someone with a purposefully arrogant or assertive manner. *No one can say Anderson doesn't know his dogs. Carminati and Naro worked hard before finding their groove. At 11 months, Naro was the youngest in training. He was aggressive, hyper and a little too stubborn. Because Carminati might describe himself the same way, the chemistry between dog and handler eventually sparked. "He's about as **attitude-y** as I am. We're a perfect fit," Carminati said. (Palm Beach Post, November 26, 2000)*

People often get our goat, but increasingly we're raging at the *things* that make us blow a gasket. This is particularly true of things that seem to have a certain frustrating quality to them:

piss-off factor *n.* (1990) An object's component or quality that has the potential to annoy or anger a person viewing or using the object. *The twist to the camera campaign, which is catching millions worldwide, is for the first time it "pops-under." . . . Advertising agency eMitch says companies in Australia are beginning to use the new, intrusive ads because they are generating a bigger reaction. "A frequency cap so people only see it once is important to minimise the **piss-off factor**. I get irritated if I see it over and over again," said eMitch's Mr Darren Patterson. (Sydney Morning Herald, July 21, 2001)*

The verb *to piss off* means to annoy, irritate, or anger, and it entered the language in the late 1960s. This was once considered a vulgarism, but these days it's not uncommon to hear it on TV and to see it in print. For example, the phrase *piss-off factor* has crashed such august publications as *Fortune* magazine and Britain's *The Independent* newspaper, and has been heard on CBC TV, Canada's national public television network.

Postal workers are the archetypal pissed-off employees. That reputation began on or about August 20, 1986, when a disgruntled postal worker opened fire on his coworkers, killing 13 of them. Over the next seven years, there were nine more such incidents involving postal workers, and a total of 34 people were killed. These gruesome statistics are the source not only of postal workers' violent reputation, but also of a phrase that today is used with dark humor:

go postal *v.* (1994) To become extremely angry, possibly to the point of violence. *Postal Service employees are no more likely to **"go postal"** than are other American workers, according to a national study released this week . . . Researchers found that the homicide rates at postal facilities were lower than at other workplaces. In major industries, the highest rate of 2.1 homicides per 100,000 workers was in retail. The next highest rate of 1.66 was in public administration, which includes police officers. The homicide rate for postal workers was 0.26 per 100,000. The most dangerous occupations: taxi drivers and chauffeurs, with a homicide rate of 31.54 per 100,000 workers.* (Austin American-Statesman, September 2, 2000)

The good news is that the workplace homicide rate is going down. According to the Bureau of Labor Statistics, there were 1,080 workplace murders in the United States in 1994, but "only" 677 in 2000 (an increase from the 651 recorded in 1999). This statistic mirrors the overall rate of workplace violence. Although there were over 802,000 incidents reported in

2000 (according to the U.S. Bureau of Justice Statistics), that figure is down from the 1,064,000 incidents reported in 1996.

The workplace isn't the only place where people go postal; they also seem to erupt on their *way* to work.

> **road rage** *n.* (1988) Extreme anger exhibited by a motorist in response to perceived injustices committed by other drivers. —**road-rager** *n.* —**road-rage** *adj. Other research, which analyzed more than 10,000 road rage incidents, reported that men ages 18 to 26 accounted for a majority of the confrontations, while women accounted for only 4 percent overall. The study, based on news, police and insurance reports from 1990–96, was conducted for the AAA foundation by Mizell & Co., an international security firm in Bethesda, Md. The research found that aggressive drivers tend to be young, poorly educated men with criminal records, histories of violence, or drug or alcohol problems. Many also have suffered recent emotional or professional setbacks. Yet, the study noted, hundreds of motorists with no such backgrounds also commit acts of road rage. (Dallas Morning News, July 1, 2002)*

The phrase *road rage* appeared only four times in the media from 1988 through 1993. In 1994 at least 10 stories appeared. Then things took off: In 1995 the number of stories jumped to over 200; in 1996 there were nearly 900; and in 1997 the number of stories shot up to over 2,000. Road rage was all the rage. And when something is all the rage, the language coughs up synonyms at a furious rate: **car rage** (1995), **driver rage** (1994), **highway rage** (1996), **motorist rage** (1996), **rental-car rage** (2000), and **taxi driver rage** (2001).

What causes road rage? Most often it's just a combination of traffic, tiredness, heat, or stress: things that could set just about anyone off given the right (or, I guess, wrong) circumstances.

However, road-ragers also tend to have histories of alcohol and drug abuse, and they quite often have psychological problems, including the following:

> **intermittent explosive disorder** *n.* (1987) A psychological disorder characterized by extreme and unrestrained outbursts of anger. *One in three of the aggressive drivers met diagnostic guidelines for* **intermittent explosive disorder,** *the scientists reported last month in* Behaviour Research and Therapy. *That compares with an estimated 2 to 5 percent in the general population.* (*Dallas Morning News,* July 1, 2002)

Road rage is fascinating in a sociological, sign-of-the-angry-times way, but it's also interesting when turned slightly and looked at from a linguistic angle. That's because the popularity of the phrase *road rage* made it extremely fertile, spawning dozens of "X rage" angers, from *air rage* to *zoo rage.* There's even a form of anger directed at all of this anger:

> **rage rage** *n.* (1996) Anger directed at people who glibly use terms such as *road rage* and *air rage. It is important that we are not drawn into the trap of believing that conditions such as "road rage," "air rage" and now "computer rage" exist in their own right: they are merely buzz terms used to describe bad behaviour for which the perpetrator must accept responsibility. Any who seek to disagree with this view could of course argue that I suffer from* **"rage rage,"** *a condition into which, sadly, I have no insight.* (*The Times of London,* June 11, 1999)

There are too many rages to investigate in detail here, but I'll look at two types in some lexical depth: *computer rage* and *cell rage.*

Think of a noun, add the word *rage* to it, and you've come up with a type of anger that *somebody, somewhere* has felt, although probably not yet written about. Here's a list of rages that *have* made the leap to print:

RAGE	ANGER DIRECTED AT . . .
air rage (1996)	Airlines and airline personnel. Also: **airplane rage** and **ground rage** (which is aimed at airport employees).
Bible rage (1999)	People who seek to change or disparage the Christian Bible.
bike rage (1995)	Bicyclists. Also: **biker rage, bicycle rage.**
concert rage (1996)	Other concertgoers (especially those talking or making other noise during a classical performance). Also: **opera rage.**
golf rage (1994)	Golfers, especially those who play extremely slowly or with little regard to golf etiquette.
grocery-store rage (1997)	Other shoppers. Also: **shopping-cart rage.**
neighbor rage (1995)	One's neighbors.
parking rage (1995)	Other motorists in parking lots. Also: **parking lot rage, parking spot rage, disabled parking spot rage.**
patient rage (1995)	Doctors, nurses, and HMOs. Also: **HMO rage.**
sidewalk rage (1997)	Other pedestrians or cyclists who use the sidewalk.
sports rage (1997)	Other fans in attendance at a sporting event, the event's officials, or the

(*continued on next page*)

RAGE	ANGER DIRECTED AT . . .
	coach or players of the other team. Also: **sideline rage,** and two hockey-specific rages: **rink rage** and **ice rage.**
surf rage (1998)	Surfers.
tax rage (1997)	Taxes and the politicians and govern-ment officials who impose them. Also: **anti-tax rage.**
telephone rage (1996)	Customer service representatives, telephone solicitors, and automated phone systems.
trade rage (1999)	The stock market, or the broker who told you to buy Pets.com (now de-funct) at $14 per share (its all-time high).
work rage (1995)	Work colleagues or bosses. Also: **desk rage, layoff rage.**
zoo rage (1998)	People who visit zoos (this is animal anger directed at humans).

Rage against the Machines

Devices have long been a source of frustration and anger. One of my favorite words is *resistentialism* (1963), the belief that inanimate objects have a natural antipathy toward human be-ings. Over the past five years or so, many people have rediscov-ered resistentialism and realized that its central idea—*les choses sont contre nous:* "things are against us"—perfectly describes our bug-ridden and glitch-filled interactions with modern ma-chines. If you've ever begged a computer to please, please give back the file containing the draft of your first novel, or pleaded with a toaster to, you know, actually *toast* the bread this time, then you are ripe for the resistential worldview.

Computers are perhaps the ultimate resistentialist device, so they generate more than their fair share of anger:

computer rage *n.* (1997) Anger or violence directed at a computer. Also: **PC rage, tech rage, IT rage, e-rage.** *Arvind Sharma, a consultant at IBM Global Services, has had a brush with* **computer rage.** *Recalling an incident he says, "I was giving this all-important presentation when my computer stalled mid-way. I became really tense. I tried fixing it but it just refused to move. I had to talk my way through the meeting. Predictably, I lost the deal. I felt like picking up a hammer and smashing the computer to smithereens." (The Statesman, Calcutta, September 29, 2001)*

Web rage *n.* (1998) Anger caused by World Wide Web frustrations such as slow downloads, nonexistent links, and information that is difficult to find. *How often do you find yourself losing your cool waiting for a Web page to load? A survey last week found that British Internet users are increasingly succumbing to* **"Web rage."** *More than half of survey respondents said they blow their stack at least once a week while surfing the Net, while 11 percent admitted to going ballistic on a daily basis. (San Francisco Chronicle, February 25, 2002)*

dot-com rage *n.* (2000) Anger caused by the perceived commercialization of the Internet. *But if* **dot-com rage** *turns out to be a factor in last week's attacks or others, I believe it should be seen not as a Robin Hood strategy to undermine the wealth of the e-commerce barons, but as a political statement akin to the protests in December in Seattle. (New York Times, February 14, 2000)*

pop-up rage *n.* (2001) Anger caused by pop-up ads that appear on some websites. *With the humble blinking banner* *routinely ignored, the "pop-up" is the latest hope for struggling websites desperate to turn a dollar. But it appears Internet users have other ideas. Eyesores. A nuisance . . . As the intrusive box springs up across the Web at the behest of marketers, "pop-up rage" is breaking out in its wake. (Sydney Morning Herald, July 3, 2001)*

Cell phones (1984)—or *mobile phones* (1965), the term preferred by those who live outside of North America—are certainly useful devices. Some of us are always late, of course, so the cell phone is great for calling ahead—it both warns the other person of our lateness and somehow absolves us of any wrongdoing. If you're in the car or walking around town, you can use the cell phone to get in a quick call or two. (However, as the writers of *Seinfeld* so cannily observed, the on-the-street cell phone call is "the lowest phone call you can make"; it's a "big hefty stinking faux pas.")

But it's also true that we're in the midst of an anti-cell backlash as people rail against the sheer ubiquity of these phones and the frequent rudeness of those who use them:

cell rage *n.* (1999) Anger directed at the users of cell phones. Also: **cell phone rage, mobile rage, mobile phone rage.** *While increasing numbers of restaurants and movie theaters are banning the devices and stories about "cell rage" are taking their place among air and road rage incidents, no stadium full of people has built a bonfire of their cell phones. (Courier-Journal, Louisville, July 17, 2000)*

The big problem is what some punsters are calling **cellfish** (2002) behavior that includes the following:

cell yell *n.* (1999) Excessively loud cell phone talking. Also: **yell phone** *n.* (1999) The cell phone into which a person is yelling. *Before the cell phone, theatergoers rushed to* *the lobby during intermission simply for a quick smoke. Now they hurry out to shout (the **"cell yell,"** it's called) into their indispensable gadgets.* (*New York Times,* August 5, 2000)

In a study titled "Aggravating Circumstances: A Status Report on Rudeness in America," published in 2002 by Public Agenda, researchers reported that 49 percent of people say they often see people using their cell phones in a loud or annoying manner.

Speaking of annoying, have you noticed that whenever another driver does something annoying or stupid, chances are that person is talking on a cell phone? They're almost as dangerous as someone who is DWI (driving while intoxicated):

DWY *abbr.* (2000) Driving while yakking—driving a car while talking on a cell phone. *Officers have their hands full already, and unless the legislature makes the fine higher than the $25 proposed in these bills, cops might reasonably conclude that the lawmakers don't think **DWY** is that big a deal.* (*Morning Star,* Wilmington, N.C., February 13, 2001)

Then there are those who see the cell phone call as a performance art piece:

stage-phoning *pp.* (2001) Attempting to impress nearby people by talking on a cell phone in an animated, theatrical manner. *Frequently seen in cafes, coffeehouses, and airports, the Dealmaker speaks loudly and appears to prefer captive audiences. He may engage in what researcher Sadie Plant, author of the Motorola report, refers to as **"stage-phoning,"** in which the caller is effectively performing for innocent bystanders.* (*Chicago Tribune,* July 17, 2002)

With cell phones now omnipresent in the social landscape, these would-be thespians appear on every street corner, coffee shop, and airport waiting lounge. (All the world really is, indeed, a stage, although I don't think this is quite what Shakespeare had in mind.) After a few minutes of their verbal histrionics and mobile melodrama, we suppress an urge to offer them the traditional actor's sendoff—"break a leg"—because, well, this time we actually mean it.

Some folks try and extricate themselves from this **cell hell** (1998) by trying to educate abusers on the virtues of proper **cell etiquette** (1998; this is sometimes shortened, most unfortunately, to **celliquette**). In some jurisdictions, the mad-as-heck-and-we're-not-going-to-take-it-anymore crowd have even banned drivers from talking while driving, and there have been rumblings that mobiles will be sent packing from office buildings and other public areas, which are to be designated as **cell-free zones** (1999):

> Bans on driving and talking on cell phones, as far as they go, are a good thing. If only there were some way to create **cell-free zones** in restaurants, movies and shopping malls. (*Sun-Sentinel,* Fort Lauderdale, Fla., August 11, 2002)

We're already seeing signs outside of some establishments that show a cell phone crossed with a diagonal red slash (that now-universal "don't even think about it" symbol). Clearly it's only a matter of time before cell phone users and smokers, elbows akimbo, will be battling for space outside of buildings. File that under "Scenes I'd Like to See."

Chapter 5

Ad Creep

Advertising may be described as the science of arresting human intelligence long enough to get money from it.
—*Stephen Leacock*

You can tell the ideals of a nation by its advertisements.
—*Norman Douglas*

Consumers are like roaches—you spray them and spray them and they get immune after a while. —*David Lubars*

Item: A Danish outdoor-media company called Nytmedie offers new parents a free baby carriage. The catch? The carriage has a corporate sponsor's logo on the side.

Item: Acclaim Entertainment offers $10,000 in U.S. savings bonds to the first family that names its child after Acclaim's new video game, *Turok*.

Item: On December 20, 1999, city councilors of Halfway, Oregon, unanimously agree to rename the town to half.com, after an Internet e-commerce site.

Item: The History Channel sticks hundreds of ad decals on sidewalks all over New York City. The decals illegally deface public property, but the agency responsible calls them "whimsical, witty, and fun."

Item: In 1999 Pizza Hut pays the Russian Aerospace Agency $2.4 million (U.S.) to place a 30-foot-tall logo on a rocket that launched part of the International Space Station.

Pizza Hut once considered using a laser to display its logo
on the moon, but abandoned the idea as "impractical."

hy do marketers do these kinds of things? One reason is
that, as the quotation by David Lubars, an executive with
the BBDO advertising agency, makes repugnantly clear, people
tune out ads after a while. And no wonder, since research shows
that people see anywhere from 3,000 to 5,000 marketing messages every day. So advertisers have to scale new heights (or,
more accurately, descend to new lows) to attract consumers' attention.

A second reason is that, put simply, these ploys work. Nytmedie claims to have received thousands of requests for the corporate baby buggies. When a Mexican restaurant in San
Francisco offered free lunches for life to anyone who had the
restaurant's name tattooed on her or his body, about 50 people
thought this was a great idea. When Sony Ericsson confessed to
hiring actors who would pose as tourists to talk up the benefits
of the company's new combination cell phone and digital camera, hundreds of (mostly negative) stories and editorials appeared in the press, a publicist's dream come true.

Advertising types expend (cynics would say fritter away) their
considerable creative talents trying to increase three things: *frequency* (the number of times a person sees an ad), *reach* (the total
number of people who see an ad), and *JPMs: jolts per minute* (the
number of times an ad really makes a person sit up and take notice). This means we now see ads in far more places than we used
to, and the ads we see are increasingly in-your-face. The result is
that marketing and advertising are rapidly becoming the dominant form of cultural expression, certainly in North America,
and increasingly in other parts of the Western world. That worries many people, but it's a boon for language hounds because it

means lots of new words and phrases, what we might call *linguistic JPMs*.

Ad Creep

Modern marketers seem to have a mania for filling every last bit of empty space on the planet (and sometimes beyond) with advertisements. This distressing trend has its own name:

ad creep *n.* (1992) The gradual expansion of advertising space to nontraditional surfaces such as floors, bathroom walls, cars, and the sides of buildings. *Media literacy professionals call it "**ad creep**"—the relentless ooze of commercial advertising into every nook and cranny of our daily lives. If you think that the hucksters haven't won their battle for "mind share" (a share of your mind, that is), think again. Do you hang up when you're put on hold and blasted with five minutes' worth of private radio, with its lousy music and obnoxious ads? Do you even blink any more when our publicly owned buses glide past, swathed in full-body wrap-around ads?* (*Toronto Star,* January 27, 2002)

Ad creep is afflicting even the traditional marketing venues of television, radio, and the print media. For example, some *New Yorker* cartoonists created a series of cartoons for Grey Goose Vodka in which the product was depicted in the artwork and even mentioned in the punch line. (For example: "He just ordered a Grey Goose Vodka. At least I'll respect him in the evening.")

In 1997 the novelist Mordecai Richler published an excerpt of his book *Barney's Version* where, on the final page, the text wrapped around a silhouette of an Absolut bottle. In 2001 Bulgari jewelers paid noted British author Fay Weldon to write

a book called *The Bulgari Connection,* which included references
to the jeweler and its products. (Interestingly, more than one re-
viewer noted at the time that Ms. Weldon appeared to have
pulled a fast one on Bulgari, since the character who is most into
the Bulgari scene is also the least likable.) This blend of fiction
and commercial is called a **bought book** (2002) or a **fictomercial** (2001):

> British writer Fay Weldon opened up a whole new financial
> can of worms with her novel "The Bulgari Connection," spon-
> sored by the Italian jewelry company Bulgari in return for a
> few mentions in the plot. Some critics wailed about the new
> field of **"fictomercial,"** but most accepted the book for what
> it is: a harmless little experiment by a talented novelist.
> (*Atlanta Journal and Constitution,* December 15, 2001)

On TV, ads are now starting to appear *during* the shows, such as
the infamous "Pottery Barn" episode of *Friends,* where the chain
paid NBC to be, in effect, the star of the show. Earning an "11"
on a scale of 1 to 10 for annoyance is a newfangled way of getting ads in front of captured boob-tube eyeballs:

> **virtual advertising** *n.* (1994) Computer-generated ads,
> logos, and products that are superimposed on a live video
> feed or inserted into a completed movie or television show.
> *Super Bowl viewers around the world are about to be hit by
> a new generation of **virtual advertising** guaranteed to make
> channel surfers fumble the remote. The computer-generated
> ads—in this case company logos such as FedEx and GM—
> will appear on television screens attached to the superimposed
> yellow bars marking the point on the field a team must reach
> for a first down.* (*Toronto Star,* January 10, 2001)

But ads are also leaving these traditional niches behind and have
crept onto innumerable other surfaces, including park benches,
fruit, library cards, cars, buses, beaches, supermarket floors, retail

receipts, and stadium names. Ad creeping marketers particularly love a captive audience, which is why it's now routine to see ads before movies (and even *in* movies, via product placements), in washrooms and elevators, and while waiting on hold:

> **on-hold advertising** *n.* (1989) Telephone-based advertising directed at consumers while they are waiting on hold. *The **on-hold advertising** industry fills a unique niche in the advertising community by seizing that captive "on-hold" audience and relaying information about the company, including the services it provides and even special sales and promotions.* (*Oakland Post,* January 20, 1999)

Taxicabs have become rolling marketing machines, with ads on the roof, the rear window, and even the hubcaps (weighted in such a way that the ad always appears right-side up). Some cab companies, clearly looking to go out of business as soon as possible, are even experimenting with interior screens that beam ads at backseat passengers.

The aesthetics of the marketing mind seem to be offended by a flat or nearly flat surface without an ad. The sides of buildings qualify, so they're increasingly being converted into ad vehicles:

> **wildposting** *n.* (1993) The poster advertising displayed on construction hoardings, buildings, and other free spaces. *Can't get Anne Robinson's shrill "You are the weakest link goodbye" taunt out of your head? Blame it on the massive guerrilla marketing campaign behind NBC's new game "Weakest Link." . . . Beyond the small screen, graffiti written in red chalk sprouted on sidewalks in New York and Los Angeles; random "**wildpostings**" appeared on construction sites and walls in the top 10 markets.* (*Daily Variety,* April 19, 2001)

Slapping up a few posters is one thing, but cutting-edge marketers create JPMs with a bolder gambit:

building takeover *n.* (1996) The use of a building's exterior surface as an advertisement. *In Silver Tab's mission to own an entire neighborhood, Bohannon enlisted the services of Michael Chesney, the 33-year-old inventor of a practice known as the "building takeover." Chesney's Toronto-based company, Murad, got its start in the 1980s painting giant advertising murals on the sides of buildings. He quickly saw the ultimate extension of his craft: to cover the entire building exterior with a single advertising message.* (Canadian Press Newswire, November 24, 1996)

Not that ads on the sides of buildings are anything new. Early in the twentieth century, it wasn't unusual to see a mural for a local business or Coca-Cola painted on the side of a barn, soda shop, or grocery store. (Some of these old ads still exist, but they can only be properly seen after it rains, so they're called **ghost signs** [1989].) Converting a building into an ad creates what media critic Rick Salutin has called "advertecture" and what journalist Naomi Klein has called the "ad as edifice." This is also called a **3-D ad** (1996), and sometimes a single building just won't cut the marketing mustard. For example, Mattel once painted an entire street—the houses, driveways, cars, sidewalks, road, even the trees—pink to "celebrate" something called Barbie Pink Month.

Guerrilla Marketing

The building takeover is a good example of an alternative type of marketing that's becoming increasingly mainstream:

guerrilla marketing *n.* (1982) A marketing campaign that uses nonmainstream tactics and locations, often in defiance of local laws or statutes. *College campuses provide the perfect venue for **guerrilla marketing**—which runs the*

*gamut from sidewalk chalking, biodegradable tree postings
and stenciling to product giveaways and spray painting logos
around campuses—since students by nature are open to nontraditional marketing schemes, say experts.* (ADWEEK,
August 7, 2000)

As you'll see a bit later in this chapter, guerrilla marketing
usually aims to be provocative and visible. But one common
guerrilla tactic is to infiltrate the consumer's consciousness by
appearing as an innocuous, nonmarketing message. An old example is the *advertorial* (1961), an advertisement designed to resemble editorial content. Here's a newer form:

advertainment *n.* (1987) An advertisement in the guise of
a movie or other form of entertainment. *Last year, BMW
released a campaign called "The Hire," featuring online short
films by famous directors like Guy Ritchie and Ang Lee. The
"advertainments" became an overnight Web phenomenon,
pulling in one-fifth more traffic to BMW's sites and breath-
ing life into streaming video as a marketing tool.* (Smart
Business for the New Economy, January 1, 2002)

Here's another example.

advergame *n.* (2000) A Web-based computer game that
incorporates advertising messages and images. *Octopi officials say advergames promote repeat traffic to Web sites and
reinforce brands in compelling ways. Because users choose to
register to be eligible for prizes, the games help marketers col-
lect customer data. And because gamers may invite their
friends to participate, the brand benefits from word of mouth.*
(Dallas Morning News, August 8, 2001)

Savvy consumers can usually see the marketing messages that
lie behind these innocent facades. So, undaunted, advertisers
have taken things to an even more clandestine level:

stealth marketing *n.* (1991) Marketing in which actors promote a product in a real-world setting while posing as regular people. *The next time an overly friendly blond sidles up in a crowded bar and asks you to order her a brand-name martini, or a cheery tourist couple wonder whether you can take their picture with their sleek new camera-in-a-cell phone, you might want to think twice. There's a decent chance that these strangers are pitchmen in disguise, paid to oh-so-subtly pique your interest in their product. Their game, known as "stealth marketing," is one of several unorthodox ploys that Madison Avenue is using to get through to jaded consumers.* (*Time,* September 2, 2002)

The Sony Ericsson ploy mentioned earlier—hiring actors to talk up the qualities of the company's latest high-tech gadget—is a perfect example of stealth marketing. Other typical examples include the Italian scooter manufacturer Piaggio hiring models to zip around town on the company's latest version of the Vespa scooter and Ford marketing its new Focus model by lending it to young, cool people such as disc jockeys, party planners, and celebrity assistants. On a more sinister level, drug companies have paid celebrities, including the actresses Lauren Bacall and Kathleen Turner, to appear on talk shows and extol the benefits of medications manufactured by the companies.

Appropriately, stealth marketing comes in various disguises. These include the **lean-over** (2000; when someone—called a **leaner** [2002]—paid by a company leans over to you to talk up the virtues of the company's product) and **under-the-radar marketing** (1996):

Now consider the following: a colorful cardboard box plastered with a well-known logo of a certain computer maker sits in your building's lobby for several days. Not only does the trademark get noticed, but residents also may assume a neighbor has made the purchase. So the computer company gets a warm association in certain consumers' minds. The feat can be accomplished simply by tipping a few doormen, said Jonathan Ressler, president and chief executive of Big Fat Inc., a Manhattan firm specializing in just this kind of **"under the radar" marketing.** While others may use this tactic, Ressler said he won't. It's a little too deceptive. "All the big advertisers want to do this," said Ressler, who counts the **"lean-over"** as part of his arsenal. (*Newsday,* December 26, 2000)

Some synonyms for stealth marketing are **reality marketing** (2001), **undercover marketing** (1992), and **underground marketing** (1993). A related ploy is **street marketing** (1987), where a company hires a **street team** (1990) or a **street crew** (1994) to hit the streets talking up the product. Nike does this constantly in urban settings to appeal to black youth, a practice the company calls **bro-ing** (1999):

Nothing in inner-city branding has been left up to chance. Major record labels like BMG now hire **"street crews"** of urban black youth to talk up hip-hop albums in their communities and to go out on guerrilla-style postering and sticker missions. . . . So focused is Nike on borrowing style, attitude and imagery from black urban youth that the company has its own word for the practice: **bro-ing.** (Naomi Klein, *No Logo,* 1999)

The goal of stealth marketing is to get people talking about the product, the idea being that you're likely to be impressed by something if you see someone trusted, knowledgeable, famous, or just plain *cool* who likes it. Setting people's chins a-wagging is an advertising niche in itself:

buzz marketing *n.* (1996) Marketing techniques designed to get people talking excitedly about a product. *As countries around the world clamp down on conventional cigarette* *advertising, tobacco companies have become enthusiastic early adopters of* **buzz marketing** *practices, such as inviting cool young clubbers to parties staffed by cigarette girls in skimpy costumes, and club rooms decorated in pack colours.* (*The Age*, Melbourne, Australia, June 21, 2002)

This is also called **word-of-mouth marketing** (1984), **influence marketing** (1985), and **peer-to-peer marketing** (1991).

The stealth marketer wants to deliver a message to the "marketee" and then have that person repeat the message to other people. This message has its own name:

roach bait *n.* (2001) A marketing message delivered by an actor posing as a regular person with the intention of having that message passed along to many other people. *Then, there's the "roach bait" technique. Under this scenario, the paid huckster doesn't necessarily buy a drink for others. He's often found sitting in a prime spot at a bar or club, very visibly drinking Brand X. He talks up the brand big-time in the hope the good word will spread.* (*USA Today*, May 15, 2001)

This creepy phrase (the process is also called **roaching**) gives you a pretty good indication of what marketers think of the average consumer. The term comes from "roach bait," a poison that's sprayed in cockroach-infested areas. A cockroach eats the bait, returns to its nest, and excretes feces that are contaminated with the poison. The original roach dies, but other roaches eat the contaminated feces and the killing cycle continues. Happily, some marketers are pushing a slightly nicer variation on this theme—**brand bait** (2001):

"Maybe only 15 kids are hit [by the Nintendo squad] at a birthday party but kids talk, a lot—at school, with SMS, by phone," Ressler says. "We know 15 kids can impact [on]

15,000 kids or 150,000 kids [through word of mouth]. You've heard of roach bait? Well, we call this **brand bait.** People have something to go back and talk to their friends about." (*The Australian,* September 27, 2001)

Here's another unpleasant-sounding variation on this theme:

viral marketing *n.* (1989) The promotion of a service or product by using existing customers to pass along a marketing pitch to friends, family, and colleagues. *By common consent, the first ever **viral marketing** campaign was the one initiated by Sabeer Bhatia and Jack Smith to advertise their free email service in 1996. They made sure that every time someone used their service to send an email it automatically included the company's website address at the foot of the message. Using this simple device, Bhatia and Smith managed to build a customer base more rapidly than any company in the history of the world, signing up 12 million subscribers in only 18 months. As you've probably guessed, the name of the service is Hotmail.* (*The Guardian,* London, April 1, 2002)

Why "viral" marketing? Probably because a biological virus replicates itself by invading a host cell and then using the cell's machinery to create new copies of the virus. So, analogously, a customer acts like a kind of "host cell" for a company's marketing message, and that customer is used to create new "copies" of the viral marketing message. I get the willies just thinking about it.

More Marketing Types

It's an unfortunate fact that there are probably as many kinds of marketing as there are marketers. These creative types live for the sheer thrill of coming up with new ways to get the word out. Here's a sampling of a few of these other marketing niches:

ambush marketing *n.* (1987) Promoting a product by associating its name with a special event even though the product or company has no official sponsorship or marketing agreement with the event. *In **ambush marketing**, corporations try to capitalize on high-profile events, such as World Cup or the Olympics, without paying pricey sponsorship fees to the organizers. The most sophisticated marketers are careful to evade legal counterattacks by not using protected trademarks such as the World Cup name or Olympic rings. Often they take a cheaper route by sponsoring national teams or individual athletes rather than the actual events.* (*USA Today*, May 29, 2002)

This is also called **ambush advertising** (1988) or **parasitic marketing** (1989).

drip marketing *n.* (1993) A direct marketing strategy that involves sending out a number of promotional pieces over a period of time to a subset of sales leads. *Anderson recommends using large-format postcards mailed repetitively in a "**drip**" **marketing** program.* (*Business Wire*, January 14, 2002)

The phrase *drip marketing* may sound as though it's based on the practice of water torture, but it actually comes from the phrase *drip irrigation*. This is an agriculture/gardening technique in which small amounts of water are fed to plants over long periods of time. Unfortunately for anyone who is the target of a drip marketing campaign, many marketers believe in something called the "Law of 29," which states that on average a "prospect" won't turn into a "client" until they've seen your marketing message at least 29 times. Perhaps it *is* a form of torture, after all.

permission marketing *n.* (1989) Marketing in which the consumer is asked for permission to be sent targeted ads based on personal data supplied by the consumer. *Most* **permission marketing** *schemes amount to little more than permission spamming. You say yes once and the floodgates open.* (*Marketing Week,* March 15, 2001)

This is also called **opt-in marketing** (1997). The opposite is **interruption marketing** (1998), advertisements that interrupt whatever the consumer is doing (watching television, reading a magazine article, eating dinner, and so on).

social-norms marketing *n.* (1997) Marketing that attempts to persuade people to think or behave like the majority of other people. *Northern Illinois University began the first* **social-norms marketing** *campaign on a college campus in 1990, using newspaper ads, posters and handouts to deliver the message that, contrary to popular belief, most students had fewer than five drinks when they partied. By 1999, incidents of heavy drinking (five or more drinks) by Northern Illinois University students were down 44 percent.* (*New York Times,* December 9, 2001)

tribal marketing *n.* (1996) A marketing strategy that attempts to create social groups or communities that are centered around a product or service. *But the Amsterdam-based former journalist said fashion fortune-tellers had lost some of their power in the past decade. Designers such as Prada and Gucci are so keenly watched they are capable of starting trends on the catwalk. And it's been 10 years since the rise of "niche" or* **tribal marketing** *in response to the cult of individualism.* (*The Australian,* March 23, 2001)

zip code marketing *n.* (1983) A marketing campaign aimed at a specific ZIP code or postal region. Also: **zip-code marketing.** *An Olathe marketing firm will commem-*

orate its 25th anniversary with an open house this week. Ruf
Strategic Solutions plans its celebration from 3 to 6 p.m.
Friday at 1533 E. Spruce St. . . . The firm's milestones in-
clude partnering with Martin Baier, known as the father of
ZIP code marketing. (*Kansas City Star,* July 25, 2001)

Outside of the United States, this technique is known as **postal
code marketing** (2001).

If you take ZIP and postal codes and combine them with
census data, opinion polls, and marketing surveys, you come up
with a new science:

> **geodemographics** *n.* (1982) The geographical segmenta-
> tion of a region based on the average lifestyles of the
> people who live in that region. —**geodemography** *n.*
> (1980); **geodemographer** *n.* (1987) *90210. Aaron*
> *Spelling made it mean something to the rest of us, but it al-*
> *ways meant something to those who lived there . . . Hey, a*
> *neighborhood like that has a rep. Now, here's a news flash: So*
> *does your neighborhood. And—surprise—your ZIP code says*
> *just as much about you. Especially to people who want to sell*
> *you something and, conversely, don't want to waste their time*
> *hawking what you're not going to buy. It's actually a science*
> *called* **geodemographics.** (*Orange County Register,* January
> 20, 2000)

The geodemographics concept is based on evidence that birds
of a feather actually do flock together. That is, people tend to
live beside or near people who have similar lifestyles. (The unofficial motto of the geodemographic crowd is "You are where
you live.") Each segment of demographic similitude—each **consumption community** (1973) in the jargon—is called a
lifestyle cluster (1978), or more often simply a **cluster** (1976),
which brings us to the inevitable marketing angle:

As a bonus for language fans, clusters come with pleasingly wacky names. Here are the 62 cluster names defined by the PRIZM (Potential Rating Index Zip Code Market) system:

Agri-Business	Hard Scrabble	River City, USA
American Dreams	Hispanic Mix	Rural Industria
Back Country Folks	Hometown Retired	Rustic Elders
Big City Blend	Inner Cities	Scrub Pine Flats
Big Fish, Small Pond	Kids & Cul-de-Sacs	Second City Elite
Big Sky Families	Latino America	Shotguns & Pickups
Boomers & Babies	Mid-City Mix	Single City Blues
Blue Blood Estates	Middle America	Smalltown Downtown
Blue-Chip Blues	Middleburg Managers	Southside City
Blue Highways	Military Quarters	Starter Families
Bohemian Mix	Mines & Mills	Suburban Sprawl
Boomtown Singles	Mobility Blues	Sunset City Blues
Country Squires	Money & Brains	Town & Gowns
Executive Suites	New Beginnings	Upstarts & Seniors
Family Scramble	New Eco-Topia	Upward Bound
God's Country	New Empty Nests	Urban Achievers
Golden Ponds	New Homesteaders	Urban Gold Coast
Grain Belt	Norma Rae-ville	Winner's Circle
Gray Collars	Old Yankee Rows	Young Influentials
Gray Power	Pools & Patios	Young Literati
Greenbelt Families	Red, White & Blues	

cluster marketing *n.* (1984) Marketing directed at neighborhoods or regions that have a specific demographic profile. *The turn to demographic information in the 1970s enabled marketers to profile potential consumers. Demographics included basic information such as age level, income level, race, ethnicity, gender, and geographical location.*

*Marketers could target certain demographic segments of the
nation, a practice called "**cluster marketing.**" It worked because people with similar incomes and races generally lived together in clusters. (Stanford Law Review, July 1, 2001)*

This is also called **lifestyle marketing** (1983), **particle marketing** (1992), **precision marketing** (1982), or **social marketing**
(1975). If you take the geographic emphasis out of geodemographics and replace it with a psychological component, you get
psychodemographics (1987):

Considering that your target market is composed of Gen Xers,
I think your name and tag line would fit with the **psychode-
mographics** of your target consumer population. (*Sacramento
Bee,* December 10, 2002)

The Brand: The Ultimate Marketing Tool

Market research has found that children often recognize a brand logo before they can recognize their
own name. —*Eric Schlosser, Fast Food Nation*

The word *brand* has a curious and yet somehow inevitable history. It's an ancient word (it appears in *Beowulf* as *bronde*) that
came into English from the Germanic term *brandoz,* a shortening of a phrase that meant "burn word." It originally referred to
a piece of wood burning at one end, or a flaming torch. By the
mid-sixteenth century *brand* had come to mean a mark made by
burning with a hot iron, usually to identify a criminal, but before long it meant a mark of ownership burned into the hides of
cattle, horses, and other animals. In the early nineteenth century
the manufacturers of some goods started burning their names
onto casks, wood, metal, and other materials, and these trademarks became known as *brands.* By the late 1800s companies

looking to differentiate themselves in the marketplace started adding logos and other design flourishes to their packages. Some products, such as Campbell's Soup and Quaker Oats, went a step further and used their logos, designs, and advertising to create a feeling—such as comfort or folksiness—about the product in the mind of the consumer. The modern concept of the *brand* was born.

Throughout much of the twentieth century, manufacturing was a two-step process: Build something, and then use branding to convince the consumer to buy that something. In the 1980s, however, the second step had acquired far more importance than the first. Suddenly building things—along with owning all the expensive equipment and employing all those expensive workers—was no longer good business. Management and marketing theorists announced that corporations that wanted to be successful must switch from being producers of products and services to being producers of brands. This switch has been so successful that the brand is now, according to journalist Naomi Klein, "the core meaning of the modern corporation."

Needless to say, this ascendance of branding has brought with it a huge lexicon of branding lingo and jargon. A complete lexicon of brand-based concepts probably would fill an entire book and certainly would be read by few people. Herewith, then, is a short but sweet glossary of a few useful branding terms:

attitude brand *n.* (1995) A brand associated with a specific lifestyle or with an assertive or arrogant approach to life. *Since markets are flooded with indistinguishable, mass-produced items, firms have tried to individualize their goods by associating them with an "attitude brand," pushing a particular lifestyle or a cool image rather than a plain T-shirt, soft drink, or shoe. (Foreign Affairs, September/October 2001)*

attribute brand *n.* (1998) A brand associated not with a product, but with a distinctive characteristic, quality, or feature of a product. *The **attribute brand** provides a point of differentiation and serves as a barrier to competitors.* (*Economic Times*, April 3, 2002)

brand ambassador *n.* (1989) A person who officially or unofficially represents a brand and attempts to extend or improve the brand's reputation. *It is critical to instill that sense of brand, and teach all employees what the new brand stands for, and how to be **brand ambassadors.*** (PR Newswire, July 30, 2002)

brand canopy *n.* (1999) The overall impression created by a brand. ***Brand canopies . . .** are a kind of spiritual home-land for their brands, ones so recognisable and grand that no matter where the individual products roam they will carry that grandness with them like a halo.* (Naomi Klein, *No Logo,* 1999)

brand equity *n.* (1982) The level of familiarity that a con-sumer has with a particular brand. *It is no accident that those with significant **"brand equity"**— such as Nike, Gap or Starbucks—became the primary targets for anti-globaliza-tion protesters.* (*Washington Post,* July 14, 2002)

brand essence *n.* (1987) The quality or nature that uniquely identifies a brand. *According to Finucane, Jeter and Garciaparra epitomize Fleet's **brand essence**—dynamic expertise—which is expressed in the bank's tagline, "Forward Thinking."* (*Business Wire,* May 17, 2001)

brand loyalty *n.* (1973) A feeling of devotion or duty to a brand. *If you're successful at reaching someone [8 to 12 years old], chances are good you've got **brand loyalty** for life, so the thinking goes.* (*Chicago Tribune,* September 4, 2002)

brand-name dropping *pp.* (1981) Attempting to impress others by frequently mentioning the brand names of goods that one owns. *DotComGuy's year-long experiment in self-imposed isolation, e-commerce and **brand-name dropping** has finally come to an end. (New York Post,* January 3, 2001)

brand steward *n.* (1992) A person or company in charge of managing a brand. *Advertising agencies are no longer the **brand stewards** of the industry. Clients now increasingly turn to management consultants or brand consulting groups. (Marketing,* September 12, 2002)

brand wagon *n.* (1988) The brand bandwagon; the current mania for focusing on branding products instead of manufacturing them. Also: **brand-wagon, brandwagon.** *In the past few years, everyone has tried to jump on the **brand wagon.** (Fast Company,* February 2002)

brandscape *n.* (1989) The brand landscape; the expanse of brands and brand-related items (logos, ads, and so on) within a culture or market. *But even the strongest critics of globalism can not live entirely outside of the **brandscape** that now constitutes the average town centre. (The Herald,* Glasgow, Scotland, February 2, 2002)

brandwidth *n.* (1995) Brand bandwidth; the maximum amount of branding a consumer is able to process; the amount of brand recognition enjoyed by a product or service. *Corporate Branding says the marketplace has a limited **"brandwidth"** and consumers and investors can cope with only so many brand names. (Financial Express,* March 23, 2000)

co-branding *pp.* (1988) Branding two different products or services from two different companies. *That's because the restaurant is half a KFC and half an A&W—the latest example of **co-branding,** a trend that's reshaping the fast-food market. (Washington Post,* May 24, 2002)

ghost brand *n.* (1993) A once-famous brand name that remains on sale but is no longer popular. Also called an **Elvis brand.** *Many of these **ghost brands** are still being sold. Ovaltine, for instance, has a new life as a hot chocolate alternative.* (*Intelligent Enterprise,* March 27, 2001)

host brand *n.* (1993) A brand that contains one or more attribute brands or ingredient brands. *When the **host brand** is new or lacks an established identity, a recognised attribute brand can generate awareness of, confidence in and preference for the **host brand.*** (*Economic Times,* April 3, 2002)

ingredient brand *n.* (1993) A brand associated with an element of, or an ingredient that goes into, a product. *It will be an "**ingredient brand,**" much like Dolby on audio equipment or "Intel inside" on PCs.* (*Financial Mail,* Rosebank, S. Africa, August 10, 2001)

passion brand *n.* (1998) A brand that resonates strongly with consumers and makes them passionate about the brand's products or services. *Vespa is a **passion brand** that has been rediscovered by style leaders.* (*ADWEEK,* April 22, 2002)

single-brand store *n.* (1987) A store that sells only a single brand of merchandise. ***Single-brand stores** now predominate in many urban centres—Nike Town, Roots, The Body Shop.* (*The Globe and Mail,* Toronto, January 15, 2000)

superbrand *n.* (1982) A brand with a worldwide scope and extremely high consumer recognition. *Every time someone does a survey, the **superbrands** that come out on top are the one-product or one-category companies, known by the names under which they trade [such as] Coca-Cola,*

McDonald's, Sony and Microsoft. (*The Guardian,* London, November 5, 1998)

The Shinola Awards (see www.shinolas.com) celebrate the best and worst in brand names, and can be very entertaining. For example, in the Junk Food category, some of the best names were Velveeta, Jell-O, Cheez Whiz, Slim Jim, and Cracker Jack; among the worst names were Droxies (formerly Hydroxies), Fruit by the Foot, Otis Spunkmeyer, Spotted Dick, and Pork Puffs. In the Magazines category, among the best names were *Vogue, Money, Fortune, Mad, Wired,* and *Rolling Stone;* the worst names included *Modern Maturity, Martha Stewart Baby, BONKERS!, Wine Spectator,* and *Zyzzyva.*

With sales messages slowly usurping society's blank spaces and with barely ethical ploys such as stealth marketing and under-the-radar marketing now becoming the norm, it's clear that the ad industry will do just about anything to boost its products' frequency, reach, and JPMs. Like horror-show zombies with arms outstretched and drooling mouths agape, marketers mindlessly move us closer to the world depicted in the film *Minority Report,* where people are identified using retinal scans and then bombarded with personalized advertising messages. Over the top, you say? It's already happening. A company in California is putting up highway billboards that can detect the radio stations to which the majority of passing cars are tuned and then tailor the billboards' messages to the presumed tastes of those drivers. A company in Toronto is putting transmitters in certain neighborhoods and receivers in certain cabs, so that when a taxi drives through one of the designated areas, the passenger sees an ad for a company from that neighborhood. This isn't just ad creep; it's ad *creepy.*

Chapter 6

Slang Goes Mainstream

I've found that there are only two kinds that are any good: slang that has established itself in the language, and slang that you make up yourself. Everything else is apt to be passé before it gets into print. —*Raymond Chandler*

Slang is, at least, vigorous and apt. Probably most of our vital words were once slang. —*John Galsworthy*

I'm everlasting, I can go on for days and days
With rhyme displays that engrave deep as X-rays
I can take a phrase that's rarely heard
Flip it, now it's a daily word.
—*Rakim*

In late 2002 the *New York Daily News* received a copy of a leaked CNN Headline News memo that offered staffers a slang glossary and urged them to "please use this guide to help all you homeys and honeys add a new flava to your tickers and dekkos." (Tickers and dekkos are CNN jargon for the graphics that appear on the Headline News screen.) The memo suggested that the writers use terms such as **whack** (bad; crazy)—the "lingo of our people"—to ensure that the screen text remains "as cutting edge" as possible.

When I heard about this, my first thought was that it was some kind of joke or hoax. In fact, I *still* think it was a publicity stunt. After all, the idea that CNN wants slang terms such as **jimmy hat** (a condom) and **fly** (sexually attractive) to appear in news headlines is so absurd that it's difficult to take seriously.

However, what was interesting about this was the fact that many people *did* take it seriously. People recognize that corporations are desperate to attract young consumers, so hearing that a big-time news organization might stoop to street slang to attract those consumers isn't very surprising.

The problem is that few (if any) news organizations or other mainstream businesses can use youth-generated slang with anything approaching credibility. With few exceptions, slang sounds authentic only when it's used by the core group: the group from which the slang originated. This is called *ingrouping:* If you know the slang and use it properly, you're in the group. Any outsiders who use the group's slang sound like they're trying too hard. This is *outgrouping:* If you don't know the slang or if you use it improperly, you're not in the group.

People who try to use slang to make themselves sound "cool" automatically make themselves "uncool." Slang serves to bond members of a group together by giving them a shared lingo, but it's also used to separate. When group members use slang, they're using it partly to differentiate themselves—the "cool" people—from everyone else—the "uncool" people. If people in the "uncool" group start to use that slang, then the words no longer serve to differentiate, so by definition they become "uncool."

Further, if it's marketers using the slang trying to attract the core group, they usually end up alienating the very people they're trying to woo. The core group of slang users almost always resent the appropriation of their lingo, so they're usually even *less* likely to become consumers of the corporation's products. What the corporation usually attracts are the wannabes: the uncool people who want to become cool and think they can get there by using the products of a company that uses cool words.

However, the fact remains that mainstream marketing, advertisements, and press releases, as well as people who should know better, such as journalists and politicians, incorporate slang into their products and text. Why do they do it?

One reason is that many of these people, especially marketing types, are barely aware they're doing it. Ever since the 1960s, many marketers have internalized the slogans and attitude of rebellion and individualism. The counterculture has become the lunch-counter culture. You can see this in ads that exhibit what one journalist has called "group coolspeak." Consumers are bombarded with countercultural commandments: Just do it! Be yourself! Be bold! Think different! Never blend in! Do exactly as we tell you! Canadian poet Ken Babstock says that

> admonishments, exhortations and calls to authenticity such as these, whose value once seemed beyond argument, have become so prevalent in Western culture, and now emanate from such dubious sources, so that they not only ring false, but have about them the X-ray glow of their own inverted meaning. We're told to think critically by looming, spotlit billboards erected by companies whose product is at best unnecessary, and at worst a direct link to human suffering. The language of resistance is owned and trademarked. (*The Globe and Mail*, Toronto, October 19, 2002)

This "hip consumerism" (as Thomas Frank called it in his marvelous book, *The Conquest of Cool*) also manifests itself in the co-optation of rebellious songs: Jaguar ads play The Clash's "London Calling"; people in spots for Carnival Cruises frolic to Iggy Pop's "Lust for Life"; the Bank of Montreal shills to the tune of Bob Dylan's "The Times They Are A-Changin'."

And, of course, marketers and others who want to "skew young" co-opt the slang of youth. The people who criticize marketers for using teen and street slang usually say that the marketing goes awry because the 30-something creative types who create the ads either get the slang wrong or use it too late, since slang changes constantly and quickly. This is true for those marketers foolish enough to use teen slang to advertise directly to teens. Not that this stops them. Consider these examples:

- A Colorado ski resort ad says, "The hill may dominate you. But the town will still be your bitch." **Bitch** is teen slang for a passive person.
- Fox Broadcasting's *Fastlane* show has a website that says, "Are you pimp enough to get inside the action? SIGN UP for FASTLANE news!" Here, **pimp** is a synonym for "cool."
- An Old Navy ad that spoofs the *Family Feud* game show closes with **"Peace out!"** (which means "good-bye").
- An ad for Breathe Right Nasal Strips uses the catchphrase **don't go there!**

However, it's more often the case that marketers are aiming their hipness at older consumers. They're saying, in effect, "Hey, yo, check us out; we talk the way we think *you* think young people talk, so we think that means you'll associate our product with young people. Therefore, if you buy our product, you'll be associated with young people too." Call it "cool by association." Sociolinguists call it *covert prestige*.

This is an import engine of language change, because it's the mechanism by which slang terms become part of the everyday lexicon. Think of all the fairly recent slang argot that now swims comfortably in the mainstream: *all-nighter, bogus, bozo, bummer, burned out, chick, cool, cop out, crash, dig, drop out, dude, ego trip, freak out, hassle, neat, put down, rip off, toast, unwind, uptight, vibes.*

But modern marketers and journalists don't want to use these mainstream terms because they no longer offer covert prestige. (The exception here is *cool,* which is still an acceptable slang term and has been for most of the 50 or 60 years that is has been in the lexicon as a synonym for things that are calm, interesting, in-the-know, or acceptable.)

To get that "hip" sensibility, the would-be slang user must walk a fine line between waiting for a term to be established enough that its use is understood and not waiting so long that the word falls out of fashion or its meaning changes. (The word *ill*, for example, has meant both "good" and "not good" in its linguistic career.) That fine line is becoming a well-trodden path as more companies and writers pluck up the courage to use slang, as you'll see in this chapter. What follows is a collection of slang terms—mostly from youth culture and hip-hop, which are becoming increasingly the same thing—that have seen some use in mainstream contexts.

Hip-hop has made a remarkable transition from an obscure urban art form in the early 1980s to what may be the dominant form of cultural expression. Hip-hop fans—they're known as **hip-hop heads** (1991)—include not only urban blacks, but also Latinos, Asians, and plenty of whites. Rappers such as Queen Latifah, Jay-Z, Busta Rhymes, and Lil' Kim promote everything from perfume to Pepsi. The hip-hop sensibility manifests not only in music, but also in fashion, TV and movie production (remember *Bulworth*?), and attitudes. It has also generated hundreds of slang terms, many of which have become surprisingly familiar, which is another testament to hip-hop's all-purpose appeal. Consider the slang terms embedded in the following movie titles:

- *Booty Call* (**Booty call** refers to a phone call made to arrange a sexual encounter.)
- *It's All About the Benjamins* (**Benjamins** are U.S. 100-dollar bills, which feature a picture of Benjamin Franklin.)
- *She's All That* (**All that** means "as good as it gets.")

The linguist Margaret Lee has studied the mainstreaming of hip-hop terms, particularly those that appear in newspaper articles. In her paper titled "Out of the Hood and into the News," which appeared in the journal *American Speech* in 1999, she illustrates the use of dozens of slang terms, including **dis** (1982; insult; short for "disrespect"), **four-one-one** or **411** (1994; information), **gangsta** (1988; gang member; criminal), **got game** (1997; has skills, especially in basketball), **you go, girl** (1990; an expression of encouragement or approval), and **you da man** (1983; you're the best).

One of hip-hop's most popular slang terms is **bling-bling** (1999), which originally referred to the massive amounts of showy jewelry worn by some rappers, but now it's the hip-hop equivalent of *glitz,* a flashy, possibly even tasteless, display of wealth. It was coined by rapper B.G. in his 1999 hit single "Bling, Bling." Soon after, the cover of *Newsweek*'s October 9, 2000 issue screamed, "Welcome to the Bling Bling Generation." In the article B.G. explains how he came up with the phrase: "I was just thinking how I like to get my shine on when I go out. You know, I've been through a lot. Life is hard growing up in the projects and seeing all kind of things kids shouldn't see. So now that I got myself out of that situation and doing well, I'm going '**bling-bling**' because I deserve to."

A McDonald's commercial from a few years back shows a bunch of guys using "bling-bling" to describe, of all things, a scratch-and-win game. There was a movie released in 2002 called *Bling Bling* ("He's got the biggest rock of them all"), and there's also a magazine called *Bling Bling.* A recent Hummer ad included the slogan "B to the L to the I to the N to the G." The media aren't afraid to use the term, either:

> Though it was the 75th anniversary—the diamond jubilee—of the Academy Awards, **bling-bling** was barely a blip on the TV screen. (*Daily Press,* Newport News, Va., March 25, 2003)

Even the *New York Times* thinks the phrase is fit to print, and used it in 21 different articles in 2002. Here's an example:

In any case, the beginning of the 21st century is turning out to be yet another cavalcade of **"bling bling."** (*New York Times,* December 16, 2002)

Another hip-hop coinage is the exuberant **boo-yaa** (also: **boo-yah, boo-yeah**), which means "excellent," although it began its life as a marker for the sound of a shotgun blast. This exclamation has found its way into a McDonald's ad promoting a tie-in to the Disney movie *Emperor's New Groove,* as well as a KFC ad with an improbably animated Colonel Sanders. ESPN sportscaster Stuart Scott has adopted "boo-yaa" as his signature catchphrase to accompany slam dunks, home runs, and hockey hits. Here's another example:

> Yo! Check it out! Phil Collins is **boo-yaa!** That's right, Phil "Ghetto Dog" Collins' hit "Take Me Home" gets extensively sampled on Bone Thugs-N-Harmony's new CD "Thug World Order." (*Chicago Tribune,* January 24, 2003)

The hipster verb **chill out** (1980), meaning to calm down, to relax, is nowadays almost always shortened to just **chill,** and it has become remarkably popular not only in youth and hip-hop circles, but in the mainstream as well. In a Doonesbury cartoon, a character is giving some potential college recruits a tour around the campus and shows them three "popular new theme" dorms named Sega, Entenmann, and Eros. The themes? "Gaming, eating, and sex. Your three major chill groups." The Food Network has a show called *Grillin' and Chillin';* a library in Boston opened the "Chillin' Zone," an after-school student lounge complete with tables, couches, television sets, and video and board games. Even the army is hip to this word:

> You know the deal—**chillin'** in front of the TV, feet up, slippers on. Lounging in those beloved sweats of yours. (Army News Service, April 14, 1999)

Both *chilling* and *chilling out* are popular with headline writers, as the following examples from a single month demonstrate:

Grillin' and Chillin' (*Creativity,* March 1, 2003)

Chilling Out May Be Secret to Atlantic Shores Boys' Success (*Virginian-Pilot,* March 2, 2003)

In the War of Winter Wear, Parents Are Dealin' with Teens Who Are Just Chillin' (*Roanoke Times,* March 3, 2003)

The Bare Facts About Chilling Out at the Beach (*Aberdeen Press and Journal,* March 5, 2003)

Parcells Would Rather Players Be Chilly than Chillin' in Locker Room (*Dallas Morning News,* March 10, 2003)

Chillin' on a Warm Day (*Guelph Mercury,* Guelph, Ont., March 18, 2003)

Chilling Out in My Hot House (*Western Mail,* Cardiff, Wales, March 22, 2003)

Chilling Out in Name of Disarmament (*Mercury,* Hobart, Australia, March 26, 2003)

Chilling Out at a Jazzy Lounge (*New Straits Times,* Kuala Lumpur, Malaysia, March 29, 2003)

Chilling Out at the Pinery (*London Free Press,* London, Ont., March 29, 2003)

The phrase **da bomb** (1990) means "very good." Radio station KDDB FM in Honolulu calls itself "Da Bomb." A U.S. Air Force document profiling the 305th Civil Engineering Squadron's Explosive Ordnance Flight, the bomb disposal squad for McGuire Air Force Base in New Jersey, was titled "Maguire Unit is 'Da Bomb.' " But my favorite use of this phrase appeared in *The Onion* in an article titled "Clinton Threatens to Drop Da Bomb on Iraq":

> In an address before an emergency session of Parliament Monday, George Clinton said he is prepared to drop **Da Bomb** on Iraq if Saddam Hussein does not loosen up and comply with U.N. weapons inspectors by the Clinton-imposed deadline of March 1.
>
> "For Saddam Hussein to refuse to let U.N. officials inspect Iraqi weapons facilities as per the terms of Iraq's 1991 Gulf War surrender is decidedly unfunky of him," Clinton said. "While the decision to drop **Da Bomb** is never an easy one, unless Saddam gets down with this whole U.N.-inspection thang and seriously refunkatizes his stance by March 1, we will have no choice but to tear the roof off Baghdad."
>
> Preparations for the military strike, dubbed Operation Supergroovalisticprosifunkstication Storm, are already under way. (*The Onion,* February 26, 1998)

Marketers and managers get these inexplicable manias for certain words or phrases. In the 1950s many things were described as *space age,* while the 1960s adjective of choice was *revolutionary.* Prefixes such as *super-, mega-,* and *ultra-* come and go like fads. Over the past few years **extreme** has been the marketers' darling, as well as the hipper variation, **xtreme** (1986). The U.S. Patent and Trademark Office lists over 1,200 trademark names that include the word *extreme* and another 600 or so that contain *xtreme* (including such unlikely names as Xtreme Golf Association, Xtreme Locker Key, and Xtreme Christians). The store shelves groan with products such as Right Guard eXtreme Sport Deodorant and Frito-Lays' Doritos eXtreme chips. The tag line for Wrigley's Xcite gum is "X-Treme mint refreshment." (I love the British commercial that shows a guy waking up with breath so horrible that a mangy dog leaps out of his mouth, suggesting the poor fellow has "dog breath.") The impetus behind this, well, extreme behavior was no doubt the infamous *X Games* (X being a common shorthand for extreme), which began in 1995 and included such **extreme sports** (1989) as sky-surfing, kite-skiing, and street luge. Perhaps the ultimate mainstream use of extreme appeared in a July 2, 2001, *Los Angeles Times* article, where Hayley Morgan, the brand manager for a company called Extreme for Jesus, said: "At his time, Jesus was a freak. He was going to parties, hanging out with prostitutes, hanging out with the dregs of humanity. . . . He definitely would have been considered **extreme**."

The word **flava** (1991) means, simply, "style," particularly in the sense of one's approach to life (think: *lifestyle*). An ad for Phat Farm clothes describes them as "Classic American flava"; ChapStick released a lip balm called "Flava-Craze"; and there's a a line of cosmetics called Mixd Flava. The media have warmed to the word, as well:

> Cabbage Patch Posse adds **flava** to Bearcats home games. (*Cincinnati Enquirer,* December 28, 2002)

> Appearing on BET with Ed Gordon Monday night was a smooth touch for Trent Lott, but I can't help thinking the senator has got to do just a tad more to convince America he's not nostalgic for the bad old days of segregation. If he really wants to reveal his heart after the Strom Thurmond unpleasantness, he's got to show more than contrition. He's got to show **flava**. (*Washington Post,* December 18, 2002)

> In all, EOL brings mad **flava** back to R&B as they charm the hearts, souls and minds of soul music fans. (*Los Angeles Sentinel,* June 10, 1998)

The phrase **for shizzle** means "for sure" (it also appears as **fo shizzle** and **fa shizzle**). The *New York Times'* James Poniewozik reported in a February 10, 2003, article that rapper Snoop Dogg introduced himself on the *Jimmy Kimmel Live* show as "Big

Snoopy D-O-double-gizzle-fo'-shizzle-dizzle." It doesn't sound like a phrase with any staying power, but on March 4, 2003, the *Chicago Tribune* ran the following headline: "Sizzle fo shizzle."

The word **hella** is an intensifier that roughly translates as "really" or "a hell of a lot of," depending on the context. The group No Doubt had a hit single called "Hella Good" in 2001 that served to bring this word into prominence:

> On most of the songs on the knowingly titled *Temporary Forever,* the center doesn't even try to hold. Passing thoughts, complex rhymes, oddball metaphors, and **hella** non sequiturs all buzz around some indeterminate point. (*Village Voice,* January 7, 2003)

> One kid went around offering everyone the butt of his ciga-rette, in case they wanted the last drag. Finally, he turned to me. Did I want it? he wondered. I didn't. But it was **hella** tight to be asked. (*Contra Costa Times,* June 30, 2002)

(In case you're wondering, the word **tight** in the previous ci-tation means "wonderful" or "outstanding," although it's still occasionally seen in its 1960s clothes where it means "close, as in a relationship.")

A **hottie** is a sexy person, and the word is now mainstream enough to have a place in some dictionaries. Marketing for the HornDog Gear clothing line is aimed at the 18- to 24-year-old crowd. The line includes sweatshirts, hats, bathing suits, and other gear emblazoned with sayings such as "HornDog Hottie." A Nokia ad touts the company's camera phone as "the new babe alert" and is headlined with the quotation "Hottie coming your way." The Web search engine Google doesn't like people using its trademarked name as a verb. Violators are sent a polite note along with a document outlining some "examples of appropri-ate and inappropriate uses of Google's trademark." In one of those examples, the appropriate use is given as "I used Google

to check out that guy I met at the party," while the inappropriate use is "I googled that hottie." Here's a press release for *Love
Magazine:*

> Valentine's Day is fast approaching. So ask yourself this: When
> a matchmaking friend introduces you to a hunk or a **hottie,**
> what do you notice first about the person? (PR Newswire,
> January 30, 2003)

The optimistic phrase **it's all good** (1994) is used to convey
the sentiment that everything's okay and that there are no prob-
lems. Rapper MC Hammer had a track titled "It's All Good" on
his 1994 album *The Funky Headhunter,* and three years later
Will Smith rapped a song with the same title on his album *Big
Willie Style.* The phrase has appeared in ads from Budweiser and
Southwest Airlines, and it made regular appearances on *The Jon
Stewart Show.* It had become so popular by 2002 that Geoff
Edgers of the *Boston Globe* described it as "the goatee of the language game: so all over the place that it's on the verge of becoming unfashionable." However, the phrase was easily
parodied long before that, as the following piece—titled "'It's all
good' used to fill uncomfortable silences"—shows:

> The popular catchphrase **"It's all good"** was liberally used to
> fill uncomfortable silences and mask insecurities at an
> Eldorado High School 10-year reunion Saturday.
>
> "The security guard gig at VisionTech is temporary, of
> course, until my application with Metro goes through," Jason
> Verner, voted Most Likely to Succeed in 1991, told former
> classmates. "But, you know, **it's all good.**"
>
> Former prom queen Rochelle Morgan invoked the phrase a
> short time later while explaining her obesity. "OK, so I'm not
> exactly the skinny little cheerleader I was 10 years ago," she told
> a former classmate in the buffet line. "On the other hand, I'm
> the happy mother of seven beautiful children. **It's all good.**"
>
> The phrase was also used to blithely justify poor life choices

and gloss over personal problems. (*Las Vegas Mercury,* May 25, 2001)

For some reason, slang always seems to generate a fistful of synonyms for the adjective *good.* Here are just a few that have surfaced over the past few years: *bad, bitchin', def, dope, fresh, ill, sick, sweet, whip,* and *wicked.* But one of the most popular—and therefore one of the most mainstream—is **phat** (1992, although the *Oxford English Dictionary* traces one sense of the word back to 1963). For example, a press release for AOL's new "Broadband Rocks" program describes it as "phat sounds to fat pipes." Radio station WBHT in Wilkes-Barre, Pennsylvania, put up a billboard with a picture of the callipygous Jennifer Lopez and the slogan "Phat Ass, Bad Ass, Kick Ass." The *Philadelphia Inquirer* ran an article about **hip-hopreneur** (1993) Russell Simmons and titled it "Phat accompli: Hip-hop entrepreneur branches out with social causes." (Note, too, that Simmons owns the clothing lines Phat Farm and Phat Farm Boys, while his wife, Kimora Lee Simmons, runs Baby Phat and Baby Phat Girlz.) Pun-loving headline writers just adore the word phat, as you can image:

Phat Profits (*Black Enterprise,* February 2003)

Survival of the Phat-est (*SF Weekly,* January 15, 2003)

Phat's in the Fire Over "Nightmare" Crowd (*New York Daily News,* September 23, 2002)

Chewin' the Phat (*Daily News Record,* September 16, 2002)

Phat Cats (*People,* July 1, 2002)

The interrogative term **whassup** (1990; also: **'sup** or **waz-zup** or **what up**), short for "what's up," is arguably the most famous of the more recent slang words. Its fame is due almost entirely to a Budweiser commercial that first appeared in 2000. The ad features five friends regaling each other with exuberant cries of "whassup" (or, really, "whaaaaaazzzuuuuuup"). It was 60 seconds of pure joy that transcended the usual commercial shtick by being authentic (the five guys are friends in real life), hilarious, and even touching in an odd way. In a December 11, 2002, interview with the *Los Angeles Times,* the commercial's director (and one of its actors) Charles Stone talked about what he was trying to achieve: "It's two guys on the telephone who appear to be talking about nothing but, if you will, are holding hands. [It's about] the grunts and nods and between words, some of those little idiosyncrasies, the funny details about being human."

Some spin-off ads appeared (including a wonderful ad in a Japanese restaurant where "wasabi" gets warped in "whassup"), and by the end of 2000 "whassup" had become a bona fide catchphrase. The media weren't even remotely bashful about appropriating it for their own uses:

Whassup with Italian swimmer Massimiliano Rosolino and his Aussie accent? (*Ottawa Sun,* September 22, 2000)

Whassup with Rupert, Barry, and Edgar and the other guys in the really, really big corner offices? (*Entertainment Weekly,* October 27, 2000)

Whassup at work? (*London Free Press,* November 1, 2000)

Linguists trot out the term *polysemic* when they come across a word that has many different meanings. The word *set,* for example, has 58 meanings as a noun, 126 as a verb, and 10 as an adjective. In hip-hop lingo, the polysemic champ is probably **yo,** which, depending on the context, can mean "hey," "what?" "check this out," "wow," "you," "your," or it can act in a general way as an accompaniment or to add emphasis to a gesture or action. The nimble nature of *yo* is amply demonstrated in a VISA commercial featuring Chinese basketball star Yao Ming that appeared during the 2003 Super Bowl:

> YAO MING: Can I write check?
> CLERK (points to sign reading "ABSOLUTELY *NO* CHECKS"): Yo.
> YAO MING (points to himself): Yao.
> CLERK (points to sign): Yo.
> YAO MING (points to "Yao" embroidered on his sweatshirt): Yao.
> CLERK (gestures to manager): Yo!
> MANAGER (acknowledges clerk): Yo.
> YAO MING: Can I write check?
> MANAGER (points to sign): Yo.
> YAO MING: Yao!
> MANAGER (points to sign): Yo!
> CUSTOMER #1 (points to Yao Ming): Yo!
> YAO MING: Yao!
> CUSTOMERS #1 AND #2 (together, pointing to Yao Ming): Yo!
> OWNER: (addressing Yao Ming): Yo.
> YAO MING: Can I write check?
> OWNER: (points to sign): Yo!

Why do writers and marketers use slang terms such as *bling-bling* and *wassup?* Besides the reasons outlined at the start of this chapter, slang also has a certain irresistibleness to anyone who loves words. Slang is language at its most frisky. It's an ebullient verbal eruption that rejects the staid locution in favor of the bold pronouncement that shows us a vital and idiosyncratic view of the world. To use slang is to see the world from this new perspective. We stop walking past our words and start dancing with them, and even though we may not have the steps exactly right, we do it anyway because we are, in the end, natural dancers of the language.

Chapter 7

Living in a Material World

The basis on which good repute in any highly organized industrial community ultimately rests is pecuniary strength; and the means of showing pecuniary strength, and so of gaining or retaining a good name, are leisure and a conspicuous consumption of goods. —*Thorstein Veblen*

In the affluent society no useful distinction can be made between luxuries and necessaries. —*John Kenneth Galbraith*

His name was George F. Babbitt. He was forty-six years old now, in April, 1920, and he made nothing in particular, neither butter nor shoes nor poetry, but he was nimble in the calling of selling houses for more than people could afford to pay. —*Sinclair Lewis*

The social history of consumption in the twentieth century and into these first few years of the twenty-first is the story of three social scientists who dedicated large parts of their lives to studying consumer behavior. The first and foremost of these is social critic Thorstein Veblen, who published his famous book *The Theory of the Leisure Class* in 1899. Veblen's theory was, in part, that the wealthy and powerful gain respect and prestige if they show off their wealth and power: "In order to gain and hold the esteem of men it is not sufficient merely to possess wealth or power. The wealth or power must be put in evidence, for esteem is awarded only on evidence."

One of the best ways for wealth to be "put in evidence" is to flaunt that wealth by purchasing expensive and extravagant goods. This is summed up by the famous phrase that Veblen coined: *conspicuous consumption.*

That works for the rich, but what about the massive middle class? Can they, too, derive some measure of respect through consumption? It turns out they can, and the man who recognized this was the economist James Duesenberry. In his 1949 treatise, "Income, Saving, and the Theory of Consumer Behavior," Duesenberry talked of the *demonstration effect,* where a consumer is more likely to purchase something if he sees his neighbor wearing, using, or driving that something. Duesenberry called this *keeping up with the Joneses.*

Nowadays, consuming patterns are a blend of conspicuous consumption and keeping up with the Joneses. In her book *The Overspent American,* economist Juliet Schor says that people today no longer look to their peers to decide their consumption patterns. Instead, they look to social groups that earn many times as much as they do: the upper-level managers in the company they work for, the characters they see on TV, the high-end lifestyles espoused by the likes of Martha Stewart and the editors of *Architectural Digest.* Schor calls this the *new consumerism*: We are what we consume.

So what are we? Well, *wasteful* is one word that comes to mind. (This may not be a coincidence. The word *consumption* also has an older sense that means "wasting disease.") We hear stories of parents buying their children $5,000 life-size Darth Vaders and $18,000 replica Range Rovers; they throw $25,000 birthday parties and $50,000 bar mitzvahs; grooms are brainwashed into spending two months' salary on the engagement ring, and brides are talked into spending tens of thousands of dollars on the wedding. Consumption, clearly, has become a kind of sporting event:

competitive consumption *n.* (1990) Purchasing material goods in an effort to exceed a standard of living displayed by one's friends and neighbors or in the media. *In the old days, women had only their local friends and neighbors to compete with and compare themselves to. Now they have a veritable plethora of feminine image standards to be threatened by. The goddess gurus, Martha Stewart and Oprah, along with all of the trash-talking hipsters on TV and the Internet, have bombarded women's collective psyche with such a nonstop barrage of nickel-and-dime neediness that the average woman cannot dare resist the pied piper siren call of* **competitive consumption.** (*Pittsburgh Post-Gazette*, December 23, 2001)

In other words, it's no longer enough to keep up with the Joneses; now we have to leave them in the retail dust. Our era is dominated by Big Wealth and Would-Be Wealth and, fortunately for new-word watchers everywhere, there's a wealth of neologisms that illuminate and reflect these times.

Emo Ergo Sum

Other than getting themselves on television, more people than ever are validating their lives through buying things. An old cartoon expressed it best: In a kind of *Let's Make a Deal* setting, a contestant faces two doors—the first says "Buy" and the second says "Die." When we purchase something tangible, some of that tangibility seems to rub off on us, giving us proof, even if only fleetingly, that we exist. The French philosopher René Descartes is, outside of mathematics circles, most famous for his dictum *cogito ergo sum*—I think, therefore I am. If he were alive today and had grown up in the affluence and materialism that has characterized the Western world for the past 50 years or so, he might have come up with a slightly different formulation: *emo ergo sum*—I buy, therefore I am.

And although online shopping has become a popular way to buy things, most folks still do their buying by heading for a physical location to exercise their credit cards. The location of choice is the *shopping mall,* a term that dates to 1963 but had its origins 400 years before in, of all things, a golflike pastime. The game was called *Pall Mall,* a name derived from the French word *pallemaille,* literally "ball-mallet." Pall Mall was played in a long alley that had an iron hoop suspended above the ground at the far end. The object was to use a mallet to drive a ball down the alley and then through the hoop in as few strokes as possible. The alleys used for the game were often tree-lined, and proved to be pleasant places to go for a stroll, especially after the game fell into disfavor. By the mid-seventeenth century the word *mall* was being used to refer to the alley itself. In the late seventeenth century and throughout the eighteenth century, *the Mall* referred to a tree-lined walk in St. James's Park in London that used to be a Pall Mall alley. By the mid-eighteenth century a *mall* was any tree-lined or sheltered walk used as a promenade. In the 1960s developers appropriated the term for their new indoor shopping centers that were designed to encourage people to walk around and browse in the shop windows.

Thirty years ago malls came in only two flavors: tiny *strip malls* and larger *shopping malls.* Now, however, there are more malls than you can shake a MasterCard at. The International Council of Shopping Centers defines no less than nine different types of shopping center (strangely, the word *mall* is rarely used by professional shopping center specialists):

neighborhood center A small shopping center or strip mall with stores that emphasize convenience and necessities, usually including a single large grocery store that acts as the center's anchor store.

(An **anchor store** [1975] is a major retailer, particularly one that brings many customers to the shopping center.)

community center A larger shopping center with some convenience stores, but with an emphasis on general merchandise, including at least two anchor stores.

regional center An enclosed mall, about twice the size of a community center, that emphasizes general merchandise and fashion stores, with at least two anchor stores.

superregional center The same as a regional center except bigger (typically, over 800,000 square feet), with at least three anchor stores.

fashion/specialty center A small shopping center that emphasizes specialty stores, especially fashion retailers, with no anchor stores.

lifestyle center A small shopping center consisting mostly of upscale specialty stores in a quaint, villagelike setting with no anchor stores.

power center A large, open-air center that consists mostly of big-box stores. (A **big-box store** [1988] is a large-format store, typically one that has a plain, boxlike exterior and at least 100,000 square feet of retail space.)

theme/festival center A midsize center that emphasizes leisure activities such as dining, entertainment, and tourism, with no anchor stores.

outlet center A large center that consists solely of manufacturers' outlet stores.

People, particularly Americans, love to shop. The International Council of Shopping Centers reports that there are over 45,000 shopping centers in the United States alone. According to the report *All-Consuming Passion,* published by the New Road Map Foundation, Americans spend an average of six hours per week shopping. (Tellingly, the authors of the report contrast this with the average of 40 minutes per week that parents spend playing with their children.) And this isn't just six hours of weekly drudgery, either. According to the *Denver Post,* in 2000, 34 percent of Americans listed shopping as their favorite activity.

Despite this competitive side, the pleasures of shopping remain elusive to most males. In 1998 *American Demographics* magazine reported on a study that asked respondents to agree or disagree with the statement, "Shopping is an experience that is relaxing and enjoyable for me. I make time to shop and browse." Of the respondents, 67 percent of women agreed, compared to just 37 percent of men. Clearly we have a

shopping gender gap *n.* (1990) The markedly different attitudes toward shopping exhibited by men and women. *Let's start with what's called the **shopping gender gap.** In the retail-store study that Paco [Underhill] showed me, for example, male buyers stayed an average of nine minutes and thirty-nine seconds in the store and female buyers stayed twelve minutes and fifty-seven seconds. This is not atypical. Women always shop longer than men, which is one of the major reasons that in the standard regional mall women account for seventy per cent of the dollar value of all purchases. (The New Yorker, November 4, 1996)*

So I suppose this makes competitive consumption a kind of **one-upwomanship** (1977):

Even in cosmetics—which is hardly the first product line that comes to mind as a status symbol—there's a structure of **"one-upwomanship."** It turns out that women are looking for prestige in their makeup case. (Juliet B. Schor, *The Overspent American,* 1998)

In the male ranks, the shopping flag is carried most proudly by the **metrosexual** (1994), a dandyish narcissist in love not only with himself, but also with his urban lifestyle. The writer Mark Simpson invented this term, and here's his succinct description of the metrosexual type:

The typical **metrosexual** is a young man with money to spend, living in or within easy reach of a metropolis—because that's where all the best shops, clubs, gyms and hairdressers are. He might be officially gay, straight or bisexual, but this is utterly immaterial because he has clearly taken himself as his own love object and pleasure as his sexual preference. Particular professions, such as modeling, waiting tables, media, pop music and, nowadays, sport, seem to attract them but, truth be told, like male vanity products and herpes, they're pretty much everywhere. (Salon.com, July 22, 2002)

The popularity of shopping might also be explained by its apparent therapeutic effects:

retail therapy *n.* (1986) Purchasing goods to make oneself feel happier or more fulfilled. *Does the prospect of acquiring something new cheer me up? I'd be lying if I didn't admit to indulging in "retail therapy," occasionally when I'm stressed or blue. Believe it or not, shopping can be healing. Years after her divorce, my mother-in-law thanked me for teaching her how to spend money on herself. It helped her rebuild her sense of self-worth. (Albuquerque Journal, May 6, 2001)*

In other words, as the bumper sticker says, "When the going gets tough, the tough go shopping." And what do the stressed and depressed purchase during these in-store therapy sessions? In some cases, almost anything will do, but more often than not a little pampering is what keeps the therapist's couch at bay:

self-gift *n.* (1984) A gift purchased for oneself. —*adj. It is not surprising that advertisers have been capitalizing on consumers' self-gift propensities for some time. For instance, both McDonald's ("You deserve a break today") and Andes candies ("The perfect little thank me") have incorporated reward self-gifts into their slogans.* (*Journal of Consumer Research,* December 1990)

The self-gift is the retail analogue to the cookie, candy bar, or other indulgence that we allow ourselves if we've done something good or just feel a bit down in the dumps. But, like eating pleasures, it's also possible to overindulge ("overconsume") down at the mall:

binge shopping *n.* (1986) A period of excessive or unrestrained shopping. —**binge shopper** *n. (1982). For a generation, "retail therapy" has offered the ultimate salvation from the stresses of modern living. But a major new study now suggests that for millions of people, binge shopping is no longer an emotional cure-all. If anything, it may make you feel worse.* (*The Observer,* London, May 6, 2001)

If these buying binges become a regular thing, then the person enters a new and not very pleasant retail territory:

extreme shopper *n.* (1995) A person who shops in a compulsive, reckless manner. *Extreme shoppers will soon find help if they "shop until they drop" at NorthPark Center. A new health education center will join the mall's mix of exclusive stores and eateries just in time for the busy—and stressful—holiday season.* (*Dallas Morning News,* October 17, 1997)

Extreme shoppers often report heightened levels of concentration and focus while shopping, and some even go as far as to compare shopping trips to drug highs and to find them (blush) "sexually stimulating" (to borrow the clinically coy phrase that *Psychology Today* used when it reported on this phenomenon in 1995). It's no wonder, then, that shopping can turn addictive:

> **shopaholic** *n.* (1984) A person who is addicted to shopping. —**shopaholism** *n.* (1986) *Donald Black, professor of psychiatry at the University of Iowa, said his research showed 89 to 92 percent of* **shopaholics** *are women and they range in ages between their early 20s and 40s. Overall, he believes 2 to 8 percent of U.S. women are addicted to shopping.* (*News-Herald,* Willoughby, Ohio, July 20, 2002)

There are even official psychiatric terms for the behavior, including **compulsive buying tendency** (1992) and **compulsive shopping disorder** (1991):

> Drug companies are always alert for new and profitable uses for their products, and now Forest Laboratories reports—just in time for the holidays—that its antidepressant Celexa is effective against **compulsive-shopping disorders.** Shop-till-you-drop seems to be a real syndrome; sufferers consumed by the need to buy are often plunged into debt as a result. Now research financed by Forest shows that within three months of taking Celexa, nearly 80% of the 21 patients studied experienced improved symptoms. (*Time,* December 25, 2000)

And just to show that compulsive shopping isn't just a modern malady, a synonym—*oniomania* (from the Greek word *onos,* "price")—was coined by the German psychiatrist Emil Kraepelin way back in 1915.

Monster Homes and McMansions

An old joke courtesy of the comedian Stephen Wright: "You can't have everything. Where would you put it?" Our shopaholism creates not only a cash flow problem, but also a storage space problem. The knickknacks, doodads, and gadgets that we'll pay for later have to be put somewhere *now*. Perhaps that explains why house sizes have increased inexorably over the past 100 years. According to Harper's Index and a report on housing trends published by the National Association of Home Builders in 2001, the median size of a new house has gone from 700 square feet in 1900 to 1,000 square feet in 1949 to 1,385 square feet in 1970 to 2,060 square feet in 1993 to 2,265 square feet in 2001.

The average new home is getting bigger, but some new homes are bigger than others:

> **monster home** *n.* (1987) An extremely large house, especially one in which the size doesn't fit in with the surrounding architecture or terrain. *Homeowners in the coalition say they see a similar shift happening in parts of Dallas and in the Park Cities, where they say **monster homes** are destroying the historic fabric of older neighborhoods. "We have beautiful homes here, absolutely beautiful," said coalition participant Carole Jones, who lives in the 300 block of Huffhines Street. "But they're small homes. To build a 7,000- to 10,000-square-foot house next to a 900-square-foot house is outrageous." (Dallas Morning News,* October 2, 2002)

> **McMansion** *n.* (1990) A large, opulent house, especially a new house that has a size and style that doesn't fit in with the surrounding houses. *"I'll bet the two favorite rooms in those **McMansions** are the kitchen and the den because they are the only intimate rooms in the house," she said. "Who can have an intimate conversation in a 20-by-20-foot foyer?" (Chicago Tribune,* June 9, 2002)

The word *McMansion* has been a part of the lexicon only since 1990, but it has already undergone a fairly significant change in meaning. In fact, the word's current meaning seems to be almost the opposite of its original sense. As the following citation shows (this is the earliest citation I could find that uses the word), *McMansion* used to mean something similar to **cookie-cutter house** (1979), that is, a house that has a bland style that's identical to all the nearby houses:

> In this dehumanizing, auto-dominated, market-research-driven age of faltering standards of service and aesthetics, our urban and suburban landscapes are becoming more homogenized and worse.
>
> What character their history and ecology might offer is being strip-mined to make way for anonymous residential projects, monolithic office towers, climate-controlled retail complexes of questionable design and awkward transportation systems—all in the abused name of progress.
>
> We are talking here of the march of mini-malls and "**McMansions**." (*Los Angeles Times*, July 17, 1990)

This fits nicely with the formation of the word, which is *McDonald's* (the fast-food chain) plus *mansion*. After all, what could be more bland and "cookie cutter" than the fare served by McDonald's?

If a McMansion has a particularly garish style, call it a **big hair house** (1995):

> Yet the newest residential rage in Dallas is the antithesis of the traditional neighborhood: the gated community. Depending on your income and level of anxiety, these private enclaves may contain golf courses, health clubs and equestrian centers, surrounded by **big hair houses** of indecipherable pedigree and protected round the clock by cameras and private police. (*Dallas Morning News*, May 2, 1999)

The phrase "big hair house" originated in Texas, which is, of course, the home of all things big, including **big hair** (1978).

The latter refers to a bouffant hairstyle, especially one in which long hair has been sprayed, permed, or teased to make it stand away from the head and give it volume. It was once seen as an emblem of rich, powerful, or glamorous women, but is now mocked as being garish and very "1980s."

As the following mini-glossary shows, houses of large sizes come in all kinds of guises:

bigfoot house (2000) or **bigfoot home** (2000) *City commissioners voted 4–3 Wednesday night to limit so-called **bigfoot houses**—large homes on small lots. The ordinance would limit all maximum lot coverage of houses, regardless of lot size, to 30 percent. The height would be limited to 30 feet. (Detroit Free Press, May 18, 2000)*

Godzilla house (1998) or **Godzilla home** (2002) *After weeks of discussion about the pros and cons of approving two homes on one lot and approving two-story **"Godzilla houses"** in one-story neighborhoods, the council has denied a South Tampa couple's expansion plans. (Tampa Tribune, March 1, 2001)*

megahouse (1981) or **megahome** (1987) *The ascendancy of the **megahouse** reflects a nationwide trend, one that began in California in the late 1980's and spread in the last decade. United States census information shows that the average size of a new single-family house sold in 1999 was almost 10 percent larger than it was a decade earlier, while the average yard size was 13 percent smaller. (New York Times, March 19, 2001)*

starter castle (1991) *Spending was starting to resemble the conspicuous consumption of the "look-at-me-'80s" as the stock market boomed. Some folks were spending like it would never end, buying everything from multimillion-dollar **"Starter Castles"** to $100,000 home theaters. (Sun-Sentinel, Fort Lauderdale, Fla., January 4, 2002)*

trophy house (1981) *Author Marjorie Garber says in her book,* Sex and Real Estate: Why We Love Houses, *that the reason we* *go to such lengths (and expense) to live at the top is because "the* **trophy house** *is the equivalent of the trophy wife—the most visible sign of success." (Sydney Morning Herald,* August 24, 2002)

The real problem with monster homes and McMansions isn't their size per se, but their size relative to their surroundings. In a neighborhood of modest bungalows, tearing down an existing house and shoehorning a multistory, 5,000-square-foot behemoth into the same lot makes the new home stick out in a sore-thumbish way. However, it's happening everywhere you look, and the process even has its own name:

mansionization *n.* (1989) The act of tearing down an existing house and replacing it with one that is bigger, especially one that is much larger than the surrounding houses. —**mansionize** *v. Today, if Goldilocks were to visit 21st-century America, she might well be amazed at the predominance of Papa Bear sizes. . . . Passing through suburban neighborhoods, Goldilocks would notice oversized new houses, many built on undersized lots despite their turrets and faux-chateau pretensions. Real-estate brokers politely call the trend* **"mansionization."** *(The Christian Science Monitor,* January 26, 2000)

This is also called **bash-and-build** (2000):

For those who value the traditional look of their towns, **"bash and build"** can have horrible consequences. Too often, as big, boxy housing replaces the older homes, the entire look of a town can change. Trees get chopped down. And a nicely landscaped street gives way to a barren architectural hodgepodge of dwellings. (*The Record,* Bergen County, N.J., December 3, 2000)

The houses "bashed" so that the McMansions can be built even have their own names:

teardown *n.* (1989) *A mounting tide of* **"teardowns"**— *older homes demolished to be supplanted by dramatically* *larger, sometimes ostentatious houses of 5,000 square feet or even 10,000 square feet—is sweeping across many of America's older neighborhoods. (Duluth News-Tribune,* October 7, 2002)

scrape-off *n.* (1995)—*adj. Developers, speculators and real-estate marketers . . . are gobbling up smaller, older and cheaper homes, tearing them down (or scraping them off) and replacing them with "trophy houses" that are three times bigger, three times fancier and three times more expensive. . . . Since January, there have been ten* **scrape-offs** *and* **scrape-off** *construction projects in Cory-Merrill, Olson says. None match [sic] the neighborhood character. (Denver Westword,* September 2, 1999)

Money: That's What I Want

Although, as you'll see a bit later, credit cards are often used to finance high-flying lifestyles, it's really money that makes the material world go 'round. Most of us, of course, don't have much money, and the odds of us ever becoming rich are too laughably small to even calculate. But that doesn't stop a lot of us:

lottery mentality *n.* (1984) The desire to obtain money without working for it; the belief that a large sum of money can solve one's problems. *When the fix is in during good economic times, even the people on the short end of the deal figure they have a shot at success. It's a* **lottery mentality,** *a get-rich-quick mania that's overflowing with false promise. (San Jose Mercury News,* March 3, 2002)

casino culture *n.* (1987) A culture in which low-percentage money-making schemes—such as high-tech stocks, day trading, and lotteries—become mainstream investment vehicles. *For only the second time in my life, I* *feel—I just know—I can be rich, too. We are programmed from birth to believe this. If we forget it from time to time, there's a whole* **casino culture** *out there to remind us—Las Vegas and Atlantic City, Wall Street, TV commercials, lotteries.* (*Washington Post,* February 28, 1999)

The casino culture came to full flower in the late 1990s with the expansion of the stock market bubble and the whole dot-com boom (see Chapter 20, "The Dot-Com Rise and Fall"). It seemed that every Tom, Dick, and Harriet believed the Internet was the key to open the door to fabulous wealth without all that much effort and time; it was, in short, a massive **get-rich-click** (1994) scheme:

The site is run by Adam Hiltebeitel, Hossein Noshirvani, and Mare Jacobson, friends who—like most twentysomethings—yearned to join the **get-rich-click** set. (*Washingtonian,* March 2000)

While people are waiting for their financial ship to come in, they often enjoy reading about whose boats are already docked. These accounts are often way over-the-top and luridly detailed (think: *Lifestyles of the Rich and Famous*), making them a kind of pecuniary pornography:

financial pornography *n.* (1984) The graphic depiction of the lives of financiers and money managers, as well as the deals they make. *In* The Four Pillars of Wisdom, *[author William Bernstein] devotes a well-deserved chapter to the financial press and its weakness for* **"financial pornography"**—*lurid coverage of star money managers.* (*Seattle Times,* August 4, 2002)

investment pornography *n.* (1994) The graphic depiction of investment success. *You know the stories: The Top Ten Mutual Funds to Buy Now, How to Double Your Money*

*This Year, personality profiles that read like fan magazines. Stock-touting pieces that praise any path to profits. We've all done these stories, in one form or another. It's **investment pornography**—soft core, not hard core, but pornography all the same.* (*Columbia Journalism Review,* March/April 1998)

wealth pornography *n.* (2000) The graphic depiction of wealth and wealthy people. *The second reason that we should watch the money media is that, once you get past the stock tips and the **wealth porn*** (Fortune's *current cover story is about the 40 richest Americans under 40, "How They Got That Way. How They Live"), there's some really good stuff in the financial press.* (*National Journal,* Washington, D.C., September 23, 2000)

The author Tom Wolfe also calls this **plutography** (1984), which combines the prefix *pluto-* (from the Greek word *ploutos,* "wealth") with the suffix *-graphy* (from the Greek verb *graphein,* "to write").

Affluenza: A Sickness unto Debt

All this emphasis on wealth and its attendant trappings has led many people to go beyond merely reading about or watching the wealthy to actually upgrading their lifestyle to appear as though they're one of them:

affluenza *n.* (1979) An extreme form of materialism in which consumers overwork and accumulate high levels of debt in order to purchase more goods. ***Affluenza** is the contagious, addictive virus that makes us believe that too much is not enough. That transforms us from "citizens" into "consumers." That* *prompts political leaders of all persuasions to beg, "Buy something, buy anything!" (Denver Post, November 11, 2001)*

This word—a blend of *affluence* and *influenza*—was coined by psychologist John Levy in 1984. It originally referred to a malady afflicting rich children who, because they are often shielded from risk and challenges, suffer from guilt, boredom, and a lack of motivation and self-esteem. The "extreme materialism" sense appeared in the mid-1990s, but the original sense lives on, although it's now usually applied to rich people in general, and it refers to an overall dissatisfaction that wealth has not made the person happy or fulfilled.

These sorts of problems seem to afflict the nouveau riche in particular, who suffer from their own malady:

Sudden Wealth Syndrome *n.* (1997) Stress and anxiety caused by the sudden accumulation of unaccustomed wealth. *Even the "winners" on the [Antiques Roadshow]— those who make it on air, tell and receive stories, discover sudden wealth—are not delivered. On television we see only their whoops and blushes. Off the set, if given the chance, they will worry out loud about family squabbles, the cost of insurance, the threat of theft. They exhibit the same "strange melancholy . . . in the midst of their abundance" that Tocqueville noticed in 1831, the same strange melancholy of new billionaires in Silicon Valley diagnosed with* **"Sudden Wealth Syndrome,"** *or lottery winners who descend into dysfunction.* (Harper's Magazine, June 2001)

It is dashedly—but not at all surprisingly—difficult to find a commentator who feels even the slightest pity for someone who "suffers" (they always put "suffers" in quotation marks) from sudden wealth syndrome (which is also sometimes called **in-**

stant wealth disorder). The more likely reaction is snide sarcasm or even outright derision. Apparently, it remains lonely (and somewhat stressful) at the top. The "wealth" part of sudden wealth syndrome has normally been associated with the riches accumulated from dot-com IPOs and the rapid rise of the Nasdaq stock market in the late 1990s. However, it also applies to lottery winners, estate heirs, and people whose get-rich-quick (or click) schemes actually worked.

Despite this syndrome and other signs that riches don't lead to happiness, people seem to be more determined than ever to emulate the rich and famous. They have their own disorder:

aspendicitis *n.* (2000) The extreme desire to emulate the lifestyle of wealthy people (*Aspen* + *appendicitis*). *My own children and I look through photo albums and reminisce about our adventures in Africa or going to Venice on the Orient Express, twice. My friends haven't forgotten my bailing them out of credit-card chaos or taking them on the* QE2 *to New York. So what happened? If* **aspendicitis** *is a disease, then I was a sufferer.* (*The Express,* London, March 9, 2000)

And if they can't do it by accumulating wealth, suddenly or otherwise, they do the next best thing: They go into debt to purchase the trappings of wealth:

Madame Bovary syndrome *n.* (2001) The tendency for a person to go into debt to support a fashionable or extravagant lifestyle. *According to the National Association of Citizens Advice Bureaux, the number of people seeking help with their debts has increased by 37 per cent over the past two years. Another report has identified something called the* **"Madame Bovary syndrome,"** *a tendency among women to live a loan-fuelled lifestyle in order to be fashionable, avoid boredom and generally bolster their feelings of self-worth—to* *have fun, in other words.* (*The Independent,* London, July 24, 2001)

In Gustave Flaubert's 1857 novel *Madame Bovary,* the eponymous heroine Emma is married to Charles Bovary, a dull country doctor who bores Emma immensely and causes her to look elsewhere for romance and to accumulate massive debts along the way to pay for her affairs and a grandiose lifestyle that is far beyond her or her husband's means. (Mme. Bovary was French, of course, so perhaps her motto was "Give me liberty or give me debt!")

Speaking of debt, the world is in the midst of a long-term love affair with the credit card. We simply cannot get enough of these small plastic bundles of purchasing power. According to *The Nilson Report,* a banking industry newsletter, worldwide there were 1.44 billion credit cards in circulation at the end of 2000. An eye-popping 1 billion of those cards are in American wallets. In 2002, 36 years after credit cards were first introduced, household debt in the United States climbed to over $8 trillion, an all-time high, and higher than the total consumer disposable income. The 2001 *Statistical Abstract of the United States* tells us that two-thirds of consumers carry persistent credit card balances and that the total credit card debt tripled in the 1990s.

Why so many credit cards? One reason is that financial institutions are lowering the bar on credit worthiness. They offer cards to credit risks, college students, even children as young as 12 years old, according to one report. If credit is a kind of drug, then these institutions are the dealers:

credit pusher *n.* (1988) A bank or other financial institution that aggressively seeks new credit card or loan customers to the point of offering credit to people who can barely afford it. *The rise in indebtedness is in large part due to credit cards. Between 1990 and 1996, credit card debt* *doubled. Credit cards, with interest rates reaching nearly 20 percent, are a remarkably lucrative part of the loan business. Debtors pay an average of $1,000 a year in interest and fees alone. And the companies look increasingly like* **"credit pushers,"** *soliciting heavily and beyond their traditional creditworthy base.* (Juliet B. Schor, *The Overspent American,* 1998)

All of this means that extreme shoppers are becoming the norm. And when the extreme shopper's binge shopping gets out of hand, he or she (although it's usually a she) becomes a problem:

problem shopper *n.* (1990) A person who can't control his or her shopping and ends up accumulating massive debts and possibly even declares bankruptcy. *Elizabeth Roach . . . pleaded guilty to wire fraud, having embezzled $241,061 from her employer to support her out-of-control shopping habit. . . . The Roach case (along with the publicity surrounding the recent arrest of Winona Ryder for shoplifting) has become a vehicle for discussion about shopping problems and* **problem shoppers.** (*New York Times,* July 21, 2002)

debt cycle *n.* (1990) The constant accumulation of debt by purchasing items that one can't afford. *The biggest problem he sees: People living beyond their means, especially people who spend more than they earn and rely on credit cards—for cash, for groceries, for impulse buys—to tide them over until they get their next paycheck. That behavior creates an escalating and often devastating* **debt cycle** *that traps consumers.* (*Denver Post,* April 9, 2001)

Which brings us to the ignoble opposite of wealth porn:

debt porn *n.* (1995) The graphic depiction of debt and people who are in debt. *The best* **debt porn** *relies on a first-person voice—"Credit Cards Ruined My Life" (*Teen *maga-*

*zine) or "Confessions of a Credit Card Queen" (*Essence*)—and*
a familiar narrative arc: temptation leads to excess leads to a
downward spiral of spending, evoked for our disapproving
pleasure. Then—wham—rock bottom: she breaks down while
forging a credit-card application; he realizes he has never
opened half his purchases. (New York Times Magazine, July 18,
1999)

Money may not buy happiness, but how we *spend* money—
whether we're responsible or reckless—can make all the difference, as Charles Dickens so aptly pointed out in *David
Copperfield*: "Annual income twenty pounds, annual expenditure nineteen nineteen six, result happiness. Annual income
twenty pounds, annual expenditure twenty pounds ought and
six, result misery."

The losers in the game of competitive consumption—the
debt-laden binge shoppers and monster home mortgage payers
and Madame Bovary syndrome sufferers—find themselves on
the wrong side of this life ledger, with misery the result for most
of them. Since they seem determined to keep up with the
Joneses, it's clear we're going to have to find those damn Joneses
and tell them to stop spending so much money.

Chapter 8

Weapons of Mass Distraction

Books are the compasses and telescopes and sextants and charts which other men have prepared to help us navigate the dangerous seas of human life. —*Jesse Lee Bennett*

Television is actually closer to reality than anything in books. The madness of TV is the madness of human life. —*Camille Paglia*

The words "Kiss Kiss Bang Bang," which I saw on an Italian movie poster, are perhaps the briefest statement imaginable of the basic appeal of movies. This appeal is what attracts us, and ultimately what makes us despair when we begin to understand how seldom movies are more than this. —*Pauline Kael*

Western culture in general, and North American culture in particular, is becoming increasingly defined by the incessant search, even the *need*, for entertainment. In between slaving for the man and sacrificing for the kids, we crave some downtime when we can shuck off our cares, thumb our noses at the world, and ingest a little candy for the eyes and the ears and sometimes even that most neglected of organs, the mind. We hunker down in our sanctum sanctora and sing, à la Nirvana, "Here we are now, entertain us."

But entertaining has become a complex business over the past 10 years or so, thanks mostly to the relentless encroachment of the Internet into our personal lives. Instead of listening to the radio, people hang out in chat rooms; instead of reading the newspaper, people read **blogs** (1999), an eye-watering ugly word that's short for *web log* (or *weblog*), an online journal or diary.

This doesn't mean that people don't indulge in the traditional pastimes, far from it. They still crave what Larry Gelbart, creator of the TV show *M*A*S*H,* has called **weapons of mass distraction** (1996). Folks still watch television, go to the movies, and, yes, they still read books. The proof that these amusements still play vital roles in our entertainment culture is that they're all busy generating new words and phrases, as you'll see in this chapter.

Books

Until recently, the Internet has had a palpable antibook feel to it, a bias that was reflected in scorn-soaked terms such as **dead tree edition** (1995) and **treeware** (1997). Some even claimed that the Internet would sound the death knell for traditional books and publishing since now any budding poet or novelist could foist self-edited scribblings on the Web for all to read.

Two problems soon put the kibosh on such talk: First, nobody could figure out how these writers could get paid and, as Samuel Johnson once said, "No man but a blockhead ever wrote, except for money." Second, even if you could figure out the money angle, nobody actually would pay these writers anything because their self-edited scribblings almost always turned out to be poorly edited drivel.

So, yes, the publishing industry is still on its feet, and in fact it's pumping out more books than ever. About 120,000 books were published in 2000, a 300 percent increase from 1975. (In the Delicious Irony department, it's worth noting that one of the most successful of the dot-coms, Amazon, built an empire based mostly on its bookselling operation: "Earth's Biggest Bookstore.")

So the death of books has been greatly exaggerated, but the publishing world still has seen plenty of changes over the past few years, particularly in the guises that books now wear. *Audiobooks* have been around for a while (they first appeared in the late 1950s; the phrase *audio book* became the word *audiobook* in the mid-'80s), but now we have two varieties: the **book-on-tape** (1989; also: **BOT**) and the **book-on-disc** (1991; also: **BOD**). The former has inspired more than one person to wonder that if a person who reads a lot is called a *bookworm* (1599), then a person who listens to a lot of books-on-tape must be a **tapeworm** (1993).

Another trend has been the *electronic book,* or **e-book** (1988), a book in a digital format designed to be read using either a computer or a specialized **e-book reader** (1998). E-books were all the rage in 2000 and 2001, but the bloom fell off the e-book rose rather quickly after people realized that computer screen text was still difficult to read and that the e-book readers were expensive, one-trick ponies.

The e-book revolution seemed so inevitable at the time that the language changed in anticipation. Within a few years (so the thinking went), using the word *book* without any kind of modifier would be confusing because people wouldn't know if you're talking about a book printed on paper or one that's printed on electrons (so to speak). So people started using the term **p-book** (1999) to refer to a "paper book" and thus help distinguish between the paper and electronic formats. (*P-book* is an example of a *retronym,* a neological category that I discussed in Chapter 1, "A Mosaic of New Words.")

While the skin of the book has changed, so, too, has its guts as new literary genres are born out of the sea foam of our writers' imaginations. For example, recent works by the likes of Don DeLillo, Jonathan Franzen, Thomas Pynchon, Salman Rushdie, Zadie Smith, and David Foster Wallace have been called **hysterical realism** (1998), a genre characterized by exceptional length, frenetic action, offbeat characters, and long digressions on topics secondary to the story:

> *White Teeth* had, in the end, no harsher critic than Zadie Smith herself. Exasperated by the enormous reputation accorded her debut, she disparaged it as "the literary equivalent of a hyperactive, ginger-haired, tapdancing 10-year-old." Her second most severe critic, James Wood, suggested the novel was an example of **"hysterical realism,"** characterised by "a pursuit of vitality at all costs." (*Evening Standard,* London, September 3, 2002)

James Wood, mentioned in the above citation, is the literary critic of *The New Republic* and is the coiner of the phrase *hysterical realism,* which appears to be a play on *magical realism* (1937). The latter may also have inspired **Kmart realism** (1986), novels written in a spare, terse style and that feature struggling, working-class characters in sterile, bleak environments:

> While brand names are frequently found in **Kmart realism,** the most crucial aspect of the genre is its subject matter: people whose lives are circumscribed by strip malls, trailer parks, rent-to-own stores, tattoo parlors, gun shops, fast-food joints and tanning salons. People whose lives are marked by rootlessness. (*Chicago Tribune,* January 25, 2002)

Before Kmart came along, this type of writing was often called *trailer park fiction* or, later, *Diet-Pepsi minimalism* or *hick chic.* These labels have been slapped on many writers over the past 15 years or so, but the ones most associated with this style are Frederick Barthelme, Ann Beattie, Eric Bogosian, Richard Ford, Bobbie Ann Mason, Mary Robison, Joy Williams, and Tobias Wolfe. The great and inimitable Raymond Carver is considered the patron saint of the genre.

Another relatively new literary genre is **steampunk** (1987), which applies science fiction or fantasy elements to historical settings and that features steam-powered, mechanical machines rather than electronic devices:

> *Arcanum* is a prime example of **steampunk,** a subgenre of science fiction that explores the displacement of ancient ways by modern technology. Like *Thief,* with its steam-powered mechanical robot guards, *Arcanum* reconfigures the fantasy genre by imagining a past of magic and sorcery clashing with a present distinguished by advanced mechanical technology. (*New York Times,* October 4, 2001)

Although there are antecedents, William Gibson's 1982 novel *Neuromancer* is generally considered to be the first example of a literary form called **cyberpunk** (1984). This science fiction subgenre places computers, networks, and electronics (the *cyber-* part) inside a future that is anarchic and often dystopian (the *punk* part; from the anarchic, dystopian punk-rock music of the 1970s). Move the setting to the past, especially the Victorian age, take out the electronics and replace them with mechanical devices, especially elaborate, steam-powered contraptions, and you have a new genre: steampunk.

Steampunk often imagines what the past would have been like if the future hadn't happened so quickly. It imagines, in other words, what engineers and inventors might have come up with if they'd had another, say, 100 years to tinker with mechanical and steam-powered machines. (Some examples: a steam-powered flamethrower; a spaceship made of steel and wood.) In other cases, steampunk envisions a historical world that has modern elements. For example, in *The Difference Engine,* Gibson and coauthor Bruce Sterling imagine a late-nineteenth-century world in which Charles Babbage was able to build his "difference engine"—the first computer—and so the computer and communications revolution occurred 100 years earlier than it did.

I should note, as well, that people are also describing other media as "steampunk," especially video games and movies. For the latter, the steampunk label has been applied to films such as *Wild, Wild West, Brazil,* and even *Edward Scissorhands.*

Another new form is **chick lit** (1996), which features books written by women and focusing on young, quirky, female protagonists:

> *The Girls' Guide to Hunting and Fishing* is the **"Chick Lit"** book of the moment, a loosely linked set of short stories centering on Jane Rosenal's romantic coming-of-age over 20 or so years. (*Orlando Sentinel,* June 27, 1999)

There's also another sense to this phrase (that dates to 1993) that means "a book written by a woman or that appeals primarily to women" and so is the literary analogue to filmdom's *chick flick* (discussed later in this chapter).

One of my favorite new book words is **bonkbuster** (1988), a bestselling novel that features numerous sex scenes, so the word combines the slang verb *bonk*—to have sex—and *blockbuster*:

> It's no longer accurate to say that the forces of Anything Goes are sweeping through American culture (if indeed they ever were). Instead, the picture is far more complex and confusing. . . . We have these high-toned sex journals in the finest bookstores, but old-fashioned Harold Robbins–style **bonkbusters** are déclassé. (David Brooks, *Bobos in Paradise,* 2000)

Bonkbusters are sometimes described as **unputdownable** (1979). The opposite of this is a book that many people purchase but few read in its entirety, otherwise known as the **unread bestseller** (1983):

> There's the National Book Critics Circle Awards, another nice "high-culture" opportunity for Jonathan Franzen, author of

jumbo **unread bestseller** *The Corrections.* (*New York Observer,* March 11, 2002)

Some classic unread bestsellers are *A Brief History of Time* by Stephen Hawking, *The Satanic Verses* by Salman Rushdie, and *Gravity's Rainbow* by Thomas Pynchon.

A few other new literary genres to note before moving on are the **autopathography** (1989), an autobiography that is inspired by or that focuses on a disease or disorder that afflicts the author; the **me-moir** (1999), a memoir that is exceptionally self-centered; and the **Judas biography** (1999), an autobiography that denigrates or betrays a former friend or spouse of the writer. This is similar to the **hiss and tell** (1996), a book in which the author expresses contempt for a person or for people with whom he or she has had a relationship.

Television

If any form of entertainment can lay claim to the adjective *universal,* it's television. In North America, 98 percent of households have at least one TV set, a number that's shocking not because it's so high, but because it implies that there are something like 2 million households that *don't* own a TV.

That doesn't mean that television gets universal respect, however. Television is a medium that is widely and passionately disparaged even by people who tune in regularly. Over the years the TV has been variously called the *idiot box* (circa 1955), the *boob tube* (1963), the *idiot tube* (1968), and more recently the **plug-in drug** (1977), the **one-eyed monster** (1980), and the **brain drain** (1995). People who watch a lot of TV are called **couch potatoes** (1979), **sofa spuds** (1986), and other variations on this theme, such as **couch tomato** (1986; a woman), **spec-tater** (1983; a sports addict), and **baked potato** (1996; a drug user).

Television's reputation hasn't been helped in recent years by the advent of *reality TV,* a term that has been around since the late 1970s and early '80s, when it referred to shows such as *Candid Camera* and *Wedding Day* (the latter being a short-lived show that featured the unromantic premise of couples getting married in a TV studio). In recent years the label has also been applied to shows such as *Cops* and *America's Funniest Home Videos,* so perhaps that's why the creators of shows such as *Survivor, The Bachelor,* and *Joe Millionaire* have tried to find some other word or phrase to be the standard descriptor of series such as these that include elements of both drama and reality programming. The winner appears to be **dramality** (2000), which in the insular world of TV programmers has already achieved "term of art" status (of course I'm using "art" here in the broadest sense of the term):

> **"Dramalities,"** they say, are satiating people's needs for sanitized gossip, Peeping Tomism, and the pathetic desire to feel superior. The programs' unrehearsed moments are like visual jazz, appealing to the near-universal desire to be on TV in a country where there is no greater achievement. (*Business Week Online,* January 30, 2003)

Fittingly, *dramality* was coined by the guy who started it all (at least in North America): Mark Burnett, creator of *Survivor.* Some other contenders that have come and gone are **reality drama** (1985), **peeping-Tom TV** (1996), **unscripted programming** (1998), and **unscripted nonfiction drama** (2001). If a celebrity is involved, call it **celebreality** (2002); if the premise of the show is to humiliate one or more people, call it **humilitainment** (2002). All of this is likely moot because, as I write this, *reality TV* is firmly entrenched as the phrase-of-choice among the couch-noscenti.

Reality TV fans crave those JPMs—jolts per minute—that I talked about in Chapter 5, "Ad Creep," and many of them would likely swear that the best way to get those jolts is to watch **adrenaline television** (1995), a live broadcast of a dramatic event:

> For several gripping hours on Tuesday afternoon, the Colorado school siege provided cable news networks with **adrenaline television**—students running from the school with hands in the air, crying parents desperate to see their children, a bloody victim dangling from a broken window as he sought help. (Associated Press, April 21, 1999)

Others turn to **stunt programming** (1987), controversial, extravagant, or gimmicky television shows designed to boost a network's ratings. Examples of **stunt program** (1994) genres include the self-explanatory **car-crash TV** (1993) and **motorcycle-crash TV** (1997), as well as **carnography** (1984), shows that contain scenes of carnage or other types of violence.

What the networks and cable operators really want is a stable of shows that qualify as **appointment television** (1988), programming for which a person sets aside time to watch, either live or on videotape:

> It's called **"appointment television,"** an entertainment goal the basic cable industry is finally achieving. Cable no longer is merely a place to find fast-breaking news coverage, old movies or specialty programming. (*Rocky Mountain News,* July 6, 2002)

A TV programmer's other goal is to generate buzz about their show (show-buzz?), particularly at work, so they'll often include a controversial or exciting segment designed to get people's chins a-wagging. If successful, such a segment is called a **watercooler moment** (1999):

> We spent three or four hours very late one night talking about how a programme can basically market itself. This involved establishing one or two **"watercooler moments"** which would get people talking the next day. (*The Observer,* London, July 1, 2001)

It's a classic workplace scene: Two or three coworkers arrive at the office watercooler more or less simultaneously and, people being the social creatures that they are, a brief—and ideally non–work-related—conversation ensues. Nowadays, these confabs are just as likely to break out in the coffee room, alongside the photocopier, or while waiting to use the fax machine. But the watercooler was long ago chosen as the symbolic location for spontaneous workplace chit-chatting. That's the idea underlying *watercooler moment.* Insert some gratuitously controversial or titillating content into a show, and the next day the watercooler conversations will begin with the phrase "Did you see last night's episode of *X*?" (This is also called **watercooler television** [1998].)

This perhaps explains why some of us are addicted to shows and media spectacles that are both annoying and compulsively watchable, otherwise known as **irritainment** (1995):

> "**Irritainment** is a word we've come up with that means something is so annoying, you can't stop watching it." A good example was the O.J. Simpson murder trial. (*Amusement Business,* June 10, 2002)

Above all, TV types want us to stay put. They want us to plunk ourselves down on the couch, tune to their station, and then stay right where we are until bedtime. Fascinating or controversial events—particularly wars—are one way to achieve this goal, and since these kinds of spectacles most often get saturation coverage on news networks such as CNN, this has come to be called the **CNN effect** (1991):

> The latest snapshot of U.S. consumers showed confidence was near a decade low even before the grim realities of war in Iraq invaded TV screens. Being glued to the news also took a toll on chain-store sales last week in what economists have come to call the **"CNN effect,"** although the long-awaited advent of spring-like weather dragged some from their couches. (*Los Angeles Times,* March 26, 2003)

The CNN effect is becoming a misnomer because people increasingly get their news from multiple sources and in short bursts throughout the day, a phenomenon known as **news grazing** (2002):

> How could the twin American institutions of the anchor and the evening news have fallen into such seeming decrepitude and peril? The standard rap cites these factors: the fractionalization of the TV audience in the 500-channel cable-satellite media universe; the fierce and ever-expanding competition of cable news, as led by Ailes and Fox; the postmodern **news-grazing** habits of the young, who turn to such antiestablishment sources as the Internet and Jon Stewart's "Daily Show" for their information fix. (*New York Times,* May 19, 2002)

In the absence of a war or a Ford Bronco chase, keeping viewers tuned to a single channel for any length of time is sublimely wishful thinking in this era of the remote control and the gnat-like attention span. Nowadays many people prefer to spend their evenings (or, at least, the commercial breaks) using the remote to leap from one channel to another, a process known as **zapping** (1983), **channel flipping** (1984), **channel grazing** (1988), or **channel surfing** (1988).

Movies

Human beings love stories. From the ancient myths to modern soaps, we have a hunger for narrative that runs deep enough to be called a fundamental human attribute. We get our stories not only from the books and TV shows that I've talked about in this chapter, but also from friends, family, and neighbors; from theater, opera, and radio dramas; and from singers, monologists, and the traditional oral storytellers who, thankfully, still exist in this harried, sound-bitten age. But when we really want to lose ourselves in a story, most of us turn to the movies, something that Americans did over 4.5 *billion* times in 2002 (1.6 billion movie tickets, 2 billion VHS rentals, and 900 million DVD rentals). Whether it's *The Lost Weekend* or *Weekend at Bernie's*, there's something about *There's Something About Mary* and other screen gems that satisfies our need for narrative.

Movies entertain and thrill and fascinate, but they can also heal, a realization that has spawned **cinematherapy** (1995), a new form of therapy or self-help that uses movies, particularly videos, as therapeutic tools:

> **Cinematherapy** is a relatively new therapeutic approach being used by many psychotherapists and counselors. It is an extension of bibliotherapy, a technique developed by psychiatrist Carl Menninger, who assigned fiction and non-fiction books to his patients to help them develop insight and coping strategies. When using a video tape, the individual can view certain segments and important scenes over and over again and use the message in the story to understand himself and his own life more accurately. (Cox News Service, July 3, 2001)

This approach has become popular thanks to the number of books that have appeared in recent years, including the 1999 book, *Cinematherapy: The Girl's Guide to Movies for Every Mood,* by Nancy Peske and Beverly West, and their 2002 follow-up book called *Advanced Cinematherapy: The Girl's Guide to Finding Happiness One Movie at a Time.* These books join a host of others in this newly formed genre, including *Reel Therapy, The Motion Picture Prescription,* and *Rent Two Films and Let's Talk in the Morning.*

Of course, most of us attend or rent a movie not to find ourselves, but to escape from the real world for a couple of hours. The traditional movie genres—comedy, drama, action, thriller, and horror—are all still with us and, when done at least passably well, are capable of giving good story. But we've also seen the birth of a few new genres in the last 10 or 15 years.

Take **screwball noir** (1991), for example, which combines antic or comedic scenes with a bleak or shadowy atmosphere:

> Rudolph's latest effort, "Trixie," is emblematic. A **"screwball noir"** about a humble woman security guard prone to malapropisms who uncovers crooked dealings in a small resort town, it's got a talented cast headed by the sublime Emily Watson. (*The Oregonian,* December 8, 2000)

This genre-bender of a phrase combines two types of movies: the *screwball comedy* (1938)—a whimsical, witty movie about the amusing antics and battles of eccentric, often romantically linked characters—and the *film noir* (1958)—a movie characterized by dim lighting, a bleak urban backdrop, and shadowy, cynical characters.

One of the most popular new genres is the **chick flick** (1992), which features themes, characters, or events that appeal more to women than to men:

> So what is a **chick flick** exactly? A movie where everyone talks a lot, preferably at the hairdresser? A movie that makes women and certain sensitive men cry faster than frying onions? (*Sunday Times,* London, October 20, 2002)

Chick flicks run the gamut from the hard-charging *Thelma & Louise,* to the whimsy-inducing *Moonstruck,* to the tear-jerking *Steel Magnolias.* It also includes the relentlessly cute *Sleepless in Seattle,* which may have invented the genre when Tom Hank's character described *An Affair to Remember* as a "chick's movie." What about the opposite type, those testosterone-drenched action movies starring guys named Arnold, Sylvester, and Bruce? Why, those are **dick flicks** (1998), of course.

The recent popularity of Jackie Chan and his jaw-dropping martial arts moves has focused attention on an obscure genre called **chopsocky** (1978), low-end martial arts films that feature mostly fight sequences with little or no plot. The word is most likely a blend of *chop suey,* a Chinese-American dish of shredded meat and mixed vegetables, and the verb *sock,* to hit somebody or something hard, especially with a fist. Higher-end chopsocky movies also make use of **wire-fu** (1997), a cinematic technique in which actors perform kung-fu moves while attached to wires and pulleys that make them appear to fly, run up walls, and so on:

> Cinematographer Peter Pau and fight choreographer Yuen Woo Ping use the technique of **"wire-fu,"** or kung-fu aided by wires and pulleys to give the characters on screen superhuman techniques. (*East Carolinian,* Greenville, N.C., March 8, 2001)

Another newly popular genre comes from, of all places, Bombay (now known as Mumbai), the center of the Indian film industry, which, according to one report, produces over 800 films a year. This has given us the word **Bollywood** (1979), the films or film industry of India, a cinematic blend of *Bombay* and *Hollywood*:

> A three-hour **Bollywood** potboiler averages a half-dozen songs. There is no current Hollywood equivalent, even though Baz Luhrmann's latest venture, *Moulin Rouge,* borrowed heavily from this genre. (*Toronto Star,* November 1, 2001)

In the movie *Sunset Boulevard,* former silent screen star Norma Desmond utters the classic line, "I'm still big, it's the movies that got small." Ms. Desmond would be shocked by how small some movies have become, with low- and even no-budget movies now a certifiable trend:

> **guerrilla filmmaking** *n.* (1985) Low-budget filmmaking that usually features a skeleton crew, no location permits, street scenes shot on-the-fly, simple props and clothing, and nonprofessional actors. *Yes, filming was intense. "We had 27 days in Toronto and the last day in Detroit when we did 25 and 30 setups," director Joe Carnahan said. "One car*

and one camera and four guys: **guerrilla filmmaking.**"
(*Boston Herald,* January 10, 2003)

A subset of guerrilla filmmaking is **microcinema** (1998), low-budget films shot mostly on digital video, edited on a computer, and then distributed via videotape or over the Internet.

Because **microcinema** opens a direct connection between filmmakers and audience, for the first time in the 100-plus-year history of motion pictures average people can shoot, edit, and perhaps even disseminate their visions without answering to anybody. (*Wired,* October, 1999)

(I should also point out that *microcinema* also refers to a small exhibition space used to display alternative and underground films.)

Computer-based film editing is the latest thing, and it's taken to its logical conclusion in the emerging world of **machinima** (1998), animated shorts or movies created entirely on personal computers and "filmed" in real-time using computer graphics rendering software or computer game technology:

A digital Walt Disney who wants to make a **machinima** film will start with a game engine, the software that generates the virtual 3-D environment in which a game like Quake II is played. . . . But **machinima** directors go a step further, discarding the game's out-of-the-box elements in favor of their own characters, scenery, story line and dialogue. (*New York Times,* July 22, 2002)

Machinima is a blend of *machine* and *cinema.* The cinema connection is clear, but why "machine"? Computers are machines, of course, so that's an obvious influence. On a more subtle level, the software that creates machinima's scenes, lighting, and actors is called an *engine* (see the usage above).

The "actors" in a machinima film—not to mention characters such as Woody and Buzz Lightyear in the *Toy Story* movies—are called **synthespians** (1990), synthetic thespians:

The **synthespian,** an artificially-created "human" actor, is the Hollywood Screen Actors' Guild's nightmare. . . . The word— and, yes, it's an awful one—was coined by LA-based digital effects expert Jeff Kleiser when he created the industry's first virtual actor (or "vactor") for his 1988 short film *Nestor Sextone for President.* (*The Herald,* Glasgow, Scotland, December 26, 2001)

Computers are also being used to perform the **fan edit** (2000), a version of a movie or other artwork that has been edited by someone other than the original artist, especially by a fan of the work or artist:

Thanks to digital technology, a delightful new art form emerged this year: the **fan edit**. . . . [T]his summer, Mike J. Nichols, a "Star Wars" addict living in Santa Clarita, Calif., used his Macintosh to make a series of merciful cuts to "The Phantom Menace"—most notably, the virtual elimination of the irksome Jar Jar Binks. Fans who obtained a copy of Nichols's "Phantom Edit" through the Internet hailed the arrival of a vastly improved (if not yet good) movie. (*New York Times,* January 6, 2002)

In a world that hits us over the head with wars and terrorist attacks and pop stars dangling their children off balconies, it's good to have a large cache of weapons of mass distraction. We need our unputdownable books, whether on paper, tape, or disc, whether in the form of Kmart realism, steampunk, or chick lit. We couch potatoes and tomatoes need our appointment television where we paradoxically distract ourselves from the real world by watching reality TV and zapping our way through the stunt programs and irritainment. And we need ("more than ever," thank you, Tom Cruise) our movies, those chick flicks and chopsockies that act as cinematherapy, making the world okay again for a couple of hours, anyway.

Chapter 9

Tales of Comfort, Security, and Privacy

Who could deny that privacy is a jewel? It has always been the mark of privilege, the distinguishing feature of a truly urbane culture. Out of the cave, the tribal teepee, the pueblo, the community fortress, man emerged to build himself a house of his own with a shelter in it for himself and his diversions. Every age has seen it so. The poor might have to huddle together in cities for need's sake, and the frontiersman cling to his neighbors for the sake of protection. But in each civilization, as it advanced, those who could afford it chose the luxury of a withdrawing-place.
—*Doris McGinley*

I f it please the reader, let me begin this chapter by introducing into evidence the following factlets:

- In 2001, according to the Consumer Electronics Agency, 25 million U.S. households had a home theater setup.
- Researchers at the NPD Group report that people bought an average of 20 takeout restaurant meals in 1984, but by 2002 that number had nearly doubled, to an estimated 37 per year.
- According to the National Burglar and Fire Alarm Association (yes, Virginia, there is an association for *everything*), approximately one in five homes is equipped with an electronic security system.
- In 2002 CNBC reported that the United States has 3.5

million security cameras in public locations such as airports, street corners, and bus stations, and there are probably another 5 or 6 million security cameras in private locations.

What do these straws in the sociological wind tell us? According to trend gurus, cultural anthropologists, and neighborhood busybodies, they're all indications that people are increasingly looking for more comfort, safety, and privacy in their lives. People, so the current thinking goes, see the world as a harsh, dangerous, and uncivil place so they're withdrawing from the world to the comfort, safety, and privacy of their own homes.

But, I hear you interject, what about the fact that the crime rate is dropping? Good point. The Federal Bureau of Investigation's Uniform Crime Reports Program tracks the *Crime Index rate,* which is a measure of the crimes reported to local police authorities in seven categories: homicide, forcible rape, robbery, aggravated assault, burglary, larceny-theft, and motor vehicle theft. The Crime Index *fell* 30.1 percent from 1991 to 2001.

So why are people hunkering down in their homes? One possible answer is that the media's reporting of crime is increasing. According to the Center for Media and Public Affairs, network news coverage of crime rose by 240 percent from 1990 to 1995.

Another possibility is simple demographics (if the word *simple* can rightly be applied to this complex social science). The stay-at-home trend first appeared in the late 1970s and early 1980s, about the time that the first Baby Boomers were reaching their mid- to late 30s. That's usually the time when people begin to lead quieter lives, and, particularly if they have children, they start to slow down and spend more time at home. So, yes, a huge chunk of the population began staying at home, but not entirely because society was becoming too scary. Rather, it was in part because the massive demographic bulge of the Baby Boom gen-

eration (see Chapter 14, "A Baby Boom Lexicon") was settling down, which they would continue to do over the next 20
years.

Whatever the reason, people are looking for more comfort,
security, and privacy in their lives, and they're coming up with
all kinds of new words and phrases to reflect that search.

The Comfort of Things

We humans sure like our comfort (which, just so you know, comes
from the Latin word *confortare,* which means "to strengthen"). We
seek out *creature comforts,* and when we're doing something we're
good at, we say we're in our *comfort zone.* We admire people who
are *comfortable in their own skins,* especially the well padded among
us who claim, eyes a-twinkling, that they're *built for comfort.* A
close call is *too close for comfort,* and help that's really no help at all
is pooh-poohed as mere *cold comfort.*

Spiritual and religious matters are traditional sources of comfort but, the material world being what it is (see Chapter 7,
"Living in a Material World"), we're increasingly turning to
things to help us feel at ease. The original comfort thing was
probably **comfort food** (1977), which refers to simple fare (especially food loaded with carbohydrates) that's comforting because the eater associates it with his or her childhood in
particular or with home cooking in general:

> Along with grits, one of the **comfort foods** of the South is
> black-eyed peas, and to start a new year they are an absolute
> necessity, at least if you are seeking good luck for the next 365
> days. (*Washington Post Magazine,* December 25, 1977)

Increasingly, we're looking for items that have a **comfort factor** (1981), some quality or characteristic that makes us feel
comfortable:

There is also no denying the **comfort factor** in the wake of the Sept. 11 terrorist attacks. . . . A remembrance of things past is always good for the soul. (*Boston Herald,* April 25, 2002)

As proof of the remarkable strength of our current "will to comfort," here's a list of some comfort things that have appeared within the last 20 years or so:

comfort architecture (1998) *Comfort architecture? It's there all right. . . . Chicago architect Kathryn Quinn sees it in the new reluctance of her clients to have a TV blasting in almost every room of the house. They want oases of quiet, she says, instead of a high-anxiety environment in which they can't escape the latest news bulletin on CNN. (Chicago Tribune,* November 4, 2001)

comfort art (1994) *In Kinkade's lush, colorful paintings it's almost always sunrise or sunset. Windows in old-fashioned cottages brim with light and smoke wisps curl from stone chimneys. There might be beautiful spring blooms on the plants and fall foliage on the trees—all at the same time. "My work is purely escapist; it's comfort art for sure," Kinkade said. (San Diego Union-Tribune,* September 16, 2001)

comfort book (1991) *Treating insomnia calls for improving habits leading to bedtime. . . . These include taking a bath, drinking milk, reading a comfort book, or listening to favorite slow music. (Manila Bulletin,* Manila, Philippines, July 26, 2002)

comfort clothes (1981) Also: **comfort clothing.** *This year the watchword in men's fashion is "comfort clothes," and nowhere is that more evident than in the underwear market.* (*Daily News Record,* New York, May 13, 2002)

comfort dog (1987) *The Cavalier King Charles spaniel is a descendant of the toy spaniels seen in 17th- and 18th-century* *paintings. At that time they were used as* **comfort dogs,** *and this holds true today. The animals were used to keep nobles' laps warm in draughty castles and on long coach rides, and acted as flea magnets to keep possibly plague-infested fleas from biting their owners.* (*Herald Sun,* Melbourne, Australia, April 13, 2002)

comfort flower (2001) *Rushing plans to expand upon such things—garden accessories, scarecrows and* **comfort flowers** *he enjoys—when he appears at the Oklahoma Garden Festival.* (*Daily Oklahoman,* January 31, 2002)

comfort furniture (1988) *Broyhill has tuned into the vintage craze with its expanding Attic Heirlooms Collection of furniture that looks right off the floor of an antiques mall. . . . "It's* **comfort furniture,"** *says Broyhill marketing director Boyd Barnhardt.* (*Houston Chronicle,* June 1, 2002)

comfort movie (1989) *I call these* **comfort movies,** *but everyone's idea of a* **comfort movie** *will be different. A time of stress is a time for the familiar. Old favorites connect us to feelings we once had of delight or coziness or peace. They evoke that earlier feeling and make us less anxious about the moment we're in.* (*San Francisco Chronicle,* December 23, 2001)

comfort music (1993) *Singer-songwriter Jeb Loy Nichols makes* **comfort music.** *It's sweet and warm and goes down like a cup of cocoa with an extra shot of sugar.* (*Boston Herald,* June 21, 2002)

comfort person (1988) *Ruba "is the queen of patience," says Reham. "The* **comfort person.** *The one you go to in a crisis."* (*Detroit News,* November 1, 2002)

comfort room (1984) *With the deck as their playground, Gus and Dianne find the sunroom is their* **"comfort room."**

It's where they begin mornings and end evenings. (*Daily Press,* Newport News, Va., August 19, 2001)

comfort scent (1992) *Within a few minutes of noon, we were taken upstairs to a large, bright room with two big tubs brimming with bubbles. Each of us was shown to a table filled with tiny vials and asked to pick a scent to be added to our bath water and massage oil for aromatherapy. I selected a **"comfort" scent** with lavender.* (*The Washingtonian,* Washington, D.C., May 2002)

comfort shirt (1998) *Keep creative stashes for sick days: Magic "Dr. Mom" elixirs include hot cocoa, peppermint tea, Popsicles, Daddy's ice pack (a grown-up cachet for feverish little foreheads), Mom's old T-shirts for a **comfort shirt** to sleep in and the king of all cure-alls, the kid's favorite kind of cookie.* (Copley News Service, January 19, 1998)

comfort snack (1990) *Daily treats are the only way to get through the nine to five, according to research which has found consumers rely on **comfort snacks** such as chocolate and cake to compensate for being in the office.* (*The Scotsman,* Edinburgh, Scotland, May 3, 2002)

comfort song (1987) *"The funny thing about Redeemer is that I used to sing it at home as my **comfort song,**"* Mullen said. *"I had no idea that others would sing it as their **comfort song,** too."* (*Orange County Register,* August 26, 2001)

comfort TV (1993) Also: **comfort television, comfort TV show.** *But by mid-September, the [Gary] Condit story was a faint memory. **"Comfort TV,"** fed by nostalgia for more innocent times, came on strong, typified by huge viewership for a Carol Burnett special.* (Copley News Service, December 28, 2001)

comfort video (1999) *Many people have at least one **comfort video**, a movie that gives them a warm glow. Maybe the same glow chicken noodle soup gives them on a rainy day. They are movies that either bring you up when you're feeling down or make you feel a happy melancholy like an old blues song.* (*Morning Star*, Wilmington, N.C., December 28, 2001)

comfort writing (1998) *Murray draws parallels between the nurturing nature of food and her play—she describes [her play]* Salt *as "**comfort writing.**"* (*Courier Mail*, Queensland, Australia, May 11, 2002)

Getting Comfy in the Cocoon

If there's a single word that encapsulates not only this desire for comfort, but also the whole people-are-staying-home-because-the-world-is-a-frightening-place viewpoint, it's **cocooning,** which was coined by trend-watcher Faith Popcorn in 1981. She defined it as "the impulse to go *inside* when it just gets too tough and scary *outside.*" This word is now well established in the mainstream and has even made the linguistic grade by getting included in a couple of dictionaries.

Ms. Popcorn, who as a professional trendmeister knows a good thing when she sees it, has even developed her own cocooning lingo. Here are some examples:

armored cocoon *n.* A home equipped with a security system and perhaps even a gun.

cocoon-hopping *pp.* Going from one cocoon to another.

cocoony *adj.* Relating to a cocoon. Also: **cocoonier.**

drive-time cocooning *pp.* Performing personal tasks (what Popcorn calls "life-maintenance chores") within one's car (a **secondary cocoon**).

hyper-cocooned *adj.* Relating to a person who leaves his or her home only rarely.

socialized cocoon *n.* A cocoon to which only close friends and relatives are invited.

wandering cocoon *n.* Any space that makes a person feel safe and comfortable while not at home.

"Drive-time cocooning" never made it past Ms. Popcorn's small circle of friends and acquaintances, but the concept of performing personal tasks in one's car is a bona fide trend. (See, for example, my discussion of *dashboard dining* and related terms in Chapter 3, "Faster Food.") Fortunately, a similarly cocoonish term has given this trend a label:

carcooning *pp.* (1989) Using one's car for working, playing, eating, grooming and other tasks normally performed at home or at the office. —**carcoon** *v., n. Academics have coined the word "carcooning" to describe how people increasingly outfit their cars for comfort, entertainment and productivity. Phone systems are built in. New stereos pull in satellite radio broadcasts and play MP3 files downloaded from the Internet.* (Associated Press, August 22, 2002)

This word is a combination of *car* and *cocooning*. If the latter means, as the *Encarta World English Dictionary* would have it, "withdrawing into a state of personal privacy in order to escape stressful everyday life," then carcooning people are escaping the stress of everyday commuting by withdrawing into a state of personal vehicular privacy.

Caves and Nests

If "cocooning" just sounds too pop-corny for your average cocktail party conversation, you can avoid it by using the following synonym:

caving *pp.* (2002) Staying inside one's home as often as possible. *Social commentators have coined a new phrase for it:* **caving.** *It describes families who prefer being at home to just about anywhere else. Even those who flee the big cities for the coast are ending up spending their days—and nights— behind four secure walls.* (*Sunday Mail,* Queensland, Australia, January 6, 2002)

As you might imagine, the "hunker-down set" (as one *Newsday* headline writer called the stay-at-home crowd) doesn't like to move. The mobility rate—the percentage of people who move in a given year—is declining steadily. According to the U.S. Census Bureau, for all of the 1950s and '60s, the rate hovered around 20 percent; by the late 1990s and into 2000, the rate had fallen to around 16 percent. Instead of moving, people are staying put and improving their existing houses:

nesting *pp.* (1981) Performing home improvements and adding new furniture and appliances in an effort to make a home more comfortable. *—adj. She and her husband, developer and builder William Gray, moved to rural Charlottesville, Va., late last year. She says she travels less, buys less for herself, and is focused on* **"nesting"***—making her home more comfortable.* (Associated Press, September 5, 2002)

Home improvement is a massive industry. Is there a research group that can give us some solid numbers on the size of the industry, you ask? Of course there is. The Home Improvement Research Institute reports that U.S. consumer spending on home improvement hit $190.6 billion in 2001, and their forecast for 2002 was $198.5 billion, an all-time record. Home improvement and home-furnishing stores are being called **nesting stores** (2002), while home design magazines are being called **nesting magazines** (2000) or **shelter magazines** (1976).

With their houses all spiffed up and cozy, people are choosing to entertain more at home, whether that means inviting friends over for dinner or hanging around watching a video. The phrase that captures this trend is **staying in is the new going out** (1997):

> Market research firm Mintel's annual report British Lifestyles 2002 makes it seem that way, concluding that **"staying in is the new going out."** The report shows spending on alcohol consumption in the home is up 56 per cent in the past five years . . . compared with just a 16 per cent increase out of home. . . . In the last five years spending on major brown goods (televisions, audio equipment and mobile phones) has risen by 42 per cent. (*Leisure & Hospitality Business,* February 7, 2002)

Oh, Give Me a Home
Where the Guard Doggies Roam

Slightly offsetting the *full-nest syndrome* (see Chapter 14, "A Baby Boom Lexicon") are the added feelings of security aging parents must feel by having a son or daughter or two hanging around the house. In most cases, however, security-seekers turn their homes into Faith Popcorn's *armored cocoon,* a cocoon style that's quickly becoming the standard model. Home security products—what Ms. Popcorn, in her book *The Popcorn Report,* called the *paranoia industries*—was an $18.7 billion business in

2001, and sales in the United States are growing at a more-than-healthy annual rate of nearly 9 percent.

An increasingly popular architectural choice is the **safe room** (1978) or **panic room** (2000), a hidden room stocked with food, medicine, and other necessities:

> In other parts of the country, new home construction is beginning to reflect a national nagging climate of fear and uneasiness that is demonstrated by homeowner requests for secret **safe rooms** or **panic rooms.** These rooms are often hidden off the master bedroom through a trap door in a closet, said Jill Shannon, director of sales and marketing at Parker Development Co. in El Dorado Hills, Calif. (*Milwaukee Journal-Sentinel,* March 23, 2003)

Alarm systems, fences, guard dogs, and panic rooms offer the individual homeowner a sense of security, but humans have long believed that there is strength in numbers. Early in the nineteenth century tycoons, industrialists, and other wealthy types kept the rest of the world at bay by building *gated communities*—streets and neighborhoods surrounded by walls and where the only entrances were guarded gates. Now, according to the National Association of Home Builders, the United States has more than 20,000 gated communities that hold more than 8 million people, or **gaters** (1995), as they're sometimes called.

Over the past 10 years or so, a new kind of gated community has appeared:

> **privatopia** *n.* (1989) A walled-in or gated community of private homes, especially one in which a homeowner association establishes and enforces rules related to property appearance and resident behavior. *Gwyther told the World Congress of Sociology in Brisbane on Monday that the middle classes are choosing these walled communities or **privatopias** as a refuge from the ravages of globalisation. "It's all*

about security. They want security of income, investment and physical security for their family. These people are quite vulnerable." (Sydney Morning Herald, July 12, 2002)

This blend of *private* and *utopia* was coined by political scientist Evan McKenzie, who published an article titled "Morning in Privatopia" in the Spring 1989 issue of *Dissent.* He also wrote a book called *Privatopia,* which was published in 1994. What's so utopian about such an area? It's the strictly enforced rules and regulations—the so-called *restrictive covenants*—that are designed to maintain certain community standards. However, as McKenzie reports in his book, many of these communities have a distinctly dystopian scent to them: Vegetable gardens are frowned on; trees aren't allowed to grow taller than the houses; dogs must weigh less than 30 pounds; even the most trivial exterior renovations require approval from the homeowners' association. The mind-numbing bureaucracy required to maintain a privatopia helps explain why the groups and committees that enforce the community rules are called **residential private governments** (1989):

Condominiums, co-ops and home-owner associations have been described as **residential private governments** exercising legislative, judicial and executive powers over those living within their boundaries. By becoming a "member," people accept regulation of conduct, lifestyle and property rights. (*New York Times,* November 22, 1989)

Urban Comforts

Rather than looking for enforced comfort and security in an armored cocoon or walled-in privatopia, many people are bucking the caving trend and are looking for safe places in the world around them:

third place *n.* (1990) A place other than home or work where a person can go to relax and feel part of the community. *In the real world . . . all communities—and therefore all members of communities—need a "**third place.**" It's not your home. It's not where you work. Those are the first two places. No, it's the place where you go to, um, be.* (*Washington Post,* September 13, 2002)

The term *third place* was invented by sociologist Ray Oldenburg and first appeared in his 1990 book *The Great Good Place,* a celebration of the places where people can regularly go to take it easy and commune with friends, neighbors, and just whoever shows up. The subtitle says it all: "Cafes, Coffee Shops, Community Centers, Beauty Parlors, General Stores, Bars, Hangouts and How They Get You Through the Day."

The concept struck a chord, and the book became surprisingly popular. Many businesses and organizations redesigned themselves to encourage people to hang out. Some, to make sure you didn't miss the point, even incorporated "third place" into their names. We now have, for example, the Third Place Coffeehouse in Raleigh, North Carolina, and the Third Place Bookstore in Lake Forest, Washington. Oldenburg even released a second book in 2002: *Celebrating the Third Place: Inspiring Stories About the "Great Good Places" at the Heart of Our Communities.*

Other people find comfort in doing things with people who have a common interest:

urban tribe *n.* (1983) A group of city dwellers who have formed a bond through a common interest, such as work or a social or recreational activity. *I began to see tribes everywhere I looked: a house of ex-sorority women in Philadelphia, a team of ultimate-frisbee players in Boston and groups of musicians in Austin, Tex. Cities, I've come to believe, aren't* *emotional wastelands where fragile individuals with arrested development mope around self-indulgently searching for true love. There are rich landscapes filled with* **urban tribes.** (*New York Times,* October 14, 2001)

Urban tribesmen and tribeswomen may love the city, but many of them come to believe that it's not the best place to raise children. They see the crime, the noise, the dirt, and the city's inherent anonymity and impersonality, and they realize that they have to make the move from urbanite to suburbanite. They have to, in other words, banish themselves from the urban environment:

urban exile *n.* (1975) A person who has reluctantly moved from a city to a suburb. —**urban-exile** *adj. Urban exiles disapprove of the suburbs in principle but find themselves living there in practice. They disapprove of the sterility, the conformity, the split-level subdivisions, the billiard-room wet bars and the blueberry bagels. But somehow, because of kids, or the need for space, or out of sheer exhaustion, they find themselves plopping down a mortgage deposit and suddenly living on one of those streets with names like Crestview Circle Court.* (*New York Times,* April 9, 2000)

Privacy Under Siege

Retreating to a bunkerlike bungalow, a patrolled privatopia, or a sterile suburb might make you feel safer, but it isn't necessarily going to improve your privacy. You'll still have to deal with telephone solicitors calling just as you sit down to dinner; homeowner associations dictating a pink flamingo–less lifestyle; and nosy neighbors eyeballing your every move.

Then there are the more sinister forms of privacy invasion that are built in to many of our modern actions:

data shadow *n.* (1967) The trackable data that a person creates by using technologies such as credit cards, cell phones, and the Internet. *It's not only spam that worries Garfinkel. It's the power that businesses wield with personal information. Take the case of a Los Angeles man who injured his leg in a supermarket; when he sued, the market used records of his alcohol purchases to malign his character. Our* **"data shadows"**—*a term coined by Columbia professor Alan Westin*—*"force us to live up to a new standard of accountability," Garfinkel writes.* (*Industry Standard*, February 21, 2000)

As the above citation says, the coiner of *data shadow* was Alan Westin, who first used the term in his 1967 book, *Privacy and Freedom*. However, it wasn't until 1992 that the term started appearing in the mainstream press.

In our movements through the world, we used to leave behind us a kind of trail strewn with documents and contracts and store receipts—the so-called *paper trail*. Now there's an electronic equivalent:

paperless trail *n.* (1994) A sequence of electronic files or transactions that document the actions of a person or organization. *Who knows what "smoking guns" are lurking in the recesses of computer systems? . . . Further complicating matters, Johnson-Laird said, is the easy transferability of computer files by such means as e-mail. Other* **paperless trails** *may be found in computer-stored or generated records, voice mail and electronic bulletin boards.* (*American Bar Association Journal*, April 1994)

As near as I can figure, the phrase *paperless trail* has also been used since about 1989 as a pun on *paper trail*, and refers to the general idea of working with electronic files (that is, without paper). In this sense, it's a close cousin of *paperless office,* a term that entered the lexicon around 1971.

What's so sinister about all this is that it enables a determined snoop to "tail" us through our daily lives:

> **dataveillance** *n.* (1988) The ability to monitor a person's activities by studying the data trail created by actions such as credit card purchases, cell phone calls, and Internet use. *Many Canadians don't realize how extensive electronic surveillance has become in the past 20 years. There are safeguards and penalties for abuse in government, but information exists in countless private-sector databases, often unsecured ones. . . . That's why Big Brother is less a concern, critics say, than the thousands of profit-motivated Little Brothers already in our midst. People who do [not] understand about* **"dataveillance"** *are often lulled by empty promises of confidentiality, especially online.* (*Toronto Star,* August 12, 2000)

Dataveillance is an inelegant blend of *data* and *surveillance.* It has been around since the late 1980s, but its use has jumped significantly over the past few years thanks to the increasingly widespread concerns for individual privacy in the Internet age. The term was coined in 1988 by Roger A. Clarke, a professor of computer science at the Australian National University. A synonym that isn't as popular, but rolls off the tongue a little better, is **consumer espionage,** which was coined by former *Wall Street Journal* reporter Erik Larson in his 1992 book, *The Naked Consumer.*

The data trail generated by our purposeful activities isn't the only scourge to our privacy; now there are accidental privacy lapses to fret about:

> **data spill** *n.* (2000) The accidental transmission or display of private online data to a third party. *Unintentional dis-*

*closures of personal information, called **"data spills,"** can occur when visitors click on a link to an external site. Browsers automatically notify the new site of the URL (Internet address) from which the user has just come, possibly disclosing private information. For example, the URL could contain a name or e-mail address, or it could communicate confidential information about personal interests (e.g., www.medicalsite.com/baldness).* (Security Management, May 1, 2001)

With our home theater systems, our takeout meals, and our security systems, we've got our armored cocoons stocked up and locked up and turned into giant panic rooms where we retreat from a world that feels increasingly cold and cruel. The brave among us attend comfort movies and hang out in third places, but the rest of us prefer to feather our privatopian nests. Yes, it may be true that staying in is the new going out because the boomers are slowing down and that this trend may reverse itself as Generation Y ages, but I'm not betting on it. The *crime* rate may be down, but the *terror* rate is up, and, after September 11, 2001, terror now seems uncomfortably close, which is likely to keep people seeking comfort, security, and privacy for quite some time.

Chapter 10

Slowing Down

Why has the pleasure of slowness disappeared? Ah, where
have they gone, the amblers of yesteryear?
—*Milan Kundera*

It is remarkable how much we all could do if we avoid hustling, and go along at an even pace and keep from attempting too much. —*John D. Rockefeller, Sr.*

There is more to life than increasing its speed.
—*Mohandas Gandhi*

The phrase *rat race* has long been used as a disparaging
metaphor for the daily struggle to survive and get ahead in a
competitive world. No one's too sure where the phrase came
from, but the *Oxford English Dictionary* offers a tantalizing clue.
It quotes a 1937 edition of the journal *American Speech* that defines a rat race as a "dance of low-grade nature." Inspired either
by suppositions about what such a dance would entail, or possibly by images of rats running aimlessly through mazes or on exercise wheels, by the 1950s *rat race* had shifted to its current
meaning and has since become a full-fledged and familiar member of the lexicon. We now talk of people paying a **rat-race
membership fee** (1997)—the costs associated with buying
clothes and other things that are needed for one's job—and of
reaching a **rat-race equilibrium** (1997)—a tacit workplace
agreement in which an employee's willingness to work long
hours for possible promotion is equal to an employer's belief

that working long hours merits promotion. (See Chapter 18, "People Who Work at the Office," for more on this phrase.)

The problem here is that while this may be called an "equilibrium," there's something decidedly unbalanced about it. Like the absurd intensity of a rat running on an exercise wheel, there's an inherent folly in racing through life working ever-longer hours and rushing from one appointment to the next. And unfortunately, as comedian Lily Tomlin once observed, even if you win the rat race, you're still a rat.

People seem to be realizing this. According to a study published by the New York–based Families and Work Institute, 63 percent of employees would like to work fewer hours. Overall, if given the choice, those employees would reduce their workweeks by an average of 11 hours. In *The Overspent American,* Juliet Schor reports on surveys from the mid-1990s showing that 75 to 80 percent of people believed the country had become too materialistic and too greedy.

Now many people are doing something about it: They're dropping out of the rat race. They're throwing up their hands, hanging up their briefcases, and cutting up their credit cards. In short, people are slowing down. What is *not* slowing down, thankfully, is the production of new words, especially new words related to this newfound slowness that people are discovering.

The New Slowness

According to the U.S. Census Bureau, between 1996 and 2000 *nonmetropolitan* (exurban and rural) areas welcomed 3.8 million people from central cities and a further 5.2 million people from the suburbs. Some of those people were chasing businesses that moved to the cheaper exurban areas, but many were former rat-racers fed up with the grit of the cities or the sterility of the suburbs. They sought the exurban or rural life because they believed it to be slower paced and more deliberate. (In Australia, people who move out of the city and settle into a seaside community are called **sea-changers.**) These urban and suburban *outmigrations* (as the census types say) are symptoms of what the writer Cullen Murphy labeled the *New Slowness.* It's "fast-free living" of the stop-the-ride-I-want-to-get-off variety. Its slogan is a simple one: **slow is beautiful** (1987).

Not that slowing down is easy for former fast-trackers. I'm reminded of a cartoon showing a woman sitting on a meditation mat talking on a cell phone. She says, "I'm crazed with this noble path—let me get back to you." Rather than putting their entire lives in slow-motion mode, people are experimenting with slowness by dialing things back one at a time:

> **selective slowness** *n.* (1997) A less hectic lifestyle created by consciously slowing down one or two aspects of one's life. *Rather than resigning ourselves to running at one break-neck speed, we have the privilege, as Manzini says, of custom-designing the flow of our lives. How does he do it? "When I am at work I'm in the machine, and there is nothing I can do to move slow. But I try to be conscious that it is not a good way to live. When I leave work," he says, "I try to switch off— slow down and do things that make me feel good, like going out to the country and relaxing. This is what you call **selective slowness.** It's the beginning of consciousness that you can escape the machine."* (Natural Way for Better Health, December 1997)

Eating is a common example of an activity where people practice selective slowness. Many people eat so fast that you wonder if they even notice the food going down. This is not only bad for them (it promotes gas and leads to overeating because the body doesn't have time to let you know when it's full), but it's also less enjoyable because there's no time to really taste and savor the food. Some people have reacted against hurried repasts and the whole fast-food culture by creating a new food movement. In 1986 Italian wine writer Carlo Petrini spied a new McDonald's restaurant in Rome's famous Piazza di Spagna and decided that enough was enough. He enlisted the help of some friends, and they vowed to fight the encroachment of fast food by promoting its opposite:

> **slow food** *n.* (1986) An agricultural and gastronomic movement that emphasizes traditional, organic growing methods and the appreciation of fine food and wine. Also: **Slow Food** —*n.* Food grown and consumed in this way. —**slow-food** *adj. Most of us think "slow food" when it takes 40 minutes to get an order of pancakes and eggs. But for a growing number of people across the globe, **slow food** is not an inconvenience but a goal—an attempt to put the brakes on our fast-food frenzied world. Instead of drive-up burgers, tacos and chicken wings, **Slow Food** followers carve out a little bit of time in their hectic schedules to appreciate locally grown food, to preserve traditional cooking techniques (which usually require patience, not speed) and to celebrate the bounty with family and friends. (Salt Lake Tribune, April 24, 2002)*

Today the slow food movement—its well-chosen symbol is a snail—has over 70,000 members in 40 countries who adhere to the movement's credo: "To celebrate the diversity of culinary traditions and culture, promoting ecologically sound food production and reviving the dinner table as the center of leisurely pleasure and social interaction."

Another way that people are practicing selective slowness is by getting a good night's sleep. The National Sleep Foundation estimates that 47 million Americans are sleep-deprived. Books such as Jill Murphy's *Permission to Nap* and James B. Maas's *Power Sleep* say that between 60 and 100 million Americans don't get enough sleep. The solution, the experts say, is to slow down and make sleeping well one of your top priorities:

> **sleep hygiene** *n.* (1979) The principles or practices that enable a person to consistently get a good night's sleep. *Just as small children need a bedtime routine, grownups can benefit from familiar night-time rituals. A warm bath, a soothing drink, listening to music or having a good conversation with your partner or a friend on the phone (as long as it's not about the day job) are all recommended. Known as "sleep hygiene," this also means avoiding napping too much during the day.* (*Evening Standard,* London, January 21, 2002)

Albert Einstein, Thomas Edison, and Winston Churchill all had regular daytime naps, which didn't seem to do them much harm. (Edison, in fact, claimed that he rarely slept in bed; he preferred to stay in his laboratory and catnap in a special chair or even at his workbench.) A nap that refreshes the mind and enables you to tackle the rest of the day with renewed vigor and enthusiasm is called a **power nap** (1980) or a **prophylactic nap** (1988):

> Dr. David Dinges, a sleep researcher at the University of Pennsylvania, is a strong advocate of **prophylactic napping**— taking what he and others call a **"power nap"** during the day to head off the cumulative effects of sleep loss. (*New York Times,* January 4, 2000)

(I know you know what the noun sense of *prophylactic* means. As an adjective, *prophylactic* describes something that prevents disease or, more generally, something that's used as a precaution.)

The corporate office seems an unlikely place to slow *anything* down. But a few truly enlightened workplaces are hoping to boost the bottom line by offering perks to improve the mental and physical fitness of their employees. For example, ARUP

Laboratories in Salt Lake City comes complete with a fitness center and a health care clinic. Workers at consulting firm Booz Allen & Hamilton get to enjoy an on-site Weight Watchers program, a gym with a personal trainer, and a basketball court.

The National Commission on Sleep Disorders says that employees' chronic sleep debt is costing businesses $150 billion a year in accidents and lost productivity. This may be why many workplaces are allowing employees to take *catnaps* (1823) during the day. They've even gone so far as to designate a separate room set up for nappers:

> **nap nook** *n.* (2000) An office or room where employees can nap during working hours. *That old adage "if you snooze, you lose" no longer applies in the business world. Napping on the job is slowly becoming acceptable—when done in the proper place at the proper time. Office workers don't have to prop themselves up in a cubicle anymore, pretending they are on the telephone when in fact they are catching some Z's. . . . Workers can take their 15-minute break in the* **nap nook,** *if one is provided.* (*Asheville Citizen-Times,* August 23, 1999)

Will workplace napping ever becoming accepted in the hard-charging North American business world? I'll believe it when I see it, but we know there's at least a pro-nap faction out there. Besides *nap nook,* there's also **nap room** (1980), **solitude nook** (1996), **wellness room** (1994), **quiet-zone room** (2002), and the very cozy-sounding **spent tent** (1998).

Exhausted employees have for many years recharged their batteries by taking a **mental health day** (1978) or a **well day** (1982), a day off work in which a person calls in sick with a pretend cold or some other fake ailment. The phone call itself is by far the hardest part. Not only does it induce acute feelings of guilt, but it also taxes the acting skills of the average person by having to falsify a scratchy voice, stuffy nose, and the general malaise of someone feeling achy all over. Some modern companies don't want their employees going through these contortions, so they allow them to take days off when needed. These are most often called *personal days,* but here's a better phrase:

> **duvet day** *n.* (1997) A company-approved day off that employees can take if they feel too tired to work. *"**Duvet days** were introduced because we realise that everyone has those days when they just cannot face work," explains Katherine Nicholls, HR manager at August.One. "In the past, these may have been days when people would have called in sick or they may have had to be pre-planned as holiday. The beauty of **duvet days** is that they are not pre-planned and people do not have to pretend or feel guilty about calling in."* (*Computer Weekly,* February 1, 2001)

The originator of the duvet day concept was a British PR firm named August.One Communications (the human resources manager of which is quoted in the above citation). It began offering this perk for the pooped back in 1997.

Balancing Work and Family

In Sloan Wilson's great 1955 book, *The Man in the Gray Flannel Suit,* a World War II veteran named Tom Rath appears to have it made: He has a good job working at a charitable foundation, a beautiful wife, and three wonderful children. But a dark cloud hangs over this seemingly idyllic life. Their house is much smaller than their neighbors' houses; they drive a 14-year-old car; their friends talk only of promotions and real estate. "I don't know what's the matter with us," Tom's wife, Betsy Rath, says one night. "Your job is plenty good enough. We've got three nice kids, and lots of people would be glad to have a house like this. We shouldn't be so *discontented* all the time."

But the Joneses must be kept up with, so Tom takes a job working as an assistant to Ralph Hopkins, the head of a large broadcasting company. Hopkins is a classic workaholic who has sacrificed everything—including his relationship with his wife and daughter—to get to the top. Unfortunately, he expects Tom to do the same. Tom would love the extra money, but he balks at the marathon hours the job requires. In a classic speech, Tom turns Hopkins down:

> I'm not the kind of person who can get all wrapped up in a job—I can't get myself convinced that my work is the most important thing in the world. I've been through one war. Maybe another one's coming. If one is, I want to be able to look back and figure I spent the time between wars with my family, the way it should have been spent. Regardless of war, I want to get the most out of the years I've got left. Maybe that sounds silly. It's just that if I have to bury myself in a job every minute of my life, I don't see any point to it. And I know that to do the kind of job you want me to do, I'd have to be willing to bury myself in it, and, well, I just don't want to.

Tom Rath's choice of family over work is the same choice that many people are considering today. I'm not talking about modern-day Thoreaus building shacks in the woods and living **off-the-grid** (1991), meaning they no longer require connections to utilities, especially the electricity and water supplies and the sewage system. No, I'm talking about people who just want less stress in their lives, more meaning, and more time for themselves and their families. In a nutshell, they want a balance between their work and their personal lives; they want **work-family balance** (1987) or **work-life balance** (1986):

> A model employee is [one] who demonstrates a healthy **work-life balance.** In every company I know, the workaholic is alive—and sick. But is this the model we should emulate? Do

company presidents proudly escort visitors through factories jubilantly exclaiming, "Yes, all my employees work an average of 20 hours each day!"? If they do, they probably neglect to mention the high turnover, above-average absenteeism, low morale, and jagged productivity levels. (*Industry Week,* August 1, 1988)

This book is built on the premise that new words commonly act as cultural signposts that give us clues about where we are and where we're going. The phrase *work-life balance* is a perfect example, as the word's linguistic career demonstrates. It first showed up in 1986, and for the next 10 years it appeared only sporadically. When I'm researching words, I often turn to the Lexis-Nexis database of major newspapers (the top 75 or so newspapers from around the world). For *work-life balance,* the database turns up 32 articles that used the phrase in the 10-year period from 1986 to 1996. Over the next six years the numbers tell a tale:

1997:	32 articles
1998:	83 articles
1999:	137 articles
2000:	476 articles
2001:	573 articles
2002:	629 articles

If the notion that newspapers reflect our lives isn't too quaint (and I don't believe it is), then this increase—particularly the explosion of articles in 2000 and beyond—must reflect something interesting that's bubbled up from the depths of the cultural stew. Could it be that the notion that our technologically hopped-up society is going too fast for some people—and not just for the usual cast of Luddites, either—is taking hold at some level?

Based on the results of a survey conducted for the Radcliffe Public Policy Center in 2000, the answer seems to be an emphatic "Yes!" Eighty-two percent of men and 85 percent of women ages 20 to 39 said that having a work schedule that allows them to spend time with their family is more important than doing challenging work or earning a high salary. In the same age groups, 70 percent of the men and 63 percent of the women said they'd be willing to give up some of their pay in exchange for more time with their families.

People are improving their work-life balance by working fewer hours, doing less business traveling, telecommuting full or part time, or pooh-poohing promotions to stressful jobs. Others are taking sabbaticals, essentially a whole bunch of mental health days in a row. (Those who can't afford sabbaticals do the next best thing: They read about them in leave-it-all-behind books such as Peter Mayle's *A Year in Provence* and Frances Mayes's *Under the Tuscan Sun,* what journalist David Brooks has called "pornography to the overstressed.")

For some, however, the rat race is an inherently stressful and family-unfriendly pursuit. These people achieve balance by going a step further:

downshifting *pp*. (1989) Quitting a high-stress job in an effort to lead a simpler life. —**downshifter** *n*. (1990) *For some, dissatisfaction with the work-and-spend culture has become palpable enough to spur them to action. They have begun "downshifting." In the years from 1990 to 1996, nearly one-fifth (19 percent) of all adult Americans made a voluntary lifestyle change, excluding a regularly scheduled retirement, that entailed earning less money. Just over half of these people, or 55 percent, consider their lifestyle change to be permanent. And nearly all of them (85 percent) are happy about the change they made.* (Juliet B. Schor, *The Overspent American,* 1998)

A classic downshifter is the actress Demi Moore. After starring in the films *G.I. Jane* and *Striptease,* Ms. Moore was the hottest female film star around. But she gave it all up for several years to raise her children in little Hailey, Idaho (population: 6,500), far away from Hollywood's big-city-bright-lights atmosphere. Or how about the singer and songwriter Cat Stevens? After a string of hits in the 1970s, Stevens had a couple of brushes with death: once from tuberculosis and once from drowning. After the second incident, he gave up the music business entirely. He became a Muslim, changed his name to Yusuf Islam, and now devotes his life to humanitarian causes.

However, it's not just film and music stars who are downshifting. Ordinary folks are cashing in their corporate poker chips by taking lower-paying but lower-stress jobs, finding work that has meaning for them, returning to school, or starting their own businesses. In the latter case, the downshifter generally becomes a new type of sole proprietor:

> **soul proprietor** *n.* (1998) A businessperson or entrepreneur who balances work with emotional and spiritual growth.
> **—soul proprietorship** *n. He says coaching reflects an accommodation of sorts between baby boomers' 1960s pursuit of personal knowledge and their 1990s pursuit of personal wealth. Bringing those urges into alignment is the secret. "If every part of your life is working in balance, you will be more successful," he says. Another executive coach I met, Wendy Wallbridge of San Francisco, coaches businesspeople to become what she calls "soul proprietors."* (Daniel Pink, *Free Agent Nation*, 2001)

This isn't to say that everybody should become a downshifter and all will be right with the world. Some people just aren't wired for slowness:

> **upshifter** *n.* (1999) A person who takes on a fast-paced, high-stress job after having previously retired or moved to

a low-stress job. — *adj.* —**upshift** *v.* —**upshifting** *pp.*
Christine retrained as a barrister and has been practising in
East Anglian Chambers for almost a year. "It's nerve-racking
work," she says, with glee. "I handle criminal cases, which are
a big responsibility. I've just left court, and my hands are still
shaking." This is the kind of stress that **upshifters** *seek, and*
it has actually been proven to be good for your health. Tests
conducted by Jos Bosch of Ohio University show that a short
burst of acute stress raises levels of immunoglobulins, the body's
defence chemicals. (*The Independent,* London, May 4,
2003)

The radical idea here isn't that some people are returning to
high-stress jobs; many folks just have the need for speed, and
downshifting is probably the worst thing they could have done
to themselves. No, the shocker is the claim that stress can be
good for you. Doesn't that fly in the face of everything we've
learned over the past 20 years about the effects of stress on the
body, particularly on the immune system? On the surface, yes,
but the Ohio University study mentioned above makes a crucial
distinction between *active stress,* such as meeting a deadline or
racing to pick up the kids from school, and *passive stress,* such as
watching horror flicks or TV war coverage. The researchers also
differentiated between *acute stress*—intense but short-lived, such
as handling an emergency at work—and *chronic stress*—less intense but longer-lasting, such as taking care of someone who is
ill. Active or acute stress boosts the immune system (at least
temporarily), while passive or chronic stress tears it down. As the
researchers whimsically put it, "A hassle a day keeps the doctor
away."

The Simple Life, Twenty-first Century Style

There's more to downshifting than just jumping off the fast track and getting on what some people call the **relax track** (1995). It also involves simplifying your life by getting rid of possessions you don't need, minimizing your consumption of the planet's resources, and generally just creating a smaller **ecological footprint** (1994). This consciously simpler lifestyle is called **voluntary simplicity**:

> All of these things are part of the—get your buzzword notebook out—"**voluntary simplicity**" movement. Catered dinner parties are out. Potluck is in. Lobbying for a pay raise is out. Trading increased salary for extra vacation time is in. People are exchanging dry-cleaning lifestyles for wash and wear ones, and they don't feel deprived. (*Florida Times-Union,* Jacksonville, August 8, 2000)

The above citation calls *voluntary simplicity* a buzzword, but there's nothing new about the phrase. It was coined in 1936 by the writer Richard Gregg:

> **Voluntary simplicity** involves both inner and outer condition. It means singleness of purpose, sincerity and honesty within, as well as avoidance of exterior clutter, of many possessions irrelevant to the chief purpose of life. It means an ordering and guiding of our energy and our desires, a partial restraint in some directions in order to secure greater abundance of life in other directions. It involves a deliberate organization of life for a purpose. (*Visva-Bharati Quarterly,* Summer 1936)

The term was reborn in 1981 with the publication of Duane Elgin's book *Voluntary Simplicity: Toward a Way of Life that Is Outwardly Simple, Inwardly Rich.* The concept was then popularized by the bestselling 1992 book *Your Money or Your Life,* written by the late Joe Dominguez and Vicki Robin, which approached voluntary simplicity from both a personal finance and a philosophical angle.

Voluntary simplicity is also called the **frugality phenomenon** (1996) and **creative simplicity** (1994). A person who practices it is called a **simple-living practitioner** (1996), a **simple-liver** (1988), or a **domo** (1991):

> Then one day while reading a book review in the newspaper, I found out what we had become—**"domos."** ... According to a recent study, Yearning for Balance, prepared for the Merck Family Fund by the Harwood Group, the road to **domodom** is filled with former yuppie baby-boomers, with 72 percent of people aged 40 to 49 agreeing with the survey statement, "I would like to simplify my life." ... Twenty-eight percent of all the respondents said that "in the last five years, they had voluntarily made changes in their life which resulted in making less money—not including those who had taken a regularly scheduled retirement." (*Yoga Journal,* August 31, 1996)

Domo is short for *downwardly mobile* or *downwardly mobile professional.* This has echoes of **yumpie** (1984)—young, upwardly mobile professional—a one-time linguistic rival to **yuppie** (1982). Therefore, you can think of a domo as a kind of anti-yuppie.

A yuppie, of course, is the ultimate *materialist* (1853), a word that for the past century and a half has referred to a person who is concerned with material wealth and possessions rather than intellectual and spiritual values. A simple-liver or domo has renounced materialism, so he or she is a **post-materialist** (1981), a term that's also used in adjectival form:

> The **Post-materialist** Downshifters are the new social elite. They enjoy a high standard of living but intend to jump off the treadmill to pursue a "simple, leisurely lifestyle which is not

defined by material wealth and possessions." (*Scotland on Sunday*, October 15, 2000)

Post-materialism (1980) is for people who have renounced materialism. If a person has *never* been into the materialism thing, call him or her an **anti-materialist** (1972) instead.

The simplicity movement is not without its doubters and critics, who dismiss it as the **self-deprivation movement** (1997):

> People have been buzzing about "the simplicity movement" for several years now. Some are doing more than dreaming of a simpler life. They're taking action—changing jobs, scaling down expectations, changing entire life philosophies. . . . The movement is not without critics. Some deride it as the **"self-deprivation movement."** (*Dallas Morning News*, August 13, 1998)

But as almost all simplicity books and articles point out, the idea isn't to do without, it's to make do with less. Authors speak of finding the "middle way" between poverty and luxury, between self-sufficiency and self-indulgence, between conservation and consumption. Simple livers aren't into deprivation. Instead, they just practice **safe spending** (1992):

> The National Center for Financial Education offers free tips on controlling holiday spending and avoiding becoming a "debt head" through the Internet at www.ncfe.org. The center also sells "credit card condoms," which slip over credit cards as guards against impulsive buying, and stickers warning to practice **safe spending.** (*Milwaukee Journal-Sentinel*, November 29, 1996)

What movements such as the New Slowness and voluntary simplicity really boil down to is this: increasing the things in your life that give you joy and decreasing the things that cause stress, anxiety, or dissatisfaction:

joy-to-stuff ratio *n.* (1995) The time a person has to enjoy life versus the time a person spends accumulating material goods. *As families become more affluent, sometimes they begin to suffer from what has come to be called "affluenza": They focus their lives around accumulating more and more stuff that they have less and less time to enjoy; their "joy-to-stuff ratio" gets out of balance.* (*Cincinnati Business Courier,* December 28, 2001)

These ideas are by no means universal, but ever-increasing numbers of people are doing the slow food thing, maintaining proper sleep hygiene, and treating themselves to the occasional duvet day. Like Tom Rath, they're stripping off their metaphorical gray flannel suits and downshifting into a state of work-life balance. These domos and post-materialists and soul proprietors are the folks you see grinning as they play in the park or saunter along with their dogs. They may look slightly crazy at first, but their joy comes from having quit the rat race and rejoined the human race.

Chapter 11

The New Activism

For every prohibition you create, you also create an underground. —*Jello Biafra*

We call ourselves culture jammers. We're a loose global network of media activists who see ourselves as the advance
shock troops of the most significant social movement of the
next twenty years. Our aim is to topple existing power
structures and forge major adjustments to the way we will
live in the twenty-first century. —*Kalle Lasn*

I'm mad as hell and I'm not going to take it anymore.
—*Howard Beale*

Virginia Woolf's idea of the "word-coining genius" (see
Chapter 1, "A Mosaic of New Words"), can be readily applied to the world's activists. By definition, activists rebel against
orthodoxy, so, consciously or unconsciously, they also seem to
rebel against orthodox words. Someone defacing a billboard to
change its message has gone beyond being a mere *graffiti artist*
and is now a **midnight billboard editor** (1993). At large-scale
protests such as in Seattle and Quebec City, the more organized
activists split not into *teams* but into **affinity groups** (1977)—
small groups of like-minded protestors who watch each other's
backs. Each affinity group has a member who fetches water and
performs other chores, but don't call that person a *gofer;* instead,
he or she is an **action elf** (2000). The more violence-prone
among the protesters—the young malcontents with their

window-smashing crowbars and acid-filled eggs—aren't mere *anarchists;* they're called the **black bloc** (1996) because they're usually garbed from head to toe in black.

Activism generates a busload of new words not only because neology comes with the territory, but also because there are lots of activists out there and lots of things for them to protest against. There are the anticorporate **globophobes** (1997) protesting globalization; the **Groucho Marxists** (1977) using humor and creativity to subvert marketing messages; and the pro-environment **green collar workers** (1984) campaigning against Western society's profligate use of the Earth's resources.

Today's busy activist rails against **brandalism** (1999)—the defacement of public buildings and spaces by corporate ads, logos, and other forms of branding; **Frankenfood** (1992)—food derived from genetically modified (GM) plants and animals; and **greenwashing** (1990)—implementing token environmentally friendly initiatives as a way of hiding or deflecting criticism about existing environmentally destructive practices.

The modern activist promotes **ethical globalization** (1995)—globalization that takes into account human rights, local democracy, and the safety of the environment; the **triple bottom line** (1995)—measuring corporate performance along three lines: profits, environmental sustainability, and social responsibility; and the **precautionary principle** (1988)—that action should be taken to correct a problem as soon as there is evidence that harm may occur, not after the harm has already occurred (often shortened to the pithy "When in doubt, don't").

This chapter takes you through many more fruits of the activists' very active word-coining genius.

Words for Activists

The word *activist* (1909)—a person who is vigorously or aggressively active in pursuit of a political or social goal—has been in the language for nearly 100 years. For a long time the word referred only to a person who used, in the words of the *Oxford English Dictionary*, "energetic action" to achieve some end. In the 1960s and '70s, however, *activist* became associated with the protest movement, and the word developed a distinctly radical tinge. Since then neologists have enjoyed combining the word *activist* with some other noun suited to the type of activism a person practiced. Nouns beginning with an "ack" sound have been particular favorites. For example, there's the blend of *hacker* and *activist*:

> **hacktivist** *n.* (1995) A computer hacker who breaks into computer systems to further an activist agenda. —**hacktivism** *n.* (2000) *It is called **hacktivism**. Across the globe, elite computer experts with some of the world's most technically innovative minds are setting their sights on ways to help human-rights causes. . . . For example, when the Chinese government shut the door to the use of the search engine Google earlier this year, a **hacktivist** devised a way to reopen it in less than a day.* (*Chicago Tribune*, November 17, 2002)

Then there's what might be called the mother of all activist blends:

> **lactivist** *n.* (2000) An activist who promotes breast-feeding over the use of infant formula. —**lactivism** *n.* (2002) *Loyal fans and followers of [pediatrician William] Sears . . . were shocked to find that his site featured prominent banner ads promoting infant formula. . . . The site has become the target of an angry letter-writing campaign by pro-*

breast-feeding parents, medical professionals and **"lactivists"** *all over the world.* (Salon.com, January 25, 2001)

This word is a satisfying blend of the prefix *lacto-,* "milk," and *activist.* A less-flattering synonym is **nipple Nazi** (1996). Here's another blend:

slacktivist *n.* (1995) An activist who seeks projects and causes that require the least amount of effort. —**slacktivism** *n.* (1995) *Mrs. Mikkelson says teachers setting up Internet projects underestimate the pleasure people get out of doing something that feels like a public service yet requires no more than a few keystrokes. "It's all fed by **slacktivism,**" she said, "the desire people have to do something good without getting out of their chair." (New York Times, May 29, 2002)*

This shortened form of the phrase *slacker activist* had a brief appearance on the Internet's Usenet service in 1995 and then didn't appear again until 2000 in a discussion concerning people whose idea of activism is clicking the "Forward" button in their e-mail software. Media references to slacktivism didn't appear until 2001.

Then there are the blends that don't quite work:

actorvist *n.* (1995) An actor who is an activist. —**actorvism** *n.* (2002). *Here's a look at some of today's most vocal celebrity* **"actorvists."** *... Susan Sarandon ... Richard Gere ... Earvin "Magic" Johnson ... Edward James Olmos ... Fred Thompson ... Harry Belafonte ... Charlton Heston ... Robert Redford ... Alfre Woodard ... Martin Sheen. (Fort Worth Star Telegram, October 16, 2002)*

raptivist *n.* (1987) A rapper who is an activist. —**raptivism** *n.* (1993) *Highly informed and articulate,* **raptivist** *veteran Boots is unrelenting in his attack on "fat cats," cor-*

rupt cops and the "American way." (*The Independent*, London, November 17, 2001)

Jamming the Cultural Signals

Since early in the twentieth century, *jamming* has referred to deliberately blocking a signal (such as a radio or TV broadcast), usually by broadcasting a competing signal on the same frequency. Over the past 20 or 30 years, the dominant Western cultural "signal" has been the marketing message. (See Chapter 5, "Ad Creep.") Over the same period, disparate activist groups have used a shared loathing of the ever-increasing marketing onslaught as an excuse to try to "jam" that signal. This meant blocking the signal, making the signal unintelligible, or changing the signal's meaning to something more subversive. Hence a new activist art form was born:

> **culture jamming** *pp.* (1984) To manipulate existing cultural images—particularly those found in advertising—to mock, refute, or subvert those images. Also: **culture-jamming.** *Radicals have a term for such behavior:* **culture jamming.** *Coined by the art-punk band Negativland to describe its parodic defacements of billboards and other mass-media outlets, the phrase encompasses any act of media sabotage, from newspaper hoaxes to computer hacking.* **Culture jamming** *is the act of infecting the mainstream from within.* (*New York Times,* December 31, 2000)

Culture jammers (1991) are also sometimes called **artistic terrorists** (1987). They believe that billboards and other in-your-face advertising usurp public spaces. They want to, in a sense, take that space back from the rich corporations and give it to the poor citizens, in what journalist Naomi Klein calls *semiotic Robin Hoodism:*

All at once, these forces are coalescing to create a climate of semiotic Robin Hoodism. A growing number of activists believe the time has come for the public to stop asking that some space be left unsponsored, and to begin seizing it back. **Culture jamming** baldly rejects the idea that marketing because it buys its way into our public spaces must be passively accepted as a one-way information flow. (Naomi Klein, *No Logo,* 1999)

These **culture jams** (1997) are also called **creative crimes** (1994), and they're created by **guerrilla artists** (1981):

The activism includes "culture jamming," whereby ads are subverted by **"guerrilla artists"** to send anti-corporate messages out to the public; jammers paint hollow skulls on the faces of Gap models, or change an Apple ad featuring the Dalai Lama and the slogan "Think Different" to "Think Disillusioned." (*The Guardian,* London, September 23, 2000)

The word *guerrilla* comes up a lot in activist tracts and manifestoes. (See also *guerrilla gardening* and *eco-guerrilla* in this chapter.) The use of this term was possibly inspired by the semiotician Umberto Eco's 1967 essay titled "Towards a Semiological Guerrilla Warfare":

[T]he receiver of the message seems to have a residual freedom: the freedom to read it in a different way. . . . The battle for the survival of man as a responsible being in the Communications Era is not to be won where the communication originates, but where it arrives. . . . I am proposing an action to urge the audience to control the message and its multiple possibilities of interpretation. . . . [O]ne medium can be employed to communicate a series of opinions on another medium. . . . The universe of Technological Communication would then be patrolled by groups of communications guerrillas, who would restore a critical dimension to passive reception.

Culture jamming takes many forms, but the idea underlying all of them is to tweak the nose of some big corporation. Jammers particularly love to take on big media companies, and the goal is something the jammers call **media-wrenching** (1991)—a play on *monkey-wrenching*, which I discuss later in this chapter. The most common form of culture jam is one that performs a *détournement*—literally, a "turning around"—a term from the 1960s Situationist movement that means to take an image, event, or message out of its regular context and to place it in a new context that changes or subverts its meaning. Jammers seem to be at their most gleeful when then apply a détournement to advertising messages, either by altering an existing ad or by creating a new ad that uses familiar marketing images to create a subversive message. This approach is the trademark of the symbolic home of culture jamming, *Adbusters* magazine, which was first published in 1989. With over 85,000 subscribers at the end of 2002, this slick and glossy publication is anything but an obscure, underground zine. It has even inspired its own terminology: The people who create these subversive ads are called **busters** (1994), and the process of creating them is called **adbusting** (1994):

> Something not far from the surface of the public psyche appears delighted to see the icons of corporate power subverted and mocked. For a growing number of young activists, **adbusting** has presented itself as the perfect tool with which to register disapproval of the multinational corporations that have so aggressively stalked them as shoppers and so unceremoniously dumped them as workers. (*Courier-Mail,* Queensland, Australia, July 21, 2000)

An advertisement with a subversive, down-with-marketing message is called a **subvertisement** (1993):

Adbusters makes an explicit connection between the commercial corruption of our mental and physical environment. . . . In one **subvertisement,** we see a person with a bar-code on the back of his neck watching TV. The tag line reads, "The product is you." (*In These Times,* November 25, 2002)

Subvertisers (2000) also call their creations **anti-ads** (1994) and **uncommercials** (1982).

Those who **subvertise** (2000) seem to have a particular dislike for billboards, which are derided as **sky trash** (1997) or **pollution on a stick** (1990):

Consider the billboard, for so long the working-class grunt in the glittering media universe. When Lady Bird Johnson wanted to beautify America, she launched a campaign against billboards. Ted Turner inherited his father's billboard company but dumped it after getting into television. When tobacco and liquor advertisers were forced off the airwaves, they took refuge on billboards. **"Pollution on a stick,"** the medium's been called. (*Fortune,* March 1, 1999)

In response, ad jammers create their own billboard subvertisements, which, since they're designed to "kill" the original corporate marketing message, are sometimes called **killboards** (1998):

In [*Adbusters*] are essays on how to be an effective "culture jammer," celebrating teenagers who protest at McDonald's and Pepsi taking over their schools' catering, plus spoofs of ads and **"killboards,"** parodies of billboards, such as one of two cowboys on horseback, one saying to the other, "Bob I've got emphysema." (*The Independent,* London, July 18, 1998)

If the jammer modifies an existing billboard to change the ad's message, it's called **billboard liberation** (1989):

Ahh the East Bay, where no corporate or government billboard is safe, and the sweet sight of **billboard liberation** is nigh! (*East Bay Express,* Emeryville, Calif., January 9, 2002)

Liberation is another word that pops up often in activist circles (or should that be activist *squares?*). For example, in 1993 a group called the Barbie Liberation Organization purchased several hundred Barbie and G.I. Joe dolls, switched the voice boxes, and then returned the dolls to the stores. That Christmas kids heard their new Barbie saying things like, "Attack with heavy firepower!" and "Eat lead, Cobra!" while the G.I. Joes chirped "Let's plan our dream wedding" and "I love to try on clothes."

The phrase *billboard liberation* is based on the antics of a group called the Billboard Liberation Front, which began altering billboards in the late 1970s. Their particular brand of **anti-marketing** (1985) is called **billboard banditry** (1993) and the pranksters don't deface the billboards, they **reface** (1986) them:

Like Gran Fury, David Collins and his helpers altered other Benetton ads in Britain, **"refacing"** rather than defacing. One depicted two attractive young women, one white, one black, holding an Asian baby between them next to the caption, "Lesbian mothers are everywhere." (*Creative Review,* October 1, 1999)

In its most literal sense, refacing an ad involves altering a poster or billboard to make a head—usually the head of a fashion model—resemble a skull, a practice known as **skulling** (1997):

Skulling is one technique: turning anorexic models on Calvin Klein billboards into death's-heads with a few deft strokes of a magic marker. (*The Globe and Mail,* Toronto, January 15, 2000)

What these activists are really talking about is a new kind of environmentalism that cleans up what they see as "pollution of the mind." It's a **mental environmentalism** (1992):

> Kalle Lasn . . . says tuning out is all about **"mental environmentalism."** "Twenty or 30 years ago, we joked about a few parts per billion of chemicals in the air or food, but got a hell of a shock when we realized these create all kinds of cancers," said Lasn, founder of the anti-consumerism magazine *Adbusters* in Vancouver. "I think we're at the early stages of a movement in the mental realm where people are finding out that things they used to joke about—like ads, erotic titillation and violent images—have a powerful effect on our mental health." (*The Hamilton Spectator,* Hamilton, Ont., April 23, 2002)

An Activism Sampler

Culture jamming attracts a lot of activists not only because it's subversive, but also because it's just plain fun. But there are almost as many ways to tweak the noses of the powerful as there are people willing to do the tweaking. In this section I give you a tour of some modern forms of activism.

Earlier I mentioned the word *actorvist,* an actor who lends his or her name to activist causes. Although it seems to be mostly actors who do this, other celebrities—from famous authors, to sports stars, to fashion models—are also getting in on the activism game in ever-growing numbers, a trend that has its own term:

> **celebrity advocacy** *n.* (1998) Active support for a cause or position by a celebrity. George *magazine and William Baldwin's Creative Coalition were honoring Michael J. Fox to raise money for the thesp's Parkinson's disease research founda-*

tion. Maria Shriver and hubby Arnold Schwarzenegger were
*on hand . . . "This is **celebrity advocacy** at its best," said*
Baldwin. (Variety, August 7, 2000)

There's usually a celebrity or two in the more peaceful parts
of the large protests that accompany summits for organizations
such as the G-8, the World Trade Organization (WTO), and the
World Bank. That's partly because protesting became something
of a fad after the 1999 WTO summit in Seattle. That protest
was a success for the activists, not only because of the sheer
number of demonstrators—most accounts put the total at
around 30,000 people—but also because the trade talks were effectively shut down and the antiglobalization movement attracted immense media attention. Protesting became the new
radical chic, and many protesters sought only to be seen at each
summit meeting, behavior that was put down by more dedicated activists with a disparaging new verb:

> **summit-hop** *v.* (2000) To attack globalization and corpo-
> rate power only by protesting at one trade-related summit
> after another. —**summit-hopper** *n.* (2001) *Wherever gov-*
> *ernments or their representatives met to discuss global issues,*
> *the protesters were there, too—from Seattle to Prague to*
> *Quebec city to Genoa. . . . At the same time, labour and non-*
> *labour activists are debating the value of what some call*
> ***summit-hopping.*** *"Our focus can't be on just going from*
> *demonstration to demonstration," says Judy Darcy, national*
> *head of the Canadian Union of Public Employees. (Toronto*
> *Star, June 15, 2002)*

So what were the hardcore activists doing instead? Much of
the time they seemed to be trying to come up with ways to inconvenience the public. The theory here is that if the average
person's day gets significantly disrupted, not only might he or
she think to ask why (so the protesters' message has a chance to

get through), but the person also might get mad enough to call or write some local politician, which just might lead to some positive action down the road.

One of the most common inconvenience tactics is to block traffic:

pickade *n.* (2000) Picketing that purposefully prevents traffic from moving or from entering or leaving a specific location. —**pickade** *v.* (2002) —**pickader** *n.* (2000) *While the IFA is protesting—and not "pickading" any of the plants—farmers will not deliver animals across those protest lines. While some factories have their own supplies, these are estimated to be less than a fortnight's kill. With relations between the two sides deteriorating, "pickades" could well be the next step.* (*Irish Times,* September 30, 2002)

Pickades are usually harmless, so some of the more radical activists think they're not inconvenient enough. Here's one way they crank up the heat:

darking *pp.* (2002) Disrupting power by cutting or short-circuiting high-voltage electrical lines. —**darker** *n.* *The term "darking" was coined last year in the Czech Republic's Moravia region, where the practice of cutting high-voltage power lines and toppling power poles was first reported.* (Deutsche Presse-Agentur, November 14, 2002)

On a less destructive note, some activists eschew power plants in favor of power planting:

guerrilla gardening *pp.* (1977) The surreptitious or unauthorized planting of flowers, shrubs, vegetables, and other flora in a public space. —**guerrilla gardener** *n.* (1988) —**guerrilla garden** *n.* (1982) *Sam Tylicki . . . didn't get permission from the city to use the property, so Tylicki is trespassing. That means the city can kick him out, along with*

his green peppers, collard greens and other vegetables. But get-
ting permission is against the philosophy of **guerrilla gar-**
dening, *an international environmental movement whose*
followers "reclaim" public space by planting fruits, vegetables
and flowers. (*The Plain Dealer,* Cleveland, September 22,
2001)

The original guerrilla gardeners were probably the gypsies,
who used out-of-the-way locations near the side of a road or path
to plant potatoes and other vegetables. They then continued on
their nomadic way and returned later to harvest the crop.

Today's guerrilla gardeners view their politicized plants as
symbols for reconnecting with the land in the face of urban
blight and as a way of green-thumbing their collective noses at
"The Man." The planting-as-protest began in the 1970s with a
New York group called the Green Guerrillas. These urban hor-
ticulturalists started off crudely by lobbing **seed grenades**
(Christmas tree ornaments filled with soil and wildflower seeds)
into abandoned, debris-filled lots. But they eventually converted
hundreds of these lots into flower- and vegetable-filled **community gardens** (1971). The movement has since spread around
the world (one slogan: "Resistance Is Fertile") and now operates
under the more general rubric of guerrilla gardening.

Note, too, that those who grow marijuana plants on public
lands are also sometimes called guerrilla gardeners. (Although,
back to the protest angle again, a few activists somehow managed to plant marijuana seeds near the British Parliament in the
annual May Day protest of 2000. By July the plants had
sprouted and were apparently growing quite nicely. Police con-
fiscated the crop immediately.)

Messing around with fax machines seems to be a common activist strategy:

black fax *n.* (1996) A black piece of paper faxed to a company as a prank or as retaliation for distributing junk faxes.

So, now I'm getting spam faxes. From advertising ranging from a periodontist in New York City, to a wireless phone company. . . . My question is: now that I know who these companies are, how terrible would it be for me to hit them back, say, with a late-night, 500-page **black fax** *(emptying their toner cartridge)? Or what if I called the periodontist and made, say, 40 different appointments for fictional patients?* (*The Guardian,* London, July 18, 2002)

mobius fax *n.* (1996) A continuous piece of paper faxed to a company as a prank or as a retaliation for distributing junk faxes. *Let the offenders know how it feels to run out of paper. Get their fax numbers and "use the* **Mobius Fax,**" *schemes Vince Nestico, who runs The Anti-Telemarketer's Source Web site. "Tape about six sheets of construction paper together lengthwise, and start the fax . . . after the fax has passed through the first page, take the opposite end of your construction paper strip and flip it over once. Tape that end to the end that has already passed through, creating a continuous strip."* (*Home Office Computing,* February 1997)

The mobius fax idea comes from mathematics, where a *Möbius strip* is a two-dimensional surface that has only one side. To create one, take a long, rectangular strip of paper, twist the ends 180° with respect to one another, and join the ends together to form a loop.

The aim of the black or mobius fax is to throw a proverbial monkey-wrench into the communications machinery of a corporation. This sense of monkey-wrench as a purposeful obstruction or hindrance (also seen in the similar idiom *to throw a spanner in the works*) has been around since about 1920, but lately it has been taken up by the activists, who now refer to any such activity as **monkey-wrenching** (1984; also: **monkey wrenching**):

The community has been bristling with anger and gripped with tension since April, when a historic drought prompted federal officials to cut off water to most of the region's 1,400 farmers. . . . Irked by the cutoff, protesters on July 4 stormed the head gates that control the flow of water into the irrigation project's main canal. In a distinctly rural act of civil disobedience, farmers took turns cranking open the gates. On three occasions in subsequent days, the irrigation **monkey wrenching** was repeated. (*Los Angeles Times,* September 16, 2001)

This phrase was almost certainly inspired by a novel called *The Monkey Wrench Gang,* which was published by the writer Edward Abbey in 1975. The book traces the exploits of some ecologically minded saboteurs as they wreak havoc in a rampage throughout the southwestern United States. They pour syrup into bulldozer fuel tanks, burn down billboards, and even cause the wreck of a coal train.

These and other of the book's techniques were taken up by **monkey-wrenchers** (1985), the most notorious of which was the Earth First! group, which made a name for itself by disabling logging trucks and driving spikes into trees to damage log-cutting equipment.

If the activists' cause is the environment, then their monkey-wrenching is called **eco-terrorism** (1980), **eco-tage** (1980)—which is short for **eco-sabotage** (1984)—or **eco-defense** (1985). The people who engage in this kind of activism have many names, including **eco-terrorist** (1987), **eco-saboteur** (1988), **eco-defender** (1988), **eco-anarchist** (1989), **eco-guerrilla** (1986), **eco-raider** (1978), **eco-kamikaze** (1990), and **enviro-extremist** (1991).

Hacktivists often throw virtual monkey wrenches into the digital works of a corporation. (One hacktivist group goes by the name of Virtual Monkeywrench.) This electronic activism has its own name:

techno-strike *n.* (1998) A protest in which a company is inundated with e-mail messages, faxes, and website hits in an effort to shut down the electronic portion of the company's business. *Last Friday, members of the Communication Workers Union and its international sister organisations attempted to flood the company's e-mail addresses, faxes and web sites in order to disrupt business. The CWU calls the action a "techno-strike." (Printing World,* February 8, 1999)

A less high-tech protest is to strike at someone with pastry:

pie *v.* (1977) To hit a person, particularly a political or business leader, in the face with a pie. *In general, pieing is a leftist activity with anarchist overtones. Targets tend to be identified with big business or forces seen as hostile to the environment, public health and/or human rights. (New York Times,* December 10, 2000)

Newsweek writer Jean Seligmann called such a delivery a **c-mail** (1998), short for cream (pie) mail.

At protest sites, activists often hang giant banners on the sides of buildings. You also see culture jammers modifying massive billboards in strategic places (such as the Billboard Liberation Front pasting the face of Charles Manson in the middle of a huge Levi's billboard). Ever wondered how they perform these tricks? They use mountaineering techniques to clamber down the side of the building or billboard, a method known as **urban rappelling** (1999):

> The Ruckus Society began with a single mission but expanded its reach. It launched in 1995 in Montana to focus on forest-saving campaigns, but in 1998 it held an action camp—a kind of boot camp to teach protest methods—on human rights that "really opened the eyes of a lot of tree-huggers to a world of different issues," Sellers said. . . . Now the society's new bag of

tricks—in addition to teaching such staples as **urban rappelling** and civil disobedience—will include high-tech tools. (*San Jose Mercury News,* April 21, 2002)

A protest whereby the activists form a human chain by linking their arms together, sometimes through plastic tubes, is called a **lockdown** (1997).

Activists planning to participate in a **lockdown** situation who anticipate hours of immobility wear an adult diaper, such as Depends. (*LA Weekly,* August 15, 2000)

If the human chain extends around a building, it's called a **quarantine** (2002).

Saturday's actions included a large rally and a march to Farragut Square, near the World Bank/IMF buildings. The march ended in a **"quarantine"**—an attempt to circle the buildings. Activists linked arms, some held together with duct tape, and sat in the road as the police presence increased to the point of a blockade that was six officers deep in some places. (*The Tartan*, Carnegie Mellon University, Pittsburgh, October 2, 2002)

This is just a small sampling of what the world's activists are up to. Taken together, these actions can be seen as part of a larger strategy in which many small acts add up to a combined force that can topple a much larger and more powerful foe. This is called the **Lilliput strategy** (1994):

In Jonathan Swift's satiric fable *Gulliver's Travels*, the tiny Lilliputians, only a few inches tall, captured the marauding Gulliver, many times their height, by tying him down with hundreds of threads while he slept. Gulliver could have crushed any Lilliputian under the heel of his boot, but the dense network of threads tied around him held him immobile and powerless. Similarly, facing powerful global forces and institutions, people need to combine their relatively modest sources of power with often very different sources of power available to participants in other movements and locations. Just as the tiny Lilliputians captured Gulliver by tying him with many small pieces of thread, the **Lilliput Strategy** weaves many particular actions designed to prevent downward leveling into a system of rules and practices that together force upward leveling. (*The Nation*, December 19, 1994)

Note that the phrase *downward leveling* refers to a process where communities and countries compete for corporate business by gradually lowering labor costs and removing regulations, thus creating what many people call a "race to the bottom."

Activists and Their Acronyms

I've always suspected that when a group of activists get together, the first thing they decide on is a snappy acronym. The ideal acronym is not only an easy-to-pronounce and easy-to-remember word, but it also should hark back to the group's purpose or beliefs. One of my favorites is BUGA-UP—Billboard Utilizing Graffitists Against Unhealthy Promotions—an acronym that sounds like *bugger-up,* which is what the group likes to do to billboards. Then there's PETA—People for the Ethical Treatment of Animals—which contains the word *pet.* Another good one, although not an activist group per se, is PEN—the international organization of Poets, Essayists, and Novelists.

One of the most fertile sources of acronyms is the **anti-growth** (1975) movement, which is against *urban sprawl* (1958) and other forms of unchecked or irresponsible development. Here's a glossary of the acronyms these folks have come up with (so far):

BANANA *n.* (1991) Build Absolutely Nothing Anywhere Near Anything. A person who is opposed to new real estate development, particularly projects close to their neighborhood. *"BANANA" is an acronym that has a chance to survive, and appeals to people like me who really don't have much use for dictatorial neighborhood organizations or strident preservationists who oppose any new development, change or progress.* (*The Times-Picayune,* New Orleans, September 18, 2002)

CAVEs *n.* (1990) Citizens Against Virtually Everything. A group of people who routinely oppose new real estate developments and other projects that they believe will harm their local area. Also: **CAVE people** or **CAVE dwellers.** *In Columbus, Gaymon and others explained, CAVEs dominated for years. They say the no-growthers opposed and prevented Interstate 85 from passing near the city. They were content to keep the city dependent on textiles and the military. They fought bond packages and sales tax boosts for improvements.* (*News & Record,* Greensboro, N.C., September 16, 2001)

GOOMBY *n.* (1989) Get Out Of My Back Yard. A person who hopes for or seeks the removal of some dangerous or unpleasant feature from his or her neighborhood. **—GOOMBYism** *n.* (2002) *The city is trying to raise taxes and it is trying to harass a legitimate business that an environmentally correct City Council finds offensive. The appellate judge coined a new phrase to describe what council members are doing: GOOMBYism.* (*Orange County Register,* February 18, 2002)

LULU *n.* (1986) Locally Unwanted Land Use. A real estate development or other construction project to which the local residents are opposed. *At the top of the list presented by the Southern Strategy committee . . . is speeding up the widening of Capital Circle, the traffic artery surrounding most of the city. Other recommendations included discouraging unattractive public projects—or **LULUs,** locally unwanted land uses—that are disproportionately located in the southern part of the county. (Tallahassee Democrat,* January 30, 2002)

NIMBY *n.* (1980) Not In My Back Yard. A person who hopes or seeks to keep some dangerous or unpleasant feature out of his or her neighborhood. *But to advocates of the mentally retarded, that kind of thinking [is] a reminder of the benighted days when all retarded people, even those who posed no threat to others, were seen as monsters and opening group homes for them triggered furious **Nimby** campaigns.* (*New York Times,* January 23, 2002)

NOPE *n.* (1990) Not On Planet Earth. A person or attitude that opposes all real estate development or other projects that would harm the environment or reduce property values. *In trying to build new refineries, "you deal with **NOPE**—Not on Planet Earth. That's the mood. 'We don't want a power station,' " said Ron Oligney, an energy consultant.* (*Dallas Morning News,* May 18, 2001)

NOTE *n.* (1994) Not Over There Either. A person or attitude that opposes new real estate development in the local community and is not open to compromise on this issue. *There is also the zealous "Nimby" (Not In My Back Yard), his eager disciple the **"Note"** (Not Over There Either) and the mega-conservationist the "Banana" (Build Absolutely Nothing Anywhere Near Anything).* (*Western Morning News,* Plymouth, England, August 23, 2002)

Today's activism landscape is dotted with a mind-spinning variety of protesters, protest techniques, and things to protest against. So it's no wonder that activists are also active word coiners: They're just trying to supply names to all the landmarks in their world. Whether you agree with the aims and tactics of these globophobes and culture jammers and guerrilla gardeners, there's no doubt theirs is a rich, creative, and angry lingo that offers many joys for new-word watchers.

The Political Correctness Wars

We cannot write off that imagery is not important. It's why in some countries poets are thrown into prison. Words have so much power. —*Audrey Thompson*

We want to create a sort of linguistic Lourdes, where evil and misfortune are dispelled by a dip in the waters of euphemism. —*Robert Hughes*

Throughout history, attempts to micromanage casual conversation have only incited distrust. They have invited people to look for an insult in every word, gesture, action. And in their own Orwellian way, crusades that demand correct behavior crush diversity in the name of diversity. —*George Herbert Walker Bush*

The purpose of Newspeak was not only to provide a medium of expression for the world-view and mental habits proper to the devotees of IngSoc, but to make all other modes of thought impossible. It was intended that when Newspeak had been adopted once and for all and Oldspeak forgotten, a heretical thought—that is, a thought diverging from the principles of IngSoc—should be literally unthinkable, at least so far as thought is dependent on words. —*George Orwell*

may as well get the tricky definition out of the way right off the top:

political correctness *n.* (1948) The conformity to liberal or progressive opinion on matters of gender, race, ethnicity, disabilities, or sexual preference, especially via the de-

liberate use of language or actions that avoid giving of-
fense. —**politically correct** *adj.* (1970) Also: **PC.**

Between the lines of this necessarily long-winded definition
lies the history of political correctness, which I view metaphor-
ically as the history of contrasting tools.

In the late 1960s and through the '70s and '80s, political correctness was used as a kind of goad, a stimulus to improve
people and society. For feminists and their gender politics and
for Black Power radicals and their race politics (to name just two
groups that adopted PC codes of conduct), political correctness
was used to prod people into behaving nonoffensively. This is
the positive side of political correctness, and its basis was most
likely the writings of Chairman Mao Zedong, particularly a
piece called "Where Do Correct Ideas Come From?" which appeared in his 1963 *Little Red Book.* The phrase "correct ideas"
often was translated into English as "correct thinking," and
most scholars believe this was the source of the "correct" part of
political correctness.

But political correctness also has been used as a metaphorical
sword, cutting down to size those who appear to be mindlessly
conforming to liberal orthodoxy. This has certainly been the
case since at least the mid-1980s, when conservatives began
using the charge of "political correctness" to slice up left-wing
opponents and their positions. Today *politically correct* is used as
a grievous insult that implies the person is a humorless, self-
righteous slave to the liberal party line. Interestingly, this negative side of political correctness first appeared in the 1930s and
'40s (although at the time it was just referred to as "correctness"). Back then it was used by leftists to criticize the old guard
on the left who adhered too slavishly to Marxist doctrine.

Whether it's used as a goad or a sword, political correctness is
very much a linguistic phenomenon, since much of what we call
political correctness is really **speech correctness** (1995). A good

example is the use of new terms to avoid older terms that explicitly refer to a person's gender, race, ethnicity, class, religion, physical or mental disabilities, or sexual orientation. Most of the new terms are familiar. For example, one of the most common (and one of the most controversial) sources of PC language change is the use of **gender-neutral** (1978) occupation names.

This linguistic neutering often is performed by revamping a word's gender-based ending—the **gender-ender** (1992). The most common replacement is to substitute *-person* for *-man. Chairman* morphs into *chairperson; fisherman* becomes *fisherperson; craftsman* is renovated into *craftsperson.* The *-person* suffix has become such an emblem of PC speech that a backlash against it has developed over the past few years and a second wave of **sex-neutral** (1976) words has appeared. The *chairperson* is now the *chair;* the *fisherperson* is now a *fisher;* the *craftsperson* is now a *crafter.*

Other occupations skipped right over the uncomfortable *person* stage and went right to their ideal **gender-free** (1978) versions. An airplane stewardess or steward is now a *flight attendant;* a fireman is now a *firefighter;* a mailman is a *letter carrier,* a *postal worker,* or the jaunty-sounding *postie.*

In other cases, however, PCers have coined new **ambigenic** (1992) words. For example, instead of the female-only *seamstress,* there's the any-gender **sewist** (1998):

> I understand how teens like to shop and try on clothes, so maybe you won't be able to make all, or even most of their clothes, but after looking through the pattern catalogs, ready-to-wear styles are available to the home **sewist** that will please a teen-ager. (*Fort Worth Star-Telegram,* March 12, 2000)

Another way that gender-enders are stripped is to replace them with the *-ron* suffix. So a *seamstress* becomes a **seamstron** (1992), an *actor* or *actress* becomes an **actron** (1992), and a *laundress* becomes a **laundron** (1992). Few of these constructions have caught on, not surprisingly, but there's one that has a chance of sticking around—the PC replacement for *waiter* and *waitress:*

> **waitron** *n.* (1980) A person who waits on tables at a restaurant. *[A person] was at a restaurant and asked a tray-carrying woman whether she was his waitress. She informed him in no uncertain terms that she was not his, or any one else's, "waitress." In fact, the restaurant had no waiters or waitresses. She was a **"waitron."** The man inquired what a **waitron** was, and the woman condescendingly educated him that a **waitron** was a gender-neutral name for a person who blah, blah, blah. When she finished her blather, the customer inquired whether she would bring him a glass of water. "Oh," she replied, "the busboy will do that." (National Review, April* 11, 2002)

Then there's the strange saga of the elusive genderless third-person singular pronoun. We have *he, his,* and *him* or *she, hers,* and *her,* and that's it. If you want to make a general statement applicable to anyone, male or female, using one of these pronouns is going to offend *somebody.* A few writers get around this by alternating pronouns: first a male pronoun, then a female, and so on. Others use relatively cumbersome constructions such as *he or she* and *he/she,* the stuffy-sounding *one,* or the funny-looking (and unpronounceable) *s(he).* My favorites are the new words that people come up with. David Crystal, in his book *The Cambridge Encyclopedia of the English Language,* lists the following attempts: *co, E, et, heesh, hesh, hir, hirm, hizer, ho, jhe, mon, na, ne, person, po, tey, thon,* and *xe.* Other proposals include *himmer, hit, ve,* and *wit.* Many people ignore all of this and just use the plural forms *they, their,* and *them.* These are gender-neutral and, if treated carefully, always can be used as singular pronouns without ambiguity. If a language purist complains, tell *them* that these plural pronouns have been used in English to refer to singular subjects for about 600 years and that the *Oxford English Dictionary* lists examples from such literary giants as Henry Fielding, William Makepeace Thackeray, and George Bernard Shaw.

What's the point of all this gender wrestling? Theoretically, a change in language can and should lead to a change in thought patterns. For example, if you use the same term for both sexes (such as *firefighter*), then (so the theory goes) you'll be more likely to treat men and women equally. Similarly, if you apply a more dignified term to a person (such as using *women* instead of *girls*), then you're more likely to view that person with respect. This applies not only to the person saying or writing the PC term, but also to the person hearing or reading it.

This linguistic sensitivity falls under the general rubric of **cultural sensitivity** (1980), and, from a language point of view, it requires that each of us practice what one writer called "vocabulary management." It means giving up **politically incorrect** (1947) phrases such as *Mexican standoff, Indian giver, go Dutch,* and even *black.* For the latter, some say that the word *black* just has too many negative connotations in the language: *black sheep, black magic, blackmail, black market, black hat* (although idioms such as *in the black* and *in black and white* are either positive or neutral). The PC term of choice is *African-American.* (Which reminds me: The denizens of Appalachia are, apparently, getting mighty tired of being called *hillbillies.* If they had their druthers, the name they'd prefer would be *Appalachian-Americans.* The black citizens of Appalachia have their own preferred term: *Affrilachian.*)

> The phrase *African-American* sounds quite modern, but it's actually over 150 years old. It was used frequently by whites throughout the United States in the nineteenth century. It wasn't appropriated by the black community until the early 1970s. The catalyst was

Dr. Ramona H. Edelin, president of the National Urban Coalition, who at the Black Political Convention in Gary, Indiana, in 1972 first proposed the use of "African-American" over "black." She repeated her proposal in late 1988, but this time her cause was taken up by the Reverend Jesse Jackson:

> Just as we were called colored, but were not that, and then Negro, but not that, to be called black is just as baseless. To be called African-Americans has cultural integrity. It puts us in our proper historical context. Every ethnic group in this country has a reference to some land base, some historical cultural base. African-Americans have hit that level of cultural maturity.

Thanks to the Reverend Jackson's high profile, the mainstream press jumped all over the story, and within a few years *African-American* had become a permanent and common part of the language. Not that the changeover wasn't without its problems. Consider, for example, the following correction that appeared in a newspaper:

> An item in *Thursday's* Nation Digest *about the Massachusetts budget crisis made reference to new taxes that will help put Massachusetts* "back in the African-American." *The item should have said* "back in the black." (*Fresno Bee,* Fresno, Calif., July 21, 1990)

The original substitution of "African American" for "black" was not a proofreader's mindless replacement but a practical joke. In any case, the correction is still hilarious.

Note, too, that this linguistic victory doesn't represent the end of the story. In the past few years, black people who were born in (or who have ancestors who come from) non-African countries—Jamaica, Grenada, even European countries such as Britain and France—have objected to the "African" adjective. Most often these people prefer to go **off the hyphen** (1998), meaning they'd rather be called just an "American" rather than an "African-American."

The sensitivity component of political correctness has also been extended beyond words and into the realm of feelings and emotions:

> **emotional correctness** *n.* (1989) Feelings or sentiments deemed to be socially acceptable. **—emotionally correct** *adj.* (1983) *Do your eyes refuse to mist over with sympathy when you read that a fertility-drug-guzzling stranger produces septuplets? Were you somewhat indifferent to the death of Diana, Princess of Wales, or, for that matter, Linda McCartney or Mother Teresa? If you answer yes to any of these questions, apparently hanging is too good for you because you are guilty of failing to comply with the dictates of* **Emotional Correctness** *(EC).* (*South China Morning Post,* November 13, 2002)

Of course, there's sensitivity and then there's just plain silliness. Take, for example, the famous case of the word *niggardly* (1571), an adjective that means "grudgingly spending or giving only the smallest possible amount." The word *niggardly* comes to us from the Middle English word *nigon* (1303), a miser, and is not in any way related to *nigger* (1786). This knowledge didn't help a fellow named David Howard, who on January 15, 1999, said the following to a couple of people: "I will have to be niggardly with this fund because it's not going to be a lot of money." His listeners thought he was making a racial slur, and the subsequent brouhaha (it received national press coverage) forced him to resign from his job in the Washington, D.C., mayor's office.

Thisism, Thatism, Ism, Ism, Ism

The suffix *-ism* is used to form nouns of various types, what H. L. Mencken called its "plentiful offspring." These include doctrines or belief systems (for example, *capitalism, stoicism*), actions (*criticism, plagiarism*), distinctive features (*colloquialism, modernism*), and characteristics (*heroism, patriotism*). The *-ism* suffix is also used to form nouns related to prejudices and discrimination. Early examples include *anti-Semitism* (1881) and *racism* (1933), which replaced *racialism* (1907). This use of the *-ism* suffix picked up steam in the 1960s and early 1970s, when the language added *sexism* (1968), *ageism* (1969), and *male chauvinism* (1970). Since then it seems that just about every human characteristic has had "-ism" tacked on to the end to form a new source of discrimination or prejudice. (In their 1991 book, *Isms,* Alan and Theresa von Altendorf decried this trend, pooh-poohing it as the "ismization of the language.") Most of these have been nonce terms that quickly faded from view. Here's a list of some that have caught on and continue to appear in media articles and elsewhere:

ISM	FIRST USE	DISCRIMINATION OR PREJUDICE DIRECTED TOWARD OR BASED ON . . .
ableism	1981	The disabled
adultism	1985	Children
alphabetism	1988	Having a name that begins with a letter that comes later in the alphabet
animal lookism	1992	Noncute animals
appearanceism	1991	Appearance
beardism	1991	Bearded men
bodyism	1991	Body size or shape
bookism	1979	People who don't read books
breastism	1991	Breast size
colorism	1986	Skin color

(continued on next page)

ISM	FIRST USE	DISCRIMINATION OR PREJUDICE DIRECTED TOWARD OR BASED ON . . .
diseasism	1990	People who are sick
Eurocentrism	1982	Non-Europeans or those with non-European ancestry
faceism	1992	People who are ugly or, at least, not good-looking
faithism	1994	Religion
familism	1986	Nontraditional families
fattism (or fatism)	1988	People who are fat
feelism	1992	Animals that are slimy, scaly, or otherwise don't feel very nice
foodism	1985	People who eat plain or unhealthy food
genderism	1984	Gender
handicapism	1979	The disabled
handism	1985	Handedness (esp. left-handedness)
healthism	1985	People who are unhealthy
heightism	1980	Height (especially small people)
heterosexism	1978	Homosexuals
languageism	1982	Non-English speakers
lookism (or looks-ism)	1978	Appearance
scentism	1991	Smell
shapeism	1991	Body shape (esp. overweight bodies)
shortism	1988	People who are short
sightism	1991	Blindness or visual impairment
sizeism	1981	Body size
skinnyism	1999	People who are skinny
smellism	1991	Smell

ISM	FIRST USE	DISCRIMINATION OR PREJUDICE DIRECTED TOWARD OR BASED ON . . .
speciesism	1975	Nonhuman species
weightism	1984	People who are overweight
wineism	1991	People who drink inferior wines
voicism	1992	Voice

Differently Languaged

If there's a poster boy, er, I mean, a poster *person* for politically correct language, it's probably the adjective *challenged*. This means "relating to a particular impairment," but its purpose is to recast that impairment in a more positive mold by emphasizing the spirit and determination required by people to deal with their disability. It originated in the shift that the word *challenge* made from noun to adjective in the early 1980s:

Bill Carney is spending this Christmas with his sons—a victory for the crippled Army veteran who convinced the courts he was a fit father even if he couldn't throw a football. And he has a message for other handicapped parents so **challenged**: "If you love 'em, if you really care, don't give up." (Associated Press, December 23, 1981)

By 1982 *challenged* had become a synonym for *handicapped*:

The DeBolts . . . have a folder of material on themselves and a list of suggested speech topics: "Love, Laughter, and Twenty Kids," "From Burn-Out to Bonfire," "Parenting in the '80s," "Society Says 'Handicapped'—We Say **'Challenged.'** " (*Washington Post,* November 4, 1982)

Adverbial modifiers began jumping on to the *challenged* bandwagon a couple of years later. The first adverb was *physically*, as in **physically challenged** (1984):

> Russel Derek, head of the LAOOC's handicapped-services department, said he thinks about six nations, including the United States, would enter competitors in the wheelchair events. He said the "**physically challenged** athletes" will train at Santa Monica City College beginning next month. (*The Globe and Mail,* Toronto, March 24, 1984)

This was soon followed by **emotionally challenged** (1985), **visually challenged** (1985), **mentally challenged** (1986), and **multi-challenged** (1990). (Language columnist William Safire once called phrases such as these "adverbially premodified adjectival lexical units.")

In the early 1990s some observers began to criticize this use of *challenged* as being too euphemistic. Invariably, the writer would go on to coin a number of facetious variations on the theme, including knee-slappers such as **vertically challenged** (1991) instead of "short," **follically challenged** (1991) for "bald" or "balding," and **circumferentially challenged** (1992) for "fat." By the time people started jamming their tongues into their cheeks and describing virgins as **hymenally challenged** (1995), the silly season had begun.

Undaunted, pro-PCers looked for other ways to put a positive spin on having a disability. One of the most enduring has been **handicapable** (1981):

> "I'm not handicapped, I'm **handicapable.**" That was the motto of Curtis Matthew Young, who was born disabled and given a life expectancy of three days. Young beat the odds and not only survived, but lived life to the fullest, his family said. (*Philadelphia News,* June 29, 2001)

Another adverb/adjective combination that proved popular was **differently abled** (1981), a locution that emphasizes what people are able to do rather than what they are unable to do. In recent years this has been shortened to **diff-abled** (1998; rhymes with *disabled*), and the handicap itself has been given a new name:

> **diff-ability** *n.* (1997) A disability, especially one that causes or encourages the person to develop different or special abilities. Also: **diffability.** *Ryals likes to focus on the positive. "As my experiences grow, I keep wanting to rephrase and change the word disability to a new word, 'diff-ability.' Throughout my life, most people noticed my deformities and looked at my disability, while my friends and family focused on my different abilities," he said.* (*Orlando Sentinel,* June 28, 2002)

All of these phrases are opaque, but the hands-down winner of the Let's See How Vague We Can Get contest is the phrase **differently challenged** (1991):

> [Actress Camryn Mannheim] went on to work with disabled people herself, becoming a sign-language interpreter some 15 years ago. Eventually, "I found myself in the arena of being an advocate for **differently challenged** people." (*Times-Picayune,* New Orleans, January 19, 2000)

A variation on this is **specially challenged** (1986).

A Politically Correct Miscellany

Despite the gloomy forecasts of the doomsayers and other professional party poopers, our culture is gradually becoming more civil and more enlightened. We no longer allow people to keep slaves; we no longer sacrifice goats or virgins to appease the powers-that-be; and we no longer use the words *leech* and *cure* in the same sentence.

Part of this ongoing enlightenment involves coming up with not only inoffensive alternatives to certain existing words and phrases, but also new words for new inoffensive actions and beliefs. This section takes you through a few of my favorite examples of this politically correct lexicon that I've collected over the years.

Let's start with the word *pet*, which at first blush seems about as inoffensive a term as there is in the language. It has referred to a domesticated or tamed animal since the sixteenth century and even has branched out to mean a favorite person, or one who is treated with special kindness. What's wrong with that? Plenty, say the animal-rights activists. *Pet* implies the human ownership of an animal, and that just won't do. The preferred term is **companion animal** (1977):

> "It's important that individual people who have **companion animals,** bring them into their homes, make them dependent on them, have a more responsible and respectful relationship than one of property owner," said Dr Elliott Katz. (*The Scotsman,* Edinburgh, Scotland, July 10, 2002)

And, of course, the words *owner* and *master* are also *verboten.* If you have a dog, cat, or other companion animal, the pro-animal set would prefer it if you called yourself the animal's **guardian** (1977) or, more generally, an **animal guardian** (1997):

> The Animal Services Commission today approved a proposal to remove all mention of pet "owners" in city literature and codes. . . . The Animal Services Department already uses **"animal guardian"** rather than pet owner in all of its documents and communications, and other cities—including Berkeley,

West Hollywood and Boulder, Colo.—have adopted similar measures. (City News Service, July 22, 2002)

While we're on the subject of animals, there was a furor a few years back about dolphins getting caught and killed by the nets that fishers were using to catch tuna. More humane (dolphane?) methods that didn't endanger dolphins were developed, and tuna caught using these methods was labeled **dolphin-safe** (1989):

> The fishermen aboard the *Azteca VI* cast a net as large as 11 football fields into the azure Pacific waters off the Mexican coast. In swam hundreds of glistening yellowfin tuna—and scores of dolphins. A dozen divers plunged into the ocean and parted the net to set the dolphins free. A decade ago, the *Azteca VI*, a Mexican tuna boat, likely would have let the dolphins drown. But new fishing techniques have reduced the mortality rate of dolphins captured in Latin American tuna nets by a dramatic 98 percent, from 132,000 in 1986 to fewer than 2,000 last year. U.S. Commerce Secretary Donald Evans will rule in the coming months on whether the drop in dolphin deaths entitles Latin American fisheries to label their canned tuna **"dolphin-safe,"** a move that would place their tuna in U.S. supermarkets. (*Newsday,* June 30, 2002)

Dolphins aren't the only marine life threatened by human fishing techniques, so similar labels that have appeared are **turtle-safe** (1990) and **whale-safe** (1996).

These are examples of **greenspeak** (1982), or what might be called "environmentally correct" speech. When the environment became a mainstream concern in the 1980s and 1990s, marketers often resorted to greenspeak to make their products more attractive to the pro-environment crowd. Labels such as **biodegradable** (1962), **environmentally friendly** (1984), **ozone friendly** (1987), and **CFC free** (1988) were slapped on products willy-nilly. Even product ingredients and materials required the stamp of correctness:

> **good wood** *n.* (1988) Wood that does not come from an endangered forest region or from an endangered tree species; wood grown on a plantation. *"Good wood" is the new buzz term in furniture. And it isn't just for eco-activists any more; home décor retailers such as Ikea and Restoration Hardware are jumping on the good-wood bandwagon, along with hardware giants such as Home Depot.* (*The Globe and Mail,* Toronto, August 12, 2000)

This is also called **ethical wood** (2000), **plantation wood** (1985), and **managed wood** (1995).

Correctness, political or otherwise, is often a tricky business. For example, African-Americans would be well within their rights to slap you upside the head if you described them as *colored* (1611), which is now universally regarded as derogatory. However, you'd be flying your PC flag high if you instead described that individual as a **person of color** (1971), a phrase that's been in the language (most often seen as **people of color)** for over 30 years.

The phrase *person of color* is an example of **people first wording** (1991). Another common example is **person of size** (1980), the gentle way of referring to a hefty person. Phrases such as these were almost certainly the inspiration behind what appears to be a presidential neologism. When referring to Muslim women who wear some kind of covering—a *hijab,* such as the *chador* or the *burka*—as a sign of piety, U.S. President George W. Bush used the never-before-heard phrase **women of cover** (2001). His first use occurred on October 4, 2001 in an address to employees of the State Department: "I see an opportunity at home when I hear the stories of Christian and Jewish women alike, helping **women of cover,** Arab-American women, go shop because they're afraid to leave their home."

The president used the phrase in subsequent speeches, and a number of media outlets picked up on it. I even found four media citations that didn't refer to the president when using the phrase: *PR Newswire* (October 18, 2001), *Buffalo News* (October 26, 2001), *The Scotsman* (June 15, 2002), and *Kirkus Reviews* (August 15, 2002).

The bureaucratic mind seems particularly suited for creating euphemisms. For example, the humble *greeting card* is now sometimes referred to as a **social expression product** (1980). Earnest PC types have a genius for coining this kind of thing, often coming up with long-winded alternatives to words or phrases that are deemed to be no longer correct. One of the strangest of these coinages to cross my desk in recent years is **OTPOTSS** (2002), which is spelled out in all its bureaucratic glory in the following citation:

> It is not just government departments that like to come up with new ways of describing homosexuals, though equalities minister Barbara Roche has this week triumphed in the field with the wonderful mouthful **"orientation towards people of the same sex,"** or **"otpotss"** for short. The phrase will replace "homosexual" in anti-discrimination laws currently being drawn up by the Department of Trade and Industry, because it was felt that using homosexual was "no longer the way forward in defining sexual orientation." (*The Guardian,* London, November 27, 2002)

Earlier I talked about gender-free language being the hallmark of PC speech. However, many feminists *want* gender-based words. Specifically, they want female alternatives to existing words that are either male in character or that contain words such as *man, men, his,* and *him.* So, for example, *women* is replaced by **wimmin** (1980), **womyn** (1980), or **wimyn** (1992), and *history* is replaced by **hystery** (1992) or **herstory** (1973):

> Let us continue to examine the recommendations given us by the advocates of Political Correctness, especially regarding **wim-**

min. Feeling puzzled? That's the new spelling of "women" proposed by feminists who strongly oppose the vilifying ending -men in this most feminine of words. The synonyms **womyn** or **wimyn** are hardly more comprehensible to the uninitiated. The singular is womban or womon. . . . Mankind—pardon me, personkind—has all too long been viewed through the distorting lens of history. The remedy is, of course, **herstory,** a term defined by the *Woman's New World Dictionary* as follows: 1. The past seen through the eyes of women. 2. The removal of male self-glorification from history. (*Swiss News,* October 1, 2000)

Keeping track of all this and ensuring that one is fully compliant with PC codes of conduct can be exhausting work:

diversity fatigue *n.* (1998) A form of mental exhaustion brought on by the constant attention required to ensure a workforce or other group is racially or ethnically diverse. *The question of television's racial and ethnic diversity in front of and behind the camera remains a hot-button issue. . . . Still, even those experiencing what might be called "diversity fatigue"—which would be, in all likelihood, just about everyone associated with the debate—had better get used to the topic, since it isn't going to be resolved any time soon. (Los Angeles Times,* January 8, 2000)

Beyond Political Correctness

The culture's current attitude toward political correctness seems to be one of derisive acceptance. On one hand, we no longer tolerate (and therefore rarely hear or see) terms such as *cripple* and *retard.* Nobody with a working brain will mourn the passing of the word *Jew* used as a verb. Moreover, phrases such as *flight attendant* and *mentally challenged* are part of the lexicon and no longer elicit second mental glances. On the other hand,

PC language is still a regular subject of diatribes and tub-thumpings across the land as pundits and barking heads rail against the euphemisms and often heavy-handed tactics of the "thought police."

Some folks believe that these opposite attitudes are in the process of being reconciled into what they hope will be a new era where the obvious linguistic indignities and insults will be scrubbed from public discourse, but where people will still be free to speak their minds on any subject. This new era is called **post-political correctness** (1996) and is often described as **post-PC** (1992) or **PPC** (1998).

Chapter 13

Of Melting Pots and Salad Bowls

Here individuals of all nations are melted into a new race of men. —*J. Hector St. John de Crèvecoeur*

Multicultural is not a description of a category of American writing—it is a definition of all American writing.
—*Ishmael Reed*

Maybe the truest thing to be said about racism is that it represents a profound failure of the imagination.
—*Henry Louis Gates, Jr.*

Is North America a *multicultural* (1941) society? Since the word describes a society that consists of a number of cultures, races, and ethnic groups, let's consider the numbers. In his book *The Clustered World,* journalist Michael Weiss reports that the United States has 300 different races, 70 Hispanic groups, and 600 Native American tribes, and nonwhites account for 25 percent of the population (over 70 million people). In Canada the 2001 census recorded over 100 mother tongues, from Arabic to Urdu, and the mother tongue of one-sixth of the population is a language other than English. (In Toronto, Canada's largest city, more than 46 percent of the population has a mother tongue other than English.) Describing societies such as these as "multicultural" almost seems like an understatement.

However, this *multiculturalism* (1957) is not without its problems. Should immigrants attempt to blend in with the dominant culture, or should they strive to preserve as much of their own culture as possible? Why do so many races and ethnic groups congregate together to create neighborhoods that are *monocultural* (1968)—consisting of a single culture? How do people who live in *bicultural* (1940)—consisting of two cultures—households combine and respect each other's traditions? What words are best used to inoffensively name or describe the members of ethnic or racial groups? Is the often imperfect English used by nonnative speakers "bad" English that needs to be corrected, or is it just another dialect? How do such societies handle and discourage racism?

The answers and accommodations generated by these questions tend to forge new ways of thinking about, and new ways of seeing, the **multiculti** (1991) world. And, as we certainly know by now, new ways of thinking and seeing always generate new words. I'll take you through some of these multicultural neologisms in this chapter.

Melting Pot or Salad Bowl?

In 1908 the playwright Israel Zangwill released a new production called *The Melting-Pot*:

> America is God's Crucible, the great Melting-Pot where all the races of Europe are melting and re-forming! Here you stand, good folk, think I, when I see them at Ellis Island, here you stand in your fifty groups, with your fifty languages and histories, and your fifty blood hatreds and rivalries. But you won't be long like that, brothers, for these are the fires of God you've come to—these are the fires of God. A fig for your feuds and vendettas! Germans and Frenchmen, Irishmen and Englishmen, Jews and Russians—into the Crucible with you all! God is making the American.

The play was a success and the *melting-pot* metaphor—that the various races and cultures that populated the United States were "melted" down into a single national culture and identity—became a permanent part of the lexicon. However, this metaphor has always had its detractors. One of the earliest was philosopher Horace Kallen, who, in his 1915 essay "Democracy versus the Melting Pot," introduced an alternative metaphor— the *orchestra:* "As in an orchestra, every type of instrument has its specific timbre and tonality, founded in its substance and form; as every type has its appropriate theme and melody in the whole symphony, so in society each ethnic group is the natural instrument, its spirit and culture are its theme and melody, and the harmony and dissonances and discords of them all make the symphony of civilization."

In the same essay, Kallen also coined the phrase *cultural pluralism,* which is the theory that for a society to thrive, it must accept and encourage multiple cultures and ethnic groups.

Since Kallen's day, a number of commentators have pointed out that the melting pot metaphor, its undoubted popularity aside, isn't a reflection of the current American reality.

For one thing, it appears that U.S. society isn't a single, cohesive unit. Instead, it seems to be an assortment of regions, each with its own distinct multicultural mix. Here's an example:

transnational suburb n. (2000) A suburb made up mostly of immigrants who maintain strong ties to their home countries. *Social scientist Mike Davis has coined the phrase "transnational suburbs" to describe an emerging phenomenon. Natives of particular Mexican villages are moving en masse into the same U.S. neighborhoods, creating de facto satellites of their hometowns. (Contra Costa Times, July 17, 2002)*

In short, the United States may be better described as a collection of **multiple melting pots** (1998):

These more diverse metropolitan areas are located in the emerging melting pot regions of the country, which, recent trends suggest, will differ sharply from the mostly white and white/black heartland regions. This represents a new demographic divide that is likely to be just as significant as now-familiar divides: city versus suburb, or urban versus rural. In the twenty-first century, immigrants will be introduced to American life in a series of **multiple melting pots**—each with its own race and ethnic personality. (*World and I,* May 1, 2001)

In other words, the U.S. motto may still be *E Pluribus Unum* (from many, one), but perhaps *E Pluribus Pluribus* is closer to the truth.

Also, for the melting pot to function, immigrants have to give up their old cultures in favor of the American Way. That is, each immigrant becomes just another ingredient in the **American stew** (1980). But there's plenty of evidence to show that many immigrants are hanging on to their cultural identity while still mixing with the larger culture. To some, this is reminiscent of the way that salad ingredients remain identifiable when mixed together. Therefore, America isn't so much a melting pot as it is a **salad bowl** (1975):

In fact, the very concept of assimilation is being called into question as never before. Some sociologists argue that the melting pot often means little more than "Anglo conformity" and that assimilation is not always a positive experience—for either society or the immigrants themselves. And with today's emphasis on diversity and ethnicity, it has become easier than ever for immigrants to avoid the melting pot entirely. Even the metaphor itself is changing, having fallen out of fashion completely with many immigration advocacy and ethnic groups. They prefer such terms as the **"salad bowl"** and the "mosaic," metaphors that convey more of a sense of separateness in describing this nation of immigrants. (*Washington Post,* May 25, 1998)

The *mosaic* metaphor mentioned in the above citation dates to at least 1966, when it appeared in a book by Michael Kraus titled *Immigration, the American Mosaic: From Pilgrims to Modern Refugees.* A mosaic (as I mentioned in Chapter 1) is a collection of small, colorful elements that together make up a picture or design, so it seems an apt metaphor. This aptness explains not only the widespread use of the mosaic trope, but also the wealth of related phrases it has spawned over the years. For example, there's **mosaic culture** (1992):

> "As an American Muslim, I am working with my community to be part of our multi-ethnic, **mosaic culture** to . . . coordinate with my countrymen and to project a united front against the terrorist threat that we face from overseas," writes Hassan Makhzoumi, a Maryland physician who is prominent in the Muslim community. (*Baltimore Sun,* October 13, 2002)

A similar term is **mosaic society** (1981):

> We also gain here a survey of how the "one and many" worked out in the past. Thomas Jefferson and other founders opposed immigration and extolled sameness. . . . When immigration increased there was "the melting pot." On the ethnic front, that gave way to the **"mosaic" society.** (*Washington Times,* July 20, 1997)

Former Canadian prime minister Pierre Trudeau coined the term **cultural mosaic** (1978) to describe his country's underlying societal metaphor:

> As the 1996 census shows, the **cultural mosaic** of Canada has grown from two main stripes—English and French—into a fabric of many hues and colors. In particular, the Greater Toronto Area has experienced dramatic changes in its demographics in the past two decades. Today, people from more than 100 countries speaking 80 languages live there, thanks to wave after wave of immigrants who settled that beautiful and

vibrant city and surrounding municipalities. (*Maclean's,* April 27, 1998)

Finally, in the 1989 New York mayoral race, candidate David Dinkins (the eventual winner) described the city as a **gorgeous mosaic** (1988) throughout his campaign (although his first recorded use of the phrase was in 1988).

Similar to the mosaic metaphor is the **patchwork quilt** (1983):

> In the **Patchwork Quilt,** assimilation into a common domi-
> nant culture is anathema, akin to cultural suicide. Advocates of
> the **patchwork quilt** say that individual sub-cultures should
> resist assimilation and aggressively agitate for power in pursuit
> of their own agenda. (*Jakarta Post,* October 2, 2000)

Those who see America's ethnic and racial makeup as more of a hodgepodge often liken it to a **crazy quilt** (1986), which is a quilt made of irregularly shaped and patterned pieces:

> Surprisingly, only one large U.S. city east of the Sierra Nevada
> boasts a non-Hispanic multiracial population larger than 5
> percent. And it's not New York, Chicago, or Miami. It's un-
> heralded Jersey City, N.J. Once a center for organized crime,
> the city now hosts a **crazy quilt** of people—from poor
> Egyptians looking for a new life to New Yorkers in search of
> cheaper housing. (*The Christian Science Monitor,* July 17,
> 2001)

The final item in this miscellany of metaphors is the **bouquet of flowers** (1981):

> Viewing our country as a melting pot is a dangerous thing. I
> prefer to view it as a fragrant **bouquet of flowers.** Imagine
> how boring the food court at your favorite shopping mall
> would be without the Mexican, Italian or Chinese selections.
> (*Hartford Courant,* January 19, 2001)

The use of the "food court" image in the last citation is fortu-itous since it gives me a way to segue smoothly into another new phrase:

> **food court multiculturalism** *n.* (2001) The practice of enjoying the attributes of several cultures other than one's own in a superficial and temporary way. Also: **food-court multiculturalism.** *Cultural conservatives have never really understood diversity, preferring to equate it with a superficial* ***food-court multiculturalism*** *and with the apparatus of co-ercion: affirmative action, political correctness and lawsuits, lawsuits, lawsuits.* (*Washington Post,* March 8, 2002)

A similar phrase is **boutique multiculturalism** (1990).

Ebonics

On December 18, 1996, the board members of the Oakland Unified School District voted unanimously to give Black English official status as a second language. The board's reason-ing was simple: Black English was a dominant vernacular since the district's student population was 53 percent black. Those students who spoke Black English needed instruction on how to "decode" their native dialect into standard English, which would better prepare them for life outside of school.

From the response this decision generated, you'd have thought the board members had voted in favor of regular tor-ture sessions. Parents, pundits, and even leaders of the black community such as Jesse Jackson, Maya Angelou, and Spike Lee condemned the move. (Sample headline: "The Ebonic Plague.") The usual criticism was that Black English was a "lazy," "infe-rior," slang dialect and that for black kids to get ahead in this world, they needed to learn only standard English. (Note that the school board caused much of its own grief by claiming that

Black English was "genetically based," a foolish and indefensible notion that pleased no one.)

The critics, in this case, could not have been more wrong. There is nothing inferior about Black English, those who speak it aren't being even remotely lazy, and it's certainly not slang. Black English is recognized by the vast majority of linguists as a legitimate language with its own grammar, phrasing, and lexicon.

Black English and its variants are also known as African-American English (AAE), African-American Vernacular English (AAVE), Black Vernacular English, **ghettoese** (1986), and, most famously, **Ebonics** (1973):

> To many white Americans, **Ebonics**—or Black English—may seem like a "mish-mash" of African American slang terms. But in reality, it is a dialect with its own set of linguistic rules. Among the linguistic characteristics of **Ebonics** is the omission of consonant sounds. For instance, the word "best" becomes "bes" and "sand" becomes "san." Words ending with "ed" such as "hugged," "messed" and "cooked," become "hug," "mess," and "cook." Another characteristic of Black English is the alteration of the "th" sound to an "f" or "v" sound, such as when "birthday" becomes "birfday" and "brother" becomes "bru-vah." Many characteristics of **Ebonics** also are seen in the Southern white, non-standard, English dialect. For instance, "R" and "L" sounds are dropped. This way, "four" becomes "foe" and "door" becomes "doe." (*Tulsa World,* May 28, 1997)

Ebonics combines *ebony* and *phonics,* and it became a lexical celebrity thanks to the Oakland school board hubbub. Each of those board members, and anyone else who supports or is a proponent of Ebonics, is an **Ebonicist** (1997):

> Words that a student doesn't know, of course, are "blocking agents" [things that prevent or hinder learning]. In remedying the problem, **Ebonicists** are characteristically enthusiastic

about redesigning language tests (Williams has an ongoing fight with the SAT) while apparently doubtful about dictionaries, which are wonderful at unblocking "blocking agents." (*The Maneater,* University of Missouri, Columbia, February 5, 2002)

The infamy of Ebonics (it was voted "most controversial" word for 1996 by the American Dialect Society) has given the wags of the world a new reason to live: coming up with humorous constructions based on the *-onics* suffix, which roughly translates as "the language, dialect, or speech patterns of." Examples are legion and run the gamut from *Alabonics* (the dialect used in Alabama), to Moronics (the speech patterns of stupid people), to Zionics (the language of Jewish-Americans). Among the more popular of these terms was the "white English" corollary to Ebonics: **Ivoronics** (1996)—*ivory* plus *phonics.* Those who thought former U.S. president Bill Clinton had his own unique way of speaking often referred to it as **Clintonics** (1991). One of the most successful of these coinages is **Bubbonics** (1996)—*bubba* (slang for a southern male, especially an uneducated "good ol' boy" or redneck) plus *phonics*— the speech patterns of the U.S. South:

The North Georgia representative, a tall, broad-shouldered man who speaks in a slow, Southern drawl he jokingly calls **"Bubbonics,"** is preaching spending restraint as he seeks the office responsible for presiding over the state Senate and appointing Senate committees. (*Florida Times-Union,* November 3, 2002)

Chinglish, Spanglish, and
Other Multicultural Englishes

As I mentioned in Chapter 1, English has a well-deserved reputation for borrowing (although seldom returning) words from
other languages. But the opposite process goes on as well:
English cheerfully lends its words to other languages.
Indonesians talk of having an *asisten* (assistant), Japanese speak
of working at a *konpyuta* (computer), and, despite the ominous
presence of the Académie Française, which seeks to keep the
French language free of vulgar *anglicismes,* the French read and
respond to *le é-mail.* The tendency for English—particularly
English technical terms—to colonize other languages is often
derided as **linguistic colonialism** (1977):

> The existence of Western words in Bahasa Indonesia, particu-
> larly English, shows that language borrowing or language
> mixing has taken place. Many feel that this is a form of **lin-
> guistic colonialism** that could threaten the survival of the na-
> tional language. This phenomenon has indeed become trendy
> at all levels from teenagers to politicians. They often either de-
> liberately or spontaneously throw in a sprinkling of English
> words in their native language. (*Jakarta Post,* October 28,
> 2002)

But people around the world aren't just borrowing English
words; they're also learning the English language at a furious rate.
The number of people who speak English is notoriously hard to
pin down—the statistics are kept unevenly from country to country, and it depends a great deal on how you define "speak." (Like
a native? Fluently? Conversationally? Enough to ask where the
washroom is?) In the fourth edition of his monumental work,
The American Language, which was published in 1936, H. L.
Mencken estimated the total number of English speakers in the
world at 191 million—174 million native speakers and 17 mil-

lion others. The most comprehensive modern survey to date, published 60 years after Mencken, appears in linguist David Crystal's 1997 book, *English as a Global Language*. Crystal says the total number of English speakers in the world may be as high as 1.8 billion, or nearly a third of the planet. Of those, only about 450 million are people who learned English as a first language, meaning that nonnative English speakers are clearly the majority.

People who learned English as a second (or third or fourth) language—those who speak what writer Joel Miller calls "Majority English"—exhibit a wide range of linguistic competency. A lucky few can boast of being fluent in English, but most speak the language in an endearingly idiosyncratic manner where the grammar, syntax, and lexicon of both English and their native tongue are combined into a new dialect. In most cases the name of this new dialect is a combination of the name of the native language and the suffix *-lish* or *-glish*. For example, the dialect that combines Japanese and English is called *Japlish*. Here's a list of the various "Englishes" that I've come across:

DIALECT	FIRST USE	COMBINES ENGLISH WITH . . .
Arablish	1984	Arabic
Chinglish	1980	Chinese
Czechlish	1994	Czech
Denglisch	1978	German (*Deutsch* plus *Englisch*)
Denglish	1998	Dutch or German (*Deutsch*)
Engleutsch	1995	German (*Englisch* plus *Deutsch*)
Espanglish	1954	Spanish (*Español*)
Finglish	1986	Finnish
Franglais	1959	French (*Français* plus *Anglais*)
Fringlish	1994	French
Hinglish	1988	Hindi

DIALECT	FIRST USE	COMBINES ENGLISH WITH . . .
Indlish	1994	Indian or Indonesian
Japlish	1980	Japanese
Konglish	1990	Korean
Manglish	1995	Malay or Mandarin
Singlish	1980	Singaporean
Spanglish	1967	Spanish
Taglish	1980	Tagalog
Tinglish	1985	Tamil or Thai
Yidlish	1980	Yiddish
Yinglish	1982	Yiddish

The Dark Side of Multiculturalism

Multiculturalism is appreciated by most people, especially those who've lived in racially or ethnically diverse neighborhoods or cities. But there are still some thick-browed Neanderthals walking around out there who judge others based on nothing more than their skin color, religion, or ethnicity. For example, you've probably heard of someone getting arrested for DWI—driving while impaired. But some bad-apple cops will pull someone over only because they are **DWB** (1991)—driving while black:

> Many young (and not-so-young) men, black or brown, know what it's like to be stopped by a police officer for doing, well . . . nothing. It's called **DWB**—Driving While Black. And it doesn't stop at being stopped. According to a recent study from the Justice Department, African-Americans and Hispanics reported that police used force or threatened to use force against them twice as often as whites said they did. (*St. Louis Post-Dispatch,* March 16, 2001)

After the September 11, 2001, terrorist attacks, a new abbreviation appeared that was clearly inspired by DWB: **FWA,** or flying while Arab:

> Today, Arab-Americans say men and women of their heritage are being interrogated relentlessly for **"FWA"** (flying while Arab). (*Orlando Sentinel,* August 18, 2002)

Both DWB and FWA are examples of **racial profiling** (1994), detaining, questioning, or arresting a person whose race is part of a profile of traits that allegedly identify the most likely perpetrators of certain crimes:

> It is no longer news that **racial profiling** occurs; study after study over the past five years has confirmed that police disproportionately stop and search minorities. What is news, but has received virtually no attention, is that the studies also show that even on its own terms, **racial profiling** doesn't work. . . . Police stops yield no significant difference in so-called hit rates—percentages of searches that find evidence of lawbreaking—for minorities and whites. (*New York Times,* May 13, 2001)

Judgments about a person based on his or her accent, grammar, vocabulary, or other language traits are called **linguistic profiling** (1998):

> One Stanford linguistics professor experienced this when he first moved to Palo Alto. When he phoned using his educated, professional voice, he would be told that the house was available—but the landlords would change their minds when they saw him in person. He is African American. He is now doing research on **"linguistic profiling"** showing that landlords and others can usually make out a caller's race and class just by their accent, and discriminate accordingly. (*The Straits Times,* Kuala Lumpur, Malaysia, July 7, 2002)

Other people judge their fellow citizens by where they live. They caution people about not going to the "bad part of town," and they might describe a person has having come from the "wrong side of the tracks." If they go so far as to label an area bad because the majority of its population belongs to a particular race or ethnic group, then they're guilty of a larger crime:

> **redlining** *pp.* (1975) The practice of refusing to serve particular geographical areas because of the race, ethnicity, or income of the area's residents. *At first, the Federal Housing Administration, the arm of the U.S. Housing and Urban Development Department that insures lenders 100 percent in foreclosure losses, reacted to racial change on the South Side by* **redlining.** *The agency, along with lenders and banks, literally drew red lines on maps of minority neighborhoods and refused to insure loans there.* (*Chicago Sun-Times,* April 5, 1999)

Areas where the majority of the population belongs to a minority group—so-called **majority-minority** (1978) areas—can also fall victim to another kind of racism, one that sees them burdened with a disproportionate number of garbage dumps, toxic waste sites, and other ugly or hazardous features of the modern urban landscape. This is called **environmental racism** (1987):

> In 1994, residents of Fulton County overturned plans for a tunnel that would have stored sewage and moved it between two treatment plants. . . . Opponents successfully portrayed that tunnel as an example of **environmental racism** because sewage from mostly white neighborhoods would be stored beneath predominantly black communities in southwest Fulton County. (*Atlanta Journal-Constitution,* July 15, 2002)

The American linguist Michael C. Haley once said that a metaphor is not "a riddle to be solved," but "it is itself a solution, a leap, a meaning, and a discovery." The metaphors we use to describe the multicultural nature of our society enable us to leap over the mundane demographic facts and discover the meaning inherent in our particular cultural combinatorics. For proponents of the melting pot or stew metaphors, meaning lies in the concept of country, and other cultures are important mostly in the way they contribute to the strength of the nation. Fans of the salad bowl, mosaic, and quilt metaphors find meaning in diversity and cultural identity, and the nation is important mostly in the way it enables individual cultures not just to exist, but to thrive and flourish. None of these metaphors will ever be "correct" (in the sense of describing society exactly), and in the end it doesn't matter if one "wins out" (whatever that means) over the others. These metaphors are useful because they give people a hook on which to hang their thoughts about the kind of society they want, a discussion that is arguably more valuable than any result that might come of it.

Chapter 14

A Baby Boom Lexicon

> When faced with unsettling developments like death, Baby Boomers always react in the same way: We sign up for self-improvement classes. —*Joe Queenan*

> I never experienced the fun and exciting parts of the whole Boomer scene—just spent a lot of time dutifully chuckling at Boomers' maddeningly pointless anecdotes about just how stoned they got on various occasions, and politely fielding their assertions about how great their music was. —*Neal Stephenson*

> Some contemporary word hunters think the current wave of offensive language was sparked by the sexual revolution of the '60s. After bouncing from bed to bed for years and abandoning all kinds of taboos, is it any surprise that the limits on baby-boomer language would collapse? —*Charles M. Madigan*

At one second after midnight on January 1, 1946, Kathleen Casey Wilkins was born in a Philadelphia hospital. In the year that followed, another 3.4 million American babies were born into the postwar world, half a million more than in 1945. It was an all-time record, and it marked the beginning of a long period of baby production that was unlike anything the world had ever seen. In 1954 births topped the 4 million mark for the first time, and they stayed over 4 million through 1964. (In 1957, 4.3 million little Winston Churchill look-alikes arrived, a record number that stands to this day.) In all, 76 million Americans were born between 1946 and 1964. Other countries experienced postwar boomlets, too. Canada, for example, welcomed over 9 million babies between 1946 and 1966. (At the peak of the Canadian boom, an average of more than four babies were born for each adult woman, a figure that, 40 years later, seems nothing short of remarkable.) But, for sheer size, no other country experienced a natal frenzy like the one in the United States, and those 76 million tykes are what we usually think of when we see the phrases *baby boom* and *baby boom generation*. (For the record, the U.S. baby boom generation now totals 78 million people, with immigration accounting for the extra members.)

The phrase *baby boom* was in use as early as 1941, but it was first used to describe the postwar baby bonanza in 1971. *Baby boomer* first appeared in 1974, and then *boomer* showed up in 1982, followed by *boomer generation* in 1984.

When reading about the boomers, it quickly becomes clear that most writers fall into one of two camps: the **boomer bashers** (1989) and those who have **boomer envy** (1991).

For the bashers, the usual boomer complaints are a glorification of the 1960s, a chronic and unhealthy self-absorption, and a dominance of the social, cultural, and political agendas. The problem with the bashers, however, is that they tend to pigeonhole the entire generation as though it were a homogeneous mass. One writer chastises boomers for "selling out" because in the 1960s they were innocent, selfless, and idealistic, and by the 1980s and '90s they'd become cynical, selfish, and materialistic. While it just might be true that some of the acid-dropping, free love–giving protesters from the 1960s are now Starbuckssipping, briefcase-toting yuppies, you can't say that a whole generation has made that change. Yippies rarely turn into yuppies. It's more likely that the 1960s activists are the same people who developed our recycling programs and spearheaded the movement toward politically correct speech and behavior. Today's yuppies are more likely to have come from those middle class, suburban kids who didn't protest and didn't care about those countercultural issues and movements that now define the 1960s.

The term *boomer envy* was coined by writer Douglas Coupland and appeared in his novel *Generation X,* where he defined it as "envy of material wealth and long-range material security accrued by older members of the baby boom generation by virtue of fortunate births." Another Coupland coinage worth noting is **bleeding ponytail** (1991): "An elderly sold-out baby boomer who pines for hippie or pre-sellout days." It's true that many boomers have done well for themselves, rising to positions of power and influence and accumulating nest eggs that guarantee a comfortable, even lavish, retirement. Is all this just because they were born at the right place and the right time? Certainly the past 50 years in North America have been a time of almost uninterrupted peace and undoubted prosperity. But you could also make a case that boomers earned their place in the sun. For example, 90 percent of baby boomers graduated from high school and more than 25 percent have at least an undergraduate degree.

Moreover, it's also true that many boomers haven't shared in the boom times. Although most boomers have fared better financially than their parents—various surveys peg the average boomer household income at around $55,000—the reality is that many have not. The American Association of Retired Persons commissioned a study in 1999 that split boomers into various categories. The "Strugglers" comprised 9 percent of the boomer population, and they had average household incomes of just $22,300; a second group, the "Anxious," had an average income of $41,000. In a 2002 survey of boomers by Allstate Financial titled *Retirement Reality Check,* more than half (52 percent) said they were worried about having enough money for retirement, and 16 percent weren't yet saving for retirement at all!

These apparent inconsistencies arise simply because this is a cohort (as the demographers like to say) that spans a wide age range. In a stretch, the oldest boomers could even be the parents of the youngest boomers. People born in the late 1940s often idolize the 1960s. I was born in 1959, but the next decade meant nothing to me other than catching frogs and learning to ride a bike. So it's not surprising that many demographers split the baby boom into two distinct groups. The people born from 1946 to 1955 are the Boomer I cohort, the **Woodstock Generation** (1975), who came of age in the 1960s; the people born from 1956 to 1964 are the Boomer II cohort, the **Me Generation** (1978), who consider the 1970s to be their formative years. Some researchers refine this and differentiate between *leading-edge* boomers—those born in the years 1946 to 1950—and *trailing-edge* boomers—those born in the years 1960 to 1964.

In any case, for over 50 years the Western world's key demographic has been the baby boom generation. This cohort has defined our culture's consumption patterns, social lives, politics, and even our language, as you'll see in this chapter.

Boomers as Permanent Kids

Although it's wrong to lump all the baby boom generation together, we still can make some general observations about the breed. For example, many boomers report that they don't feel as old as their age. They seem to have internalized Bernard Baruch's famous adage, "To me old age is always 15 years older than I am." Or, to turn this around, some boomers enjoy doing things that would normally only appeal to people 15 years younger than they are:

adultescent n. (1996) A middle-aged person who continues to participate in and enjoy youth culture. *For die-hard*

video-game connoiseurs [sic] *the Golden Age ended on 1 February, when Sega announced that the Dreamcast was to cease production after just three years. Stung by Sony's success since 1995 with PlayStation, the veteran video-game firm had put all its energies into a final charge on the hearts and minds of kids and **adultescents** with an affordable, technologically advanced new console.* (Independent on Sunday, London, December 30, 2001)

Such a person is also called a **kidult** (1988) or a **babydult** (2002). Adultescent has a fraternal twin—**adulescent** (1998)—that has appeared in various lists of "hip new words" since 1998 but hasn't caught on. (One problem might be that although it's easier to say than the cumbersome *adultescent,* it's pronounced just like *adolescent,* which is confusing.) Here's one of the few "natural" citations that I found:

It's micro-scooters and Wheatus CDs ago-go for the **"adulescents,"** or "kidults"—those whose clothes, activities and interests are exactly the same as those of youth culture. (*Irish News,* August 10, 2001)

Futurist Faith Popcorn has identified a related trend where boomers stick with or go back to the products and interests of their youth. She calls this **down-aging** (1990):

Turntables are a product of a trend Popcorn calls **down-aging.** Nostalgic for their carefree childhood, baby boomers find comfort in familiar pursuits and products from their youth. (*Tulsa World,* January 13, 2002)

For some baby boomers, middle age is a turbulent time not unlike their adolescence. Their bodies are changing in surprising ways; they feel inexplicable and uncontrollable surges of anger; they alternate between bursts of energy and bouts of enervation; relationships are in flux. It's as though middle age and adolescence have been conflated, both in fact and in word:

middlescence *n.* (1979) The turbulent, rebellious middle age of the baby boom generation. *Most baby boomers don't feel fully "grown up" until they are into their 40s. When our parents turned 50, we thought they were old! But today, women and men I've interviewed routinely feel they are five to 10 years younger than the age on their birth certificates. Fifty is what 40 used to be; 60 is what 50 used to be. Middle age has already been pushed far into the 50s—in fact, if you listen to boomers, there is no more middle age. So what's next? Welcome to* **Middlescence.** *It's adolescence the second time around.* (*U.S. News & World Report,* June 9, 1995)

This blend of *middle age* and *adolescence* was popularized by Gail Sheehy in her 1995 book, *New Passages.* As she says in the above citation, these youth-oriented boomers seem to have a mental block about the phrase *middle age.* If asked, they'd probably tell you that it sounds *old.* So these boomers work around middle age by extending the definition of "youth" to include their 40s and even their 50s. In that case, 40-something boomers aren't in middle age, they're in **mid youth** (1995) or **middle youth** (1997):

Unlike some people, I know I will someday be ol . . . ol . . . less young than I am now. In fact I already know I'm no longer a kid. I cheerfully admit that I am well into my **middle youth.** (*San Francisco Chronicle,* January 2, 2001)

A good example of boomer middlescense appeared in the August 12, 2002, issue of *Fortune* magazine, where it was noted that the average age of a rider of a Harley-Davidson motorcycle had climbed from 38 to 46 in just the previous decade. What could be more youthful than cruising around town on a hog? Of course, many Harleys are expensive, so only the well heeled can afford them, leading to the new epithet, **rubbies** (1988), or rich urban bikers (they're also called **RUBs**):

"More people pick up motorcycling when they're in their late 40s than at any other age because they have the time and they have the money," says Alvarez, who has already logged 27,000 miles on his 2-year-old Harley, including a recent 3,000-mile trek to Mississippi and back. Next month, he's off to Florida. The rise in affluent buyers, probably traced to the 1980s when publishing mogul Malcom Forbes made biking a chic activity, has brought on a new acronym: **"rubbie."** (*The Plain Dealer,* Cleveland, September 24, 2000)

Rubbies are part of a go-go class of boomers called **zoomers** (1999), defined roughly as those aged 50 and over who are passionate about travel and leisure:

You call this retirement? Forget quiet lolls in a porch rocking chair, with morning golf followed by afternoon naps and "early bird" suppers. The first of the 78-million-strong baby boom generation turn 55 this year. And just as they changed life as we know it in recent decades—from music to marriage to mutual funds—this healthy, wealthy, and wise band of **"zoomers"** is charging toward retirement at its own breakneck speed. (*U.S. News & World Report,* June 4, 2001)

Another way that boomers indulge their inner children is by playing sports, not only golf, but higher-impact sports such as snowboarding—where the younger crowd calls them **grays on trays** (1997)—tennis, track, inline skating, baseball, basketball, hockey, even marathon running. (In the 2001 New York City Marathon, 40 percent of the participants were between the ages of 40 and 54.) Boomers are so sports-crazed that they represent nearly a third of all sports participants, despite comprising just over 29 percent of the population. The problem, though, is that the bodies of those in their 40s and 50s aren't as supple or as resilient as they were in their 20s and 30s. This makes injuries a boomer phenomenon that's common enough to have produced its own term:

boomeritis *n.* (1999) Injuries to older, amateur athletes, especially those who are part of the baby boom demographic. *Forty-four-year-old Rick Gardner admits he did all the wrong things. Didn't change into sneakers. Wasn't wearing his leg braces. Hadn't played in a while. The consequences of all that didn't become clear, though, until he went for the long rebound and felt the excruciating pop in his knee. Yep, he'd blown it out. Gardner, who lives in Norfolk, didn't know it at the time, but he also was suffering from a larger societal ailment dubbed "**Boomeritis.**"* (*Virginian-Pilot*, Norfolk, Va., July 26, 2001)

This word was coined by Dr. Nicholas A. DiNubile, an orthopedic surgeon at the Hospital of the University of Pennsylvania, Philadelphia. According to a report released in April 2000 by the Consumer Product Safety Commission, sports-related injuries among boomers increased 33 percent between 1991 and 1998. The commission estimates that there were more than 1 million "medically attended" injuries to baby boomers in 1998 (which cost an estimated $18.7 billion to treat).

Many boomers refuse to go gently into that good night of old age. They seek to "intervene in the aging process," as one doctor put it. They're looking for **permayouth** (1999), an appearance of youthfulness maintained over time by using cosmetic surgery and other methods:

People are suffering psychological damage because of society's obsession with **"permayouth,"** an expert said today. The hopeless battle to stay young is driving increasing numbers of men and women into cosmetic surgery clinics in a vain bid to maintain their looks, said psychologist Dr Eileen Bradbury. (Press Association, London, June 9, 1999)

Boomers attend **Botox parties** (2001), social gatherings at which a doctor injects the participants with Botox (botulinum toxin) to reduce or remove facial wrinkles. Botox has been called "the five-minute face-lift," but real face-lifts are popular boomer options, too. According to the magazine *American Demographics,* 20 years ago the average age of a face-lift recipient was 60, but now it's 50. Thirty-five percent of female boomers have used antiaging cosmetics, and 53 percent hide their gray with hair color. In yet another *Generation X* coinage, Douglas Coupland calls this **Dorian Graying,** which he defines as "The unwillingness to gracefully allow one's body to show signs of aging":

> I don't wear makeup to work any more and I am amazed at the uninvited guests that have taken up residence around my face. . . . Look at me. I'm **Dorian Graying** and I laugh, because 40 feels much different than what it looks like. (*Toronto Star,* August 18, 2001)

Vanity plays a big part in this trend, but it has a practical side, as well. Studies have shown that if people look "too old," they're less likely to land a job or get picked for promotion. In other words, they hit their graying heads on the **silver ceiling** (1999):

> Laid off this year from a high-tech firm, public relations manager Judy Piercey expected to land another job quickly. With more than 15 years in the business, the 49-year-old considered herself experienced. Potential employers just considered her old. Like more baby boomers today, Piercey found herself grappling with a new and daunting barrier: the so-called **silver ceiling.** Worrying that employers saw her age as a liability rather than an asset, Piercey left her college graduation date off her resume and noted she had more than 10 years of experience instead of 15. (*USA Today,* August 16, 2001)

Boomers as Permanent Parents

Another characteristic of many boomers is that they delay life's
passages for as long as possible. We've seen so far how they've delayed (some would say bypassed) middle age. Some delayed
adulthood by staying in school for undergraduate and graduate
degrees. Then they delayed having kids. In the 1960s the average age of a first-time mother was 21.8 years. By 2000 that age
had risen to nearly 25 years old.

Delaying the parenthood thing also means that one is still
parenting later in life. Combine this with the happy fact that
our parents are living longer, and many boomers are caught in
the middle of two responsibilities:

> **sandwich generation** *n.* (1978) People who must care for
> both their children and their parents; people who have
> finished raising their children and now must take care of
> their aging parents. *"The **sandwich generation** is being
> chewed on at both ends," Novelli said. The boomer generation
> is struggling to help support aging parents and pay college tu-
> ition for their children. (Pittsburgh Post-Gazette, November
> 20, 2002)*

Another name for this is the **squeezed generation** (1986). A
similar idea from a financial angle is the **triple-squeezed generation** (1990), who must pay college expenses, save for retirement, and support aging parents.

Fortunately, boomers don't tend to have big families. (That
is, the baby boom was a boom because a lot of women had a
few babies, not because a few women had a lot of babies.)
Throughout the 1970s and '80s, women in the United States
had a bit fewer than two children on average over their lifetimes,
which is a 40 percent drop from the birthrate in the 1950s. The
number of people per household has dropped from 4.8 in 1900

to 3.7 in 1950 to 2.6 in 2000. This has given rise to a new kind of family:

> **beanpole family** (1987) A family whose living members come from many generations, but with few members in each generation. *Family relationships are expected to be dramatically altered by the ageing society. With people having fewer children and living longer, the whole notion of family will change. Widely extended families of cousins of similar age will be replaced by "beanpole" families of many generations.* (*The Observer,* London, May 12, 2002)

A *beanpole* is a thin, straight stick that helps support a climbing bean plant. Since at least 1837 wisecrackers have used this term as a synonym for a lanky person. In the phrase *beanpole family,* it's used to contrast the standard image of a family's living members as a wide, bushy tree. Determinedly eschewing metaphor, many demographers prefer the term *verticalized family.*

The boomers started having kids in the 1970s, but by the late '70s enough of them were getting pregnant that it created another boom, called the **baby boom echo** (1980), which now refers to those born since 1978. (Note, however, that there is no such thing as definitive in the fuzzy science of demographics. Some authorities place the generation's initial birth year at 1980, others at 1982. Some demographers even say the generation stopped in 1995 and that the kids born since then are the *millennium busters* or *millennium kids.* At this point we shrug our shoulders, say "Oy!" and move on with our lives.) They're also called **Generation Y** (1993) because they came after Generation X (people born from 1965 to 1977). Another term is **nexter** (1998):

> While there is wiggle room of a year or so, here are the basic generation names and the born-between years for each: WWII

or the GI generation, 1909–1932; swing or silent generation, 1933–1945; baby boomers: 1946–1964; Generation X or Xers, 1965–1977; and, Generation Y or **nexters** or millennials, 1978–2002. (*Austin American-Statesman,* October 19, 2002)

Nexter is a tribute to big-time corporate marketing. In the late 1990s, Pepsi aimed its "Generation Next" ad campaign directly at the youth market, even securing contracts to place vending machines—and, controversially, lots of advertising—in schools throughout North America. This youth focus caused the phrase *Generation Next* to become a synonym for *Generation Y,* and before you know it a marketing slogan appeared to have a demographic seal of approval. Members of this group became known as *Generation Nexters,* then *Gen-Nexters,* and finally just *Nexters* or *nexters.*

Quite a few nexters and Generation Xers are overweight, leading some to snicker that they comprise **Generation XL** (1995):

Meet **Generation XL.** Like college freshmen who get fat from too much dorm food and too little activity, many cubicle potatoes lead very unhealthy lives. They have erratic eating habits and indulge in too much late-afternoon or late-night high-fat snacking. They are only half joking when they say their only physical activity is surfing the Internet. (*Contra Costa Times,* Walnut Creek, Calif., March 19, 2001)

With boomer kids now in their late 20s and early 30s, it's not surprising that a good chunk of them are having kids of their own, thus turning their parents into grandparents. In fact, more than a quarter of the baby boom cohort—around 20 million of the 78 million boomers in the United States—now have grandkids to dote on. They're now **grandboomers** (1996):

Given the "boom" in baby boom, by the year 2006, there will be 80 million grandparents in the U.S. Nearly half of them will be boomers—the youngest, best educated and most active generation of grandparents in history. Already, the average age of first-time grandparents is a spritely [sic] 47. And these **"grandboomers"** are giving a whole new look to the role. (*The Globe and Mail*, Toronto, November 30, 2002)

When the boomers' kids have left home, the parents might experience the *empty-nest syndrome* (1972), the depression that often occurs after all the kids have moved out. But many nests are no longer empty as adult children return home like so many swallows to Capistrano. It's hard for young singletons to make it on their own in the cold, cruel world, so many are retreating from the fray to the safe and comfy confines of Mom and Dad's. Many of these kids don't seem to be in any hurry to leave home once they return there. So boomer parents now have a new concern:

full-nest syndrome *n.* (1986) The stress and worry experienced by parents who have adult children living at home. *The **full-nest syndrome:** The most striking evidence of the delayed adulthood trend is the increasing share of young adults living in their parents' homes until well into their 20s. The 1990 census revealed that 21 percent of 25-year-olds were living with one or both parents, up from 15 percent in 1970. Some young people are not moving out at all before their mid-20s, but many more are doing an extra rotation through the family home after a temporary or lengthy absence.* (*American Demographics*, May 1996)

An adult child who returns home to live with his or her baby-boomer parents is called a **boomeranger** (1987):

Though many students only stay for a few months, others linger at home even after they are on their feet financially. They are attracted by a room of their own, disposable income, and eager-to-help baby-boomer parents who are welcoming their "**boomerangers**"—as they are being called—back to the nest. (*The Christian Science Monitor*, July 9, 2001)

He or she is also called a **boomerang child** (1988) or a **boomerang baby** (1989), and collectively they're called the **boomerang generation** (1986).

Parents never stop being parents, of course, but most look forward to the day when they can stop *parenting*. However, for these **full nesters** (1983), the end of parenting duties seems a long way off, indeed:

lifelong parenting *pp.* (1987) Taking care of one's adult children, especially those who show no desire to live on their own. Also: **life-long parenting.** *Nearly one in four Britons in their 20s still lives with their parents and two-thirds accept parental handouts after leaving home, a report published yesterday by the Social Market Foundation reveals. It shows a trend of "**lifelong parenting**," with many children holding an "open return ticket" to their parental home. Over half of those who live with their parents do not want to move out.* (*The Independent*, London, October 21, 2002)

To avoid lifelong parenting, many parents move to smaller homes that are conspicuously lacking in guest room accommodations. These parents are **down-nesting** (1991; yet another term coined by Douglas Coupland in his *Generation X*):

Sure, there had to be a few sacrifices. My family drove a smaller car and, with three grown-up children gradually heading out the door, moved into a smaller, mortgage-free townhouse, a manoeuvre [sic] sometimes called "**down-nesting.**" (*Toronto Star*, September 23, 2001)

As if kids returning to the nest wasn't enough, some boomers end up with one or more parents returning home. These are called, of course, **boomerang parents** (1996). This means that some **boomerang family** (1991) households have four generations under one roof: the boomer couple, their parents, their children, and their grandchildren. This is the sandwich generation with an extra layer, so call it the **triple-decker generation** (1998) or the **club sandwich generation** (1991):

> When Jackie Erckert describes herself, she tells people she is not part of the sandwich generation. She says she is part of the **club sandwich generation.** That's because she represents one of four generations living under the same roof in a single-family house near Riverside Park. "In our home we have my 81-year-old mother, who has had a stroke. There is me, in my 50s; my son and his wife, in their late 20s, and their four sons—7, 6, 4 and 3. (*Buffalo News,* June 9, 2002)

Whether you're a boomer, a boomer basher, or are just plain boomer envious, chances are that the baby boom generation has affected your life in some way, for good or ill. And that's just fine with the adultescents, zoomers, and grandboomers who make up the Woodstock/Me Generation. Above all else (to risk one of those generation generalizations that I complained about at the top of the chapter), this is a self-absorbed cohort that likes being the center of attention. Boomers have been the subject of the nation's conversation for nearly 60 years, and with the youngest of them only in their early 40s, boomers will likely remain the stars of the show for quite some time to come.

Chapter 15

What's New about Getting Old

Living in an age when scientific and technological "miracles" are almost a matter of course, it's easy to overlook just how remarkable a thing aging is. But consider one startling fact: Throughout 99 percent of all the years that humans have walked this planet, the average life expectancy at birth was less than 18 years. In the past, most people didn't age—they died. —*Ken Dychtwald*

Old age is like everything else. To make a success of it, you've got to start young. —*Fred Astaire*

Forty is the old age of youth; fifty, the youth of old age.
—*Victor Hugo*

In Chapter 14, "A Baby Boom Lexicon," I mentioned that the U.S. baby boom generation was 78 million strong. With their ages spread out over 19 years, that works out to an average of just over 4 million people per year. So from 2011, when the first boomers turn 65, to 2029, when the last of them reaches that chronological milestone, something like 11,000 people *per day* will hit the official retirement age. And the good news is that most of those seniors can expect to live for quite some time. In 1900 life expectancy was between 45 and 50 years. Now, thanks to advances in medicine, improved diet, and the proven cardiovascular benefits of shuffleboard, the average 65-year-old can expect to live another 17 or 18 years.

This is a roundabout way of saying that we're going to be seeing *way* more seniors everywhere we go. In 1946, when the U.S.

baby boom began, there were 11 million people aged 65 or older. According to U.S. Census Bureau prognostications, in 2011 there will be 40 million people who are 65-plus, and by 2029 that group will hit 70 million. That's a lot of Golden Girls and Boys.

This senior tsunami is going to have a ripple effect all through society. Will there be enough workers to pick up the slack created by these retirees? Will there be enough public pension money to support the tens of millions of seniors who'll need it? Can restaurants handle massive numbers of people wanting to eat dinner at five o'clock in the afternoon? These and many other concerns are generating much discussion in congressional hearings, boardrooms, and around the dinner table. And these discussions are generating new words at a furious rate, as you'll see in this chapter.

Words for Seniors

What words should we use to label or describe a person who's getting on in years and is now a bit long in the tooth? Well, I suppose we could use euphemisms such as *getting on in years* and *long in the tooth*. For those who prefer more direct locutions, *old man* and *old woman* have been in the language for hundreds of years, but those are perhaps a bit *too* direct. In a slightly gentler vein, there are also *oldster* (1818) and *old-timer* (1888). More recently we've seen the politically correct phrase *older adult* (1969), which isn't quite as bad as the smirk-inducing PC coinages, **chronologically gifted** (1985) and **rich in age** (1991).

Probably the most popular term nowadays is *senior* (1380), which still has a faint euphemistic aura about it, probably because it at least avoids any direct reference to the word *old*. *Senior* has also spawned many phrases over the years, including *senior citizen* (1938) and relatively new coinages such as **senior discount** (1977), **senior fare** (1980), **seniors' home** (1983), and **senior moment** (1996). The latter, in case you've forgotten, is a momentary lapse in memory, particularly one experienced by a senior citizen. In 2000 it was voted Word of the Year by the staff at *Webster's New World College Dictionary.*

If you want to get truly euphemistic, use the adjective *mature,* or variations on that theme. See, for example, the name of the magazine once published by the American Association of Retired Persons (AARP): *Modern Maturity.* (Interestingly, AARP briefly published a magazine called *My Generation* that was aimed at older baby boomers. Whether this was a nod to the 1965 song by The Who isn't clear. Either way, it was an ironic reference since the song includes the famous line "I hope I die before I get old." Perhaps that's why AARP's current publication is now called simply *AARP The Magazine.*)

Someone who was clearly trying to suck up to seniors came up with the happy phrase *golden ager* way back in 1961. This comes from the phrase *golden age,* a period of great prosperity or achievement. Clearly the sucking up worked because seniors continue to embrace the phrase to this day. The similar phrase *golden years* was coined in 1960 by Del Webb, the builder of the world's first retirement community in Sun City, Arizona. (Talk to seniors for any length of time and inevitably one of them will say something like "I'd like to strangle whoever came up with the term 'golden years.' There's nothing *golden* about them." I'm sure Mr. Webb is sorry.)

As you can see, choosing words to refer to seniors and to old age is a hazardous proposition, and it's only going to get worse as more baby boomers join the club. As I mentioned in Chapter 14, many boomers don't even like the *idea* of being old, much less the reality of it. An indication of what we can expect comes from a 2002 study titled *Recasting Retirement,* published by Civic Ventures and Temple University's Center for Intergenerational Learning. The study asked people ages 50 to 70 what words they preferred to label themselves. The study concluded that "the descriptors that seemed to be most relevant and appealing to people had less to do with age than with credibility and the acknowledgment of accumulated wisdom and life experience." Here are the four most popular terms from the study:

- The Experienced
- Advisors
- Coaches
- Wise Ones

I don't know, somehow I can't picture someone saying "Excuse me, do you offer a Wise Ones' discount?"

The study also found that people don't like terms that were connected with aging or that divided life into sections, including the following:

- Elderly
- Third Agers
- Third Actors
- Retired People
- Older Boomers
- Older People

One can imagine, then, that the melancholic term **late lifer** (1991) isn't too popular in senior circles, especially among baby boomers.

The appearance of **third ager** (1988) on the list is a bit surprising since it comes with a positive pedigree. It's the lexical offspring of the phrase **third age** (1972), which was designed to put a positive spin on old age. The idea is that after youth and middle age comes not a period of decline, but a time of wisdom and freedom that should be welcomed as a new stage of life:

> In his 1999 book "Prime Time," [Marc] Freedman . . . gives voice to the millions of baby boomers poised on the precipice, the transition from middle age to . . . to what? Freedman calls it the **third age**; those of us who have made the leap are **third agers.** The term acknowledges the statistical reality of the modern life span. Retirees, especially those retiring in their 50s, have fully a third of their life left. For many, if not most, there will be many years of healthy, active living. (*Seattle Times,* April 1, 2001)

As I mentioned in the previous chapter, boomers are clinging to their youth by stretching its definition to include their 40s and 50s. However, some folks believe that combining the words "youth" and "50-something" in the same sentence is downright silly. Instead, they take a more realistic approach that extends the concept of *middle age* from the traditional 40s into the 50s and even the 60s. At these older ages, they call this their **second middle age** (1981):

> This event is a 16-day multi-sport competition for people 50 years of age and older. Sixty-five athletic and non-athletic events ranging from tennis, golf, track and field and bowling to bridge and baking are scheduled. . . . Experts agree the key to reaching a healthy **"second middle age"** is staying physically, mentally and socially active with events such as these. (*Sun-Sentinel,* Fort Lauderdale, Fla., December 9, 2001)

Another pro-senior term making the rounds is **prime-timer** (1986), which certainly has a nicer ring than *old-timer*:

> [I]f you're a young-timer . . . learn to accept help without feeling threatened. The older worker doesn't want your job. The **prime-timer** is happy to take care of the day-to-day duties

while you focus on the bigger picture. (*Milwaukee Journal-Sentinel,* November 24, 2002)

Of course, there are always a few insensitive young punks who prefer to look upon the aged with a jocular disdain that produces unflattering terms such as **wrinklies** (1982) and **crumblies** (1982):

> When Ronald Reagan was campaigning for the U.S. presidency, he was asked: "What about the issue of age?" His reply: "I refuse to take advantage of my opponent's youth and inexperience," put things in the right perspective. Some teenagers started to call their parents "the **wrinklies**" or "the **crumblies.**" The parents responded by calling their offspring "the pimplies." It was amazing how quickly the name-calling stopped. (*The Express,* London, September 12, 2002)

The boomers who are now entering the senior stage are the "young old," but 20 years ago they were just the "young." Many of them were, in fact, the young, urban professionals that inspired the term *yuppie.* Those who haven't moved to the country or retired are now the *senior urban professionals,* the **suppies** (1986):

> West Point Market, Akron, Ohio, has been using experiential marketing techniques for some time. Today 30 to 50 tour buses a year come by to see the store. "Grocery shopping is not something that most men and women like to do," says Russ Vernon, chairman, West Point Market . . . Vernon describes his customers as **SUPPIES**: senior, urban professionals. (*Grocery Headquarters,* March 1, 2001)

Another popular semiacronym for seniors is **woopie** (1986) or, curiously, **whoopie,** which is a *well-off older person*:

> Yet the majority of the old are self-sufficient, middle-class consumers with more assets than young couples and with both time and talent to offer society. Poverty is now more a condi-

tion of the young than the old and sociologists discern the emergence of a potent cohort of **woopies**—well-off older people. (*New York Times,* May 24, 1998)

A near synonym is the acronym **WOOF** (1991), short for *well-off, over 50:*

Not surprisingly then, King Size targets the older customer, or what [president Jessie] Bourneuf calls a **WOOF**—well-off, over 50. "They go to Florida, have leisure time, like comfortable clothes and drive luxury cars because they're big." (*Daily News Record,* New York, March 19, 1991)

For some reason, a bunch of these yuppielike terms flourished in the late 1980s, only to sink back into the linguistic muck. Among these were **muppies** (1985), *mature upscale postprofessionals;* **sippies** (1986), *senior, independent pioneers;* and **yeepies** (1987), *youthful, energetic elderly people.*

Active Seniors

The seniors of yesteryear with their stereotypical blue rinses and white shoes and pants up to here were a sedentary lot. Other than a game or two of horseshoes and the odd night out at the bingo parlor, they mostly sat around and had a ball reminiscing about their good times and beginning most sentences with "In my day . . ." That's probably all that *you'd* be up for, too, if you'd lived through a depression and a world war or two.

Twenty-first-century seniors seem to be taking a different approach that involves not taking this aging thing lying down. To them, "graying is playing" (another phrase coined by Del Webb), so they're determined to stay as active as they can:

active adults (1980) *On July 31, Pulte will mark the one-year anniversary of its purchase of Del Webb Corp., the na-*

*tion's largest builder of housing communities for **active adults**. (Detroit News, July 14, 2002)

active aging (1980) An aging process in which people remain active physically and mentally. Also: **active ageing.** *Unfortunately, there are hosts of physiological changes we go through as we age. Many were thought to be unavoidable. However, some of these changes can be modified if we take an "active aging" approach to our lifestyles.* (Richmond Times-Dispatch, March 21, 2002)

The people who practice active aging have their own names:

active old (1987) *What will Americans do for recreation in the next century? "It's unlikely that we'll see much growth in physically demanding activities, despite the image of the new 'active old' in the media," says Warnick. "It's more likely we'll see growth in passive recreation, such as visiting theme parks and taking cruises."* (AScribe Newswire, February 2, 2000)

OPALs (1988) Acronym for Older People with Active Lifestyles) *They might not be as in-your-face with their consumer demands as the young folks, but Older People with Active Lifestyles (**OPALs**) have enough ready cash that businesses are now courting them.* (Tulsa World, June 16, 1997)

Retirees often retire to *active-adult* residences—which are also called, unmemorably, *independent senior living homes*—most of which are built with seniors in mind and only accept people over a certain age, usually 55. (In some developments, only one person in the household has to be at least 55.) However, some areas turn into retirement communities accidentally. Any apartment building or neighborhood where most of the residents have grown old is called a *naturally occurring retirement community,* or **NORC** (1987):

One in four retirees lives in a place where at least half of the residents are older than 60. Contrast that with 6 percent who reside in golden-year nirvanas like Leisure World. Seniors are just like other generations, says University of Wisconsin-Madison Prof. Michael Hunt. They want to be with their peers, "but they also want to be part of the larger community, without the stigma" of being labeled old. Hunt coined the term **NORC** in the 1980s after surveying Madison apartments where the bulk of residents topped 60. (*U.S. News & World Report,* June 4, 2001)

NORCs are "naturally occuring" because many people prefer to **age in place** (1979), a bit of sociology-speak that means continuing to live in your home as you grow old rather than moving to a seniors' residence, nursing home, or your kid's basement. For example, according to a 2001 survey by the American Society of Interior Designers (of all people), approximately 70 percent of folks 55 or older said they were "extremely likely" to stay in their current home. In a 2000 survey sponsored by AARP, 89 percent of respondents 55 or older said they would prefer to stay in their current residence for as long as possible. If you get enough of these **stay-puts** (1985) in the same neighborhood, a retirement community will occur naturally. In some cities (such as New York and Chicago), NORC is an official designation and these communities receive funding for nursing visits, social activities, transportation, and other senior services.

Travel is a big deal for seniors, especially retirees and empty-nester couples with lots of time on their hands. A retired person who travels extensively, particular in a recreational vehicle, is called a **gray nomad** (1997):

Grey nomads—retirees who have decided to hit the road instead of sitting around wondering just how long they have left—have taken over the highways and tracks of Australia in the past decade. (*Sun Herald,* Sydney, Australia, January 12, 2003)

Retired Seniors

In the 1880s German chancellor Otto von Bismarck established the first pension plan in Europe and set the qualification age at 65 (or possibly 70; accounts differ). This was despite the fact that the average worker's life expectancy in those days was a mere 45 years. In any case, 65 became the standard age for retirement, and was used 50 years later, in 1935, when the United States began its Social Security program (when the average life expectancy was 61).

There is much talk these days of *early retirement* (1957), which means stopping working before the statutory retirement age. But in fact the trend seems to have shifted in the opposite direction. Thirty years ago the average age of retirement was 65. That number dropped steadily down to 62 years, but it has now edged back up to 63 years.

Why the rebound? Mostly because many seniors either want or need to keep working and, since most are still healthy, because they *can* keep working. According to the 2000 U.S. census, 4.5 million people over the age of 65 were still working, up substantially from the 3.8 million over-65s who were still on the job in 1997. And this trend is likely to continue. In a survey of **pre-retirees** (1980), AARP reported in 1998 that 80 percent of boomers planned to keep working after 65.

Note, however, that "working" doesn't necessarily mean "working full time." Lots of seniors don't want to quit their jobs cold turkey, so they take the gradual way out:

> **phased retirement** *n.* (1977) The gradual reduction in an employee's working hours as a transition toward retirement. *The looming problem ahead for business is what many economists are starting to call the brain drain, as well-educated and highly skilled boomers begin to make plans to retire. Watson Wyatt's Schieber said that while many*

*boomers—who make up one-third of the workforce—are de-
vising their exit strategy, many employers face being left without key workers. "By 2010, we could have a labor shortage of
up to 10 million workers," he said. "The big challenge for employers will be how to get workers to stay around longer. We
believe part of the solution will be* **phased retirement** *programs with people working an extra two or three years, part
time." (Washington Post, December 8, 2002)*

This is also called a **tapering-off** (1980) program.

Instead of a slow slide into retirement, some employers offer
a kind of trial run where the worker "retires" for a few months
to see how it feels. This is called a **rehearsal retirement** (1980):

> Polaroid has developed what it calls a "flexible work alterna-
> tive" to help senior employees make decisions about retire-
> ment. For example, mature workers can take a **"rehearsal
> retirement,"** a leave of absence for three to six months. They
> are entitled to come back to the same job, no questions asked.
> (*Baltimore Sun*, September 29, 1998)

A similar idea is the **boomerang job** (1998), where a worker
retires but remains "on call" so that he or she can come back to
the company as needed:

> A variation on phased retirement is the so-called **"boomerang
> job,"** in which an employee retires for a few months or a year,
> then bounces back to the company with limited hours. An ex-
> ample is the Monsanto Co.'s so-called Retiree Resource Corps.
> Retirees who participate are called back as needed, with a data-
> base tracking their skills and hours. Monsanto figures
> boomerangers cost 12 to 15 percent less than temporary work-
> ers. (*Baltimore Sun*, September 29, 1998)

Monsanto's Retiree Resource Corps is an example of a **retiree
pool** (1977), a group of retired workers that a company can call on:

Programs like **retiree pools,** job sharing arrangements, part-time work, part-year work, and telecommuting are all attempts to retain older employees by reducing job responsibilities and/or hours worked. (*Government Finance Review,* October 1, 2002)

This is also called a **retire-rehire** (1994) program.

Any job that bridges the gap between a person's career occupation and full retirement is called, appropriately, a **bridge job** (1988):

> In listing what they wanted from **"bridge jobs"** in the later stages of their working lives, the workers surveyed by AARP said they hoped for employment that could sustain them, offer new experiences and provide paid time off and a flexible schedule. Nearly 70 percent of the 45-plus workers said they planned to work in some capacity during their traditional retirement years. (*Times Union,* Albany, N.Y., October 20, 2002)

Those whose bridge job involves working at a McDonald's restaurant are called **McSeniors** (1987).

> On Tuesday, the U.S. House approved a measure to boost Social Security benefits for older Americans who continue to work. Indeed, many seniors without substantial savings or pensions must take low-paying jobs. And those who take those jobs at McDonald's are now being called **"McSeniors."** (*Chicago Tribune,* December 10, 1995)

So Many Seniors

When the first baby boomers turned 40 in 1986, the media were awash in stories about the coming **middle-age boom** (1985). Now, with the oldest boomers already 55 and edging toward 60, the current concern is the coming **old-age boom** (1981), also known as the **retirement age boom** (1993) or simply the **age boom** (1993):

> The shortage of health-care workers comes as the country is undergoing a demographic shift known as the **"Age Boom."** With . . . medical advances contributing to the longevity of the oldest citizens, the surging demand on health-care resources threatens to outstrip supplies by the end of the decade. (*St. Louis Post-Dispatch*, August 18, 2002)

This is also called the **age shift** (1977). For some commentators the nouns *boom* and *shift* aren't strong enough because they think the aging of the population is a pretty big deal. They prefer more sensational phrases such as **demographic time bomb** (1978), **age crisis** (1989), or even **age quake** (1988). However, my favorite phrase is **geezer glut** (1997):

> Now we boomers are over or nearing 50. Though we're still more numerous than any other generation, it's getting silly to speak of us as the baby boom; we're destined to be the **"geezer glut"**—the most tiresome generation in history. (*Las Vegas Review-Journal*, June 1, 1997)

One consequence of the age boom is that many places in the world will begin to look a lot like Florida:

> **Floridization** *n.* (1996) Having a rapidly increasing percentage of senior citizens in the population of a specific geographical area. (Also: **Floridisation**.) *Although the percentage and the sheer volume of elders and people with disabilities living in the United States in the 21st century is increasing, their distribution will vary across the country; the* **Floridization** *of the country will happen in pockets.* (*Nursing Homes*, February 1, 2000)

Why pick on Florida? According to the 2000 U.S. census, the percentage of people aged 65 and over in the United States is 12.4. In Florida alone, however, the percentage of those who are 65-plus is 17.6, the highest of any state. (Hence its unofficial nickname, the "Retirement State.") However, by 2025, it's estimated that 39 out of the 50 U.S. states will have the same or a higher proportion of seniors that Florida does now.

Of course, with great population size comes great political power, and seniors' groups are among the fiercest lobbyists in the land. This new clout is being called **age power** (1988) or **gray power** (1976):

> The face of America is changing. Have you noticed that today wherever you go, you see a silver sea of gray heads with a few balding ones bobbing up in their midst? We dominate the scene in airports, on cruise ships, in restaurants, at the theater and in the shopping malls. Our senior generation is the largest and most affluent of the over-50 population in history and our numbers will increase dramatically with the "boomers" coming of age. . . . We walk, we exercise, we don't smoke, we try to eat right, and we are becoming a **gray power** to be dealt with. (*Corpus Christi Caller-Times,* April 9, 2002)

Seniors as Elders

As you saw earlier, the word *elderly* (1611) comes with lots of negative baggage since it brings up images of frail **super seniors** (1977), the oldest of the old. Strange, then, that these negative images are not projected onto the word *elder,* which has been in the language for at least 1,000 years. Perhaps that's because *elder* means many different things. It's not only an old person, but also a patriarch, a church official, a craftsman, a senator, or just someone older than someone else.

Whatever the reason, *elder* is a positive term, so much so that it has even morphed into a verb:

elder *v.* (1991) To share wisdom and knowledge with people who are younger than oneself. *Thus, we affirm the success of **eldering** or "saging," not aging. Although we admire and love our young, significant wisdom lies with our elders. Those who can recognize this wisdom and incorporate it in their lives, can feel proud of themselves and enjoy life to its fullest.* (*Sun-Sentinel,* Fort Lauderdale, Fla., April 7, 1995)

The state of being an elder is called one's **eldership** (1977) or **elderhood** (1980):

"Too many adults want kids to stop playing and do more, accomplish things, take classes, never be bored. We are robbing them of childhood." Similarly, Thomas said the cult of adulthood pressures older people "to keep producing" whether they retire or not. Our society is "robbing elders of **elderhood**," he said. (*Chicago Tribune,* October 6, 2002)

Childhood is the source for *elderhood,* and a similar linguistic mechanism has converted *childcare* (or *child care*) into **eldercare** (1980) or **elder care**:

One of the best-kept secrets in **eldercare** is adult day services—places where physically and memory-impaired adults can spend the day, have a meal, participate in activities designed for their abilities and—often most important—give their caregivers a break. (*Seattle Times,* August 14, 2002)

A nice tie-in to the whole active aging, graying-is-playing trend is that lots of seniors are getting hitched. I suppose there's no reason why you can't call these freshly hitched seniors *newlyweds,* but lots of folks prefer the more specific term **elderweds** (1990):

In fact, at 65 and thanks to many medical breakthroughs, Ah Kong has a lot of life in him yet. Many of his friends are joining a burgeoning international community of **elderweds,** or those who marry in their 60s, 70s or even 80s. (*The Straits Times,* Kuala Lumpur, Malaysia, January 8, 2002)

Many communities understand that their senior population will increase in the years to come. To prepare for their local age booms, these communities have built low-cost homes for retirees, added ramps to building entrances, and even slowed down their traffic signals to allow for slower-moving seniors. These places describe themselves as **elder-friendly** (1990) or **elder ready** (2000):

To gain **Elder Ready** status, a city must demonstrate that it changed to help the elder population, defined as people 60 years and older, in categories such as transporation, medical services and law enforcement. A city awarded the designation can post signs proclaiming itself **"elder-friendly"** and receive support from the state. (*Business Journal,* July 5, 2002)

Finally, the elderly who are healthy, wealthy, and, optionally, wise are called the **wellderly** (1981):

Medical advances mean older people figure to be more active than before. Dr. Weinstein calls them the **"wellderly"**—retirees with more money and better health than any previous crop. (*Dallas Morning News,* February 15, 2000)

Seniors and Grandparenting

In 2001 an AARP survey found that 15 percent of grandparents provided child care for their grandkids while the parents worked, and nearly 25 percent baby-sat their grandchildren at least once every couple of weeks. These seniors have jumped from parenting to **grandparenting** (1981). Grandmothers, in particular, seem to do a lot of this, and people have taken to calling them **granny nannies** (1987):

> For those fortunate enough to have willing and able parents, the so-called **"granny nannies"** often fill a need by watching kids part-time or during irregular hours such as nights or weekends. (*Seattle Times,* October 16, 2002)

In some households grandparents are the primary or sole caregivers for their grandchildren. These are described as **skipped-generation** (1991; also: **skip-generation**) households:

> The past decade has seen a marked rise in grandparents across the board acting as parents. Often, they are the first safety net for children who are abandoned, whose parents are deemed unfit due to drugs, alcohol, violence or mental illness, whose moms and dads aren't much more than babies themselves. The AARP found the trend significant enough that it founded the Grandparent Information Center in 1993 to assist these caregivers, especially those in **"skipped-generation"** households, where a grandparent is raising a grandchild with no parent in the home. (*Pittsburgh Post-Gazette,* November 25, 2001)

This form of **kinship care** (1990) is becoming commonplace. Recent data from the 2000 U.S. census estimates that nearly 2.4 million grandparents in the United States are raising their children's children. In contrast to what may be a conservative estimate, according to a 1998 survey commissioned by AARP, one out of every nine grandparents—about 8 million out of a total of 70 million—takes care of one or more grandchildren.

Rather than looking after their kids' babies, some grandmothers are looking after their *own* babies. After a **granny pregnancy** (1994) and a **granny birth** (1994), these post-menopausal women become **granny moms** (1993) or **granny mums** (1993):

> Moves to outlaw pregnancies for older women were debated after an outcry over the work of Dr. Severino Antinori. The storm initially broke in Britain after a 59-year-old business-woman gave birth to twins after artificial fertilization at Antinori's Rome clinic. Antinori subsequently revealed that an Italian, Rossana Dalla Corte, who will be 63 in February, is pregnant. Grazia Zuffa, a senator of the Democratic Party of the Left, said, "It seems hypocritical to me that there is this outcry over **'granny-mums'** but if an elderly man fathers a child, it is seen as a sign of virility." (*Los Angeles Times,* December 30, 1993)

These women are also called **menopausal moms** (1987) or, somewhat less kindly, **Methuselah moms** (1994).

With seniors soon to be numbered in the tens of millions, it's a safe bet that this will be a diverse bunch. So it's appropriate that we now have lots of new words and phrases with which to describe members of the senior set: third ager, prime timer, suppie, whoopie, WOOF, OPAL, active adult, stay-put, gray nomad, pre-retiree, McSenior, super senior, elderwed, wellderly, granny nanny, and granny mom. Just don't call them *old.*

Chapter 16

Relationships and Marriage

If Miss means respectably unmarried, and Mrs. respectably married, then Ms. means nudge, nudge, wink, wink.
—*Angela Carter*

Writing is like getting married. One should never commit oneself until one is amazed at one's luck.
—*Iris Murdoch*

I know one husband and wife who, whatever the official reasons given to the court for the breakup of their marriage, were really divorced because the husband believed that nobody ought to read while he was talking and the wife that nobody ought to talk while she was reading.
—*Vera Brittain*

The realm of relationships is a complex world that combines "the same old, same old" with "the new new thing." In the Some Things Never Change department, for example, human beings still practice what sociologists call *homogamy* (1874), the tendency for people to marry and mate with other people who share similar socioeconomic characteristics (such as social rank, race, and a love of all things chocolate). It's also still true that the more education you have, the more likely it is that you'll get married.

According to *American Demographics* magazine, for the past 30 years people with bachelor and graduate degrees have had marriage rates that are anywhere from 10 to 20 percentage points higher than those of people who didn't graduate from high school. (Insert your own ironic comment here about people with *bachelor* degrees having higher *marriage* rates.)

"What's new?" you ask. Well, for one thing, the institution of marriage isn't quite the institution it once was. In 1950 roughly 67 percent of American adults were married. By 1980 that number had dropped to 62 percent, and in 2000 it was down to 56 percent.

But what *marriages* lack in numbers, *weddings* more than make up for in dollars. In 1990 the average cost of a wedding was an eyebrow-raising $15,000. By 2002, according to Conde Nast Bridal Group, that average was a jaw-dropping $22,360, a nearly 50 percent increase in just a dozen years.

Also, the age at which people first get married has had a roller-coasterish ride over the past 100 years or so. If asked nicely, the U.S. Census Bureau will tell you that, in 1890, the median age for a first-time bride was 22 years old and for a first-time groom it was 26.1. These averages dropped steadily all through the first half of the twentieth century and reached their lowest point in the 1950 and 1960 censuses, when the median age for women bottomed out at 20.3 and the age for men hit its nadir of 22.8. But the averages have risen quite quickly ever since, with the women's median age pegged at 25.1 in the 2000 census and the men's age at 26.8.

These are but a few of the ways that the nature of relationships, from dating, to marriage, to divorce, is changing. This chapter examines the words and phrases that reflect these changes.

The Dating Game

The biggest change in the dating scene over the past 10 years or so has been the role that technology plays in getting people together. For example, it's no longer rare to come across a couple

who first met while conversing in an Internet chat room or via
e-mail. This isn't surprising, since most surveys show that at least
75 percent of us rate intelligence and a sense of humor as the
most important mate traits, both of which are readily apparent
in text-only Internet forums. Conversely, only about a third of
us rate attractiveness as a crucial characteristic (and on the
Internet, as the joke goes, no one knows you're a dog).

A budding e-romance gets to the next level with an exchange
of phone numbers or a nerve-wracking face-to-face (F2F in chat
lingo) meeting, which is often referred to, unappetizingly, as a
fleshmeet (1996):

> The Opera Forum is a closely knit group. With 40 or so active
> participants scattered across at least a dozen states and three
> continents, and many more lurkers, members have organized
> two official group **"fleshmeets,"** and several members have at-
> tended the opera together in various cities. (*New York Times*,
> October 4, 2001)

(The world's geeks and technophiles have a reputation for
being, oh, let's be nice and say, *socially challenged*. According to
the stereotype, they'd rather code than converse, and if they
must do the latter, they'd rather do it online than in person.
That this is true is borne out by their willful tendency to coin
mildly repulsive words for things like the real world—for example, **meatspace** [1995]—and getting together with people in the
real world—*fleshmeet*. Of course, another stereotypical geek trait
is a lack of personal hygiene, so perhaps their face-to-face meetings result in an olfactory ambiance ripe enough to inspire only
nauseating neologisms.)

Spending time together in the real world as opposed to the
online world is called **face time** (1996, although sales types have
used *face time* to mean "time spent face-to-face" since at least the
early 1980s):

John and Heather duly dispatched their pictures, both of which showed pleasant, open, plumpish faces. Both liked what they saw, but there still remained the underlying worry that neither might be the person they said they were. It was not until eight months after they first made computer contact that the couple finally secured what is termed **"face time"**—a meeting in person. (*Daily Telegraph,* London, May 10, 1996)

Technology is not only helping couples meet, but it's also helping couples who've already met learn about each other, although in a somewhat clandestine way. On January 15, 2001, the *New York Observer* ran a story about this new form of dating research: using the Google Internet search engine to look for information related to a new or potential girlfriend or boyfriend. The article was titled, "Don't Be Shy, Ladies—Google Him!":

On a recent, freezing December night, I met a great guy at a bar in midtown. He was thick-haired and handsome, smart with a good sense of humor and, on top of that, he was an excellent dancer. As I waited in the coat check line, we flirted and exchanged business cards. A few hours later, I **Googled** him.

Like many of my twentysomething peers in New York's dating jungle, I have begun to use Google.com, as well as other online search engines, to perform secret background checks on potential mates. It's not perfect, but it's a discreet way of obtaining important, useless and sometimes bizarre information about people in Manhattan—and it's proven to be as reliable as the scurrilous gossip you get from friends.

Ever since, people have been using **Google** as a verb in this sense. (There's also a more general sense of the verb that means "to use Google to search for information." As I mentioned in Chapter 6, Google Inc. frowns upon this usage, but this verbal cat is already out of the trademark bag.) This has also been called **Google dating** (2002), and the latest definition of *blind date* is to go out with someone without having first Googled that person.

A few years ago the *Washington Post* reported that Japanese teenagers were meeting potential girlfriends and boyfriends by *random dialing*: dialing numbers harum-scarum on their cell phones and talking to anyone who "sounds cute." Around the same time, a new device took Japanese teens (a famously faddish bunch) by storm:

> **love beeper** *n.* (1998) A device that comes in "male" and "female" versions and that beeps if another person with an opposite-sex beeper comes within range. Also: **lovegety.**
> *Those chirps you hear on the streets of Tokyo these days are . . . the latest in lusty technology: the **love beeper**. . . . The Lovegety even has three settings to let your intended know your intentions: "karaoke," when you're in the mood to croon; "chat," for that thing some people actually do outside the Internet; and "friends," for, well, those times when you really do want to rub your back legs together. If someone's sending "karaoke" when your beeper's set for "chat," the red light flashes; if you're both on the same wavelength, it's a green light to l'amour. (Moscow Times, June 6, 1998)*

A similar device was the *MatchLinc,* which stored the answers to 64 personal questions. Using an infrared link, the device compared one person's answers with those on another person's MatchLinc and then pronounced a compatibility score (from "perfect" to "forget it").

All this technology might (and I emphasize the word *might*) be helping turn strangers into couples, but once they get to that stage, people still need to do the emotional heavy lifting to make a relationship work. Many people just can't do it:

batmobiling *pp.* (1995) Putting up emotional defenses when a relationship becomes too intimate. *Meredith (Gillian Anderson) is a frosty, uptight theatre director being romanced by an architect (John Stewart), but she is, as we say in the 90s,* **batmobiling**; *her defenses are up.* (*The Guardian,* London, August 6, 1999)

This word comes from the shield that protects the Batmobile, the vehicle used by comic book hero Batman. Batmobiling types often prefer their own company, which is why they have no trouble ending relationships. They've somehow managed to avoid the **single stigma** (1999), the belief that there is something inherently wrong with being single:

Don't fall for the **single stigma.** There's nothing wrong with being single and, contrary to how you might feel, you've got lots of company. (*The Plain Dealer,* Cleveland, February 13, 2000)

Having "lots of company" is an understatement. The U.S. Census Bureau's Current Population Survey for 2000 tells us that there are more than 96 million single people over the age of 15. Of those, the number of people who have *never* been married was 59.9 million, up from 52.5 million in 1990. That's a lot of **never-marrieds** (1977):

Here's another drawback for the **"never-marrieds"**: Some surveys show that married people, especially men, live longer than their unmarried counterparts. (*San Antonio Express-News,* June 30, 2002)

If there was a "likely-never-will-be-married" category, here's a guy who'd fit right in:

toxic bachelor *n.* (1995) An unmarried man who is selfish, insensitive, and afraid of commitment. *I hope no one*

gave you The Rules for Christmas, girls, because I'm afraid
that the idea that men could be brought to heel, like dogs, is
completely over. There is a triumphalist whiff of testosterone
*in the air—the **toxic bachelor,** formerly known as the cad,*
the rake, the bounder and the ladykiller, is back in town.
(*Independent on Sunday,* London, January 6, 2002)

This phrase was coined by Candace Bushnell in one of her original "Sex and the City" columns for the *New York Observer* in
the mid-1990s.

Such a man dreads the **DTR** (2001), the "define the relationship" conversation:

Each week we sat in the car/And had another **DTR** . . . Excuse
me, I said, when my students read their work aloud. Don't you
mean CTR? No, they said. We mean **DTR**—as in "Define the
Relationship." And then my student Ted added that they are
to be avoided at all costs. (*Deseret News,* February 6, 2003)

The toxic bachelor is often a **himbo** (1988), a man who is
good-looking, but unintelligent or superficial:

After three Garbage albums, Manson hasn't yet become a tedious pop princess. Undeniably charismatic, she can be distin-
guished from most of the pop world's thrusting teens and
vainglorious **himbos** by one easy test: she has opinions.
(*Sydney Morning Herald,* January 25, 2002)

The word *himbo* is the result of a linguistic sex-change operation
that sutured the male pronoun *him* onto the usually feminine
insult *bimbo.* (Although *bimbo* is often dressed in a gender-
neutral suit that gives it a meaning similar to *bozo;* that is, a stupid or useless person.)

Himbo is a better blend than the less intelligible *mimbo* (male bimbo) mix that was coined in a *Seinfeld* episode. Although that neologism should have been forgotten, the power of the show was such that *mimbo* has had a steady run in the media since it first appeared in 1994. In fact, the *Seinfeld* writers had a singular genius for coming up with new words that illuminated the quirks and little-noticed truths of the dating scene. Here's a sampling:

bad-breaker-upper *n.* A person who breaks up with other people in a mean or messy way. *There's a short window of breakup opportunity between Thanksgiving and Christmas. . . . If you miss that . . . you're better off waiting until after New Year's. It's just kinder. And you don't want to be labeled the **bad-breaker-upper.*** (*Maryland Gazette,* January 1, 2003)

face-to-face breakup *n.* A breakup that occurs in person. *Obviously, some relationships warrant a **face-to-face breakup,** but if it's a minor relationship, you can make it over the phone.* (*Chicago Tribune,* November 21, 2001)

get-out-of-relationship-free card *n.* Something that enables a person to easily end a relationship. *If the contestants weren't so forgettable, "Temptation Island" would be a fun, trashy show. It's a **get-out-of-relationship-free card.*** (*Charlotte Observer,* January 20, 2001)

pre-emptive breakup *n.* A breakup performed before the other person can break up with you. *Mr. Shear's new songs . . . —like "The Last in Love," about a **pre-emptive breakup**—are two-character vignettes.* (*New York Times,* March 17, 1998)

relationship killer *n.* A mistake or action that dooms a relationship. *Though easier to repair, even long-term relationships cannot withstand the more serious mistakes, such as betrayal.*

(continued on next page)

> *Richardson and Vidaurreta refer to irreparable relationship mistakes as **"relationship killers."*** (Scripps Howard News Service, June 6, 2002)
>
> **separatée** *n.* A person who is separated (cf. *divorcée*). *The imaginative "Suddenly Single" program . . . positions The Envoy Club as a sympathetic heartbreak hotel offering distraught divorcées and/or **separatées** an aromatherapy candle . . . and a session with a psychic.* (*Real Estate Weekly,* June 16, 1999)
>
> **spongeworthy** *adj.* Worthy of having sex with, particularly when it requires the use of a contraceptive sponge. *One can easily imagine* A History of the Wife *spawning several more interesting and focused books, like* A History of Marital Contraception (*note the set of cervical caps, circa 1925, lined up in a row like bowler hats; and who knew that women were deeming men **"spongeworthy"** as early as the 1840's?*). (*New York Observer,* January 19, 2001)

A member in good standing of the never-marrieds club is the **quirkyalone** (2000), a person who enjoys being single and so prefers to wait for the right person to come along rather than dating indiscriminately:

Today is International **Quirkyalone** Day, a four-city, two-continent celebration of what it means to be single and happy, not dependent on a relationship for self-worth. (*San Francisco Chronicle,* February 14, 2003)

A similar term is **leather spinster** (1998), a heterosexual or asexual woman who is happily unmarried and has no desire to seek a mate.

Marriage: Nuptial Neologisms

As I mentioned at the top of the chapter, the number of people who are married has dropped steadily since the 1950s, to the point where it's possible that by 2010, the unmarrieds will out-number the marrieds for the first time ever. That seems likely *unless* you also consider another rapidly growing demographic category: *unmarried partners*. According to the U.S. Census Bureau, in 1960 there were 439,000 "unmarried-couple" house-holds, a number that includes unmarried partners *and* people who were just friends who shared a roof. By 2000 the number of households that consisted of unmarried partners had jumped to 3,820,000, nearly a ninefold increase. (For comparison, the total number of unmarried-couple households was 4,736,000.) So while fewer people may be getting married, there are plenty of others who are shacking up together instead.

None of this is to suggest that marriage is in any way irrele-vant. Surveys show that 90 percent of high school seniors want to get married someday. In movies and television shows, people who don't want to get married are more often than not por-trayed as neurotic, while the marriage-friendly singles are shown as smart, romantic types who just haven't found Mr. or Ms. Right. Our culture glorifies marriage and looks down on singles and mere cohabiters. We live in a **marriage culture** (1991), which is splendidly illustrated by the following excerpt from *The Marriage Movement: A Statement of Principles,* a 2000 doc-ument signed by over 100 writers, researchers, religious leaders, and pro-family types:

> Whether an individual ever personally marries or not, a healthy **marriage culture** benefits every citizen in the United States: rich or poor, churched or unchurched, gay or straight, liberal or conservative, parent or childless, African American,

Hispanic, Anglo, Asian or Native American. Marriage is not a conservative or liberal idea, not a plaything of passing political ideologies. Marriage is a universal human institution, the way in which every known society conspires to obtain for each child the love, attention and resources of a mother and a father.

Pamela Paul, writing in her book *The Starter Marriage,* calls this **matrimania** (2000):

Paul cites a "marriage culture" that promotes **"matrimania."** "Not only is it a lonely world out there on your own, but choosing to be there is downright un-American." (*USA Today,* January 29, 2002)

So plenty of people still get married every year. The United States hosted 2.3 million marriages in 2001, a number that, surprisingly, hasn't changed much since the early 1970s. (So why are there fewer married people now? Because the *marriage rate* has fallen. In the 1940s the rate was about 13 marriages for every 1,000 people. By 1970 the rate had fallen to 10.5, and in 2001 it was down to 8.5.) That's a lot of ceremonies to plan, and it's a lot of stress for the betrothed, particularly a fiancée who *really, really* wants her wedding day to be just right:

bridezilla *n.* (1995) A bride-to-be who, while planning her wedding, becomes exceptionally selfish, greedy, and obnoxious. (*Bride + Godzilla*). Also: **bride-zilla.** *The tricky thing about **Bridezillas** is that their transition from sweethearts to creatures from hell cannot be foreseen, not even by the future husbands. "They are perfectly normal women— until they get a ring," says Ms. Spaemme. "They run around screaming: 'It is my day! Bow down and kiss my feet!' They demand attention, gifts and money and treat family and friends like servants." (Dallas Morning News,* August 27, 2002)

When the bridezilla goes on a rampage, she is said to be **going bridal** (2000), a nice play on *going postal* (which I discussed in Chapter 4, "Modern Angst and Anger").

Bridal showers are part and parcel of the wedding preparations, of course, but you can bet your average bride-to-be wouldn't be at all pleased if a certain kind of gift-giving becomes popular:

> **regift** *v.* (1995) To give as a gift something that one received as a gift.——**regifter** *n. Call it tacky, rude, maybe even thoughtless, but "regifting" is about as ritualistic as giving away that lump of jellied fruit every year. A two-year study of appalling habits has found that most Americans have done it. According to the study, reported in Bernice Kanner's book* Are You Normal?, *54 percent of Americans rewrap, rebox and resend unwanted presents.* (*Wilmington Star-News,* December 3, 1995)

The verb *regift* is yet another *Seinfeld* coinage. *Regift* (and the noun *regifter)* appeared in the episode titled "The Label Maker," which first aired on January 19, 1995. It took a while, but regift eventually embedded itself in the language. The proof? I found dozens of media citations that used the word without referencing its Seinfeldian origins. That's not surprising since the word fills a language gap and succinctly describes something that the majority of us have done.

Despite all the gift-giving that goes on not only in the various prewedding showers, but also at the ceremony itself, weddings can still cost a couple an absurd amount of money. (It's not called the **marital-industrial complex** [1993] for nothing.) In 1999 a man named Tom Anderson tried to change all that. He's a Philadelphia entrepreneur who was getting married at the same time that he was trying to start a business. "It occurred to me that a startup company and a startup couple both need launch money," he told the *New York Times* in 2000. He must be quite a salesman because he talked two dozen companies into paying for all but $4,000 of the wedding's princely $30,000 price tag. A newswire picked up the story, and Mr. Anderson and his bride ended up on the *Oprah Winfrey Show*. Thus was assured the popularity of a new kind of wedding:

> **sponsored wedding** *n.* (1995) A wedding in which some or all of the costs, products, or services are provided by local businesses in exchange for exposure or publicity. *Batista and Robinson, who have daughters aged 4, 2, and 1, saw a rerun of that "Oprah" segment last year. They looked at each other and nodded. Yes, they decided, as if thinking in unison, they'd do it. Of course, few brides are as ambitious as Batista. She was deter-mined to have the first fully* **sponsored wedding**—*an event that would cost the couple nothing at all. It took a year of ex-treme persistence [but] she persuaded approximately 35 business owners to give away goods and services valued at $40,000.* (*Philadelphia Inquirer,* September 1, 2001)

If "sponsorship rites" (as one headline-writing punster called a sponsored wedding) are out of the question, some people cut their wedding costs to the bone by not inviting anyone. Or, more specifically, by inviting people to attend only from the comfort of their own home:

> **Webcast wedding** *n.* (2000) A wedding ceremony broad-cast via streaming video over the World Wide Web. *When Lori Dickinson and Tyson Reiser walk down the aisle on Wednesday evening, most of their guests will be in pyjamas. The couple, from Waterloo, Ont., will say their vows in a Las Vegas chapel with 10 of their closest friends and family on hand. But another 40 or 50 people will be at home, watching the wedding live on the Internet after Ms. Dickinson, 28, and*

*Mr. Reiser, 30, sent out e-mail invitations for the **Webcast wedding** to family and friends in British Columbia, Calgary and Manitoba.* (*The Globe and Mail,* Toronto, February 4, 2002)

This is also called a **Web wedding** (2000) and **Net nuptials** (1997).

The opposite idea is to move the entire wedding, lock, stock, and napkin rings, to an exotic locale:

destination wedding *n.* (1990) A wedding that takes place out of town, usually at a vacation resort. *With parents not necessarily footing the wedding bill these days and couples looking for more wedding bang for the buck, **destination weddings** can be a thrifty alternative. A couple can save travel expenses with a wedding-honeymoon combination trip, and a smaller guest list can mean substantial savings.* (*Times Union,* Albany, N.Y., June 30, 2002)

In 1996, 65,000 couples opted for destination weddings to avoid the usual hassles associated with wedding ceremonies (guest lists, bands, drunken uncles, and so on). In a 2002 study by Conde Nast Bridal Infobank, 8 percent of couples said they were planning a destination wedding, which translates to roughly 180,000 such remote ceremonies, almost triple the number from just six years earlier. Destination weddings have an added benefit of giving the couple an instantly romantic location for their honeymoon, which is why these things are also called **weddingmoons** (1995):

A budget planner is included and costs can be cut by planning ahead and scrimping on little things in order to splurge when it matters. Many couples today are opting for **"weddingmoons"**— combining their wedding and honeymoon into one special trip. (*Sunday Advocate,* Baton Rouge, La., February 3, 2002)

Another variation on this theme is the **familymoon** (1999), a honeymoon in which the bride and groom also bring their children from previous marriages:

"We didn't want Conner to feel excluded," said New Yorker Craig Linden, whose 5-year-old stepson joined the couple for their wedding and honeymoon in Hawaii. "It was a **familymoon**." (*Ventura County Star*, August 19, 2001)

Gay Relationships

The subculture of gays and lesbians has always had a strong linguistic component to it, most notably in the words they use to describe each other. For example, the word *gay* has been in the language since the early fourteenth century, and for hundreds of years it meant "lighthearted, joyful, merry." By the 1930s, however, male homosexuals had begun using the word to describe their own kind, and by the 1950s the word was firmly entrenched (in America, anyway) as a euphemism for a homosexual. Consider, too, the word *queer*, which first appeared as a homosexual slur in the 1920s, but by the 1980s it had been appropriated by the gay community ("We're here, we're queer, get used to it!")

The gay community also isn't shy about coining new words. For example, one of the most popular gay neologisms is **gaydar** (1992), an intuitive sense that enables someone to identify whether another person is gay:

Not only is the architecture gorgeous in South Beach, but so are the people. The week I was visiting, the Art Deco District was crammed with the kind of thin, neat European men that can put even the sharpest of **gaydars** to the test. (*Boston Globe*, March 23, 2003)

Note, too, that gaydar also refers to the gay take on the love beeper theme. It was a device that came with a "gay/lesbian" switch on the back and that beeped if another person with the device on the same setting came within range.

Another useful coinage is **gayby boom** (1990; pronounced GAY-bee), a sharp increase in the number of gay parents, which includes lesbians having babies and same-sex couples adopting children:

> But gay leaders have also begun fighting for a slate of family rights including social security, medical benefits, inheritance, child custody and even gay marriage. For a growing number of homosexual men and women, such family concerns are a day-to-day reality: a new generation of gay parents has produced the first-ever **"gayby boom."** (*Newsweek,* March 12, 1990)

Gays sometimes condescendingly refer to straights as **breeders** (1981), but if the hetero person is one who wonders what it would be like to be with a gay, then they call that person **bi-curious** (1992; also: **bicurious**):

> Jill Hanrahan and Michael Wynter lived as a couple for 2½ years. Nowadays they're the best of friends. Wynter is an "out" bisexual while Hanrahan is in a committed straight relationship. She admits to being **"bi-curious,"** even though she says she can't imagine ever having a proper relationship with another woman. (*Sydney Morning Herald,* February 25, 2003)

(For the record, **bi** [1972] is short for *bisexual* and refers to a person who is attracted to both sexes.) A woman might succumb to **bi-curiosity** (1990) when she goes off to college, only to revert to a straight lifestyle when she returns home. In this case she's a **LUG** (1993), a lesbian until graduation:

> **LUG** is what gay America calls a modern social phenomenon: Lesbians Until Graduation, women who experiment with gay sexuality for just as long as they are cocooned within the world

of higher education, then nervously ditch it the second they leave in favour of marriage, kids and/or jobs. (*The Guardian*, London, June 21, 2002)

A former lesbian is often labeled a **hasbian** (1990):

Say that you'd only just got used to telling your friends your daughter was a lesbian and do not relish having to inform them that she is now a **hasbian**. (*The Dominion*, Wellington, New Zealand, November 20, 1995)

This word appears to be a play on the phrase *has-been*, a person who was once important or popular but is now largely forgotten. Given such a less-than-flattering association, can there be any doubt that this word was coined by women who are still lesbians? A much rarer synonym for this term is **wasbian** (1999).

Another oft-seen gay coinage is **gay vague** (1997), advertising designed to appeal to gays but in a subtle way that wouldn't be noticed by most straight consumers:

And on the night of [Ellen's] coming-out party, Volkswagen ran an intriguing commercial featuring two young men driving a Golf hatchback. The pair stop to pick up a chair discarded at the curb. Michael Wilke . . . calls the add **"gay vague."** "Many people turned to each other and said, 'What's going on here? Are they a gay couple?' " Wilke said. "Generally, straight people who watch the ad presume they are roommates; gay people who watch the ad presume they are a couple." (Knight Ridder, September 6, 2002)

Finally, consider **post-gay** (1991), a movement with the goal of enabling homosexuals to define their identity by something other than their sexual preference:

But this is McGinley's moment, and he's seized it with a fearlessness that's hard to resist. Even more than Tillmans and

LaBruce, he's the perfect embodiment of the **post-gay** sensibility: a horny queer kid who's not alienated, not conflicted, and not apologetic. Though his subjects are primarily male, their sexuality isn't really an issue. (*Village Voice,* March 11, 2003)

D-I-V-O-R-C-E

Ask just about anyone what's happening with divorce these days and they'll probably tell you that things are bad: Marriages don't last and more people are getting divorced than ever before. That marital pessimism is probably based on two grim-looking statistics from the U.S. Census Bureau and the National Center for Health Statistics (NCHS):

1. The number of people who are divorced rose to 21.6 million people in 2000, a 30 percent leap from the 16.6 million divorcés and divorcées in 1990.
2. The number of divorces in 2001 was a little over 1.1 million, or about half the number of marriages.

All the first stat really tells you is that people continue to get divorced, which is no surprise. As for the second stat, the number of divorces has been half the number of marriages since the late 1970s, which is the source of the entrenched idea that the "divorce rate" is 50 percent. However, when you look at the *real* divorce rate—defined as the number of divorces per 1,000 people (that is, the total number of married and unmarried adults)—a different, and more optimistic, picture emerges. In 1980 the divorce rate was 5.2. It fell to 4.7 in 1990 and then dropped again to 4.0 in 2001, a decrease of about 25 percent over 20 years.

Or look at it another way: In 2001 there were 56 million marriages in the United States and 1.1 million divorces. So less than 2 percent of marriages failed in that year, a comfortingly small percentage that has remained fairly constant for the past 25 years or so.

I should point out, however, that the news is much more pessimistic for first marriages, especially in the early days. According to the NCHS, the probability of a first marriage ending in divorce or separation within five years is 20 percent. (For the sake of comparison, note that the probability of a breakup within the first five years of unmarried partners living together is nearly 50 percent.) This finding has inspired a new coinage:

> **starter marriage** *n.* (1994) A first marriage that lasts only a short time and that ends in a clean divorce: no children, no property, no acrimony. ***Starter marriages,*** *like all marriages, are meant to last forever. But they don't. Instead, they fizzle out within five years, always ending before children begin.* (Pamela Paul, *The Starter Marriage,* 2002)

Starter marriage is meant to be a play on *starter home* (1976), a home that's inexpensive enough to be affordable to first-time buyers, but requires some maintenance and repair work. The big difference is a young couple knows from the beginning that a starter home requires much work, but it's unlikely that a couple embarking on what will turn out to be a starter marriage have any thoughts about "repairing" their relationship. The flaws in a starter marriage are apparent only after the fact. For this reason, many people prefer one of the many starter marriage synonyms, particularly *first marriage,* or one of the more recent coinages, such as **icebreaker marriage** (1999), **practice marriage** (1995), or **training marriage** (2002).

Some people remain married but seek a divorce in the hereafter, so to speak:

> **postmortem divorce** *n.* (2003) A stipulation that one must be buried separately from one's deceased spouse. *A*

*growing number of Japanese women trapped in unhappy mar-riages, for whom divorce and separation are unthinkable, are opting for freedom beyond the grave by secretly arranging to be buried apart from their husbands. "In Japan, many women stay with their husbands even though their feelings towards him are cold and they sleep in separate rooms. That way they are economically supported by their husbands," said Haruyo Inoue, a writer who has coined the term "**post mortem di-vorce**." (Daily Telegraph,* London, February 22, 2003)

Wedding ceremonies are getting so expensive that you wouldn't think people would have even the barest inclination to fork out more dollars for a ceremony to mark a divorce, but it does happen:

unwedding ceremony *n.* (2001) A formal ceremony held to celebrate a couple's divorce and to acknowledge their married life. *Now that divorce is an established cultural tra-dition, and no longer stigmatised as a shameful moral failing, increasing numbers of incompatible Americans are choosing to solemnise the break-up of their marriages with an "**un-wedding ceremony**"—often in church with a reception af-terwards—which acknowledges their shared life and marks their amicable separation as a couple.* (Sunday Express, London, June 17, 2001)

Unwedding ceremony appears to be hot off the lexical presses, with the above citation being the earliest I could find. What isn't new, however, is the idea of having a ceremony for a divorce. In fact, I've been able to trace the phrase **divorce ceremony** back over 20 years:

To divorce lecturer and author Rabbi Earl Grollman of Temple Beth El in Belmont, Mass., divorce can be even more trau-matic than death. "The big difference is, death has closure, it's over," says Grollman, who performs **divorce ceremonies** for families. "With divorce, it's never over." (*Newsweek,* February 11, 1980)

A divorce ceremony of any kind ought to help ease the pain of a failed marriage, particularly if it means the couple can remain friends (or, at least, not enemies). But many newly divorced people require more formal counseling, such as therapy sessions or the new **divorce recovery programs** (1986) that can now be found in most major centers:

> The Rev. Marilyn Dickson runs Northway Christian Church's **divorce recovery program,** one of the longest-running of its kind in Dallas. She says she's seen more older people attending the sessions in recent years, and they often face different issues than younger participants. The financial issues in pre-retirement years, the fear of facing the rest of life alone, and adjusting to a whole new reality later in life are just some of the differences. (*Dallas Morning News,* September 15, 2002)

To almost any divorcée, the man she was once married to is now her *ex-husband.* But some women don't like the harsh *ex-* prefix, so they've come up with an alternative name:

> **wasband** *n.* (1990) A woman's ex-husband. *Her husband of more than two decades—a musician in the r&b band in which she sang when she was 18—didn't like the idea of Marie setting off on a new career. He's now her "**wasband,**" as she puts it.* (*Boston Herald,* May 10, 2002)

So far no one's come up with an equivalent neologism for an ex-wife. However, we do know what to call the current wife of a woman's ex-husband and the ex-wife of a woman's current husband. In both cases, call her a **stepwife** (1990; also: **step-wife**):

> "We never really knew what to call each other," Ms. Oxhorn-Ringwood said. "When Evan was a kid, I would call Louise my ex-

husband's new wife, but after 10 years I couldn't do that anymore. We came up with **stepwives** to describe the relationship between ex-wives and current wives." (*New York Times,* May 12, 2002)

The above citation hints that the women mentioned—Louise Oxhorn and Lynne Oxhorn-Ringwood—coined the term *step-wife,* but that's not true. That honor goes to writer Phyllis Stevens who published a novel called *Stepwives* in 1990.

In a world of fleshmeets and face time where you Google someone you've met with your love beeper in the hope that he doesn't turn out to be a batmobiling toxic bachelor or himbo who's a bad-breaker-upper, it's amazing that *anyone* gets together, much less gets married. But our marriage culture ensures that matrimony remains a desired state, even if rushing into things does lead to more starter marriages and unwedding ceremonies. At least the exes can divide the spoils from their sponsored weddings, as long as the guests don't do too much regifting.

Chapter 17

People Who Work at Home

> Perhaps the rapid development of household microcomputing systems would make it possible to conduct business at home, combining motherhood, and even fatherhood, more readily with commerce.
> —*editorial from* American Demographics, *January 1979*

> I call it Digital Marxism: In an age of inexpensive computers, wireless handheld devices, and ubiquitous low-cost connections to a global communications network, workers can now own the means of production. —*Daniel Pink*

> A man is a success if he gets up in the morning and does what he wants to do. —*Bob Dylan*

> I wonder why a company pays to transport a 170-pound body twenty miles downtown when all it needs is the body's three-pound brain. —*Peter Drucker*

Until about 200 years ago, most people worked in the place where they lived. Farmers had their fields and livestock right outside the door, and tradespeople of all descriptions had their tools inside the house: Weavers weaved on handlooms, spinners spun on spinning wheels, bakers baked in ovens. Workers who needed more room—blacksmiths with their anvils and forges, woodworkers with their saws and benches—most often had a workshop next to the house. Home was work and work was home, and separating the two would never have occurred to most people.

All that changed when the Industrial Revolution came rumbling along. Its muscular machinery mass-produced goods formerly crafted by hand, and the great bulk of its hulking factories and warehouses required huge tracts of land outside of cities and towns. The world's butchers, bakers, and candlestick makers had no choice but to leave their homes to ply their trades (or, more likely, some repetitive and soul-destroying subset of a trade) in these faraway enterprises. As a result, for the better part of 200 years, most workers have been leaving their homes and hi-ho, hi-hoing their way to work.

But now a "post-Industrial" revolution is taking shape as a steady stream of workers abandon their traditional employment locales and bring their work home. In 2002, 13 million corporate employees in the United States worked at home at least once a week, and 4 million of those were working at home full time. By some estimates there may also be as many as 24 million home-based businesses, and roughly three out of four employees say they aspire to work at home. That steady stream is beginning to look more like a raging flood.

For language hounds, raging sociological floods have the added advantage of churning up lots of new words and phrases, and I'll take you through a bunch of them in this chapter.

In the early 1970s, the OPEC oil embargo shocked North America into looking for new ways to save energy. University of Southern California researcher Jack Nilles wondered if there were ways to use technology to reduce the amount of commuting that workers had to suffer through each day. Nilles estimated that cutting commuting trips by 20 percent would save nearly 200,000 barrels of oil per day. In 1973 he submitted a report to the National Science Foundation and in the process coined a new word:

> **telecommuting** *n.* (1973) Using communications technologies as a substitute for commuting to the office. *Studies have shown that federal managers are skeptical of **telecom-***

muting, *partly because it complicates efforts to staff offices*
and carry out unexpected tasks. But Wolf has argued that
telecommuting *will cut down on traffic congestion, air pol-*
lution and real estate costs. (*Washington Post,* May 23, 2002)

Telecommuting means working at home instead of the office of
one's employer, especially while maintaining a connection to the
office via telephone, fax, and Internet connection. By the late
1970s firms such as Blue Cross/Blue Shield, Control Data, and
Continental Illinois had instituted **work-at-home** (1978) programs for data-entry clerks, insurance adjusters, computer programmers, and other **telecommuters** (1975).

No one knows who the first telecommuter was, but a case
could be made that it was none other than John D. Rockefeller,
the Standard Oil tycoon. According to biographer Ron
Chernow in *Titan: The Life of John D. Rockefeller Sr.,* Rockefeller
liked to work at home: "By his mid-thirties, he had installed a
telegraph wire between home and office so that he could spend
three or four afternoons each week at home, planting trees, gardening, and enjoying the sunshine. Rockefeller didn't do this in
a purely recreational spirit but mingled work and rest to pace
himself and improve his productivity."

There are millions of telecommuters, so it's not surprising
that this species of worker comes in a variety of forms, including the following:

hard-core telecommuter *n.* (1991) Someone who
telecommutes at least 20 hours per week. *We find that just*
1.5 per cent of non-agricultural workers are "hard-core"
telecommuters, *spending at least 20 hours per week at home.*
These results suggest strongly that telecommuting is a part-
time endeavour. Only 22 per cent of the 7 million workers we
classify as telecommuters work more than 20 hours per week
at home. (*Urban Studies,* April 1, 2002)

high-tech telecommuter *n.* (1993) Someone who telecommutes using a modem or high-speed connection (as opposed to, say, just a phone). *She's resident painter in a remote "media ranch" on the mountain's Pacific Ocean side, above meandering Lobitos Creek. It's a 21st century commune that may signal an emerging trend in an area whose bucolic—and increasingly expensive—ambience has been growing in popularity among **high-tech telecommuters** from Silicon Valley and San Francisco's Multimedia Gulch. (San Francisco Chronicle, April 27, 2000)*

wage-and-salary telecommuter *n.* (1999) Someone who works at home but is employed by a company (as opposed to a self-employed worker who is on contract with a company). *The Bureau of Labor Statistics' tally of job-related home workers is the most conservative, based on its 1998 Current Population Survey. By the BLS's reckoning, the number of people who said they performed some of their work at home for their primary job in 1997—including everyone from teachers catching up on lesson plans, to **wage-and-salary telecommuters** on the company time clock, to those who were self-employed and operating home-based businesses—increased since 1991, the last time such data was collected, but modestly, up from 20 million to 21.4 million. (American Demographics, June 1999)*

Other synonyms for the telecommuter include **work-at-home agent** (or simply a **home agent**; both terms are from 1990) and **stay-at-home worker** (1981). If the home is on the range or in some other rural setting, then the homeworker becomes a **modem cowboy** (1993) or **modem cowgirl** (1997):

Bozeman, Mont., has more than 60 high-tech firms in a town of 35,000. Freed by FedEx and the Internet, **"modem cow-**

boys" (and cowgirls) move here for our high environmental quality. (*Washington Times*, September 17, 2000)

If an employee takes some paperwork or a notebook computer from the office and spends an hour or two working at home, he or she's a **day-extender** (1994). (The latter reminds me of a cartoon by Bruce Eric Kaplan. It shows Death sitting in an easy chair with a scythe while his wife glares at him from the couch. There are corpses lying around the living room. The caption is "So I brought a little work home with me. Big deal.")

What kinds of jobs do these stay-at-homebodies have? Telecommuting doesn't work for all jobs, but there are some that are more appropriate than others, including: accountant, architect, attorney, auditor, bookkeeper, computer programmer, data entry clerk, graphic artist, insurance broker, journalist, lobbyist, researcher, salesperson, systems analyst, technical writer, and telemarketer. When the first data-entry clerks began working at home in the late 1970s, they were often known as **cottage keyers** (1981):

> Some people could not work at all except at home. "I have a small child and don't have to get a baby-sitter," said Terry Medlin of Columbia, S.C., one of Blue Cross-Blue Shield's four **"cottage keyers."** (*New York Times*, March 12, 1981)

Why *cottage?* That bit of whimsy was probably inspired by the futurist Alvin Toffler, who coined the phrase **electronic cottage** in his 1980 book *The Third Wave*.

Although some 70 percent of large U.S. corporations (greater than 5,000 employees) have or plan to have telecommuting programs, there are still many that don't. If an employee has permission from his or her boss to work at home, but the company has no official telecommuting policy, that employee is a **closet telecommuter** (1992):

> Boothe is trying to get a handle on how many of BellSouth's 60,000 employees telecommute. The company believes it has

many **"closet telecommuters,"** people who have been working from home with only a nod from their direct supervisor. (*Atlanta Journal and Constitution,* August 11, 1997)

Somewhat more radically, these "nudge, nudge, wink, wink" homeworkers are called **guerrilla telecommuters** (1988):

Actually, most companies get into telecommuting as the result of the **"guerrilla" telecommuters.** Trina Hoefling of Telecommuting Success in Denver, a management consulting organization on telecommuting, said, "We find that telecommuting usually starts in pockets, nooks and crannies of the organization, a shotgun or guerrilla approach. Then the company says, 'We're going to lose this employee, so we'll let her work from home.' They realize that it's working, so they want to scale it up." (*Boulder County Business Report,* March 1997)

Telecommuting is a subset of a broader concept:

telework *n.* (1981) Work performed by an employee while away from the office. —*v.* (1990). *Telework proponents often tout the social and environmental benefits of working outside the office, such as more time for family and less traffic congestion and air pollution. Little attention, however, has been drawn to what proponents say is **telework's** most important benefit: increased employee productivity.* (*Washington Technology,* January 21, 2002)

Viewing telework as anything job-related that is done out of the office sounds pleasingly definitive, but the truth is that there is no consensus on the meanings of the words *telework* and *telecommuting.* Some people use them interchangeably to refer to working at home; some take the "commuting" part of telecommuting and infer that it must only deal with work situations that reduce or eliminate an employee's commute.

Jack Nilles—who became one of the leading proponents of

telecommuting after his report was published—told me that he started using the word *teleworking* more often beginning in the early 1980s because most European languages didn't have a word for "commuting." Teleworking remains the word of choice in Europe to this day.

And although the *tele-* prefix implies that this type of work requires a dial-up connection to the Internet or to a corporate network, most people use the broader sense of "at a distance" (the Greek word *tele* means "far away"). So telework is, literally, "work at a distance." It will come as no surprise that a synonym for telework is **distance work** (1994):

Telecommuting advocates are pushing hard for a bill that would provide state grants for **distance work** in rural areas— jobs that would allow people to work from a home computer. (*Saint Paul Pioneer Press,* March 2, 2000)

A much older synonym is **remote work** (1981):

Too much work and a corporate culture that demands workers put in "face time" at the office are the biggest barriers to telecommuting and other forms of **remote work,** according to WFD, a Boston human-resources research and consulting firm that has been tracking workplace flexibility and **remote work** for more than 10 years. (*Atlanta Journal and Constitution,* January 6, 2002)

The number of **teleworkers** (1982) or telecommuters is difficult to pin down, but estimates range from 13 million (according to the U.S. Bureau of Labor's Current Population Survey) to 31 million (according to research firm In-Stat/MDR) in the United States alone. This is up from about 3 million U.S. teleworkers in 1990. In 2002, The research firm the Gartner Group estimated there would be 137 million **distance workers** (1987) worldwide in 2003.

Here are a few more synonyms for teleworkers and telecommuters:

nomad (1993) *Through interviews and focus groups with all levels of professionals, the project team learned a lot about how employees worked and how those workstyles may change in the future. Based on what they heard, they categorized employees as **nomads** or settlers. **Nomads** are out of the office at least 60 percent of the time; settlers spend more of their time in the office. (Facilities Design & Management, January 2002)*

remote agent (1989) *Ball credited the success of Alpine to maintaining their original plan, with the premise that their employees would be able to do absolutely every aspect of their job from the comfort of their homes, with nothing more than telephone and Internet access. . . . "For many reasons, using **remote agents** is the future of the customer service industry. It is simply a more efficient and more effective business model," he said. (Denver Business Journal, April 19, 2002)*

road warrior (1988) *Telecommuting also includes overseas contract workers on a second shift while the home office sleeps and **"road warriors"** who may not have a permanent office and do much of their work from a laptop. (Herald Sun,* Melbourne, Australia, February 6, 2002)

What about those who are responsible for keeping an eye (sort of) on a company's teleworkers? Not surprisingly, most often they're called **telemanagers** (1988):

According to Smith, voice mail is the remote manager's most critical tool. One **telemanager** she worked with never provided contact information or alternative contacts for her staff or clients in case of emergency. (*Home Office Computing,* October 2000)

As seen in the above citation, telemanagers are also called **remote managers** (1986). Another common synonym is **virtual manager** (1993):

> The No. 1 reason why managers decline overseas assignments is a relatively new one, according to the PWC survey: they don't want to fracture a spouse's career. The second most common explanation is that they don't want to disrupt their children's education. Not surprisingly, **virtual managers** report much less stress than employees who commute or relocate. (*Time,* April 9, 2001)

If you could mind-meld with a few telemanagers to determine their *real* concerns about telecommuting, I'm sure the item that generates the most fear and loathing would be the sneaking suspicion that their remote employees are slacking off. They're concerned, in other words, that their teleworkers will **teleloaf** (1997):

> Despite concerns that telecommuters will **"teleloaf,"** just about every study shows a 15 to 25 percent increase in productivity. (*Sun-Sentinel,* Fort Lauderdale, Fla., March 29, 1999)

In some cases, the opposite seems to be true: Home-based employees tend to work *longer* hours than they did at the office. If they go too far, then they're said to be suffering from a malady called **teleworkaholic syndrome** (1999):

> With fewer distractions, [telecommuters] get more done. That sense of accomplishment, however, gives way to the **teleworkaholic syndrome**. . . . Because they are producing more, and may view telecommuting as a perk, they feel they have to always do more work in order to justify their situation. (*Boston Globe,* January 17, 1999)

Most teleworkers fall somewhere in the middle. According to the 2001 Telework America study done by the International

Telework Association and Council (ITAC), 72 percent of telemanagers reported that their teleworking employees "slightly or greatly"
increased their productivity after they started working at home.

Besides improved productivity, most telecommuters also report
that overall their work-at-home lives are better than when they
worked at the office. According to studies done by ITAC and Ekos
Research, roughly 70 percent of telecommuters say their lives have
improved since becoming telecommuters. If there's a downside,
it's that many homeworkers feel a sense of loneliness and isolation,
a phenomenon called **watercooler withdrawal** (1999):

> It's even been found that workers who miss the office cama-
> raderie (it's called **watercooler withdrawal**) can be made
> whole with just a day in the main office every week or two.
> (*Bangor Daily News,* June 8, 2000)

It's becoming increasingly clear that a lot of other people are
looking for a **zero-commute** (1998) lifestyle. Back in 1999 the
Michigan Small Business Development Center estimated that a
home-based business starts every 11 seconds in the United
States, and Wells Fargo Bank estimated that 69 percent of all
new businesses were based in the home. The American
Association of Home-Based Businesses figures that in the
United States there are about 24 million home-based businesses.
Finally, according to the research firm Yankelovich Partners, no
less than 73 percent of Americans aspire to work at home.

A person who starts a business is an entrepreneur, of course,
so it makes a bit of sense that a person who starts a home-based
business would be called a **homepreneur** (1992; also: **homepreneur**):

> Many people are eager to escape the corporate jungle to em-
> bark on the adventures of a home-based business. But there are
> some unique obstacles that challenge **"homepreneurs."**
> (*Calgary Sun,* October 25, 1999)

If the homepreneur works alone, you might prefer to use the term **solopreneur** (1998):

> Still, for marketers like Phelps, tracking down telecommuters—even those who have informal arrangements with their employers—is easier than finding their **solopreneur** brethren. At least telecommuters are tethered in some way to the mother ship. **Solopreneurs** are floating throughout the galaxy. (*American Demographics,* June 1999)

A solopreneur or an entrepreneur who creates a business that has only a few employees is called a **micropreneur** (1994; also: **micro-preneur**):

> These new archetypal American workers are abandoning the office for the home office, the boss for clients and the colleague in the next cubicle for support networks of like-minded **"micropreneurs."** (*Australian Financial Review,* June 8, 2001)

If the entrepreneur is a stay-at-home mother, then she's a **mompreneur** (1987; also: **mom-preneur, mamapreneur, mama-preneur, mumpreneur, mum-preneur**):

> The playground . . . is a clearinghouse for matching child-care providers with prospective employer families. It's a networking hub for the many **mompreneurs** who work from home. (*Washington Post,* August 23, 2001)

More generally, a home-based businessperson is called an **open-collar worker** (1988), a play on *blue-collar worker* and *white-collar worker*:

> Home-based entrepreneurship is attracting growing numbers of recruits to its ranks. These **"open-collar workers"** come from a variety of backgrounds: lifelong entrepreneurs, homemakers, downsized workers, graduate students, stay-at-home parents, homebound disabled people and retirees. (*Los Angeles Times,* May 20, 2001)

OTHER X-COLLAR WORKERS

Black-and-blue-collar workers	Football players
Black-collar workers	Miners (esp. coal miners) and oil workers
Brown-collar workers	UPS employees
Dog-collar workers	Graphic artists or designers
Frayed-collar workers	Workers having trouble making ends meet
Gold-collar workers	Professionals or those with in-demand skills; employees over 55
Gray-collar workers	Skilled technicians; employees whose job descriptions combine some white and some blue collar
Green-collar workers	Environmentalists
Pink-collar workers	Secretaries and clerical staff
Scarlet-collar workers	Female porn shop operators
Steel-collar workers	Robots

The word *freelance* was coined in 1820 by Sir Walter Scott in *Ivanhoe*: "I offered Richard the service of my **Free Lances,** and he refused them—I will lead them to Hull, seize on shipping, and embark for Flanders; thanks to the bustling times, a man of action will always find employment."

He was talking about mercenary knights of the Middle Ages who, in "bustling times" would sell their warrior skills to the highest bidder. By the end of the nineteenth century, the word had come to mean a self-employed journalist or writer. Nowadays it refers to anyone who is self-employed. If the person works on jobs or contracts in multiple fields with multiple companies, she's a **portfolio worker** (coined by Charles Handy in his 1993 book *The Age of Unreason*):

Portfolio workers, on the other hand, change jobs frequently. Their clear goal is to expand and upgrade their skills with each new job. They enhance their resumes with bigger and more challenging accomplishments. (*Hamilton Spectator,* May 25, 2002)

The opposite would be a freelancer who does all his or her work for a single company—a **permalancer** (1996):

The **permalancer** phenomenon started in New York and has yet to catch on in L.A., but it exists on both coasts. The term refers, of course, to people who work freelance for a company, but on a permanent basis. In the world of postproduction and visual effects, the category describes a new breed of digital artists who work primarily at one or two houses but are not officially on the payroll. (*SHOOT,* February 5, 1999)

A **lone eagle** (1992) is a freelancer who works in a small town or rural area.

This growth in small towns and rural areas reflects the increasing gentrification of the West. Gentrification is happening as entrepreneurs and freelance professionals—**"Lone Eagles,"** free agents and professional nomads—increasingly move to remote places beyond the urban setting. (*Rocky Mountain News,* June 16, 2001)

In the United States, freelancers submit their taxes using Internal Revenue Service form number 1099, so of course these workers are called **1099ers** (1996) and are said to be part of **Generation 1099** (1999):

Members of **Generation 1099** spend an inordinate amount of time hustling, invoicing and politely harassing accounts payable. And unlike full-time employees, who have taxes withheld, **1099ers** are responsible for paying their own state, Federal and Social Security taxes, and shelling out huge amounts for health insurance—if they have it at all. (*New York Times,* August 15, 1999)

A freelancer who is online and uses the Internet to connect and communicate is an **e-lancer** (1998):

The fundamental unit of such an economy is not the corporation but the individual. Tasks aren't assigned and controlled through a stable chain of management but rather are carried out autonomously by independent contractors. These electronically connected freelancers—**e-lancers**—join together into fluid and temporary networks to produce and sell goods and services. When the job is done—after a day, a month, a year—the network dissolves, and its members become independent agents again, circulating through the economy, seeking the next assignment. (*Harvard Business Review,* September/October 1998)

The home-based worker needs somewhere to work, of course. The more casual homeworker sets up shop on the kitchen table, dining room, or coffee table, but most people have an official home office, or what some call a **hoffice** (1989).

Social scientists are busy predicting that we'll increasingly retreat from the rat race into hybrid home/office spaces, or **"hoffices,"** from which computer and telecommunications gear will let us live our professional and personal lives via wire. (*Newsweek,* June 16, 1997)

One of the hottest real estate buzzwords of the late 1990s and early 2000s is **live/work building** (1992), a structure built from the ground up to act as both a home and an office. Such a building is clearly aimed at the "HO" part of the **SOHO** (1991)— Small Office/Home Office—market, although it would also be suitable for most of the even smaller **TOHO** (1994)—Tiny Office/Home Office—market:

Owners of **SOHO** businesses must be driven by self-discipline. There is no time clock to punch, yet it is still critical to get to work regularly, even if that simply means walking down a hall in your home. (*Computer User,* August 1, 2001)

[T]he rise of the tiny office/home office (**TOHO**) can be attributed to major corporations sending people home to work for at least part of the week. (*Channel Business,* April 24, 2000)

SOHO refers to a business sector that consists of two entities: "small offices," which are small businesses, each of which works out of an office; and "home offices," which are home-based businesses, each of which, again, uses an office. SOHO is also used to refer to an individual small business or home-based business, or it can refer to the actual offices used by such businesses.

What's the difference between a "small office" and a "tiny office"? No one's really sure. The most common numbers are that a tiny office has just one or two employees, while a small office has up to a couple of dozen or so. If a home has two offices to accommodate a work-at-home couple (and, according to research firm IDC, the United States has about 1.5 million such twosomes), Daniel Pink, in his book *Free Agent Nation,* calls this a *HOHO* setup: His Office/Her Office.

The home office is just one of the work locales used by a more general class of independent worker—the **free agent** (1992). The term became famous thanks to an article that Pink wrote for the magazine *Fast Company* in December 1997: "*Free agents* gladly swap the false promise of security for the personal pledge of authenticity. 'In free agency,' says Burish, who now designs training programs, 'people assume their own shape rather than fit the shape of some corporate box.' "

This class of worker includes anyone who has forsaken working full time for someone else. It includes the self-employed, freelancers, temporary workers, and those running their own

microbusinesses (1980). Traditional workers practice *vertical loyalty*, or loyalty to one's boss or employer. Free agents, however, practice **horizontal loyalty** (1992), which is loyalty to one's peers, colleagues, and customers:

> [W]ork has become more emotionally complex. Gone are the days of "vertical loyalty" to authority figures or institutions. Today's workers value **"horizontal loyalty"** to colleagues and to projects, providing their talent in exchange for opportunity. (*HR Magazine*, September 1, 2001)

In his book *The Brand You 50*, Tom Peters calls this *Rolodex loyalty*.

> I've worked out of my home since 1991. My "commute"—a single flight of stairs—takes about 20 seconds. A "traffic jam" is when my wife, who also works at home most of the time, and I pass each other on the stairs. An "interruption" is when the dog comes into my office for a pat on the head. The "cafeteria" is the kitchen, where I can make myself a latte or cappuccino whenever I feel like it. The "boardroom," in the summer, anyway, is the deck behind the house. It's a life that suits me to perfection, and a gang of Blue Meanies couldn't drag me back to a "real" office.

Chapter 18

People Who Work at the Office

Democracy divides people into workers and loafers. It makes no provision for those who have no time to work. —*Karl Kraus*

In a hierarchy every employee tends to rise to his level of incompetence. —*Laurence J. Peter*

In his 1962 book *The Organizational Society*, political scientist Robert Presthus examined how employees accommodate themselves to the culture of a corporation or organization. He categorized workers into three distinct types:

- *Upward-mobiles*—These employees are at one with the goals and beliefs of the organization. They identify with the corporate culture and even derive strength from being a part of that culture. They're happy, motivated workers who like their jobs and believe that they will rise in the corporation by doing what is best for the corporation.

- *Indifferents*—These employees accept the corporate culture, but they aren't passionate about it and they certainly don't identify with it. Instead, their identities are focused outside of the workplace in their personal lives. For these employees, their job is only a means to an end, which is to lead a satisfying life off the job. They seek security instead of power or success. They won't rock the boat, but they won't row any more strenuously than they have to.

▪ *Ambivalents*—These employees have their feet in two accommodation camps. On one hand, they're dedicated to their profession or to the work they do and are highly motivated to improve their skills. On the other hand, they reject authority and hierarchy and refuse to adapt to the corporate culture. They're usually prickly and grumpy because their superior skills don't translate into workplace success.

Researchers are clearly fond of these overgeneralizations and love to come up with their own classification schemes. One group divided employees into Institutional Stars, Corporate Citizens, Lone Wolves, and Apathetics, while another more whimsical bunch came up with the categories Chatterboxes, Sharks, Plot-icians, and Snoops. Most classifications create a hierarchy, such as the Star Workers, Solid Performers, and Goof-offs scheme proposed by one management guru. This jibes with what has become the most common worker classification scheme: Lions, Horses, and Dogs. (Managers, it is said, are supposed to feed the Lions, ride the Horses, and shoot the Dogs.) For the purposes of this chapter, I've created my own taxonomy: Ladder-Climbers, Slackers, and Bozos.

Ladder-Climbers

For many years, the way you got to the upper echelons of the business world was by assiduously climbing the *corporate ladder.* The people who do this—the *ladder-climbers* (1870)—are usually both ambitious and talented (although many a corporate rung has been scaled by those who simply know whose shoulders to stand on or whose coattails to hang onto).

But even these *careerists* (1910) have to start somewhere, and the best start is often one where a new hire doesn't have much of a learning curve:

plug and play *adj.* (1997) Describes an employee who immediately fits in with his or her new company. Also: **plug-and-play.** *In their quest for* **"plug and play"** *workers, companies look on university and college campuses for new employees.* (*Hamilton Spectator,* June 18, 2002)

In the computer world, *plug and play* (1984) is used to describe a device that works automatically after it's attached to the computer. You "plug" it in, and then you can immediately "play" with it without having to go through a tedious or confusing installation process. (As is often the case with these things, the theory is nice, but the practice doesn't live up to the hype. Until recently the ongoing flakiness of plug and play caused many a cynic to call it "plug and pray," instead.)

Continuing the objectification theme, we go from new-employee-as-easy-to-install-device to new-employee-as-easy-to-prepare-food:

oven-ready *adj.* (1997) Describes a new employee who needs little or no training or preparation. *The poaching culture is back with a vengeance. Everybody's looking for what former Computing Services and Software Association director general Rob Wirszycz once called* **"oven-ready** *people"— people with the skills and experience to hit the ground running.* (*Computing,* August 31, 2000)

These ready-to-roll employees usually waste no time becoming **fast-trackers** (1977), meaning their path to the top is quicker than that of the average corporate bear. (They are, in other words, on the *fast track* [1968], a term that comes from horseracing circles where it refers to a dry, hard racetrack that's conducive to fast running.) Here's another fast-tracker:

hi-pot *n.* (1980) A young executive who is deemed by the company to have high potential for rapid advancement. *GM will choose its high-potential candidates—its* **"hi-pots"**—*very* *early in their careers and put them on a faster track than ever be-fore. (Automotive Industries, November 1, 1999)*

Of course, getting yourself on the fast track is one thing, but actually running fast is quite another. It helps if you don't have to lug a lot of personal baggage:

zero-drag *adj.* (1999) Describes a highly motivated em-ployee who has few personal responsibilities and so can work long hours, travel frequently, or be called in to work with little notice. *The ideal **zero-drag** employee is young, unmarried and childless with no responsibilities and an ea-gerness to do well. (Boston Globe, March 11, 2001)*

In physics, *drag* refers to the resistance experienced by an ob-ject moving through a fluid medium (such as air). *Zero drag* is an ideal state where the object experiences no resistance at all, much like an eager, no-spouse, no-kids, no-pets employee. And these unfettered workers can offer the company an added bene-fit—they can work whenever they're needed:

clockless worker *n.* (1997) An employee who is willing to work at any time, day or night. *The New Economy has set many formerly 9-to-5 companies on a slippery slope that has employees working late, then into the night, then all night. In most offices, the phenomenon is voluntary, with **"clockless workers"** enjoying the flexibility of being able to work any-time. (The Christian Science Monitor, September 25, 2000)*

Campbell Soup—not the first company that comes to mind when the phrase "cutting edge" is mentioned—is nevertheless all over this trend. In a recent press release, the company cited the rise of the "Clockless Worker" as one of the reasons it was repositioning soup as an any-time-of-the-day meal. "Soup isn't just for lunch anymore," the company declared.

No matter when they eat their soup, salaried types don't get paid overtime, so when work happens outside of 9 to 5 (or beyond the standard eight hours, whenever that might happen), these employees are essentially working for free:

> **off the clock** *adj.* (1989) Describes a work-related task that is performed outside of normal office hours for no pay. Also: **off-the-clock.** *The Creative Club of Kansas City on Thursday will play host to its third event since coming to town. The event, from 5:30 to 9 p.m. at the Velvet Dog, will showcase "off the clock" work of employees at Hallmark Cards Inc. who work in the creative area. (Kansas City Star,* July 23, 2002)

Note, however, that while highly motivated employees may be willing to work off the clock, lots of wage slaves are forced into doing this by their employers. In recent years companies such as Wal-Mart, Micron, and Taco Bell have been accused of this. Here's a citation that demonstrates this darker side of unpaid overtime:

> Examples of **off the clock** work employees have reported doing include: preparing food and cleaning before clocking in, waiting after the start of their shift to clock in because business was slow, continuing to work after clocking out to finish cleaning and other chores, and/or waiting for the manager to count the till after clocking out. (*Business Wire,* February 1, 2000)

The clockless worker often takes advantage of the **night economy** (1997), the economic activity that occurs throughout the night in most major cities. This is particularly true of certain high-flying executives:

> **flexecutive** *n.* (1994) An executive or professional whose hours and place of work are flexible. *New York is no longer the only world city that never sleeps. Since 1985, the number*

of people who work through the night has quadrupled. No one wants to go to sleep on the same day as they wake up any more. Forget shift workers. The new buzz word is "flexecutive"—the professional who plays the "night economy" and doesn't let the small fact that it is three in the morning stop him or her from making their fortune. (*The Observer,* London, February 4, 2001)

Those clockless hi-pots who take advantage of their zero-drag lifestyle invariably work long hours. But does working long hours always lead to a promotion? That depends. In particular, it depends on whether the boss believes that a person deserves a promotion just because he or she is always at the office. If so, then a strange sort of balance is achieved:

> **rat-race equilibrium** *n.* (1997) A workplace balance in which an employee's willingness to work long hours for possible promotion is equal to an employer's belief that working long hours merits promotion. *According to the standard theories, unreasonable work weeks are self-defeating . . . because workers get tired or demand high overtime rates or simply rebel. However, according to a newer model, some businesses manage to develop what economists call a "rat-race equilibrium." The rat-race occurs when managers use a willingness to work long hours as a sign of some tangible yet much-desired quality that merits promotion.* (James Gleick, *Faster,* 1999)

Most *rat-race* (1937) runners work long hours because they have lots of work to do. Among the more ambitious, the extra work is self-generated in an attempt to impress one mucky-muck or another. But for many employees, the extra work often is caused by waves of **downsizing** (1981), where the survivors' "In" baskets groan under the weight of the tasks—the ***ghost-work*** (2002)—that those who were laid off used to perform.

Not only that, but those who remain fear for their jobs, so a growing number of people are putting in great gobs of overtime for no other reason than they feel they have to:

presenteeism *n.* (1994) 1. The feeling that one needs to work extra hours even if one has no extra work to do. *Today Patricia Hewitt, the Trade and Industry Secretary, will make a speech to the Work Foundation criticising Britain's long-hours culture, the "**presenteeism**" that demands that we be at work whether we have something to do or not. (The Times of London,* May 29, 2002) 2. The feeling that one must show up for work even if one is too sick, stressed, or distracted to be productive. *Based on a 1999 analysis of 17 diseases, researchers found that lost productivity due to **presenteeism** was, on average, 7.5 times greater than productivity lost to absenteeism. For some conditions—notably allergies, arthritis, heart disease, hypertension, migraines, and neck/back/spine pain—the ratio was 15 to 1, 20 to 1, or even approached 30 to 1. (Occupational Health & Safety,* April 2002)

Presenteeism is a play on *absenteeism* (1922), the chronic or repeated absence of an employee from work. It often leads to Employee Pet Peeve #37: The person who brings their newly hatched cold or flu to the office and ends up infecting everyone else. It's also the source of Employer Pet Peeve #6: The sick-at-work employee whose productivity is as bad as their health. A recent study by AdvancePCS of Texas estimated that the top five ailments that employees often bring to work—headache/pain, cold/flu, fatigue/depression, digestive problems, and arthritis—cost employers more than $180 billion a year. Go home, people!

Presenteeism is a passive please-don't-fire-me strategy. A more active strategy is to acquire new skills, and some of the more gung-ho types practically make a career out of it:

learning a living *pp.* (1988) Constantly acquiring new knowledge and skills to improve job prospects and promotion opportunities. *Learning a living—or learning as a way to increase career opportunities and rewards—has gripped the marketplace. And it is happening through formal and informal study, either face-to-face or online. The first essential is to know how to learn quickly and constantly as the requirements within jobs change.* (*Weekend Australian,* October 14, 2000)

Others whose *ho* isn't quite so *gung* learn what they need to know when they need to know it:

just-in-time learning *pp.* (1990) The acquisition of knowledge or skills as they are needed. *Rather than having employees take time away from work to sit through traditional classroom courses, many companies are using technology-based, self-guided tutorials and databases that allow users to focus on "nuggets" of information as needed to perform specific tasks and solve problems as they crop up. . . . Just-in-time learning incorporates Web- and intranet-based applications as well as CD-ROMs, satellite channels and videotapes.* (*Computerworld,* April 3, 2000)

The learning of new skills now has its own one-word moniker: **skilling** (1981), which seems to have had its origin in a pun:

Furthermore, gourmet cooking schools in the United States are booming, and such a phenomenon couldn't have come soon enough for this nation's restaurant owners. Because of tougher immigration laws and higher salaries in Europe, the general drift of great chefs from the Continent to this country has slowed to a trickle. Finally, high-class American restaurants are looking for indigenous talent. The question everyone's asking seems to be: "Who's **skilling** the great chefs of America?" (*The Christian Science Monitor*, February 26, 1981)

Note, however, that the verb *deskill,* to convert a workplace from one that uses skilled labor to one that does not, has been in the language since about 1941.

Skilling has since taken on many forms:

cross-skilling *pp.* (1989) Learning skills and knowledge across multiple departments, disciplines, or industries. *Cross-skilling isn't just about being able to move comfortably from, say, finance to marketing, but also moving across different industries, for example, from retail to manufacturing, or across different cultures by becoming an international manager, capable of operating anywhere in Europe, the USA or South East Asia.* (*Evening Standard,* London, July 14, 1998)

multi-skilling *pp.* (1983) Being proficient in multiple areas of expertise within an organization or profession. Also: **multiskilling.** *I would like to see changes in shifts and more nurses trained to work in casualty and on other wards— multiskilling would mean staff could move around within the hospital or even between different hospitals where a need arises.* (*Bath Chronicle,* Bath, England, March 30, 2002)

universal skilling *pp.* (2001) Being proficient in all areas of a business or profession. *The company's decision to pursue an extreme form of multiskilling, effectively "universal skilling," required an enormous commitment of resources.* (*Labour & Industry,* December 1, 2001)

up-skilling *pp.* (1984) Upgrading one's knowledge and skills. *Technology-in-use changes by 80 per cent every 10 years, which is less than one quarter of the average working life—that rate of change and productivity considerations dic-*

*tate major **up-skilling** and professional development of the workforce. (Irish Times, September 19, 2000)*

Yet another strategy to avoid the job-cutting block is to become what at first blush appears to be the perfect cog in the corporate machine:

Stepford worker *n.* (1992) An employee who exhibits blind loyalty to the company and an uncritical devotion to company policies. Also: **Stepford employee** (1994). *When I was working in a corporate environment, I would put on my little corporate suit—a **Stepford Worker**—and I went in there and did what was expected. (Fast Company, May 2001)*

The use of *Stepford* as an adjective is based on Ira Levin's 1972 book *The Stepford Wives* (later made into a movie of the same title). The women of Stepford (a New York suburb) are creepily content with their lives as wives, mothers, and housekeepers. And no wonder: It turns out they're all automatons, robots programmed by their husbands to embrace "traditional" wifely duties and conform to their husbands' norms. Ever since, *Stepford* has been used to describe someone who goes through life mindlessly or uncritically.

Slackers

Your average Stepford worker isn't lazy, per se, because he routinely does what's expected of him. However, he suffers from a kind of mental laziness because he won't ever think critical thoughts about the company. That laziness makes him at least a part-time member of the society of *slackers* (1898), those shirkers of duty and avoiders of exertion.

With the omnipresent threat of layoffs, modern-day workplace slacking has taken on some remarkably subtle forms. For example:

> **undertime** *n.* (1983) Time that an employee takes off work to perform non–work-related tasks; the salary or wages earned while performing such tasks. *It may be the worst-kept secret in the workplace: People are working more* **undertime**—*stealing time off during the day to compensate for heavier workloads and more stress.* **Undertime** *can take many forms, from hours spent away from the office on errands or shopping to chunks of time spent at your desk surfing the Internet.* (*Wall Street Journal,* April 18, 2002)

Undertime is often taken as a form of compensation. That is, people working in downsized corporations often end up doing the work of two or three people. This requires them to work unpaid overtime, so they get their revenge by doing paid undertime.

I talked about *telecommuting*—doing office work at home—in Chapter 17, "People Who Work at Home." Now there's a new breed of telecommuter who's using undertime to put a different spin on this old idea:

> **reverse telecommuting** *pp.* (1997) Performing personal tasks at the office. —**reverse telecommute** *v.* (1998) *Telecommuting brings the office to the home.* **Reverse telecommuting,** *as the name suggests, brings the home to the office.* (*Straits Times,* Kuala Lumpur, Malaysia, September 7, 1997)

This is also called **homing from work** (1998), since it's the opposite, in a way, of working from home. In other words, employees grab their personal to-do lists, bring them into work, and then take undertime to do things like pay bills, make doctors' appointments, and shop online. And who can blame them?

People just don't have enough time to do everything after work, especially if they have kids. Also, some things just have to be done during the day while other people are doing *their* work.

A computer term that has made the leap from the technical arena to the mainstream is *multitasking* (1966), which means performing two or more tasks at once. If a person keeps up the appearance of being hard at work while actually doing something non–work related, then he or she is actually performing a specific kind of multitasking:

> **multislacking** *n.* (1998) Also: **multi-slacking. —multi-slacker** *n.* (1998) *Multislacking is the workplace equivalent of a child bent over a textbook with a comic book propped behind it. As a kid, if a teacher came up behind you, you'd be caught hands down. But '90s **multislackers** can keep one or two work-related screens at the ready on the nanosecond someone—your boss, say—walks by. With one mouse click, the work screen is up and running, the play screen sent into the cybervoid.* (*Boston Herald,* June 22, 1998)

Scott Adams, creator of the Dilbert comic strip, made an immeasurable contribution to the multislacker world by coming up with what he calls the Total Work Equation:

Real Work + Appearance of Work = Total Work

In his 1998 book *The Joy of Work,* Adams also coined a closely related word—**multishirking**—which means doing two or more non–work-related tasks at once:

> **Multishirking.** All you need for this is a hands-free headset for your telephone. Once you're properly equipped, you can make personal phone calls while simultaneously using your computer for personal entertainment. . . . **Multishirking** is not only fun, it doubles the odds that an observer will think you're

doing at least one work-related activity. (Scott Adams, *The Joy of Work,* 1998)

If taken too far, multislacking and multishirking can lead to **eye service** (1995), working only when the boss is watching you. This is a play on the old phrase *lip service* (1644), which refers to services offered but not performed.

Slacking that only involves surfing non–work-related websites (an activity performed by 80 percent of young men and 60 percent of young women, according to one study) has a couple of its own terms:

cyberslacking *n.* (1997) Also: **cyber-slacking.** —**cyberslacker** *n.* (1999) —**cyberslack** *v.* (2000) *Tread carefully if you access the web at work. The Internet police are moving in to crack down on "cyberslacking" employees. Websense, a US company that makes software that spies on workers' Internet use [claims that] 70 per cent of all Internet porn traffic occurs during the nine-to-five working day, and 30 to 40 per cent of Internet surfing on corporate networks is not business-related. The Websense software monitors and reports on employees' Internet use and identifies the dreaded **cyberslackers.*** (Canberra Times, April 15, 2002)*

cyberloafing (1996) Also: **cyber-loafing.** —**cyberloafer** *n.* (1996) —**cyberloaf** *v.* (1997) *In the brave new world of cyber-spying, very little is private and whatever you write may come back to haunt you. Just ask the employees of Xerox Corp. In October 1999, 40 employees at locations across the U.S. were fired for "cyber-loafing" on company time. (Austin American-Statesman, January 12, 2001)*

People have been working two jobs probably for as long as there have been jobs to work. (At the end of 2001, according to the U.S. Bureau of Labor Statistics, 7.3 million Americans juggled two jobs.) If a person has a day job, then their second job is usually worked in the evening or at night, which led to the term *moonlighting* (1957). (This term sure paints a pretty picture, but, if you'll allow me to pick a nit, I have to wonder just how many of these second jobs were actually worked outside under the light of the moon.) Nowadays, however, many two-job workers prefer to keep their evenings free:

> **sunlighting** (1983) Working on another job while taking time away from one's day job. *Allowing an employee to reconfigure her day can lead to free agency. First, she takes work home and leaves early on certain afternoons. Then she arranges to telecommute three days per week. Then, while she's telecommuting, she begins moonlighting—or "sunlighting," if she's working on side gigs during the day.* (Daniel Pink, *Free Agent Nation,* 2001)

If you have the chutzpah to do your sunlighting at the office (say, by making phone calls or answering e-mail related to the other job, or by working on the job's website), then you're doing what one wag called *fluorescentlighting*.

One of the preferred ways to slack off at work is to extend one's lunch hour:

> **long-lunching** *pp.* (1987) Taking an extra-long lunch break. —**long-luncher** *n.* (1981) *Industry figures show consumption of beer has fallen from its mid-1970s peak, while wine drinking has steadily moved towards recapturing its golden days in the **long-lunching** mid-1980s.* (*Canberra Times,* May 8, 2002)

It's common for harried workers to try to cram in as many errands as possible during lunch—going to the bank, picking up dry cleaning, making bail for one's no-account brother-in-law—so it's almost inevitable that a few minutes here and there will have to be tacked on to the break. But other workers really don't relish returning to what they perceive as a soulless or useless job, so they put off the moment for as long as possible. These workers have been **dilberted** somewhere along the way:

> **dilbert** *v.* (1998) To cause a person to become bored or cynical about work. *Can you imagine efficient private companies still working only with paper? How many man-hours must be **dilberted** away? How many delays? How many errors—or flat-out frauds?* (*Arkansas Democrat-Gazette,* March 27, 2002)

This verb comes from the name *Dilbert,* the bored, cynical main character in the comic strip of the same name. Dilberted workers are expert *clockwatchers* (1911): They arrive at work no earlier than they have to, and they leave work no later than they have to. But not all office slackers are so cynical. Sometimes they're just suffering from a temporary but all-too-common malady:

> **post-vacation hangover** *n.* (1991) A feeling of sluggishness and disorientation that occurs when you return to work from a particularly long or adventurous vacation. *I'm always looking for new and better ways to combat the **post-vacation hangover.** You know, that sluggish I-don't-want-to-be-here feeling.* (*Sun-Sentinel,* Fort Lauderdale, Fla., September 29, 1997)

For those first few days after a vacation, sufferers prefer just to sit quietly at their desk all day long. However, for **no-getters** (1994; the opposite of a *go-getter*), this is a permanent state, making them the office equivalent of a *couch potato* (1979):

> **desk potato** *n.* (1988) A person who sits at a desk for all or most of the time he or she is at the office. *Too much work, too little exercise: it is a very big problem in this country. More than one in six Canadian workers can now offi-*

*cially be called a **"desk potato."** The Council for Health and Active Living at Work is urging employers to promote physical fitness at work.* (*Canada AM,* September 1, 2000)

The ultimate in employee slacking would be, of course, to not be employed at all. Or, more accurately, it would be to get laid off from one's job and receive a semihefty severance package so that one could lay about at home while, in effect, still getting paid. This sounds *real* good to some folks:

layoff lust *n.* (2001) The extreme desire to be laid off from one's job. *A new term has entered the language: "layoff lust," the sudden desire to be sent away with a severance package, providing time at last to search for meaning and cultivate the soul.* (*Atlantic Monthly,* April 2002)

Bozos

One way to get yourself laid off is to become dispensable, and here's one tactic you could follow:

strategic incompetence *n.* (1985) Job performance that is purposefully incompetent. *Some people are geniuses at avoiding hard work. Either through ignorance or **strategic incompetence,** they are constantly shunting their responsibilities onto someone else. It's easy to identify these flawed individuals. If you delegate something to them, they always return it to you half done. They bounce the problem back at you.* (*Plain Dealer,* Cleveland, March 2, 1993)

If you encounter a strategically incompetent person, you'd be well within your rights to call that person a *bozo* (1916), meaning someone who is foolish or clownish. Some companies have a real bozo problem:

bozo explosion *n.* (1991) The large number of inept employees that a company ends up with when it hires an incompetent executive, who in turn hires incompetent managers, who then hire incompetent workers. *Ed Colligan, who was then Palm's vice president of marketing . . . was also responsible for many mottos that were far more clever, including "Avoid the **bozo explosion**" (if you hire one clueless manager, you're dead; that person will hire more bozos, and they'll hire more). (New York Times, June 7, 2001)*

In hacker circles, a **bozon** (1995) is a unit of stupidity. For example, a particularly clueless person would be said to have a "high bozon count." This notion of an ignorant or stupid person "not having a clue" became popular during World War II. Nowadays we describe such as person as being **anti-clueful** (1998), and we say that he or she needs to be hit with a **clue stick** (1999) or a **clue-by-four** (1992).

Another popular variation on this theme is **clue train** (1994; also: **cluetrain**), a metaphorical train on which an ignorant or incompetent person needs to ride. This phrase was popularized a couple of years ago by the publication of *The Cluetrain Manifesto* on the Web (see www.cluetrain.com) and in book form.

Humans love to come up with clever insults, especially for the stupid, the ignorant, and the inept. I'll close this chapter with a small sampling of a few choice epithets that recently entered the language:

404 *adj.* (1995) This code is roughly equivalent to saying that for a certain person "the lights are on, but no one's home." It comes from the error message displayed when a Web browser can't locate a page: 404 Not Found. The requested URL was not found on this server. *It's rather silly that teen flicks are racking up huge box office numbers and*

Hollywood's acting like it's some earth-shattering phenomenon. Studio execs, you're so **404.** *(Buffalo News,* March 5, 1999)

i-dotter *n.* (1985) A person who is overly fastidious and detail oriented. Synonym: **t-crosser.** *"She had a very lively and a good sense of humor,"* said Delores Kane, *a fellow retired branch librarian. "She liked work done right, but she was not a nit-picker, an* **i-dotter** *or a* **t-crosser.***"* (*Chicago Tribune,* September 1, 1985)

induhvidual *n.* (1995) A stupid person; a person who does or says something stupid. *The deliciously ironic bit, though, was the comment from a Transit Workers Union representative who thought Muni drivers would experience less stress. These are the same* **induhviduals** *who can't be bothered to pull their behemoths into the block-long bus zones fiercely defended by $250 fines.* (*San Francisco Chronicle,* November 30, 1999)

torpedo *n.* (1997) An inept employee who quits to go work for a rival company. *An incompetent coworker leaving—with some encouragement—for a competing company is a* **"torpedo."** (*Chief Executive,* January 1, 2001)

The ranks of the average corporation are populated with workers and managers who commute from every corner of society. So it's not surprising that a survey of worker types reveals a workforce that's not only diverse, but that also mirrors the types of people found in society as a whole as well as their distribution through the population. The high end of the bell curve holds the upwardly mobile elite, the ladder-climbing fast-trackers who are always upskilling to make themselves plug and play; the fat middle of the curve is brimming with desk potatoes who, while glad to have a job (the layoff lust crowd excepted, of course), are indifferent to the goals of the corporation and spark their creativity only by trying to find safe ways to engage in the necessary tasks of cyberslacking, sunlighting, and long-lunching. The low end of the curve is the realm of the bozo, the i-dotter, and the induhvidual. These clue-challenged are tolerated, perhaps, because they make everyone else look good, a perception that can survive only so much 404 behavior until the torpedo must be launched.

Chapter 19

The Modern Workplace

> From time to time, social critics have bemoaned the falling
> rates of community participation in American life, but they
> have made the same mistake. The reason Americans are
> content to bowl alone (or, for that matter, not bowl at all)
> is that, increasingly, they receive all the social support they
> need—all the serendipitous interactions that serve to make
> them happy and productive—from nine to five.
> —*Malcolm Gladwell*

> This little box will be your home for sixty hours a week. It
> comes with an obsolete computer and a binder about safety
> hazards. Your challenge is to look busy until someone gives
> you a meaningful assignment. —*Scott Adams*

I f you've been working so hard lately that you feel as though
you're practically *living* in your cubicle, that's at least a linguistically appropriate feeling. That's because the word *cubicle*
comes from the Latin term *cubiculum,* which roughly translates
as "bedroom." That was how *cubicle* was used in English until
around the sixteenth century. About 300 years later cubicles
resurfaced as small sleeping areas that were separated using
wooden partitions that didn't quite reach the ceiling.

The office cubicle as we know it today was the brainchild of
a fellow named Harold Probst, who worked for the Herman
Miller company in the 1960s. Before Probst came along, offices
were arranged *bullpen* style, with desks out in the open in regi-
mented rows, the workers lined up like so many galley slaves.
Probst saw much wrong with this design, including what he

memorably called the "idiot salutation problem": the constant interruptions caused by every Tom, Dick, and Harriet saying "Hello" to you as they walked by.

His solution was to use panels and tall storage units to give each worker their own private area, and thus the modern cubicle was born. (Later someone asked Probst if he thought of himself as the "Father of the Cubicle." He answered, "My God, that's about as interesting as being the father of the Pet Rock.")

Cubicle Culture

We live in a syllable-cutting society, so it's not surprising that the three-syllable *cubicle* is often chopped down to the one-syllable **cube** (1980):

> "Managers love cubicles; employees hate them," says Barbara Hemphill, a professional organizer from Raleigh, N.C., who has helped many a "Dilbert" cope with life in a **"cube"** over the last 20 years. (*New York Times,* January 20, 2002)

Those with a more sardonic view rarely let a few extra syllables get in the way of a word that hits just the right note of disdainful mockery, which explains the popularity of Douglas Coupland's famous coinage from his book, *Generation X*: the **veal-fattening pen** (1990):

> A lot of what is happening today with [instant messaging] is a duplicate of what we saw with the early online services, CompuServe being the classic example. People like computer chat, even if it's with someone who's on the other side of your **veal-fattening pen** partition. (*InfoWorld,* June 3, 2002)

This agricultural motif may help explain why the collection of cubicles in an office is often called a **cube farm** (1997):

An overly chatty neighbor lurks, waiting for an opportunity to make small talk with a busy colleague. Glancing through the open side of a 5-foot-high cubicle, he spots his prey and strolls in. Work stops. That's one of the drawbacks of life in a **cube farm,** the standard working environment for millions of office-bound Americans. (*Denver Post,* October 21, 2002)

Cube farms are notoriously difficult places for the uninitiated to navigate. Each corridor, each intersection, even each cubicle looks the same as any other, so it doesn't take much for an office wanderer to get lost, which has no doubt inspired *cube farm* synonyms such as **cube maze** (2001) or **cubical maze** (1996) and **cube warren** (2002).

This **cubicle culture** (1996) is populated by many curious creatures, but perhaps none is more curious than the inquisitive **prairie dog** (1996), a person who pops a head over a cubicle wall in response to any loud or interesting noise or simply to chat with a neighbor (a behavior known as **prairie dogging**):

Have you had enough of the **"prairie dog"** in the next cubicle who keeps popping up and down behind the partition to see or hear what you're up to? (Newhouse News Service, May 30, 2002)

The corridors that define the cube maze are also the inspiration behind the name of another modern workplace type:

corridor cruiser *n.* (1993) A worker who spends a lot of time walking through office corridors, usually en route from one meeting to another. —**corridor cruising** *pp. The emerging Tablet PC user will be the "corridor cruiser" and not necessarily someone in a small business, he said. "The target market for Microsoft is clearly the enterprise user—from desktop to boardroom and back," Smith said. (Computer Reseller News,* June 10, 2002)

The functional opposite of the corridor cruiser—or the synonymous **corridor warrior** (1999)—is the **nester** (1985), a person who personalizes the cubicle with family photos, personal knickknacks, posters, and other non-business bric-a-brac:

> John Wesselhoeft has a name for people who scatter family photos, cutesy coffee mugs and piles of papers around their offices. These people are **nesters,** Wesselhoeft said. (*Rocky Mountain News,* January 12, 2002)

Settling into a cubicle is easiest if the nester doesn't have a **cube-mate** (1989), a person who shares the cubicle space. In that case, nesters can take full advantage of their cubicle's otherwise drab cloth walls to hang pictures, posters, and those photocopied jokes, lists and sayings—called **xeroxlore** (1985)—that are the staple of any office setting. But some cubicle dwellers use their wall space for a more serious purpose, which is to display their degrees, certificates, and awards, as well as photographs in which they appear with famous people. This is called an **ego wall** (1985):

> Now that she is a grandmother . . . she has replaced some of her comfy office chairs with a crib, a bassinet and other accouterments of designer infancy. Family photos abound. Playfully, Saban also maintains what she calls her **Ego Wall**: rows of pictures from her days as a model and disco singer with the improbable name of Flower. (*Los Angeles Times Magazine,* September 23, 2001)

This is also called a **me wall** (1991). Note, too, that a **grip-and-grin** (1977) is a photograph that shows two people shaking hands and smiling at the camera. (It also refers to a photo of a contest or event winner smiling while receiving one of those huge, oversize checks.) If a person has a wall that contains nothing but these kinds of pictures, call it a **grip-and-grin ego wall** (2002). Since these kinds of walls work better in an office instead of a cubicle, some say that cube denizens have **wall envy** (2000).

Finally, the fact that most cubicle walls are only four or five feet high means that, at least theoretically, things can be easily tossed from one cube to another. Such antics are frowned on in all but the most fratlike offices, of course, but this potential ability has led to a popular business idiom:

> **throw it over the wall** (1985) To pass a project or problem to another person or department without consulting with them or coordinating the transfer in any way. *Craig Estep . . . says that the root of the CitationJet problem was "engineering would design the airplane and **throw it over the wall** to manufacturing who would take what they got" and move on to production—a classic failure. (Fortune,* May 1, 2000)

The Flexible Office

In the early 1970s some enlightened employers realized that there was no earthly reason why every employee had to put in their eight-hour days from 9 to 5. As long as the company received its eight hours work for eight hours pay, an employee ought to be free to begin the day at 7 A.M. or at 10, depending on their relationship with their alarm clock. This new arrangement provided a welcome flexibility, so it was called **flextime** (1972) or **flexitime** (1973).

The 1980s saw a further flowering of employer flexibility when some sharp-eyed managers noticed a puzzling phenomenon: At any given time, the **occupation rate** (2001)—the percentage of desks and work areas that are occupied—was quite low. (Some recent studies show that about two-thirds of work areas are unused at any given time.) So if employees are wandering around anyway, why not institute the spatial analogue of flextime? The result was **flexplace** (1984), a program that gives employees the flexibility to work from the office or from another location such as a branch office or at home (other variations are **flex-place, flex place,** and **flexiplace**):

> In fact, "face time is almost anachronistic," says Emmett Seaborn, principal, Towers Perrin. "What was accepted in the baby-boom generation five years ago—being in the office as a demonstration of value creation—now has the appearance of being outdated. Today, if you are not working outside the office, employing flextime and **flexplace** opportunities you are probably not perceived as a performer. This is very true for the next generation, Generation Y, which actually scoffs at the notion of having to be in the office to do work." (*Workforce,* December 1, 2002)

If the employee never has to go into the office, you can describe him or her as **office-free** (1991):

> Computer experts and insurance analysts say that severe cost pressures are prompting many companies and industries in the New York region and around the nation to move faster at spinning out their employees as high-tech road warriors. Most notably, I.B.M. is about to start an entirely **office-free** sales force in New Jersey. (*New York Times,* February 8, 1994)

Although even with the shackles of an office-bound life removed, employees still need to do some work. If their work is portable, then all they need is a **mobile office** (1980):

> The solution was a **mobile office,** in which he could at least draft his reports. "I built a small one-person office in the back of a Chevy Astro van by removing most of the seats and installing a computer, TV/VCR, color printer and laser printer," Mr. Connolly said. "It's powered with an inverter, an electrical

device that takes 12-volt current from the alternator and converts it to 110 volts. With the motor running, I can run them indefinitely, or by battery, for about 30 minutes." (*Cincinnati Enquirer,* December 22, 2002)

This type of ad hoc office is also called a **virtual office** (1983) or an **instant office** (1982). For many salespeople, "the office" is wherever they can fire up their laptop or make a call. Increasingly, however, mobile workers are relying on special locations called **telework centers** (1981; also: **telecenter)** that rent out offices or cubicles equipped with office supplies, electronic tools, and Internet access:

> The Washington area, with its hair-pulling traffic delays and huge pool of federal workers, has long been the focus of efforts to promote alternative work schedules. The region is home to more than a dozen government-financed **telework centers,** where employees in the public or private sectors can rent a cubicle or computer-equipped office space for about $25 a day. (*Washington Post,* October 7, 2001)

The typical telework center is a government-funded location that not only offers a workstation and access to the Internet, but also many of the standard office accoutrements, including printers, photocopiers, image scanners, and voice mail. Many even have a receptionist who can sign for courier packages and process incoming mail.

If the worker just needs to make a quick stop to check messages, download e-mail, or send a fax, he or she might prefer a **touchdown center** (1997):

> [British Telecom] buildings already have **touchdown centres** in most major cities, where people can program in their own phone number and plug in their laptop. (*Sunday Herald,* Edinburgh, Scotland, January 21, 2001)

The New Office Landscape

In the 1950s a German design firm called Quickborner Consulting came up with the concept of *Burolandschaft,* or the *office landscape,* which became a bona fide fad in office design circles. Burolandschafters believed that the typical office setup of the day—with managers in offices and employees in rows of desks—was too hierarchical and too rigid. They advocated a more open, egalitarian design where teams—managers and their employees—sat near each other in *islands.* Desk arrangements looked random, but they were set up to facilitate the flow of communication between workers and departments. Some privacy was provided by movable acoustic screens, and the surroundings were made more pleasant with the addition of potted plants and nice carpets.

Unfortunately, this "landscaping" didn't stay in its idealistic form for very long. Managers wanted some acknowledgment of their status, so they were gradually returned to their coveted offices; employees complained about a lack of privacy—particularly **acoustic privacy** (1984), the state or condition of having external sounds reduced or eliminated—so more movable screens were added until eventually Harold Probst's newfangled cubicles became the norm.

So now the typical **officescape** (1983) is a series of manager offices along the building's outer walls and collections of cubicles or desk islands on the interior. At its most extreme, this office design incorporates only one style of office and one style of cubicle, a one-size-fits-all approach called the **universal plan office** (1992) or **universal planning** (1994):

In the eighties and early nineties, the fashion in corporate America was to follow what designers called **"universal planning"**—rows of identical cubicles, which resembled nothing so much as a Levittown. Today, universal planning has fallen out of favor, for the same reason that the postwar suburbs like Levittown did: to thrive, an office space must have a diversity of uses—it must have the workplace equivalent of houses and apartments and shops and industry. (*The New Yorker,* December 11, 2000)

As the author of the above citation (Malcolm Gladwell) says, universal planning is on the outs. The accountants and facilities managers may have loved it—it's cheap and it's easy to move people to and fro if all the offices and cubicles are the same—but employees hated it for the same reason they'd hate shopping for shoes in a store that carried only one size.

Another trend that led to the death of the universal plan was the newfound popularity of the mobile worker. Managers realized that there was no need to keep a desk on hand for every mobile employee. Why not "downsize" the office by getting rid of the workstations, cubicles, and offices used by wandering workers? But what about when one of these employees needs to use a desk for a day or two, or even just for an hour? To handle this, some companies keep a few unassigned desks that mobile workers can reserve in advance. (The only rule? No doodling on the blotter.) Since this is not unlike reserving a room in a hotel, this practice is known as **hotelling** (1991; also: **hoteling**):

A third-year associate with PricewaterhouseCoopers, Paul has been working out of client offices for the past six months. Now between assignments, he has relocated for a four-day stretch in the firm's downtown San Diego high-rise. Paul reserved his favorite private corner desk—the one that affords him an expansive view of San Diego Bay. He knows, though, that this view is only temporary. He will be leaving for another client's office soon. . . . Welcome to the concept of **"hoteling,"** where employees make reservations for work space, check in for an afternoon, a day or a week, and then move along to make room for someone else. (*San Diego Union-Tribune,* April 17, 2002)

This is also called **free-addressing** (1988) or **hot-desking** (1991), a phrase that also comes in verb and noun flavors, all of which you see here:

> Christopher Middleton, who joined IBM recently as a manager for smaller businesses, found **hot-desking** a culture shock, but a positive one. . . . Like many others who **hot desk,** he finds he gravitates to the same desk when he comes into the office. . . . In another multi-national company, one manager who disciplined herself to file everything on her laptop and dispensed with hard copies nevertheless still stuck a small picture of her family on the panel next to "her" **hot desk.** (*Daily Telegraph,* London, October 10, 2002)

The phrase *hot-desking* probably comes from the practice of *hot-bunking,* which is used on most naval vessels and submarines, particularly in wartime, where space is limited and sailors grab whatever bunk is available when the previous shift vacates the sleeping quarters.

Both free-addressing and hot-desking also apply to an office where *no* employee has a permanent desk, which is known as a **non-territorial office** (1985):

> According to visionary consultants and architects, isolated little rooms and musty, cellular offices have no place in the network society. Innovative offices with sexy names like **"non-territorial" office,** "club office" and "fun office" are better suited to modern "knowledge workers." Because, increasingly, office workers do not—or do not have to—put in an appearance at the office, the occupation rate drops. The efficient handling of space and facilities requires the sharing of workplaces. The central office is increasingly assuming the character of a meeting place, and this demands a great degree of open space, and cosy corners. (*Journal of Corporate Real Estate,* December 2001)

An office with this type of arrangement is also called an **alternative office** (1992) or a **just-in-time office** (1987).

Does it work? Yes and no. IBM used hotelling to shrink its Cranford, New Jersey, facility from 400,000 square feet to a positively svelte 100,000 square feet. On the other hand, the Chiat/Day advertising agency had to abandon its free-addressing scheme when workers complained about the lack of structure.

Malcolm Gladwell says that the current thinking among innovative office designers is to make the workplace resemble a vibrant urban neighborhood that encourages interaction. Chiat/Day's failed experiment with a non-territorial office has been abandoned in favor of the "urban office" concept, as Gladwell explains:

> The agency is in a huge old warehouse, three stories high and the size of three football fields. It is informally known as Advertising City, and that's what it is: a kind of artfully constructed urban neighborhood. The floor is bisected by a central corridor called Main Street, and in the center of the room is an open space, with café tables and a stand of ficus trees, called Central Park. There's a basketball court, a game room, and a bar. Most of the employees are in snug workstations known as nests, and the nests are grouped together in neighborhoods that radiate from Main Street like Paris arrondissements. (*The New Yorker,* December 11, 2000)

This type of workplace is most often called a **lifestyle office** (1999):

> **"Lifestyle offices"** are the buzz concept in architectural circles. The 24-hour economy and changing employment patterns are having a radical impact on office life. Work space and social space are overlapping and the office is becoming an extension of our other lives. Companies are creating leisure and relax-

ation zones—spaces that also double as informal meeting points for the exchange of ideas. So you could find a bar at your workplace—somewhere to unwind after you have closed down your computer. Or there may be a basketball net, allowing you to leap up and down and combat office stress. (*Evening Standard,* London, May 20, 2002)

The cubicle—the symbol par excellence of the modern workplace—has come a long way from its humble beginnings as a kind of bedroom. Old Harold Probst probably had no idea that he was the creator of an officescape that included inhabitants such as prairie dogs, corridor cruisers, and nesters; landmarks such as veal-fattening pens, ego walls, and hot desks; and actions such as universal planning, hotelling, and hot-desking. Ah, if only his invention had solved that pesky idiot salutation problem.

Chapter 20

The Dot-Com Rise and Fall

But how do we know when irrational exuberance has unduly escalated asset values, which then become subject to unexpected and prolonged contractions? —*Alan Greenspan*

In a hurricane, even pigs can fly. —*Anonymous*

In his book *The Devil's Dictionary,* Ambrose Bierce defined *positive* as "Mistaken at the top of one's voice." The editors at *Wired* magazine must be a positive bunch, indeed, because they spent much of the last half of the 1990s shouting to anyone who would listen that, thanks to the high-tech revolution, immense riches and unending happiness would soon become the new human condition.

If, while we're hunkered down here on Hindsight Road, we can look up, way, way up, and just discern the faint outlines of a high-water mark for this so-called New Economy, what we're probably seeing is the July 1997 issue of *Wired*. The cover showed an illustration of Earth with a smiley face superimposed on the Western Hemisphere and a flower dangling hippielike from its mouth. Below it, the words "THE LONG BOOM" bellowed, along with one of *Wired's* trademark subtitles-with-attitude: "We're facing 25 years of prosperity, freedom, and a better environment for the whole world. You got a problem with that?"

The problem, of course, was a little something called the business cycle, the death of which had been greatly exaggerated. To be fair, *Wired* wasn't alone in its failure to learn from history.

Dozens, nay, hundreds of pundits and prognosticators also saw nothing but blue skies from now on. Their collective inability to look down once in a while and see the bubble on which the economy was sitting harmed more than their reputations. It also humbled many a newly minted millionaire and, worse, cost lots of average Joes and Josephines substantial portions of their savings. (In a nice example of journalistic symmetry, the cover of the June 9, 2002, issue of the *New York Times Magazine* was emblazoned with the headline "The Long Hangover: Paying the price for the boom.")

Only two groups of people profited through the entire boom and bust: lawyers (of course) and language lovers. Why the latter? Because both the ride up and the ride down generated great gobs of new lingo. Most of these coinages were as substantial as the air molecules or electrons via which they were first disseminated, but a few are worth recording for posterity, which is what I'll do in this chapter.

The Dot Boom

Throughout the 1990s, many words and phrases competed to be the linguistic poster boy for the New Economy. E-commerce, B2B, and others made their pitches, but one phrase in particular seems to have become lodged in the popular consciousness:

> **dot-com** *n.* (1994) A company that runs its business on and derives its revenues from the Internet. Also: **dot com, dot.com, dotcom,** and **.com.** *In 1998—according to Competitive Media Reporting, which tracks ad spending— the **dot-coms** spent $324 million on TV advertising. By the end of June, they had already spent $399 million and were expected to drop a whopping $2 billion on ads for the new fall season. Already, the companies have driven the average*

price per 30-second ad during next month's Super Bowl to nearly $3 million. (Florida Times-Union, January 4, 2000) —adj. (1996) Of or relating to such a company. *You can't turn on the television, listen to the radio, or drive down the highway without being bombarded by advertisements for* **"dot com"** *companies. (Boston Globe,* October 7, 1999)

The term comes from the addresses these companies use on the Internet, such as SellMyPoorMothersSoulForADollar.com and NotOldEnoughToVoteButWorthABillionDollarsAnyway. com. With these cyberspatial signposts (which are called *domain names* by the Net's tall-forehead types), you include the dot in the pronunciation, which means a name such as rutabagas.com would be pronounced as "rutabagas dot-com." For years TV shows, radio programs, and cocktail party conversations were riddled with references to "this dot-com" and "that dot-com." So it's natural that the "dot-com" part would eventually morph into a generic marker for these Internet companies.

For a bit of variety, dot-coms have had other aliases, as well:

e-tailer *n.* (1997) An Internet-based retail operation. Also: **etailer.** *Now, if stock peddlers have their way, it's the turn of Internet retailers—or* **e-tailers,** *as they're known. (Washington Post,* April 22, 1997)

Netco *n.* (1997) An Internet-based company. Also: **netco.** *The government should have created at least a* **Netco** *to own and operate the network for use by all service providers. (Exchange,* August 22, 1997)

new chip *n.* (1998) A relatively young technology company. *Blue chips vs.* **new chips***; Bedrock investors used to sneer at tech stocks, decrying the neophytes who eagerly snatched them up. Now, they've been transformed, loading up on these hot new shares. (Wall Street Journal,* March 12, 2000)

An e-tailer does business in the online world only. However, there are retailers that have their corporate feet in both the online and offline worlds, which leads us to a term that is a close cousin of dot-com:

> **dot-bam** *n.* (1999) The Internet version of a traditional offline retailer. Also: **dot bam, dot.bam,** and **dotbam.**
> *The report says online retail is strong in many industry cate-gories, including computers, autos, books, sporting goods and catalog sellers. What's significant is that many analysts pre-dicted a sharp drop after the Christmas season. But that didn't happen, which is welcome news for today's surviving e-tail-ers—and downright encouraging for **dotbams** stepping up their Web efforts.* (InternetWeek, June 19, 2000)

The "bam" part is an acronym that stands for *bricks-and-mortar,* an old (nineteenth-century) adjective used to describe some-thing made of bricks. The 1990s saw a resurgence of this term with a more specific meaning: of or relating to something that has a physical presence in the real world, which provides a use-ful contrast to those entities that have a virtual presence in the online world. Bricks-and-mortar businesses have also been called **stores with doors** (1999) and are said to engage in **face-to-face sales** (1991).

For a dot-bam, the adjective-of-choice is **clicks-and-mortar** (1999), a fun play on bricks-and-mortar, where "clicks" (as in computer mouse clicks) denotes the online portion and "mor-tar" stands in for the real-world end of things. Poetry fans might prefer the rhyming **clicks-and-bricks** (1999), and they'd no doubt appreciate that an employee who moves from a tradi-tional company to a dot-com is said to move **from bricks to clicks** (1999). And those gung-ho retailers that sell stuff online, in a physical store, *and* through a catalog? Folks are describing them as **tri-channel** (1999) and the experience as **multi-**

channel shopping (1999). (In biz-speak, a *channel* is a method by which goods are distributed or sold.)

As online businesses, it's easy to forget that dot-coms and dot-bams are more than just pretty websites. They actually have people working for them, doing whatever it is that dot-com people do when they're not playing Frisbee indoors or drinking Jolt cola. The generic name for such a worker is an obvious one:

> **dot-commer** *n.* (1997) A person who works for a dot-com company. Also: **dot commer, dot.commer,** and **dotcommer.** *Sure, the stereotype still exists of Doritos-scoffing programmers hunched over computer keyboards and spouting technical gobbledegook. But most **dot commers** are young, savvy, entrepreneurial. And mobile. (South China Morning Post, April 30, 2000)*

A person who hires dot-commers is called a **nerd rustler** (1998), and a recruiting campaign that targets another dot-com is called a **nerd raid** (1997).

If you're the person who founded the company in the first place, you have your very own term:

> **entreprenerd** *n.* (1984) A person with programming, engineering, or other technical skills who builds an online business around a product created with those skills. *In his black jeans and Joe 90 specs, Salem is one of a new breed of entrepreneurs who are finding that in the alternative reality called cyberspace, anything is possible. At first blush these virtual prospectors—the **"entreprenerds,"** as they are occasionally described—seem a very different species to the generation of sharp-suited opportunists who rode the dizzy boom of the Thatcher years. (The Guardian, London, October 4, 1999)*

This term combines the words *entrepreneur,* a businessperson who launches new companies, and *nerd,* a person who is tech-

nically skilled, often obsessively so. It was likely coined by
Robert Levering, Michael Katz, and Milton Moskowitz in their
1984 book, *The Computer Entrepreneurs*. Here's a similar term:

> **yettie** *n.* (2000) A young person who owns or runs a tech-
> nology company. *The **yettie** represents a new branch of
> business culture in the corporate evolutionary tree.* (*Sunday
> Times,* London, February 13, 2000)

This comes from the mischievous phrase *young, entrepreneurial,
tech-based, twenty-something* and is a play on *yuppie (young,
urban professional*). It also contains deliberate echoes of *yeti,* a
hypothetical apelike creature that is supposed to inhabit the
Himalayas. The yeti is a close cousin of North America's abominable snowman, so you often see the adjective "abominable"
and the noun "yettie" in the same sentence (or else shooting's-
too-good-for-'em puns such as "the abominable showman").

As the dot-com feeding frenzy took hold, the people running
these companies starting becoming very rich, indeed:

> **sneaker millionaire** *n.* (1999) A young person, particularly
> one working in a technology-based industry, who is finan-
> cially wealthy. *Lately Gordon has been selling million-dollar
> homes to **sneaker millionaires.*** (*Newsweek,* August 9, 1999)

If the person isn't that young (and, hence, is less likely to wear
sneakers to the office), a more general term is **millionerd** (*millionaire* + *nerd;* 1996). If the person's wealth is tied up in stock
options (in other words, he or she is rich only on paper), use **op-
tionaire** (*options* + *millionaire;* 1999), instead.

Investors are often leery of companies run by people who can
still remember what puberty was like. So dot-coms try to as-
suage these fears by providing a bit of age balance:

> **gray matter** *n.* (1995) Older executives with extensive
> business experience, especially those recruited by a new

company trying to appear more established. **Gray matter**: *Older, experienced people who are hired by young firms.* (*Dallas Morning News,* December 25, 1995)

This is a play on the original sense of *gray matter* : intelligence or brains (from the general color of brain tissue). In this case, the "gray" part refers to the most likely hair color of these older employees. In fact, such a person is also often called a **gray hair** (1986) or, since baldness is often associated with age, a **no hair** (2001).

Age balance is one thing, but new companies also need knowledge balance, as well. That's because most new dot-coms are started by programmers or engineers who wouldn't know a balance sheet if it bit them in the pocket protector. Here's how many new companies make up for this lack:

knowledge angel *n.* (2001) An individual with extensive knowledge in one or more aspects of business who helps a new company that lacks expertise in those areas. *About 50 advisers, called* **knowledge angels,** *are expected to provide hands-on expertise for clients.* (*Daily Deal,* New York, February 8, 2001)

Why an "angel"? Generally, an *angel* is a kind person or one who provides guidance. More to the point, a knowledge angel is most likely a play on the term **angel investor** (1976), an individual who makes a significant investment in a new company. Alternatively, the company might hire a **virtual manager** (1999), a consultant or manager from another company who provides management expertise for a new business.

These new companies are often called *startups* (1960), a term that can refer to any new business venture, but applies particularly to companies that are still looking for financing. If an angel investor isn't hovering over the startup, then the company's managers need to plead with a *venture capital* (VC) firm to supply the money. Here's a list of new words that are related to this stage in a dot-com's life:

burn rate *n.* (1984) The rate at which a newly formed company spends cash on startup costs, research and development, and other expenses. *Not long after Paul Brockbank took over as CEO of Ah-ha.com, prospects did not look good. At a* **burn rate** *of nearly $150,000 per month, the money was almost gone.* (*Utah Business,* November 1, 2000)

drive-by VC *n.* (1999) A venture capital firm or investor that supplies money to a new company, but does not offer any other type of support or expertise. *"We're trying to be the antithesis of the* **drive-by VC**," *Tobin said. "It's our intention to nurture those companies as a network."* (*Business Journal,* June 30, 2000)

incubator *n.* (1980) A company that helps a startup business by providing office space and equipment, arranging financing, and offering business guidance. *"**Incubators** are the future of business," said Howard Morgan, vice chairman of Pasedena-based Internet* **incubator** *Idealab. "The model has created a way for start-ups to hit the ground running by learning from and collaborating with other companies in the* **incubator**." (*Los Angeles Times,* January 3, 2000)

restartup *n.* (1995) A company that is unsuccessful with its initial business, but has enough capital to start a new business. Also: **re-startup.** *Crosspoint Solutions, Inc. of Santa Clara, CA, an FPGA* **"re-startup,"** *has named Robert Blair president and CEO.* (*Semiconductor Industry & Business Survey,* May 8, 1995)

venture catalyst *n.* (1988) A firm or person that obtains financing for new companies that would otherwise not have access to venture capital. *Garage.com is part of a new and emerging group of so-called* **venture catalysts.** *Armed with more than just a catchy name, the catalysts help funnel some of Silicon Valley's venture capital to startups that for various reasons can't otherwise get their hands on it.* (Fortune, April 12, 1999)

vulture capitalist *n.* (1978) A venture capitalist who supplies financing under extremely onerous terms. *Venture capitalists are offering the companies they bankroll increasingly hard-knuckled deals that leave little wealth for a start-up's managers or original backers. . . . Some entrepreneurs agree to the harsh new terms simply because they have no other way to raise cash to survive. But other managers now shun the investors, whom they call* "**vulture capitalists,**" *bent on picking the meat off a young or struggling start-up.* (New York Times, July 28, 2002)

The Dot Bust

From a linguistic point of view, the New Economy fuss was mostly about generating buzzwords. If you were brave enough to read the press releases and websites of these companies, you'd have to wade through such warm-the-cockles-of-an-MBA's-heart gems as e-tailer, tri-channel, and burn rate (to name three that you've seen so far in this chapter).

But then the dot-com boy wonders started making boy blunders. (My favorite example is an outfit called computer.com, which blew more than half of its venture capital—over $3 million—on a few Super Bowl commercials. Not surprisingly, the company is now out of business.) And once the frenzy turned into a fizzle, we saw the emergence of a new linguistic entity that

I like to call the *anti-buzzword*: a twist on an existing buzzword that pokes fun at the original concept.

With dot-com, for example, you see some wonderfully (and wickedly) inventive wordplay:

dot-coma *n.* (1999) The moribund state of the technology industry as a whole, or of a failed or failing dot-com in particular. *The lackluster debuts were part of an overall **dot-coma** that hit the Internet sector in trading yesterday.* (*Seattle Times,* July 31, 1999)

dot-commiserate *n.* (2000) What people who have been laid off or fired from a dot-com, or who are directly affected by a dot-com failure, do when they get together. *Web Integrators **Dot-Commiserate** Over High-Profile E-tailer Failures.* (*Computer Reseller News,* April 24, 2000)

dot-commode *n.* (2001) The metaphoric toilet into which a dead dot-com has fallen. (A *commode* is a chair or box-shaped piece of furniture holding a chamber pot covered by a lid.) *The bitchin' '90s are . . . financed by idiots throwing money down the **dot commode**.* (*Daily Bruin,* Los Angeles, February 20, 2001)

dot-compost *n.* (2000) What remains after a dot-com goes under. *Here are a few sites we wouldn't mind seeing on the **dot-compost** heap.* (*USA Today,* June 13, 2000)

dotcom-uppance *n.* (2000) The just and richly deserved demise of a dot-com. Also: **dot-comuppance** and **dotcomuppance.** *Dotcom-uppance; Investors in rush to get back to the old economy.* (*Daily Mail,* London, April 19, 2000)

Other wordsmiths, clearly reveling in the dot-com downturn, resorted to rhyme, assonance, and alliteration:

dot-bomb *n.* (1999) A failed dot-com. Also: **dot bomb** and **dot.bomb.** *Layton addresses how . . . companies . . .*

*that are unable to sustain a profit can quickly go from "out-standing dot.coms to potential **dot.bombs.**" (Business Wire,* October 11, 1999)

dot-carnage *n.* (2000) The widespread and indiscriminate slaughter of dot-coms. Also: **dot carnage** and **dot.carnage.** *The **dot-carnage** will also clear the path for the next boom, which techies say is sure to come. (USA Today,* June 22, 2000)

dot-com Darwinism *n.* (2000) Survival of the fittest as applied to the dot-com species. ***Dot-com Darwinism;** E-retailer die-off is predicted. (Austin American-Statesman,* April 13, 2000)

dot-com deathwatch *n.* (2000) A vigil kept over a dying dot-com. *Now it may separate survivors from those bound for the **dot-com deathwatch.** (Business Week,* June 5, 2000)

dot-com graveyard *n.* (2000) The metaphorical resting place of deceased dot-com companies. Also: **dot com graveyard, dot.com graveyard,** and **dotcom graveyard.** *Brandwise joins **dot-com graveyard.** (News and Observer,* Raleigh, N.C., May 27, 2000)

dot-dead *adj.* (2000) Of or relating to a defunct dot-com company. Also: **dot.dead** and **dotdead.** *Dot.com can be very dangerous. It can be dot.com or **dot.dead.** (Malaysia Economic News,* April 27, 2000) —*n.* (2001) Such a company. *Some of you took the plunge and went to a dot-com, which is now a **dot-dead.** (CBS News,* February 21, 2001)

dot-gloom *n.* (2000) The feeling of despair or despondency that characterized the dot-com downturn. Also: **dot gloom** and **dot.gloom.** *Internet World trade show convenes amid **dot-gloom.** (San Jose Mercury News,* October 26, 2000)

dot-gone *adj.* (2000) Relating to a dot-com company that is no longer in business. Also: **dot.gone, dot gone,** and **dotgone.** *By next year, when Super Bowl XXXV rolls around, a lot of these dot-coms may be **dot-gone.*** (*San Francisco Examiner,* January 30, 2000) —*n.* (1998) Such a company. Also **dot-goner.** *Many of today's much-hyped "dot coms" will soon be "dot gones."* (*The Record,* Bergen County, N.J., December 21, 1998)

People who don't like dot commers very much prefer to call them **dot communists** (2000) and are said to be suffering from **dot-com rage** (2000): anger caused by the perceived commercialization of the Internet. If that rage reaches a boiling point, the person might decide to stop going online altogether, at which point he or she would become a **not com** (1999).

Another New Economy buzzword that has come under linguistic attack since the dot-coms started dropping like flies is the adjective **B2B** (1996). This is short for *business-to-business,* and it describes transactions in which one company sells a service or product directly to another company. This became one of the more notorious buzz-abbreviations, so it was inevitable that the world's wiseacres would take those infamous initials and twist them into something more fitting for the times:

B2B: back-to-banking
B2B: back-to-basics
B2B: back-to-business school

And since there were lots of other "B2-whatever" buzzwords (such as **B2C,** business-to-customer), the fun didn't end there:

B2C: back-to-consulting
B2M: back-to-Mom's
B2P: back-to-parents

B2R: back-to-reality
B2S: back-to-school

That "back-to-school" crack is a shot at the relative youth of many of the dot-commers. Here are two more digs:

dot snot *n.* (2000) A young person with an arrogant and self-important manner because he or she has become rich by creating a dot-com company. Also: **dot-snot.** *The results of that obsession are . . . a lot of excessively rich kids—referred to locally as "dot snots"—who wander around town as if they own the place.* (*PC Magazine,* May 9, 2000)

sneakers-up *adj.* (2001) Of or relating to a deceased dot-com. Also: **sneakers up.** *More than 200 dot-coms have already gone sneakers-up.* (*New York Times,* February 11, 2001)

Sneakers up is a play on the idiom *belly-up:* of or relating to a failed or bankrupt company. This idiom also plays a role in a new abbreviation:

MTBU *n.* (1986) Maximum time to belly-up; the maximum number of days, weeks, or months that a company is expected to survive. *Investors keep track of how much money their portfolio companies have on hand, and how long they can survive without an additional infusion. This is the MTBU—"maximum time to belly-up."* (*Boston Globe,* November 12, 2001)

Someone with a tech background must have come up with this one because it's almost certainly a play on the abbreviation *MTBF,* Mean Time Between Failures, which is a measure of the average time (usually in hours) between failures for devices such as computer hard drives and printers. Here's another phrase that has a similar meaning:

fume date *n.* (1994) The date on which a company runs out or is expected to run out of cash. *Was it a success? The WebTaggers guys say they will not know until the wire transfer date, Aug. 15, when WebTaggers anticipates that funds from investors will have traded hands. After that? Jan. 1, 2001, the "fume date," which no one really wants to think about—the point at which, if no venture capital is coming in, the partners must admit defeat.* (*New York Times,* June 7, 2000)

It's likely that this phrase came from the idiom *running on fumes,* which refers to something (usually a car) that is so low on gas that it must be running on whatever fumes remain in the tank. Since a startup company's relationship to money is analogous to a car's relationship to gas, the date that a company runs out of money would be its "running on fumes date," or just its fume date. And if a startup shelves its plans to file an IPO (initial public offering; selling the company's stock to the public) and, instead, files for bankruptcy, then it's better to call it a **startdown** (2001).

Tech stocks weren't helped one bit by the litany of corporate scandals that dominated the business pages in late 2001 and through much of 2002. Enron was the poster company for these scandals, which led to a new term:

Enronomics *n.* (2001) A fiscal policy or business strategy that relies on dubious accounting practices, overly optimistic economic forecasts, and unsustainably high levels of spending. *Democratic National Committee staffers urge candidates to run against "Enronomics," an albatross even worse than recession that they hope to hang around Republican necks.* (*USA Today,* January 23, 2002)

Punsters and wordsmiths had a field day with the Enron name in 2002, coining variations such as **Enronitis, Enronic,**

Enronish, Enronian, Enronista, Enronism, Enronize, End-ron (a play on *end-run*), **Enron-around** (a play on *runaround*), and Enron as a verb.

When dot-com stalwarts such as WorldCom, Tyco, and Global Crossing also succumbed to accounting scandals, the nightly newscasts featured one executive after another paraded around in police custody, a practice that came to be known as the **corporate perp walk** (2002):

> Another week, another **corporate perp walk.** Two former WorldCom executives were led by government agents to federal court in Manhattan, where they face charges related to that company's misstatement of billions in expenses. (*New York Times*, August 4, 2002)

If these corporate scofflaws weren't being led away in handcuffs they were being summoned to testify before various congressional committees. Unfortunately, they never did say very much:

> **Fifth Amendment capitalist** *n.* (2002) An American executive who invokes the Fifth Amendment of the U.S. Constitution to avoid giving testimony regarding possible wrongdoing at his or her company. *We haven't reached the stage yet where the alleged Enron culprits are being called "Fifth Amendment capitalists," but it's probably fair to suggest that those who have used and will be using the legal protection will likewise be assumed to be guilty in doing so.* (*Baltimore Sun*, February 13, 2002)

The U.S. Constitution's Fifth Amendment is usually invoked by a person who does not want to testify before a court of law or other body because the testimony would somehow incriminate that person. This phrase is a play on the term *Fifth Amendment Communist* that was popular when Joseph McCarthy was hunting communist witches in the 1950s.

If a company didn't go sneakers-up during the dot-com Dark Ages, chances are good that its stock price tanked during those dire days. And since most technology companies are listed on the Nasdaq (National Association of Securities Dealers Automated Quotations) exchange, the value of the Nasdaq Composite Index suffered correspondingly. In fact, in the two-year period from early 2000 to early 2002, the index value fell over 60 percent. This led to a new verb:

Nasdaq *v.* (2001) To decline sharply in value or quantity. *Yet while his quarterback rating has **Nasdaqued**, Griese has been criticized for not making enough big plays.* (*Denver Post,* October 28, 2001)

What's not quite so new is the general term for when technology stocks head south:

tech wreck *n.* (1989) A sharp drop in the value of technology stock prices. *But, step gingerly, observers say, because the emerging Internet landscape in Europe is rife with uncertainty, much like the landscape in the U.S., where Internet-focused mutual funds lost between 40 percent to 60 percent of their value within a month during the **tech wreck** this spring.* (*Chicago Tribune,* June 25, 2000)

If an employee's stock options hadn't come due (that is, if the employee wasn't *vested*), then he or she was stuck with these:

underwater options *n.* (1976) Stock options in which the strike price (the price at which the employee is contracted to buy the shares) is higher than the current stock price. *Confronted with the shortcomings of their options strategies, tech companies might be expected to look around for alternatives. But they're not. The few companies that are talking publicly about dealing with their employees' **underwater options** are desperately looking for ways to dial back the clock*

to the way things were before the Nasdaq bear arrived.
(*Fortune,* June 26, 2000)

In other words, the options were not only worth less than the paper on which they were printed, they were simply worthless.

Those employees with even less luck ended up being laid off or fired (or, to use the preferred tech company euphemism, *uninstalled*). By late 2001 tens of thousands of knowledge workers had become knowledge job-seekers. With so many kindred souls wandering the streets, someone had a good idea:

> **pink-slip party** *n.* (1987) A party where each attendee is a person who has recently lost their job, particularly because of a failed or downsized dot-com. *Failure chic has spawned a cottage industry of failurenalia. Academics are writing books about failing. The VH-1 and E! Entertainment cable channels have shown programs about it. An Internet marketing firm called Thehiredguns.com sponsors* **pink-slip parties** *where casualties can get together and "dot-commiserate."* (*New York Times,* August 20, 2000)

If there's a totem pole of the dot-com downtrodden, the low person on it would have to be any student who was promised a high-tech job upon graduation, but then had the offer yanked out from under them. Some of these unfortunates did get a silver (or, I guess, green) lining:

> **apology bonus** *n.* (2001) A bonus paid by a dot-com to a college student who was promised a job before the downturn and now can't afford to be hired. *What is the "apology bonus," and is it becoming a trend?* (*Business Wire,* April 27, 2001)

Did anything good come out of the dot-com debacle? Many people believe that it served to weed out a huge number of companies that probably shouldn't have been in business in the first place. On a more general level, some people have come to see the technology sector in a new light, a sober and realistic view that they're calling, with metaphorical fingers crossed, **post-crash realism** (2001).

Chapter 21

The Art and Science of Politics

The new, old, and constantly changing language of politics is a lexicon of conflict and drama, of ridicule and reproach, of pleading and persuasion. Color and bite permeate a language designed to rally men and women, to destroy some, and to change the minds of others. —*William Safire*

The class of confidential communication commonly called "leaks" play, in my opinion, a vital role in the functioning of our democracy. A leak is, in essence, an appeal to public opinion. Leaks generally do not occur in dictatorships. —*Richard Neustadt*

The story of politics in the 2000s is a tale of contradiction, of seemingly irreconcilable trends, of immovable objects duking it out with irresistible forces:

- When elections roll around, people flock to the sidelines in droves—U.S. presidential election turnout was a paltry 51.2 percent in 2000, up from the mere 48.9 percent who turned out in 1996, but typical for most presidential elections in the twentieth century. (The anomaly was the 1960 Kennedy-Nixon contest, which persuaded 62.8 percent of people to vote.) In state and municipal elections, barely a third of the voting age population bothers to exercise their franchise, and in some municipalities voter turnout is as low as 5 percent. And yet we're awash in political news and information: Read any major newspaper or watch any major network news broadcast and most of the stories will have a political slant.

▪ People say they're disgusted with negative campaign tactics, but negative campaigning works because the "victim" almost always drops in the polls after an attack.

▪ Some people complain about politicians who make decisions based on what the latest polls say, while others berate their elected representatives for not listening to the people.

These and a host of other conflicts are at the heart of what some wags calls **democrazy** (1989), a democracy that has absurd or inequitable characteristics or in which senseless or unjust events occur. These tensions may have sociologists and members of the **punditocracy** (1987) scratching their heads, but word-watchers aren't complaining because conflict is the grease that keeps the word coinage machines humming, as you'll see in this chapter of the latest political words and phrases.

Politicians

The word *politician* is based on the adjective *politic,* which in turn comes to English via a Greek word meaning "citizen." That sounds like a noble pedigree, but the earliest incarnation of *politician* is a negative sense that means "a shrewd schemer; a crafty plotter or intriguer." This meaning was active in the late sixteenth century and still exists today in the phrase "office politician," someone who engages in *office politics* (1917). The sense of politician that refers to a person who makes politics his or her profession doesn't appear until about 40 years after the original negative sense.

Politicians are also often called *politicos* (1630; from the Italian—or possibly the Spanish—word *politico*), which has the slightly negative connotation of a politician who's merely a time-server. For veterans of the political wars, *politician* is often shortened to *pol* (1942; pronounced *pawl*).

These days politicians are given lots of other titles, the cruder examples of which I'll leave to your imagination. Most of these coinages are reflections of a politician's actions or policies. For example, a politician who supports initiatives and policies that harm the environment is called a **pollutician** (1992), a chuckle-inducing blend of *pollution* and *politician*:

> [I]t's my personal feeling that the next wonder of the world will be the discovery of a sincere **"pollutician,"** elephant or donkey. (*Press Journal,* Vero Beach, Fla., March 19, 2001)

A less cynical blend is **businesscrat** (1995), a Democratic Party politician with strong private-sector credentials:

> Senator Bob Kerrey (D-Neb.) couldn't have said it any better. As chairman of the Democratic Senatorial Campaign Committee, he's scouring Corporate America for a few good execs willing to run for the Senate next year. . . . The new **Businesscrats** will have to get used to being loyal Democrats. Most have donated to the GOP as well as the Democratic Party. (*Business Week,* February 13, 1995)

On the right side of the political spectrum there's the **theocon** (1989), a conservative who believes that religion should play a major role in forming and implementing public policy:

> Libertarians distrust Bush's tough law enforcement measures; neocons have split with the White House over foreign policy; cultural pessimists underestimated America's spirit; **theocons** still embrace public religion, a concept instantly outdated by Sept. 11. (*Slate Magazine,* December 3, 2001)

This word combines *theological* and *conservative* to form a nice play on *neocon,* a word that entered the language surprisingly recently, in 1979 (although *neoconservative* dates to 1964).

Today's electorate can tell a hypocrite when they see one and will often coin a word or phrase in honor of the hypocrisy. One of my favorites is the **SUV Democrat** (2001), a politician—particularly a member of the U.S. Democratic Party—who talks about energy conservation but who owns and drives a fuel-inefficient sport utility vehicle.

> Not to her great credit, U.S. Sen. Dianne Feinstein owns a gas-guzzling SUV, even though she believes in global warming and doesn't want to drill in Alaska's Arctic National Wildlife Refuge. In fact, last year the *Los Angeles Times* reported that she owned three SUVs. Which makes her your perfect **"SUV Democrat."** (*San Francisco Chronicle,* May 10, 2001)

One of the reasons that people—particularly young people—are turned off politics is that they believe all politicians are the same. (I call this the "Meet the new boss; same as the old boss" school of political philosophy.) They see George H. W. Bush raising taxes and Bill Clinton cutting welfare, and they conclude that "They're all the same." The language reflects this with the term **Demopublican** (1980), a politician who could be a member of either the Democratic or the Republican Party:

> No person's property or freedom is safe when the **"Demopublicans"** are in session. (*Herald-Sun,* Durham, N.C., February 16, 2003)

Similar constructions are **Demican** (1986) and **Democan** (1990), as well as **Republocrat** (1977), **Republicrat** (1980), and **Repubocrat** (1988).

Voters

Every few years, the politicians polish up their speeches, pucker up their baby-kissing lips, and belly up to the stump to embark on another campaign to win over that inscrutable and elusive creature known as the voter. Out of necessity, politicians must treat voters as generalized entities (because, they'll tell you, you can't please all of the people all of the time), and that often means coming up with labels to represent the average citizen. So we have *the man in the street* (1831), the *woman in the street* (1976), *everyman* (1906), and *everywoman* (1945). There's also *John Q. Public* (1937), *Jane Q. Public* (1977), and *John Q. Citizen* and *Jane Q. Citizen* (1983). Joe is a popular first name for the average bear, and his names have included *Joe Blow* (1924), *Joe College* (1932), *Joe Average* (1936), *Joe Lunchpail* (1965), *Joe Six-Pack* (1970), and *Joe Citizen* (1986), to name just a few.

Today's politicians and pollsters have an unseemly fixation on a particular segment of the electorate known as *swing voters* (1966), independent voters who can decisively influence the outcome of an election. The United States, in particular, elevates the swing voter to mythic status, and with every election cycle the strategists and other big thinkers anoint a new demographic as the Key to Winning the Election.

In the 1994 midterm elections, for example, the swing voter was the **angry white male** (1990), a middle-class white male, particularly one who feels angry because his wages are stagnant or falling, his job isn't secure, or he feels that other groups are getting greater benefits than he is:

> According to census statistics, the weekly earnings of a man smack in the middle of the wage distribution dropped about 15% between 1973 and 1992. That certainly helps explain why the famous **angry white male** voters of 1994 were so angry. (*Rocky Mountain News,* December 29, 1994)

The 1996 presidential election gave us the famous **soccer mom** (1982), a white suburban woman who is married and has children:

> As all alert citizens know by now, politically, this is the Year of the **Soccer Mom. Soccer moms**—those harried, frazzled,

overburdened (but still game and cheerful) women—are this year's critical group of swing voters. Great minds (Dick Morris', for example) have studied them, and vast sums of money have been spent on learning how to woo and win their votes. (*Fort Worth Star-Telegram,* September 15, 1996)

This term's arc through the media is interesting. From its first appearance in 1982 through the end of 1989, "soccer mom" appeared six times in the media. From 1990 through 1995, the phrase showed up about 80 times. Then, in 1996, this suburban symbol was trotted out in no less than 1,150 stories. That impressive spike was due to the incredible amount of ink devoted to the soccer mom demographic in the U.S. presidential election of that year—although, as *Boston Globe* columnist Ellen Goodman pointed out after the election, soccer moms accounted for a mere 6 percent of the electorate, so it's likely that the only thing they were swinging were the side doors of their minivans.

The 1998 midterm elections gave the boot to the soccer mom and replaced her with the **waitress mom** (1996), a married woman who has children, works in a low-income job, and has little formal education:

Forget the suburban, well-educated soccer moms of 1996. "It's actually the **waitress moms** who will decide this election," Democratic pollster Celinda Lake told a forum on women and turnout. These women like the Democrats' views on education, health care and Social Security, but polls show a majority of them are unlikely to vote. (*USA Today,* October 14, 1998)

For the 2000 presidential election, yet another female demographic was trotted out for politicians to fawn over: **WMWMs** (2000), the white married working moms:

In fact, 2000's key voters appear to be white married working moms—in political junkie jargon, **"WMWMs,"** "WM squared," or "WMx2"—because they back Bush by a giant margin that has Democrats wringing their hands. (*New York Post,* August 20, 2000)

Moms, apparently, eschewed silly demographic labels in the 2002 midterm elections, so their husbands picked up the slack in the form of **office park dads** (2002), married suburban fathers working white-collar jobs who represent roughly 15 percent of the U.S. electorate:

"The new blue-collar worker, the new Reagan Democrat, is the **'office park dad,'** " said Simon Rosenberg, executive director of the New Democratic Network. "They're (baby) boomers and busters . . . these are people who make $60,000 a year, and they're struggling to make it in the new economy." (*San Francisco Chronicle,* August 13, 2002)

In 2002 Democrats also focused their attention on the **NASCAR dad** (2002), a white working-class father:

Although politics and pole position might seem an unlikely mix, analysts say Democrats could be on to something. Candidates in recent years have coveted the votes of so-called soccer moms, but pollsters recently have begun extolling a group dubbed **NASCAR dads**—the political demographic du jour. (*Dallas Morning News,* September 16, 2002)

The Republicans, meanwhile, were more concerned with the affluent husband-and-wife team of the **Patio Man** (2002) and the **Realtor Mom** (2002) who live in **Sprinkler City** (2002), a fast-growing outer suburb or exurb:

Republicans were told to pursue **Patio Man** (fond of fancy grills) and his wife **(Realtor Mom),** who live with their kids in **Sprinkler City** (the outer suburbs). (*Sarasota Herald-Tribune,* January 13, 2003)

Campaigning

Once politicians and parties switch into **campaign mode** (1979), both the fur and the neologisms start flying. The latter is a product of what has come to be called **campaignspeak** (1985) or **electionspeak** (1990): the insiderish lingo and jargon favored by political operatives and back-room movers and shakers.

For example, polls are an integral part of any election campaign. Not only do third-party researchers conduct polls to gauge the current support of each candidate—which is duly reported in the media, resulting in some cases in **horse-race journalism** (1983): media coverage that focuses on poll results and political battles instead of policy issues—but the candidates and parties also poll constantly to see which way the political winds are blowing. One strategy employed by in-house pollsters is the **naked re-elect** (1993), a polling question in which respondents are asked whether an incumbent politician deserves to be re-elected:

> Since it is now unclear where the district's constituents will be, Jones asked all Utahns if Matheson has done a good enough job to be re-elected next year, or should someone else new get a chance to serve. Such a question is known as a **"naked re-elect"** in political jargon because there is no opponent listed opposite Matheson. (*The Bulletin's Frontrunner,* August 2, 2001)

As the above citation mentions, the "naked" part of a naked re-elect comes from the fact that the question doesn't mention a specific opponent. Instead, the question simply asks if a particular politician deserves to be re-elected or if someone else should be given a chance to serve.

In recent years, however, a new kind of poll has crawled out from under the research rock:

push poll *n.* (1994) A series of calls, masquerading as a public-opinion poll, in which people who support a particular candidate offer negative information about a rival candidate. *A legitimate public-opinion poll seeks to tally the views of the respondents, while a **push poll** gets its name from its intention to push voters away from an opponent and toward the candidate who paid for the calls.* (*New York Times,* September 13, 1998)

Push polling (1994) is a nasty bit of business, but it's just politics as usual in this age of negative campaigning, where slamming an opponent's character—which is sometimes called **character fragging** (1992; fragging is military slang for "killing")—often is seen as a better strategy than slamming his or her policies. This campaign curmudgeonry is fueled by **opposition research** (1977), a euphemism for potentially scandalous information uncovered while researching a political opponent. Political junkies almost always shorten this phrase to **oppo research** (1992) or just **oppo** (1990). Also: **OPO** or **opo**:

> Griffin works the **oppo** beat for the Republican National Committee, but he's not some shadowy operative whispering shady tips over the phone. As the man in charge of investigating the opposition, the research chief blasts his findings to the entire press corps in mass e-mailings, then sits back and watches the negative stuff spread like a computer virus. (*Washington Post,* February 16, 2003)

Parties and candidates often delegate the delicate business of opposition research to an **oppo firm** (1994) that specializes in this sort of political muckraking. (These outfits are sometimes described as "full service," whatever that might mean.) These firms, or the in-house **oppo units** (1992), are staffed with **oppo researchers** (1992) or **oppo guys** (1996), political operatives who specialize in digging up dirt on opponents:

We see the Bush's "oppo" [opposition] research team, mobilized during the first presidential debate, pouncing on every word from Gore to poke holes into it. "We make the bullets," smiles **oppo guy** Mark Corallo as staffers look up whether or not Gore actually did vote this way or that in the past. (*Toronto Star,* November 2, 2000)

Oppo is often disseminated using **attack ads** (1982) or by placing a strategic phone call or three to the media, but the most common mode is the **attack fax** (1990), a fax transmission—usually sent to the media—that attacks the ideas or conduct of an opponent:

During her quarter-century career as her husband's closest political partner, Clinton helped develop the legendary **"attack fax"** or "instant reply" that proved so effective during the 1992 and 1996 presidential campaigns. (*Hartford Courant,* November 2, 2000)

Faxes, of course, seem hopelessly archaic and low tech to our twenty-first-century sensibilities, which are better able to process the latest way that a candidate can "go negative": the **attack e-mail** (2000):

"Mrs. Dole has gone from negative attack ads against Erskine Bowles' wife to negative **attack e-mails,**" said Bowles spokeswoman Susan Lagana. (*Charlotte Observer,* October 18, 2002)

Dishing political dirt has become so common that it even has its own verb: **Bork** (1987), which means to attack a political opponent in a particularly vicious, partisan manner:

With judges leaving, and new appointees facing the chilling prospect of being **"borked"** if they are not politically correct, the ranks of the judiciary could diminish to critical levels without it, stalling the judicial system. (*Florida Times-Union,* February 27, 2003)

This verb is named after Judge Robert H. Bork, whom Ronald Reagan nominated for the U.S. Supreme Court in 1987. The nomination was rejected by the Senate after Judge Bork's enemies launched a series of vicious attacks in the media, and within a few months the judge's name had become a verb that is now a standard part of the political vernacular.

When a candidate **plays the negative card** (2000), his or her opponent has two choices: take the high road and stick to the issues, or practice **jujitsu politics** (1992) and reply to the attack with a counterattack. Doing the latter might satisfy the candidate's desire for revenge, but an escalating negative campaign can lead to a particularly nasty end:

> **murder-suicide** *n.* (1998) Negative campaigning that damages both the targeted opponent and the politician who initiated the campaign. *A candidate's shelling of an opponent often ricochets back on himself. A classic example was the 1998 "murder-suicide"—a characterization coined by Davis strategist Garry South—when gubernatorial aspirant Al Checchi destroyed both his and Rep. Jane Harman's candidacies with relentless attack ads.* (*Los Angeles Times*, April 4, 2002)

Campaigns and elections sometimes become indelibly associated with particular words and phrases. The 1992 U.S. presidential campaign gave the world the slogan "It's the economy, stupid," which has been gleefully borrowed by headline writers and other wags ever since. (Examples: "It's the environment, stupid"; "It's the tax cut, stupid"; "It's the deficit, stupid"; "It's the stupidity, stupid.") The 1996 campaign hosted the coming-out party for the *soccer mom* (which I discussed earlier in this chapter). The 2000 election will forever be associated in people's minds with a previously obscure four-letter word: **chad.** This humble word entered the language in the 1940s and was content to remain in the shadows. It refers to either the tiny bits of paper left over from punching data cards (in which case it's also called *computer confetti* or *keypunch droppings*) or the perforated strips of computer paper that have been separated from a print-out. It's the punched-out bits of data cards that became the focus of the 2000 election because in Florida, where the close vote required a manual recount, the ballots were of the punch-card variety. As long as a card was perfectly punched there was no problem, but that didn't happen in many cases, resulting in an entire taxonomy of chad. Apparently, there's chad and then there's *chad*:

dimpled chad This is the same as a pregnant chad.

hanging chad A chad in which only one corner remains attached to the card.

loose chad A chad that's completely punched out.

pregnant chad A chad that's only indented slightly and is still fully attached to the card.

swinging chad (or **swinging-door chad**) A chad in which two corners remain attached to the card.

tri-chad A chad in which three corners remain attached to the card.

These are all semiofficial designations that were actually used in the manual recounts. The basic rule was that a ballot with a pregnant (or dimpled) chad was not counted, but a ballot with a hanging chad, a swinging chad, or a tri-chad was counted. Some of the controversy—inevitably dubbed **Chadgate** (2000)—lay in the fact that in most cases, ballots with the latter three chad types would not have been counted by the machine method because the attached chad likely would block the hole when the card was fed through.

The 2000 election also highlighted a few other new words and phrases. For example, a map of the election results appeared to show America divided into two regions: the South and the heartland voted for Republican nominee George W. Bush, while the West Coast and the industrial regions in the North and Northeast voted for Democratic candidate Al Gore. Since Republican states are traditionally shown in red and Democratic states are shown in blue, pundits of both political stripes soon began talking of **red states** (2001) versus **blue states** (2001):

> In the last election there were the **red states** (George W. Bush) and the **blue states** (Al Gore). Some see the division as between Middle America and the two coasts. Other dichotomies are cited as rural and urban, small town and big city, religious and secular. (*The Times Union,* Albany, N.Y., June 21, 2002)

Early on election night, when it appeared that his blue-state Electoral College votes would fall shy of the red-state votes, Gore called Bush to concede the election to him. Within minutes, however, it became clear that the Florida result was going to be too close to call and that a recount of the ballots would take place. Gore then called Bush back and offered him an **unconcession** (2000), a statement that retracts a concession:

> The 2000 presidential election was over for about an hour early Wednesday morning, the interval between when Democratic nominee Al Gore called Republican George W. Bush to concede and when he hit redial and called in his **unconcession.** (Cox News Service, November 10, 2000)

Although the noun *unconcession* first appeared in 2000, the verb **unconcede** actually goes back to 1996, when on election night Republican presidential candidate Bob Dole prematurely sent a concession fax to news organizations and was forced to unconcede.

The Florida recount turned into a full-fledged imbroglio when voters started complaining that the ballots had been confusing and that they thought they voted for the wrong candidate. (My favorite voter quote: "I did find [the Palm Beach ballot] confusing and I'm a member of Mensa.") Lots of people also voted for more than one candidate, a phenomenon known as **overvoting** (1983):

> Election officials who use punch card systems similar to the one in Palm Beach County expect that a certain number of ballots will have more than one hole punched in a given race, a practice called **"overvoting."** (*New York Times,* November 9, 2000)

The whole mess also gave the world a new verb:

> **Florida** *v.* (2000) To cheat someone or something, particularly out of an election victory. *Among Democrats, the new phrase for being cheated out of one's hard-earned desserts by shameless political machinations: "I got **Florida'd."** (San Francisco Chronicle,* November 17, 2000)

Spinning

All human endeavors have an element of art to them, where by "art" I mean a high level of skill. We have the "art of war," the "art of the deal," and even "the art of motorcycle maintenance, Zen and." Political skill is most often seen in the art of **spin** (1977), which means to convey information or cast another person's remarks or actions in a biased or slanted way so as to favorably influence public opinion. As a noun it refers to the information provided in such a fashion.

This stalwart member of the political lexicon probably came from phrases such as "putting a positive (or negative) spin" on something. In turn, this notion of influencing direction almost certainly made the leap from sports such as baseball and billiards where players impart spin on a ball to change its course.

A person who is an expert at influencing public opinion in this way is a **spin doctor** (1984) or a **spinmeister** (1986), and the language that person uses is called **Spinnish** (1988):

> "Inclusion"—decoded from the original **Spinnish**—is the hallmark buzzword of a GOP eager to evade its share of responsibility for the fact that American law continues to stink with racial and ethnic classifications. (*Weekly Standard,* May 17, 1999)

Some call this spin doctor lingo **camouflanguage** (1988), which is language that uses jargon, euphemisms, and other devices to camouflage the true meaning of what is being said.

A **spinner** (1984) will sometimes book a **spin appointment** (1992) with a journalist or other person he or she wants to influence. Often, however, there is a common area where **spin doctoring** (1986) happens—usually a press center or the lobby of the building where a candidate's debate takes place—and this is called **spin alley** (1988) or **spin valley** (1988). It's here where the **spin patrol** (1984) mounts its **spin operation** (1988) with a simple goal in mind: to achieve **spin control** (1984). It has to be careful, however: If it starts spinning too soon—for example, if it's trying to get in some **preemptive spin** (1989)—it might be accused of **premature spin** (1992).

This assumes, of course, that an issue is even **spinnable** (*adj.;* 1990), meaning that it's capable of or susceptible to being influenced by biased or slanted information:

> Imagine that bin Laden remains on the run, his continued freedom inspiring Muslim fundamentalists across the Arab world. Even in the clever political jargon of Washington, it is a stretch to consider such an outcome **"spinnable."** (*South China Morning Post,* September 26, 2001)

Spin is an oral art form that relies on the speaker to spout pithy phrases with a frequency calculated to ensure the message sinks into the listener's consciousness. But some spinning also occurs in written form, usually as stat-filled handouts or faxes. This is called **paper spin** (1992). A related form is **spin journalism** (1998), news stories or facts presented in a biased or slanted way in an attempt to influence public opinion:

> Sir Malcolm Rifkind, the Scottish Tories' general election campaign leader, last night launched a scathing attack on the culture of so-called **"spin journalism,"** as the Conservatives continue to suffer a wave of bad press over claims of internal splits and plots. (*The Herald*, Glasgow, Scotland, April 28, 2001)

Finally, there's the mind-bending concept of **Zen spin** (1999), to spin a story by not doing any spinning at all:

> The benefits of spin were being canceled out by the press's resistance to it. Often we reacted by spinning even harder, but I was beginning to see the virtue in just letting stories go—**Zen spin.** (George Stephanopoulos, *All Too Human*, 1999)

Leaking

If spinning is the political art form, then leaking is its craft. The verb *leak*—to disclose secret or confidential information through unofficial channels for political purposes—is very old. It dates to at least 1859, while the variation *to leak out* dates to 1832. (The noun sense—that is, the information disclosed—only goes back to the 1930s.)

A leak, by definition, is given to a reporter with the understanding that it is *not for attribution,* meaning that the reporter is not allowed to divulge the identity of the leaker. Journalists want to appear "in the know," so they rarely state outright that they were the beneficiary of a leak. Instead, they'll pepper their prose with certain code phrases that indicate the presence of a leak: *senior government official; a source close to X; an informant who asked that his name not be disclosed.* Using these unknown sources is called **blind sourcing** (1995):

> But the prolific **blind sourcing** in Miller's article to "senior American officials," "foreign scientists," "American officials," "an administration official," "administration officials," and "an informant whose identity has not been disclosed" calls into immediate question who talked to Miller about the alleged Madame Smallpox and why. (*Slate Magazine,* December 6, 2002)

Most of the information that a **leakee** (1978) receives comes in the form of an **unauthorized leak** (1975), although many governments now see the wisdom behind the occasional **authorized leak** (1977), which is a leak approved by the government as a way of getting information into the public realm without having to commit itself to the content of the leak:

> Aides for a White House that has denounced **"unauthorized leaks"** put together a plan for which news organizations would be the recipient of **authorized leaks** about the budget. (*Washington Post,* January 6, 1999)

Leaks come in many different forms and serve many different purposes. In the 1980s researcher Stephen Hess (in his book, *The Government/Press Connection*) classified leaks into six distinct types:

> **animus leak** A leak used to embarrass another person, often as a way of settling a grudge. *It's not an **animus leak** intended to hurt somebody.* (*Slate Magazine,* January 29, 2003)
>
> **ego leak** A leak that serves to boost the self-esteem of the leaker. *There are some leaks that are plain **ego leaks**; in*

fact, I think that's the biggest category in Washington, people leaking information who are really saying in a sense, "I'm important because I have important information." (*MacNeil/Lehrer NewsHour,* May 12, 1986)

goodwill leak A leak designed to ingratiate the leaker with a reporter, in the hope that the reporter will then provide favorable coverage down the road. *Miller could have worked back to administration officials who gave her multiple **Good Will Leaks** confirming what she had learned rather than stonewalling her.* (*Slate Magazine,* December 6, 2002)

policy leak A leak for or against a policy in an attempt to garner more press attention for that policy. *If Pentagon and State Department **policy leaks** were smart bombs, Iraq would be a smoldering parking lot by now.* (*Wisconsin State Journal,* August 2, 2002)

trial balloon leak A leak that reveals some or all of a potential policy as a way of assessing public opinion regarding that policy. *This week [British Prime Minister Tony Blair] appeared to be stirring the possum, proposing a UN Security Council–type elite body comprising Germany, France and Britain sitting above what would be an increasingly unwieldy grouping of 25 or 27 leaders once the new entrants were admitted. Under the plan, floated in a **trial balloon leak** to the press, the special council could take executive decisions in between full council meetings.* (*Australian Financial Review,* January 24, 2002)

whistle-blower leak A leak that exposes corruption or wrong-doing. ***Whistle-blower leak:** usually by career civil servants outraged by waste, dishonesty or a cover-up and eager to expose the scandal.* (*Philippine Daily Inquirer,* November 25, 2002)

Hess also recognized a seventh leak type: the *no-purpose leak,* which is a leak that occurs only because politicians are naturally garrulous people. They love to talk, and sometimes when they do they unintentionally disclose information.

With the help of new words, the apparent contradictions of the political world come into focus. People are increasingly turned off politics because they see that it's now closer to a kind of competitive sport played with ruthless intensity by oppo guys, spin doctors, and ego leakers. The interchangeable Demopublicans and Republocrats vie on the playing field of public opinion not to do good works, but to paint the electoral map with an increasing proportion of blue states or red states. Their push polling and attack faxes, their camouflanguage and trial balloon leaks, are tricks to win the hearts and minds—but mostly the *votes*—of the soccer moms and waitress moms, the office-park dads and NASCAR dads. The media revels in all this because horse-race journalism is dramatic and simple and their job as leakees gives them insider status. All of this breeds voter cynicism and apathy, which is a shame because politics is worth paying attention to, if only so that Joe Six-Pack and Jane Q. Public can keep a wary eye on those who represent them.

Chapter 22

Fightin' Words

Modern war needs modern lingo. —*William Safire*

We can best help you to prevent war not by repeating your words and following your methods but by finding new words and creating new methods. —*Virginia Woolf*

World events only have a major effect on our language when they transform the daily lives of millions of Americans, the way World War II did. —*Geoffrey Nunberg*

A language is a dialect with an army and a navy.
—*Max Weinreich*

War has always been one of the most prolific sources of new words. Not only do military organizations generate more than their fair share of jargon, but soldiers seem to have built-in slang generation mechanisms that I assume are implanted during basic training. Not only that, but there's something about war words that make us want to adapt them for everyday use. Our conversations, memos, and business plans are studded with verbs such as *annihilate, entrench, outflank,* and nouns such as *barrage, foray, ration.*

Generally speaking, the larger the war, the more terms it adds to the language. World War I (a term, by the by, that didn't enter the language until 1939) was a long, horrific conflict that produced a long list of new and newly popular words, including *amputee, basket case* (a bit of British black humor that originally referred to a person who was a quadruple amputee), *camouflage, ceasefire, dogfight, front line, GI* (from *government issue*), *home front, lousy* (as in infested with lice), *no-man's land, shell shock, strafe, trench coat,* and *walking wounded.*

Another major conflict, World War II, populated the lexicon with dozens of new terms, including *beachhead, black market, blackout, blitz, blockbuster, bloodbath, evacuate, firepower, flak, foxhole, fraternization, gizmo, gung ho, hit the sack, intercept, jeep, kamikaze, scorched earth, snafu,* and *task force.*

Vietnam, by contrast, was a relatively small war, so its list of new words is comparatively short: *boat people, body count, collateral damage, dove, friendly fire, grunt, hawk, MIA,* and *surgical strike.* Similarly, the first Gulf War was short-lived so it gave us just a few new terms, such as *smart bomb, weapons of mass destruction,* and, most famously, *mother of all————,* which came from Iraqi president Saddam Hussein's claim that the coming fight would be "the mother of all battles." (See the Appendix for a long list of the various *mother of all* constructions that have a appeared since the first Gulf War.)

All wars large and small generate massive numbers of new words and phrases, but only a few of those set up shop in the language and even fewer branch out to create satellite offices in nonwar settings. As you'll see in this chapter, the "war on terror" is no different. It's still too early to tell which of the following words and phrases have linguistic staying power, but I've tried to concentrate on those terms that have remained popular over the past year or two.

September 11, 2001

After those hijacked airliners slammed into the World Trade Center towers, the Pentagon, and an empty Pennsylvania field on September 11, 2001, few observers gave much thought to what these events meant for the future of the language. Heck, most people were too busy thinking about what these events meant for the future of the *world*. But language changes in unconscious ways, too, so lots of words related to the events of that awful day started showing up without anyone really noticing.

The prime example of this "behind the scenes" neology is the term that is now most closely associated with that day—**9/11**:

> "Some days, I just want a normal life like other women," said Kristen Breitweiser, who lost her husband, Ronald. "I want to go food shopping. I want to bake an apple pie. I don't want to be a **9/11** widow for the rest of my life." (*New York Times,* September 9, 2002)

This term became a part of the lexicon literally overnight. By September 12, 2001, most of the world knew or could easily figure out what *9/11* meant. This was even true (although to a lesser extent) in countries such as Canada, Britain, and Australia, where "9/11" means November 9. Dozens of newspapers and magazines used *9/11* in their September 12 editions, so trying to figure out who coined the term is meaningless. Here's a typical example from that day:

> "Remember Pearl Harbor" became the rallying cry of a generation of Americans battling for freedom against tyranny after a Dec. 7, 1941, Japanese attack. . . . "Remember **9/11**" will be the rallying cry of this generation of Americans standing for freedom against terrorism. (*Duluth News Tribune,* September 12, 2001)

In a result that was a surprise to no one, *9/11* was voted "Word of the Year" for 2001 by the American Dialect Society. (The phrase voted "Most Inspirational" was *let's roll,* the last known words of Todd Beamer, a passenger on the hijacked flight 93, which crashed into an empty field rather than into its intended target, which may have been the White House.) *9/11* was also voted "Most Likely to Succeed," which is an interesting prediction (and one that is by no means guaranteed to come true). Strangely, *9/11* didn't generate very many phrases of its own. Here's one:

> **Generation 9/11** *n.* (2001) The generation of people who were enrolled in high school or college on September 11, 2001. *After the deadliest attack on American soil in the history of the republic, the generation that previously seemed direction-less and without a fitting title now had one—**Generation 9/11**. "After Sept. 11, there was a definite change," said Luke Punzenberger, president of Marquette University Student Government. It's something I can't put my finger on. You walk down campus and it just feels different."* (*Marquette Tribune*, Milwaukee, Wis., November 16, 2001)

This phrase appears to have been coined by whatever *Newsweek* editor decided to title that magazine's November 12 cover story "Generation 9-11." There are citations in the media prior to November 12, but they're all discussing the forthcoming *Newsweek* article. I did manage to find a couple of dozen articles that used *Generation 9/11* (or *Generation 9-11*) without referencing the *Newsweek* piece, so it's possible that this label may have some longevity.

Besides *9/11*, many people also used the less ambiguous phrase, **September 11**, particularly as part of longer phrases, such as *the events of September 11* and *the terrorist attacks of September 11*. There's also **September 11 syndrome** (2001), feelings of anxiety and dread associated with the terror attacks:

> According to Dr. [Harriet] Braiker, Americans on the whole have shown remarkable "surface resiliency" in carrying on with their daily lives in the short- and long-term aftermath of the September 11 attacks. But she voices concern about the acute levels of anxiety that lurk beneath the surface, and specifically takes the Bush administration to task for actively contributing to that nervous-

ness—"keeping us on a shaky footing for reasons known only to the White House"—and not taking obvious and somewhat simple steps to alleviate it. She refers to this uncertainty as part of the **"September 11 Syndrome"**—a term she coined to describe the nationwide anxiety epidemic that resulted from the aftermath of that terrible day, and of a nation still waiting for the other shoe to drop. (*Business Wire,* September 5, 2002)

For a while after 9/11, people used the phrase **so September 10** (or **so 9-10**) to describe something that seemed naive, innocent, or clueless in a before-the-attacks kind of way:

But perhaps the most memorable line I've heard came on the radio recently. Daphne Brogden is the former producer for nationally syndicated radio physician Dr. Dean Edell. Brogden, who now has her own Direct-TV movie show, called her old boss the other day to offer this story. Brogden says she was at a rock concert with her sister after the New York and Washington attacks. The band's vain lead singer was preening and mugging on stage. After observing this behavior and hearing the singer repeatedly plug his new CD, Brogden told Edell her sister turned to her and said, "That's **SO Sept. 10.**" (*CBS MarketWatch,* October 4, 2001)

You don't see *so September 10* very much these days, and in fact it was replaced for a while by **so September 12** (2003), which describes something that's reminiscent or evocative of the day after the terrorist attacks:

Tired of the now **"so Sept. 12"** look of Semper Fi and "I Love New York" T-shirts, other au courant celebrities have taken a different, yet equally fatuous, turn in their attire of choice. Recently, such luminaries as Ben Affleck, Minnie Driver and Jennifer Blanc have been spotted in Christ apparel, T-shirts emblazoned with the following legends: "Jesus Is My Homeboy"; "I Love Jesus" and "Jesus Hates Your Botox." (*The Globe and Mail,* Toronto, January 11, 2003)

Will *9/11* find a permanent niche in the language? The sheer ubiquity of the term means that it probably will stick around for a long time. The more straightforward *September 11* is almost certainly doomed since, now that we've seen a few other September 11s go by (2002, 2003, etc.), saying just the month and day is becoming more ambiguous unless some other context is provided.

Post-9/11 Words

Thinking back to September 11, 2001, and the days that followed, one of the things that struck me as a language watcher was how much people struggled with words to describe either the enormity of the attacks or the depth of their feelings about the terrible results. A mute shock quickly became everyone's natural state, and when words did come, "It was like watching a movie" became the standard refrain.

When the politicians found their voices, they did strange things, like resurrecting archaisms such as *evildoers* (1398) and foisting upon us foreign-sounding words such as *homeland* (1670). We all struggled with the proper pronunciation of *Al Qaeda* (it's al KAY.duh), we found out what the *Taliban* was, and we learned the difference between a *burqa* and a *chador*.

We also started using some old words and phrases in new ways. For example, in the aftermath of the collapse of the World Trade Center towers, the resulting debris field became known almost immediately as **ground zero** (the firefighters, police, and construction types who worked there also called it "the pile"). *Ground zero* (1946) has been around for a while and traditionally has referred to the area underneath an exploding bomb, particularly a nuclear weapon. The earliest media citation I could find for this new sense of the phrase was an ABC News transcript of a show that aired at 3:05 A.M. on September 13, 2001:

At 11:01, the journey in began and the landscape changed through streets filled with dust and ash, past trucks waiting to haul away debris, exhausted police and firemen with dazed looks into a nightmare set in another world that was named for the center of a nuclear blast, **ground zero.** (*ABC News Special Report: America Under Attack,* September 13, 2001)

Another phrase repurposed in the post-9/11 period was **weapons-grade** (1990), an adjective meaning "extreme; intense":

And you were just on a ride? You were not down there for some of that **weapons-grade drugs** they have there? (National Public Radio, December 18, 2001)

This adjective is normally used to describe a fissionable material—such as uranium or plutonium—that's of suitable quality to be used in the making of a nuclear weapon. In the months after 9/11, however, we were exposed, so to speak, to dozens of references to a nasty bit of business called **weapons-grade anthrax** (2001). This is a deadly virus that was being sent in powder form via the mail and causing sickness, death, and terror around the country. The anthrax virus is nasty enough in its regular form (if *regular* can be used for something so deadly), but the *weapons-grade* flavor uses extremely small spores (a few *microns*—millionths of a meter—in diameter). Their tiny size means that the spores are easily spread and inhaled, which is what makes them suitable to be used as a weapon.

Soon, however, people were taking up the **weapons-grade** adjective and applying it to more mundane objects. Besides the drugs reference in the above citation, I've also seen *weapons-grade* used to modify the following things: tequila, salsa, peanut butter, charisma, cheddar cheese, slap-shots, punctuation (!?), and, ahem, certain intestinal gases, referred to in semipolite society as *wind.*

By the way, the anthrax-by-mail scare resulted in a new phrase that shined brightly for a few months:

collateral mail *n.* (2001) Mail that contains or has been tainted by a noxious substance, especially the anthrax virus. *Greg Poland, a professor of medicine and infectious diseases at the Mayo Clinic in Rochester, Minn., said that although "no envelope is airtight" and any powder inside could be squeezed out in processing, the probability of a significant number of anthrax spores escaping is low. . . . So far, he said, no anthrax cases have been caused by what he called "**collateral mail**."* (*Washington Post*, October 24, 2001)

This euphemistic phrase was itself based on another euphemism, the notorious *collateral damage*, a term that military double-spokespersons use to refer to the unintentional harm to civilian life or property that occurs during a military operation. The source of the euphemism is the word *collateral*, which in this sense means "additional but secondary" (collateral comes from the Latin *collateralis*, literally "side by side with"). Given this, *collateral mail* didn't quite work because the inherent harm in such mail is implied only via the phrase's relation to collateral damage. Of course, attempting to undergird militaryspeak with a rational etymological support is almost always a foolish exercise. But I digress.

On March 19, 2002, the *Washington Post* ran an article claiming teenagers were appropriating the words of the post-9/11 world as the raw material for slang:

Their bedrooms are "ground zero." Translation? A total mess.
A mean teacher? He's "such a terrorist."
A student is disciplined? "It was total jihad."
Petty concerns? "That's so Sept. 10."
And out-of-style clothes? "Is that a burqa?"
(*Washington Post*, March 19, 2002)

Now it's true that teenagers tend to be more verbally daring than their elders. And we've seen that *so September 10* was a phrase with some currency, although not just among teenagers. But *ground zero* for a messy bedroom? *Burqa* for a nonstylish article of clothing? Nope, sorry, thanks for playing, though. Although the *Post* story cites an outfit called the "Center at Georgetown for the Study of Violence" as the source, there is simply no evidence that anyone other than a couple of smart-aleck teenagers were using these slang terms.

A *real* post-9/11 trend was that people were scared to death that another attack was imminent. The anthrax scare didn't help matters, nor did airline passenger Richard Reid, who on December 22, 2001, tried to detonate a bomb in his shoe, which led to a new phrase:

> **shoeicide bomber** *n.* (2001) A suicide bomber who conceals the bomb inside one of his or her shoes. Also: **shoe-icide bomber, shuicide bomber.** *As is often the case, Jay Leno had the best line about the airline passenger who tried to ignite explosives in his shoes while in flight: "This is something new—a **shoe-icide bomber."** (Ventura County Star,* December 29, 2002)

This phrase is a play on **suicide bomber** (1991), a person who deliberately kills himself or herself while detonating a bomb. As the above citation suggests, it was probably coined by comedian Jay Leno—or, more likely, by one of his writers. Either way, it's a clever coinage that was given the "Most Creative" award for 2001 by the American Dialect Society.

The overall sense of around-the-corner doom was helped by the U.S. government's regular warnings about possible attacks using things like **dirty bombs** (1977) and crop dusters loaded with biological weapons. After a while, people grew used to these warnings, and possibly even a little tired of them:

threat fatigue *n.* (1991) Ignoring or downplaying possible threats because one has been subjected to constant warnings about those threats. *Over all, the decision against a public alert represents a significant shift in the thinking of senior government officials over the last several months. Some officials said they had become concerned about the process after several public warnings were issued last fall based on hazy intelligence reports that offered no guidance on how anyone could respond. They said they feared that such alerts might be causing "threat fatigue" among Americans, who have been bombarded by so many unspecific warnings that they no longer arouse much concern.* (*New York Times,* June 30, 2002)

Of the several dozen media citations I found for *threat fatigue,* all but five appeared since June 30, 2002, when the FBI warning about a possible July 4, 2002, terrorist attack was leaked to the media. Interestingly, the phrase was previewed by Homeland Security director Tom Ridge in an interview earlier in the month:

There's benefit to reminding America of the longtime implications of this challenge. A greater challenge is how we deal with the information we want to share with America, because there is a concern about **threat fatigue.** (*National Journal,* June 8, 2002)

The War on Terror

It's still too early to see the big picture of the post-9/11 world. I'm not a historian, but if I had to guess what elements that big picture will contain, I'd start with probably the most obvious conclusion: The events of September 11, 2001, moved the concept of terrorism in most Americans minds from the "abstract" list to the "real" list. Terrorism no longer happened to people halfway around the world who were embroiled in centuries-old conflicts that few understood. Instead, terrorism was something that had now happened on American soil and so could happen anywhere in the Western world. The West had come face-to-face with an extreme form of terrorism called **hyperterrorism** (a word coined on September 12, 2001):

> Confronted with an act of **hyperterrorism,** the world's sole hyperpower has shown itself to be hyper-fragile. Its vulnerability has stunned most Europeans more used—the French most of all—to denouncing America for its arrogance, its power and its unilateralism than to lamenting its weakness. If America is revealed to be a "giant with clay feet"—illustrated graphically by the collapse of the twin towers of the World Trade Center— could Europe be the next and even more vulnerable target? (*Financial Times,* London, September 13, 2002)

(Another coinage, **theoterrosim** [2001], which refers to Al Qaeda's brand of religion-based terrorism, didn't catch on.)

That big picture also may show another attitude shift: the resolve actually to *do* something about terrorism. Thus the **war on terror** (originally 1984, but first used in this context on September 13, 2001) was born:

> All these formulations are important, but **"war on terror"** is the one that has caught on. . . . The phrase meets the basic test of Presidential rhetoric: it has entered the language so fully, and framed the way people think about how the United States is reacting to the September 11th attacks so completely, that the idea that declaring and waging war on terror was not the sole, inevitable, logical consequence of the attacks just isn't in circulation. (*The New Yorker,* September 16, 2002)

The problem, though, was that conventional military strategy and hardware didn't apply. This was a new kind of warfare:

asymmetric warfare *n.* (1995) Warfare in which the combatants have markedly different military capabilities and the weaker side uses nonstandard tactics such as terrorism. *In Afghanistan, precision bombing missions guided by elite U.S. foot soldiers coordinating with ragtag rebel groups "turned the Northern Alliance into a conquering army," said Andrews, a Green Beret captain in Vietnam. In the process, the theory of **asymmetric warfare** was turned on its head. The theory said that rogue states and terrorists would not face the United States in conventional battle and would resort to attacks on civilians. The United States would have to hunker down in defense. But Green Berets draped in shawls riding into battle on horses and CIA operatives prowling back alleys to buy off defectors showed the United States can take the offensive in unconventional warfare.* (*Miami Herald,* December 26, 2001)

A similar idea is **fourth-generation warfare** (1989), where at least one side uses nontraditional tactics and is composed of a nongovernmental military force.

One of the problems with battling hyperterrorism is that the opposing force does not have an identifiable country or area to target. An organization such as Al Qaeda is an amorphous collection of "cells" in countries all around the world. It's not from or associated with a particular country or geographic area, so it's **a-geographic** (1996):

It is not bin Laden but Al Qaeda that turns out to be unkillable. Before 9/11, Al Qaeda was a hierarchical body with a central command and, in Afghanistan, a country of its very own. Now it has neither country nor command, and a new, diffuse and decentralized organization has taken its place—"Al Qaeda 2.0," as Peter Bergen calls it. This new Al Qaeda is, if not "virtual," then at least **a-geographic.** (*New York Times,* December 29, 2002)

Asymmetric warfare does not involve one side's tanks shooting at another side's tanks. Instead, the "weaker" of the two opponents uses nonstandard military techniques, such as flying jet-fuel-loaded airplanes into buildings and, most chillingly, deploying nasty biological agents:

bioterrorism *n.* (1989) Terrorism that uses biological weapons. *Out of $1.5 billion devoted to counterterrorism by the federal government during the last fiscal year, Wickland said, only $40 million went to the U.S. Centers for Disease Control and Prevention for bioterrorism preparedness.* (*Seattle Post-Intelligencer,* September 29, 2001)

An example of a **bioterrorist** (1991) is a **smallpox martyr** (2001), someone infected with the smallpox virus who deliberately attempts to spread the disease to other people and start an epidemic:

The simplest way to deliver the deadliest bio-weapon of all, smallpox, is also the most low-tech and efficient. All you need is a suicide volunteer, and we now know they are legion. Infect him in Baghdad or Karachi or the Gaza Strip; have him sit out the virus's two-week incubation period until he begins to cough and get woozy. Then buy him a plane ticket from New York to Los Angeles, or from Chicago to Atlanta. All he has to do is watch the in-flight entertainment and emit the occasional cough. A sneeze works, too. Such a person is now referred to by public-health officials with a disconcerting name: the **smallpox martyr.** (*New York Times,* December 15, 2002)

A **biothreat** (1984) in general and a **bioweapon** (1984) in particular are made possible by a sinister new branch of biology:

dark biology *n.* (1997) Scientific research related to biological weapons. *Unlike nuclear physics, where it is relatively easy to gauge the intent of research programs, "the only way you can tell the difference between good biology and **dark biology** is in the application," she said. And by then, it is potentially too late.* (*Government Executive Magazine,* January 22, 2002)

The phrase *dark biology* was coined by the science writer and novelist Richard Preston. If you're interested in dark biology (and feel like scaring yourself silly), you should read one or more volumes of Preston's self-described "trilogy on dark biology": *The Hot Zone* (1994), *The Cobra Event* (1997), and *The Demon in the Freezer* (2002).

Thwarting bioterrorists and their bioweaponry to maintain our **biosecurity** (1986) is the mandate of the new **antibioterrorism** (1998) procedures:

Leading senators have agreed on a $3.2 billion **antibioterrorism** bill, twice as much as President Bush has proposed spending. The money would go for stockpiling vaccines and antibiotics, increase food inspections, give money to the Centers for Disease Control and Prevention, and help state and local governments prepare for bioterrorism, said Sen. Bill Frist, R-Tenn. (Associated Press, November 14, 2001)

Gulf War II

In 2002 and 2003 the war on terrorism targeted Iraq and its alleged program to build *weapons of mass destruction* (1937). Those who emphasized Iraq's destructive potential often were criticized as being excessively phobic about Saddam Hussein's intentions:

Iraqnophobia *n.* (1990) An unusually strong fear of Iraq, especially its ability to manufacture and use biological, chemical, and nuclear weapons. Also: **Iraqnaphobia, Iraqniphobia.** *Now that September is here, President Bush can launch his "initial public offering" of stock in his newest product,* **Iraqnophobia.** (*The Tennessean,* September 14, 2002)

This word is a play on *arachnophobia* (1925), an unusually strong fear of spiders. Not surprisingly, this term first appeared the last time Iraq was in the news, when it invaded Kuwait in 1990. The movie *Arachnophobia* was playing in theaters at the time, so the initial references were jokes that played off the movie's title.

Before the war began, the Pentagon told news organizations that they would be able to insert some of their journalists into military units to provide coverage of that unit during the war. This process was called **embedding** (2002), and the inserted journalists were called **embeds** (2002):

> Would-be war correspondents, nicknamed **"embeds,"** are being put through reporter boot camps, supervised by U.S. military personnel or by private companies staffed with ex-soldiers. (Newhouse News Service, February 11, 2003)

Independent journalists who weren't **embedded** (2002) were known, curiously, as **unilaterals** (1990):

> The Anglo-American coalition, along with its Kuwaiti allies, have never been keen on the **"unilaterals,"** as they call the independent journalists. All privileges were given instead to the carefully selected group of official "embedded" journalists who travel with U.S. or British military units. (*The Globe and Mail,* Toronto, April 1, 2003)

The Iraq war unleashed a flood of new military jargon, most of which is likely to be quickly forgotten once the war fades into history. One phrase that might stand the test of linguistic time is **shock and awe** (1996), a military strategy in which massive amounts of firepower are unleashed early in a conflict in an effort to force the enemy's regime to collapse or surrender:

> "The attack to kill Saddam and his leadership is a classic case of **shock and awe**," said Harlan Ullman, a chief architect of the strategy and co-author of the 1996 book **"Shock and Awe."** "Cut off the head of the emperor and the empire goes. Even if it misses, it sends a signal." Ullman says he invented the term **"shock and awe"** but that the concept draws on military strategists from Sun Tzu to the Prussian military thinker Carl von Clausewitz. (*Atlanta Journal and Constitution*, March 22, 2003)

Another possibility is **decapitation strike** (1982), a military attack designed to kill the enemy's leaders or knock out their ability to communicate with and control their troops:

> The bombing raid, which lasted no more than 30 minutes, was what military officials call a **decapitation strike.** The apparent aim was to kill the Iraqi dictator and either prompt his army to surrender or, at the very least, create chaos in the upper echelons of Iraq's leadership at the outset of the war. (*Baltimore Sun*, March 20, 2003)

My personal favorite that emerged from the fog of warspeak was **gorilla snot** (2001), a gluelike substance that is spread over sand to prevent a dust cloud from forming whenever a helicopter takes off or lands.

The result of the war was what the U.S. administration had wanted all along: **regime change** (1980), getting rid of Saddam Hussein and his cronies who controlled Iraq. Even before the war, however, this phrase was taken up by the public at large and used as an ironic reference to a change of leadership, particularly in business, politics, or sports:

> As you might have heard, we've had a **regime change** here at the paper. We knew something was up Wednesday when all

the TVs in the building suddenly went black, then showed the *Star Tribune* flag with patriotic music playing. Then the middle managers were dragged from the building in shackles and loaded into black vans—some sort of retreat, I guess. Next thing you knew we had a new editor. (*Star Tribune,* Minneapolis, May 19, 2002)

The phrase *regime change* has been used in military and diplomatic circles for many years. It became a household term early in 2002 when members of the Bush administration began using the phrase conspicuously when discussing their policy toward Iraq. Secretary of State Colin Powell used the term in congressional hearings in early February, and White House spokesman Ari Fleischer began using *regime change* regularly in press conferences around the beginning of March. Whether it was the prospect of war with Iraq or the unabashedly euphemistic scent carried by the phrase, it struck a chord, and suddenly references to "regime change" were everywhere you looked.

What interests me, however, is the shift the phrase has taken to more mundane contexts. Whether it's the retirement of a business executive, the defeat of a politician, or the firing of a coach, wags from all walks of life are planting their tongues firmly in their cheeks and referring to these leadership moves as "regime changes." Clearly war remains, as the linguist Eric Partridge once observed, "ever . . . an augmentor of vocabulary."

Appendix

New Trends in Prefixes, Suffixes, and Modifiers

We go through this every time a new technology emerges. It took a while before people could stop talking about horseless carriages, electric iceboxes and electronic brains. But in the end, those hybrid names always wind up sounding quaint, and so will all those compounds with "cyber," "e," "virtual" and the rest. If we were smart, we'd drag them all to the trash icon of history right now. —*Geoffrey Nunberg*

We've had Filegate and we've had Travelgate. We've had so many gates, I think it's time to show [Bill Clinton] the front door. —*Bob Dole*

Ever since Saddam Hussein (who apparently has the Mother of All Oedipus Complexes) vowed to engage the allies in the aforementioned Mother of All Battles, the phrase has become the Mother of All Metaphors. . . . Frankly, I'd like to see him sentenced to the Mother of All Hangings, not only for the terrible things he has done, but for coining the Mother of All Annoying Catch Phrases. —*Jerry Zezima*

As I described in Chapter 1, new words are formed in many ways, but probably the most common is to combine an existing word with an affix (a prefix or a suffix) or another word or phrase (a modifier). This appendix examines the prefixes, suffixes, and modifiers that have been used most commonly over the past few years to create new words.

Prefixes

Slapping a prefix onto the front of an existing term is probably the easiest way to coin a new word, particularly when the neologism names something that differs in some specific quality from the thing named by the existing term.

For example, many new technological things are electronic or online versions of existing things, so the new items are easily named by tacking on one of the half dozen common technological prefixes: *e-*, *cyber-*, *Net-*, *i-*, *info-*, and *techno-*. Unfortunately, it's so easy to use these prefixes that a movement against their use has developed. This backlash has been going full throttle since the tech meltdown began in 2000, but it began before that. For example, in their 1999 book, *Wired Style*, authors Constance Hale and Jessie Scanlon plead for some restraint in their entry for the prefix **e-**: "Please, resist the urge to use this vowel-as-cliché." The prefix **cyber-** fares no better, with Hale and Scanlon calling it "terminally overused." The use of the **info-** prefix is now so common that John Seely Brown and Paul Duguid, writing in their 2000 book, *The Social Life of Information,* call this process *infoprefixation.*

Perhaps this antitechnology-prefix trend explains at least in part why many "real-world" prefixes have become extremely popular. For example, consider the prefix **bio-,** which means "life" or "biology." Elsewhere in the book I've mentioned *bioterrorism, biothreat,* and *biosecurity.* In recent years we've also seen coinages such as **biobreak** (computer geek-speak for a trip to the bathroom); **biodiesel** (a truck and bus fuel made from discarded restaurant grease); **biofraud** (the fraudulent manipulation of data in a biological study or survey); **biodiversity** (the diversity of plant and animal life in a particular niche or region); **biometrics** (the identification of an individual based on biological traits, such as fingerprints, iris patterns, and facial features); **biomimicry** (manufacturing principles and practices that mimic natural materials or processes); **bionomics** (the merger of biological and economic theory); **biopharming** (using genetically modified plants to grow pharmaceuticals); and **biopiracy** (the patenting of plants, genes, and other biological products that are indigenous to a foreign country).

Another oft-used prefix these days is **eco-,** short for "ecological" or "ecology," which has been in the language since at least the word *ecosystem* showed up in 1935. In Chapter 11, "The New Activism," I talked about *eco-terrorism, eco-tage, eco-sabotage, eco-defense, eco-terrorist, eco-saboteur, eco-defender, eco-anarchist, eco-guerrilla, eco-raider,* and *eco-kamikaze.* Other eco-coinages include **eco-efficiency** (the ability to manufacture goods efficiently and with as little effect on the environment as possible); **eco-porn** (a corporate advertisement that extols the company's environmental record or policies); **eco-scam** (an ecological argument or policy supported by lies or inaccurate facts); **eco-tech** (technology designed to alleviate environmental problems and reduce the use of natural resources); and **eco-tourism** (tourism that promotes or displays ecological thinking or living).

One of my favorite new prefixes is **Franken-,** which means, "genetically modified" (GM). As I explained in Chapter 1, this prefix was first used in the word *Frankenfood,* coined by Paul Lewis in 1992. Mr. Lewis was inordinately pleased with his prefix, as you can see in an interview he gave a few months after his coinage first appeared:

> "I'm proud of this word," [Paul Lewis] says. "It has a phonetic rhythm, it's pithy, and you can use the 'Franken-' prefix on anything: 'Frankenfruit,' say. You can say, 'We're breathing Frankenair.' 'We're drinking Frankenwater.' 'It's a Frankenworld.' " (*Boston Globe,* October 14, 1992)

Frankenfruit has ripened into a mature member of the language, but the others he mentioned—*Frankenair, Frankenwater,* and *Frankenworld*—didn't take. That's good, because it's hard to imagine how air, water, and the world can be in any way "genetically modified." *Franken-* coinages are on more solid ground when they stick to their GM roots. Some that have caught on are **Frankenbean, Frankencorn, Frankenfish, Frankenforest, Frankenplant, Frankenrice, Frankentomato, Frankensalmon,** and **Frankentree.**

Another productive member of the prefix brigade is **Mc-,** short for "McDonald's." McDonald's itself, of course, uses this prefix with a giddy abandon: *McLean Deluxe, Chicken McNuggets, Mayor McCheese, Egg McMuffin, McDeal,* and *McPizza,* to name just a few. (One commentator has said that the point of all these *Mc-* terms was to create an entire *McLanguage* that people would associate with McDonald's.) But the rest of us are using *Mc-,* as well, to mean either "relating to McDonald's" or "lowbrow; vulgar; lightweight." In this book I mentioned a few of these *Mc-* constructions: *McJob, McMansion,* and *McSenior.* There are in fact dozens of these terms, including the following that I've stumbled on in my travels: **McChild care, McChoose, McContraceptive, McCouch, McDentist, McDoctor, McExistence, McFrankenstein, McLawsuit, McLibel, McLife, McMoviemaking, McPaper** (*USA Today*), **McParody, McSatan, McScapegoat, McSports, McSpotlight, McStable, McStory, McSushi, McTeacher, McTheater, McTherapy, McTwist, McUnion, McVegan, McWork, McWorker,** and **McWorld.**

The word *spokesman,* a person who speaks on behalf of other people, especially an organization or movement, has been in the language since the mid-sixteenth century. *Spokeswoman* entered the lexicon about 100 years later. The language assembly line that began punching out gender-neutral terms in the 1960s produced *spokesperson* around 1972. Since then, the prefix **spokes-** has led a busy life identifying dozens of different kinds of mouthpieces, including the following: **spokesalien, spokesath-**

lete, **spokesbeaver, spokesbug, spokescake, spokescat, spokescow, spokescritter, spokesdog, spokesdrinker, spokesduck, spokesdude, spokeseagle, spokesfruitcake, spokesgal, spokesgiraffe, spokesgolfer, spokesguy, spokeskid, spokesmodel, spokesmom, spokesmouse, spokesobject, spokespuppet, spokesrabbit, spokestoddler,** and **spokeswarbler.**

A prefix that has been very fashionable over the past few years is **meta-,** which comes from the Greek *meta,* "beside; after." Meta- has a number of meanings, but the trendy one is "beyond; transcending" and it's used to designate an object that analyzes or describes similar objects. For example, a *meta-language* is a language used to analyze or describe another language, and a *meta-fiction* is fiction that analyzes or comments on the nature of fiction. Here are some other meta- constructions that I found while examining just one month's worth of articles in a media database: **meta-column, meta-commentary, meta-concept, meta-drama, meta-feeling, meta-homecoming, meta-information, meta-layer, meta-monster movie, meta-movie, meta-museum, meta-myth, meta-narrative, meta-problem, meta-race, meta-science fiction, meta-scientist, meta-search, meta-semaphore, meta-slasher, meta-space, meta-story, meta-thoughts, meta-translation,** and **meta-video.**

The German prefix **über-,** "super," has become extremely popular in the last few years, to the point where a proto-backlash is forming: In January 2003 the *New York Times* ran an article titled "Ach du Lieber! Don't You Wish Über Was Over?" It went on to list 15 *über-* constructions, including *über-burger, über-producer,* and *über-caterer.* Here are a few others that I found when looking through just a week's worth of articles in a media database: **über-athlete, über-bitch, über-brain, über-bungalow, über-chef, über-city, über-competitive, über-computing, über-conservative, über-database, über-exclusive, über-freshman, über-grunge, über-hubris, über-issue, über-Jewish, über-lawyer, über-liberal, über-linebacker, über-**

lobbyist, über-luxe, über-modern, über-paranoid, über-pop-
ular, über-publicist, über-star, über-successful, and über-
trendy.

Suffixes

Just as tossing a prefix onto the front of a word is a natural form
of language construction, so, too, is hooking up a suffix to the
back of a word. In fact, certain suffixes are among the most
common of neological generators.

Consider, for example, the suffix **-gate,** which is used in
building names for scandals, especially a scandal that has a sinister, even criminal cast to it. The Watergate scandal was, of
course, the archetype for this. According to *Safire's New Political
Dictionary* by William Safire, shortly after Watergate there was a
wine adulteration scandal in France that was called *Winegate.*
This was followed in short order by *Koreagate, Lancegate,
Applegate, Billygate,* and *Irangate.* Three of my favorites have
been *Floodgate*—based on a 1978 scandal involving congress-
man Daniel Flood; *Pearlygate*—a scandal involving a televange-
list or minister; and *Gategate*—used several times over the years
in scandals involving, of all things, gates. In recent years we've
seen **Bimbogate, Chinagate, Filegate, Tailgate, Travelgate,
Whitewatergate, Zippergate,** and, of course, **Gennifergate,
Paulagate,** and **Monicagate.**

Another impressively busy suffix is **-ware,** short for "software." This suffix has programmed into the language such clas-
sics as *freeware* (free software), *shareware* (software that you try
for free and then purchase if you plan to keep using it), and *va-
porware* (a software product that has been announced but not
delivered). Some of the dozens of recent variations include
abandonware (software code that is lost because the company
that wrote the code has gone out of business); **beerware** (soft-

ware in which the purchase "price" is to buy the developer a beer, drink a beer in the developer's name, or send the developer a case of beer); **careware** (software in which the "price" is to do a good deed or donate something to charity); **coasterware** (software so bad or useless that it never gets installed); **fritterware** (feature-laden software that seduces people into spending inordinate amounts of time tweaking various options for only marginal gains in productivity); **herdware** (computer software that tracks cattle herds); **malware** (computer viruses and other software designed to damage or disrupt a system); **retroware** (software that's two or three versions earlier than the current version); **shovelware** (content from an existing medium, such as a newspaper or book, that has been dumped wholesale into another medium, such as a CD-ROM or the Web); **slideware** (a much-hyped software product that currently exists only as a series of slides in a sales or marketing presentation); **spyware** (software that surreptitiously sends data to an individual or a company when the computer on which the program is installed is connected to the Internet); and **terrorware** (software used by terrorists).

The suffix **-free** comes in handy when you want to describe something as lacking a particular quality or feature. The model for this is *fat-free,* which nowadays has umpteen healthy variations, including *calorie-free, cholesterol-free, salt-free, MSG-free,* and even *peanut-free.* Nonnutritional varieties I've seen are **content-free** (a message or communication that is big on style but almost totally lacking in substance); **fact-free** (a scientific endeavor that doesn't take into account real-world constraints, such as chemical or biological data); **friction-free** (an extremely efficient capitalist market in which buyers and sellers can find each other easily, can interact directly, and can perform transactions with only minimal overhead costs); and *office-free* (see Chapter 19, "The Modern Workplace").

We live in a world where, it seems, everyone is addicted to

something. Fortunately, we can easily label these addicts by tacking on the **-aholic** (also: **-holic, -oholic**) suffix. The original model for this is *alcoholic,* which gave us *workaholic, foodaholic,* and *chocoholic.* Some addicts that have come to light recently are **controlaholic, grungeaholic** (grunge music addict), **javaholic, milkaholic, smokeaholic, surgiholic** (plastic surgery addict), and **Webaholic.** Elsewhere in this book see *shopaholic* (Chapter 7) and *teleworkaholic* (Chapter 17, "People Who Work at Home").

The Spanish suffix **-ista**—like its English counterpart *-ist*—is used to designate a person who practices a particular skill or profession (such as a *barista,* a coffee server), who is a devotee of someone or something (such as a *Sandinista* or a *Zapatista),* or who is associated with a particular action, movement, or thing (such as a *torista,* a bullfight fan). A member of the fashion industry, or a person who is obsessive about fashion, is often called a **fashionista.** Someone who attempts to recall an elected politician is a **recallista.** A graffiti artist is a **graffitista.** Fans of British prime minister Tony Blair are **Blairistas,** while the devotees of U.S. president Bill Clinton were often called **Clintonistas.**

On January 19, 1991, *Saturday Night Live* cast member Rob Schneider created a character named Richard Laymer, an office worker whose desk was in the room containing the photocopier. His shtick was to banter inanely with anyone who came into the room to make copies. In particular, he'd come up with off-the-cuff nicknames for each person. For example, once when a character named Steve entered the copy room, Richard greeted him with the following verbal riff: "Steve! The Steveman! Steve-o-rama! Steve-o-ramovich! Steve-oh! Steverino! Steve-oooooh! Steverolo! The Steve-meister! The Stevenator! Steeeeeve!"

These improvised linguistic solos almost always included a variation on the person's name that ended with the suffix **-meister,** German for "master." When talking in this way became a fad for a time in the early 1990s—one columnist dubbed it

Laymer's syndrome—the *-meister* compound became the signature label. Laymer's syndrome was eradicated long ago, but the *-meister* suffix lives on and is probably as popular today as it was back then. (A variation on the theme is the suffix **-ster,** which has proven to be at least as productive.) A search of just one month's worth of media articles revealed the following *-meister* compounds: **ad-meister, chat-meister, cliché-meister, horror-meister, hype-meister, image-meister, mix-meister, music-meister, piano-meister, pitch-meister, pop-meister, rap-meister, scam-meister, sleaze-meister, spin-meister, stunt-meister, style-meister, swing-meister, trend-meister, Web-meister, whimsy-meister,** and **word-meister.**

The *Oxford English Dictionary* defines *lallapaloosa* as "something outstandingly good of its kind" and gives an earliest citation from 1904. It also includes the variant spelling *lollapalooza,* which was taken as the name of a multiband, alternative music tour that has run every summer since 1991. It was extremely popular, which no doubt contributed to the rise of the suffix **-palooza,** which, depending on the context, denotes a large gathering, a musical concert, or something excessive. The following *-palooza* compounds all appeared in the media in early 2003: **acoustic palooza, advice-a-palooza, balloon-a-palooza, Blues-a-palooza, can-a-palooza, candy-palooza, cruise-a-palooza, dog-a-palooza, fun-a-palooza, local-palooza, lollipop-palooza, loop-a-palooza, opinion-palooza, pet-a-palooza, polar-palooza, Pokey Palooza, Pope-a-palooza, price-a-palooza, pumpkin-palooza, Santa-palooza, serv-a-palooza, Shakespeare-a-palooza, shoes-a-palooza, slam-bam-a-palooza, snack-a-palooza, snooze-a-palooza, touchdown-palooza,** and **vodka-palooza.**

Another suffix to watch is **-rati,** which indicates the elite or the intelligentsia of a particular group. The original is *literati*: the literary intelligentsia or the educated class. Recent variations on the theme include **belligerati** (writers and other members of the intelligentsia who advocate war or imperialism); **chatterati** (the elite members of the chattering classes); **cinerati** (cinema intelligentsia); **digerati** (digital intelligentsia); **jitterati** (overcaffeinated digerati); and **journarati** (journalism intelligentsia).

Entertainment may be the closest thing the Western world has to a universal creed. Whether our brow is high, low, or right in the middle, we all like to been entertained (bearing in mind that one person's entertainment is another person's irritant). A sign of entertainment's universality is that people often discard the "enter" part of the word and use **-tainment** as a new suffix. Here are some examples that have been coined in recent times: **advertainment** (an ad as a kind of entertainment); **agri-tainment** (farm-related entertainment); **eater-tainment** or **eat-a-tainment** (restaurant-going that also includes entertainment such as wall-mounted memorabilia, video displays, or live music); **edu-tainment** (entertainment that is also educational); **kiddie-tainment** (entertainment aimed at children); **infotainment** (entertainment that also imparts information); **irritainment** (entertainment and media spectacles that are both annoying and complusively watchable); **humilitainment** (entertainment that involves humiliating people); **militainment** (news coverage of, or television shows about, war or the military); **murder-tainment** (a fictional murder mystery, particularly one on TV); **promo-tainment** (a promotional ad presented as a form of entertainment); **retail-tainment** (retail shopping that is fun or entertaining); **retro-tainment** (old movies and TV shows); **sports-tainment** (sports-related entertainment); and **ubi-tainment** (ubiquitous entertainment; entertainment that is accessible in any location, as from a wireless Internet connection).

In Chapter 16 I told you about a creature named *bridezilla,* a bridal monster created by the maniacal need to have "the perfect day" and who'll walk over anyone and everything to get it. This word is a combination of *bride* and *Godzilla,* the fictional mutant dinosaur created by U.S. hydrogen bomb testing in the Pacific that, in numerous films in the 1950s and 1960s, would wade onto land and destroy everything in his path. The popularity of the original Godzilla and his high-tech update that appeared in the 1998 movie has spawned a monster of a suffix—-zilla—which is used to refer to anything that's monstrous either in size or in behavior. Internet types, in particular, seem to love this suffix. There's *Mozilla,* a Web browser; *Go!Zilla,* a file download program; and, according to a site called DaveZilla.com, there are at least 1,000 websites that have *-zilla* in the address. Here are some recent *-zilla* constructions: **Bart-zilla, butt-zilla, cod-zilla, coffee-zilla, drive-zilla** (a hard disk drive), **Gotti-zilla, mom-to-bezilla, mom-zilla, panic-zilla, sewer-zilla, Shaq-zilla, shred-zilla, tent-zilla, Todd-zilla,** and **turkey-zilla.**

Modifiers

Neologists harness prefixes and suffixes to create new words and new compounds, but there are also full-fledged words and phrases that can be put to good neological use. For example, in Chapter 12, "The Political Correctness Wars," I talked about the adjective *challenged* and how the PC crowd has used it to form constructions such as *physically challenged, emotionally challenged,* and *mentally challenged.* In other chapters we've seen the phrase *just-in-time* used to mean "when and where something is needed": *just-in-time lifestyle, just-in-time learning,* and *just-in-time office.* The word *challenged* and the phrase *just-in-time* modify the preceding or following word, so these types of formatives are called *modifiers.* Here's a look at a few other modifiers that have hit the lexical radar screen in recent years.

In the 1960s anthropologists coined the phrase *alpha male* to refer to the dominant male in a group, particularly a group of primates. Since then the modifier **alpha** has been used as a superlative that generally means "most dominant" but can also take on other meanings depending on the context. Here are some examples: **alpha earner** (a wife who earns all or most of her household's income); **alpha geek** (the person with the most technological prowess in an office or department); **alpha girl** (the dominant member in a group of girls; a girl who bullies other girls); **alpha mom** (the dominant woman in a group of mothers); **alpha pup** (market research jargon for the kid who is deemed by his or her peers to be the "coolest" in their school, neighborhood, or town); and **alpha talent** (the most popular or most talented performer).

Sometimes the world changes in spectacular ways and we get what business buzzwordists call a *paradigm shift*. Most of the time, however, things change gradually in slow, almost imperceptible increments; this slow change is well described as **creep,** a modifier that you saw in Chapter 5, "Ad Creep," where I defined *ad creep* as the gradual expansion of advertising space to nontraditional surfaces such as floors, bathroom walls, cars, and the sides of buildings. Another common use of this modifier is **bracket creep,** which refers to the gradual movement of taxpayers into higher tax brackets because of inflation. Now people also speak of **device creep,** the gradual increase in the number of electronic devices in a person's life. **Jargon creep** is the tendency for the use of jargon terms to expand into different contexts and to spawn variations on the original terms. There's also **mission creep,** the process by which a mission's methods and goals change gradually over time. Another example is **title creep,** the gradual devaluation of executive job titles by assigning those titles to ever-larger numbers of employees (for example, those companies where it seems that every second employee is a vice president).

On February 12, 1981, the *Associated Press* ran a story titled

"Two Men Killed in Drive-by Shootings," which appears to be the first time the phrase *drive-by shooting*—shooting a person from a moving vehicle—appeared in print. Since then the phrase **drive-by** has been used as a modifier that describes something done in a quick-and-dirty manner. For example, in Chapter 20, "The Dot-Com Rise and Fall," I mentioned *drive-by VC,* a venture capital firm or investor that supplies money to a new company, but does not offer any other type of support or expertise. Many other such phrases have appeared over the years, including recent sightings such as **drive-by birth, drive-by commentator, drive-by downloads, drive-by editing, drive-by lawsuit, drive-by parent conference, drive-by patriotism, drive-by politics, drive-by shirting, drive-by surgery,** and **drive-by voice mail.**

One of the most popular modifiers of all time has got to be **mother of all** (from Iraqi leader Saddam Hussein's 1990 Gulf War nonprescient phrase, *the mother of all battles*), which means, depending on the context, "best; greatest; most intense." Hundreds of *mother of all* constructions have appeared over the years, from **mother of all asteroids** to **mother of all zinfandels.** Someone once described the luncheon meat Spam as "the mother of all chopped, shaped, artificially flavored and colored food-substance products." In searching just a week of media articles, I found the following examples: **mother of all bad draft picks, mother of all briefings, mother of all colds, mother of all compromises, mother of all cover-ups, mother of all dilemmas, mother of all droughts, mother of all economic development tools, mother of all injustices, mother of all lawsuits, mother of all mistakes, mother of all political battles, mother of all rallies, mother of all reality shows, mother of all scams, mother of all scandals, mother of all seizures, mother of all speeches, mother of all statements,** and **mother of all traffic jams.**

When I was thinking of possible titles for this book, I briefly considered *New Word Nation*. I liked its snappy rhythm, the pleasing alliteration, and the natural tie-in to my contention that new words reflect our culture. But then I started noticing lots of other books with "Nation" in the title. In my own book collection I saw **Corporation Nation, Free Agent Nation, Fast Food Nation,** and **Suburban Nation.** In the bookstores I saw **Asphalt Nation, Credit Card Nation,** and **Prozac Nation.** Clearly **nation** had become a popular modifier. Checking Amazon.com, I found oodles of "Nation" titles: **Adoption Nation, Alien Nation, Cardinal Nation, Chili Nation, Confederate Nation, Cornbread Nation, Database Nation, Doonesbury Nation, Gun Nation, Hawaiian Nation, Hellfire Nation, Imagine Nation, Lost Nation, Midnight Nation, Nonprofit Nation, Pinocchio Nation, Poker Nation, Prison Nation, Redneck Nation, Restless Nation, Ritalin Nation, Rogue Nation, Salmon Nation, Tattoo Nation, Voyeur Nation,** and **Wireless Nation.** On TV Michael Moore had a show called *TV Nation.* In print I saw references to **bloviation nation, food nation, hip-hop nation** (or **double-h nation**), **IM nation, knowledge nation, open-source nation, peeping-Tom nation, plastic nation, surveillence nation, thumb nation,** and Janet Jackson's album *Rhythm Nation.* Now I'm waiting for someone to write a book called *Nation Nation* that discusses this phenomenon.

Early in the seventh season of the TV show *Seinfeld,* we learn about a man whom Jerry describes, in what will prove to be one of the show's bigger understatements, as "a little temperamental." That man is a purveyor of soup called the Soup Nazi, and he remains one of the show's most memorable characters. The Soup Nazi is also at least partially responsible for the popularity of the word **Nazi** as a modifier. It's used to describe someone who is fanatically devoted to a cause or movement, particularly in a dogmatic, tyrannical manner. Some recent sightings of this modifier are **body Nazi** (an exercise fanatic); **femi-Nazi** (conservative commentator Rush Limbaugh's putdown of radical feminists); **fitness Nazi** (a physical fitness fanatic); **health Nazi** (someone obsessed with being healthy, particularly by not smoking or being exposed to cigarette smoke); **list Nazi** (someone who is a stickler for the rules of an Internet mailing list); **smoke Nazi** (antismoking fanatic); and **tobacco Nazi** (another antismoker).

A while back, General Motors ran an ad that claimed, "This is not your father's Oldsmobile." The idea, I think, was to convey that the new model was more modern, more up-to-date, than the old model, so it would appeal to youth—a son or daughter—rather than age—the father. That idea of something appealing to youth instead of age is at the heart of the modifier **not your father's,** which remains surprisingly popular to this day. I checked a month's worth of recent media articles and found the following: **not your father's Army food, not your father's Astroturf, not your father's ATM, not your father's battlefield, not your father's burger, not your father's cell phone, not your father's classical music, not your father's duplex, not your father's grandparents, not your father's heavy metal, not your father's law firm, not your father's military, not your father's NASCAR, not your father's Navy, not your father's NBA, not your father's neighborhood association, not your father's NFL, not your father's police station, not your father's recession, not your father's Republican party, not your father's science-fiction novel, not your father's solar technology,** and **not your father's suburbs.**

The word *pornography* comes from the Greek *pornographos,* which means "writing about prostitutes." It entered the language in 1857 and only a few years later took on the general sense of any sexually explicit material, which is how the word has been used since. Surprisingly, the short form *porn* has only been in the language since about 1962. Since then, however, **porn** (along with the longer **pornography**) has become an incredibly popular modifier that means "the graphic depiction of something." In this book I've mentioned several *porn* constructions, including *debt porn, financial pornography, investment pornography, leisure porn, time porn,* and *wealth pornography.* Here are a few others I've seen in my media excursions: **choco porn** (graphic depictions of chocolate and chocolate-based foods); **disaster porn** (movies that revel in gratuitous violence; media coverage that focuses on large-scale disasters); **domestic porn** (books, magazines, and TV shows that display images of domestic perfection); **eco-porn** (a corporate advertisement that extols the company's environmental record or policies); **food porn** or **gastroporn** (the suggestive pictures and prose used to describe recipes in upscale cookbooks or menu items in fancy restaurants); **gadget porn** (drooling coverage of high-tech or high-end gadgetry); **political porn** (detailed, behind-the-scenes descriptions of political events); **weather porn** (TV shows or movies that feature extreme weather); **wedding porn** (graphic depictions of lavish weddings and receptions); **wine porn** (over-the-top descriptions of wines and wine tastings).

Index

About the Author

hudson taylor

Paul McFedries is the president of *Logophilia Limited* and has written over 40 books that have sold nearly 3 million copies worldwide. These books include many titles in the Complete Idiot's Guide series, including *The Complete Idiot's Guide to a Smart Vocabulary* and *The Complete Idiot's Guide to Windows.* McFedries is also the proprietor of Word Spy, a website and mailing list devoted to the study of newly coined and evolving words, with over 10,000 subscribers and 100,000 users a month.